Fundamental Concepts for the Software Quality Engineer

Also available from ASQ Quality Press:

Software Quality Professional
A Quarterly Journal Published by ASQ, edited by Taz Daughtrey

Root Cause Analysis: Simplified Tools and Techniques
Bjørn Andersen and Tom Fagerhaug

101 Good Ideas: How to Improve Just about Any Process
Karen Bemowski and Brad Stratton, editors

Success through Quality: Support Guide for the Journey to Continuous Improvement
Timothy J. Clark

Quality Problem Solving
Gerald F. Smith

The Certified Quality Manager Handbook, Second Edition
Duke Okes and Russell T. Westcott, editors

Six Sigma for the Shop Floor: A Pocket Guide
Roderick A. Munro

Six Sigma Project Management: A Pocket Guide
Jeffrey N. Lowenthal

Principles and Practices of Organizational Performance Excellence
Thomas J. Cartin

To request a complimentary catalog of ASQ Quality Press publications, call 800-248-1946, or visit our Web site at http://qualitypress.asq.org .

Fundamental Concepts for the Software Quality Engineer

Taz Daughtrey, Editor

ASQ Quality Press
Milwaukee, Wisconsin

Fundamental Concepts for the Software Quality Engineer
Taz Daughtrey, Editor

Library of Congress Cataloging-in-Publication Data

Fundamental concepts for the software quality enginer / Taz Daughtrey, Editor.
    p. cm.
  Includes bibliographical references and index.
  ISBN 0-87389-521-5 (alk. paper)
  1. Computer software—Testing. 2. Computer software—Reliability. I. Daughtrey,
Taz, 1949–

QA76.6 .F858 2001
005.1—dc21   2001004987

© 2002 by ASQ

10 9 8 7 6 5 4 3 2

ISBN 0-87389-521-5

Acquisitions Editor: Annemieke Koudstaal
Project Editor: Craig Powell
Production Administrator: Gretchen Trautman
Special Marketing Representative: David Luth

ASQ Mission: The American Society for Quality advances individual, organizational, and community excellence worldwide through learning, quality improvement, and knowledge exchange.

Attention Bookstores, Wholesalers, Schools and Corporations: ASQ Quality Press books, videotapes, audiotapes, and software are available at quantity discounts with bulk purchases for business, educational, or instructional use. For information, please contact ASQ Quality Press at 800-248-1946, or write to ASQ Quality Press, P.O. Box 3005, Milwaukee, WI 53201-3005.

To place orders or to request a free copy of the ASQ Quality Press Publications Catalog, including ASQ membership information, call 800-248-1946. Visit our Web site at www.asq.org or http://qualitypress.asq.org .

Printed in the United States of America

 Printed on acid-free paper

American Society for Quality

Quality Press
600 N. Plankinton Avenue
Milwaukee, Wisconsin 53203
Call toll free 800-248-1946
Fax 414-272-1734
www.asq.org
http://qualitypress.asq.org
http://standardsgroup.asq.org
E-mail: authors@asq.org

Contents

Introduction

These resources are offered to practitioners seeking to apply the principles of quality to the development and use of software and software-dependent systems. The popular media are constantly highlighting various spectacular failures or threats from ill-conceived or poorly designed computerized systems. One must search harder to learn of success stories, much less of the methods that contributed to those successes. Here are experience-based reports of software quality practices that have proven effective in a wide range of industries, applications, and organizational settings.

The articles in this volume span the Body of Knowledge established for the American Society for Quality's Certified Software Quality Engineer (CSQE). This content is not meant to provide any comprehensive treatment of that Body of Knowledge or to serve as a primary study aid for those preparing to take the CSQE exam. It is organized around the structure of, and relative emphases within, the Body of Knowledge.

The distinctive value of the CSQE is that it is built on extensive validation against actual practice. The American Society for Quality (ASQ) demands a rigorous process—first simply to determine the validity of a specialization area, and then to identify the success factors for its pursuit. The Software Quality Engineering Body of Knowledge spans the materials found essential for professionals applying quality principles to software-based systems. Periodically, this Body of Knowledge undergoes a full recalibration to ensure it continues to reflect the current state-of-the-practice.

Each of the eight sections of this book are devoted to one of the areas within the current Software Quality Engineering Body of Knowledge. These topical areas are:

- Standards, Principles, And Ethics
- Quality Management
- Software Processes
- Project Management
- Measurement
- Inspection And Testing
- Audits
- Configuration Management

Either two or three articles were selected for each section, reflecting the relative importance of the topics as weighted in the CSQE examination.

This collection is designed to be a tool—a means of equipping software quality practitioners for growth in technical skills, personal competence, and professional image. The significant information contained can contribute to individual and organizational success in the pursuit of software quality.

Most of these contributions originally appeared in *Software Quality Professional*, a journal I have been privileged to edit since its first issue in 1998. I appreciate the efforts of the journal's Associate Editors, Editorial Board, and technical reviewers for providing the evaluations and recommendations that helped bring these articles to their current useful form. SQP's production staff, from manuscript coordinators to copy editors to the graphics and digital specialists, all contributed to the process that eventually brought forth these presentations.

Other contributions were initially presented at the International Conference on Software Quality, an annual series of conferences organized by the Software Division of the American Society for Quality. These presentations were first evaluated by the Program Committees of the 1999 and 2000 conferences. The material was further refined under the editorship of Tom Griffin, ASQ Software Division Publications Chair.

Dedication and cooperation among its staff and many volunteers allows ASQ to promote the principles and practices of quality improvement and to achieve its mission of being "recognized throughout the world as the leading authority on, and champion for, quality." The ASQ Software Division, which includes some 5000 professionals worldwide, is dedicated "to improve the ability of individuals and organizations to satisfy their customers with quality software products and services through education, communication, research, outreach, and professional development." This work is a part of that effort.

A volume such as this one is possible only because of the direct work and indirect support of many individuals, including ASQ staff, Society member volunteers, and a wide circle of colleagues, friends, and family. I salute them all, and I welcome the readers of this book into the community of software quality professionals.

Taz Daughtrey
Lynchburg, Virginia

PART ONE

Standards, Principles, and Ethics

A professional is one who professes something. To "profess" is to "affirm," to "claim one's belief in." What do software quality professionals affirm? What do such individuals claim to believe?

Competence is clearly central to this identity. Quality professionals value not mere adequacy, but the pursuit of excellence. They affirm personal accountability in what they do, and they strive for individual and organizational improvement.

The publication you are reading right now is one mark of that striving. The individuals who have written articles are sharing their insights for the good of the profession. Those of us involved in assembling the material are motivated to support the drive toward excellence. And you, the reader, are exhibiting a strong commitment to personal improvement.

Watts Humphrey begins our collection by offering both a framework and the experimental data on taking personal responsibility for building in quality during software development. **"The Software Quality Profile"** describes how the Personal Software Process and Team Software Process have been employed to save substantial development time and produce products with fewer defects. Individual software engineers have been trained to pay careful attention to, and make detailed measurements of, their work in order to isolate and remove sources of mistakes. Based on thousands of such exercises, Humphrey shares results on key variables that are related graphically in quality profiles.

The elements of a software product that describe its quality ("fitness for use") can be treated within various frameworks, which David Miller calls "quality models." His **"Choice and Application of a Software Quality Model"** presents six such commonly used models and elaborates on the strengths and weaknesses of each. Miller advises an organization to select and use the one model that most directly addresses the quality factors important to that organization's business goals. Definition, specification, and measurement of factors contributing to quality are seen as crucial to agreement on goals and priorities.

"Risk Management Supporting Quality Management of Software Acquisition Projects" presents experiences of a major global automaker as shared by Gerhard Getto. He argues for using risk management as a driver for the software acquisition process. Experiences gained in an ongoing business process re-engineering project have shown that the risk management process, in particular, must be adapted to the constraints imposed by the project organization. Risk management allows one to act before difficulties turn into real problems.

1

The Software Quality Profile

Watts S. Humphrey, The Software Engineering Institute,
Carnegie Mellon University

*T*he software community has been slow to use data to measure software quality. This article addresses the reasons for this problem and describes a way to use process measurements to assess product quality. The basic process measures are time, size, and defects. When these data are gathered for every engineer and every step of the development process, a host of quality measures can be derived to evaluate software quality. Extensive data from the Personal Software Process are used to derive the profiles of software processes that generally produce high-quality software products. By examining these profiles, one can judge the likelihood that a program will have defects found in its subsequent testing or use. Examples are given of defect profiles, together with guidelines for their use.

Key words: data, defect, measurement, profile, process, PSP, quality, software engineering, TSP

INTRODUCTION

Without numbers, quality programs are just talk. There are four reasons why the software community has been slow to use numbers for software quality.

1. There is no generally recognized definition for quality measures.
2. Even when one knows what numbers to use, the data are not easy to gather.
3. Even with data, it is not obvious how to interpret and use the numbers.
4. People are reluctant to measure the quality of their personal work.

This article addresses these questions and gives examples of software quality data that can readily be gathered and used by trained engineers. While focusing on measuring and controlling the defect content of programs, other quality measures are important to customers. Defect content, however, must be measured and controlled before other quality aspects can be effectively addressed. Some of the material in this article is taken from two textbooks written by the author to introduce process methods in undergraduate and graduate software courses (Humphrey 1995, 1997). The rest comes from some yet unpublished work with development teams.

THE SOFTWARE QUALITY PROBLEM

Software quality is becoming increasingly important. Software is now used in many demanding applications, and software defects can cause serious damage and even physical harm. While defects in financial or word-processing programs can be annoying and costly, people are not killed or injured. But when software-intensive systems fly airplanes, drive automobiles, control air traffic, run factories, or operate power plants, defects can be dangerous. People have been killed because of defective software (Leveson 1995).

While there have not been many fatalities so far, they will almost certainly increase. In spite of its problems, software is ideally suited for critical applications since it does not wear out or deteriorate. Computerized control systems are so versatile, economical, and reliable that they are the common choice for most systems. Therefore, software engineers must consider that their work could impact the health, safety, and welfare of many people.

The Risks of Poor Quality

Any defect in a software program can potentially cause serious problems. While it may seem unlikely that a simple error in a remote part of a large system could be disastrous, these are the most frequent sources of trouble. The problem is that systems are becoming faster, more complex, and automatic. Catastrophic failures are increasingly likely and potentially more damaging (Perrow 1984).

When designing large systems, difficult design issues are carefully studied, reviewed, and tested. As a result, the most common causes of software problems are simple oversights and goofs. These are typically mistakes made by software engineers. While most of these mistakes get caught in compiling and testing, engineers inject so many defects that many still escape the testing process and are not found until the product is used.

The problem is that software engineers often confuse simple with easy. They believe their simple mistakes will be simple to find. They are often surprised to learn that such trivial errors as omitting a punctuation mark, misnaming a parameter, or incorrectly setting a condition could escape testing and cause serious problems in actual use. These are, however, the kinds of things that cause many of the problems software suppliers spend millions of dollars finding and fixing.

The quality of large programs depends on the quality of the smaller programs of which they are built. Thus, to produce high-quality large programs, every software engineer who develops one or more of the system's parts must do high-quality work. This means that all the engineers must be committed to quality. When they are committed, they will track and manage their defects with such care that few, if any, defects will be found in integration, system testing, or by customers. The Software Engineering Institute (SEI) has developed the Personal Software Process (PSP) and the Team Software Process (TSP) to help engineers work this way.

MEASURING SOFTWARE QUALITY

Software quality impacts development costs, delivery schedules, and user satisfaction. Because software quality is so important, it is necessary to first discuss what is meant by the word quality. The quality of a software product must be defined in terms that are meaningful to the product's users. What is most important to them and what do they need?

Defects and Quality

A software engineer's job is to deliver quality products to customers at their planned costs and on their committed schedules. Software products must also meet the user's functional needs and reliability. While the software functions are most important to the program's users, these functions are not usable unless the software runs. To get the software to run, however, engineers must remove most of its defects. While there are many aspects to software quality, the first concern must be with its defects.

Defects are important because people make mistakes. Experienced programmers typically make a mistake for every seven to 10 lines of code they develop (Humphrey 1996). While the programmers generally find and correct most of these defects when they compile and test their programs, there still can be defects in the finished product.

What Are Defects?

Some people mistakenly refer to software defects as bugs. When programs are widely used and applied in ways their designers did not anticipate, seemingly trivial mistakes can have unforeseeable consequences. As widely used software systems are enhanced to meet new needs, latent problems can be exposed, and a trivial-seeming defect can become dangerous. While the majority of trivial defects have trivial consequences, a small percentage can cause serious problems. Since there is no way to know which of these mistakes will have serious consequences, they all must be treated as potentially serious.

The term defect refers to something that is wrong with a program. It could be a misspelling, a punctuation mistake, or an incorrect program statement. Defects can be in programs, designs, or even the requirements specifications or other documentation. Defects can be redundant or extra statements, incorrect statements, or omitted program sections. A defect is anything that detracts from the program's ability to completely and effectively meet the user's needs. A defect is an objective thing; it is something one can identify, describe, and count.

Simple coding mistakes can produce destructive or hard-to-find defects. Conversely, many sophisticated design defects are easy to find. The sophistication of the design mistake and the impact of the resulting defect are largely independent. Even trivial implementation errors can cause serious system problems. This is particularly important since most software defects are simple programmer oversights and mistakes. While design issues are always important, newly developed programs typically have few design defects compared with the number of simple oversights, typos, and goofs. Therefore, to improve program quality it is essential that engineers learn to manage the defects they inject in their programs.

The Engineer's Responsibility

The software engineer who writes a program is best able to find and fix its defects. It is important that software engineers take personal responsibility for the quality of the programs they produce. Writing defect-free programs, however, is challenging and takes effective methods, skill, practice, and data. By using the PSP, engineers learn how to consistently produce essentially defect-free programs.

The importance of careful engineering practices is illustrated by the system-test data for the Galileo spacecraft shown in Figure 1 (Nikora 1991). In more than six years of system testing, the Jet Propulsion Laboratory (JPL) found 196 defects in this 22,000 lines of code (LOC) system. While only 45 of these defects were judged to be fatal, many noncritical defects had to be removed before some of the critical defects could be uncovered. System testing is like peeling an onion; the outer layers must be removed before the critical problems can be found. Since the Galileo spacecraft mission was successful, it is likely that most of the product's defects had been removed.

By following sound engineering practices, PSP-trained engineers remove most of their defects before integration or system test. Systems built using these methods routinely have less than 0.2 defects per thousand lines of code (KLOC) found in system test. When compared with 8.9 defects per KLOC found in Galileo, it is clear that the PSP teaches engineers to peel away layers of defects before they release their code.

The PSP and TSP

The PSP was developed by the SEI to help small software groups and engineers understand and improve their capabilities. It provides process scripts, forms, and standards that guide engineers through the steps of planning, tracking, and doing software work. The PSP is introduced with a textbook and course in which engineers complete

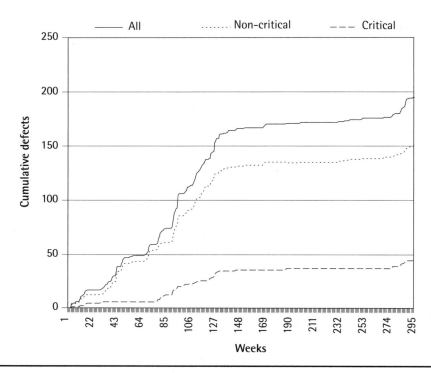

Figure 1   Galileo system test defects.

10 programming exercises and five analysis reports (Humphrey 1995). The PSP is being taught at several universities in the United States, Europe, South America, and Australia, and it is being introduced by a growing number of software organizations.

The TSP was developed because many engineers had trouble applying the PSP to projects of more than one or two engineers (Humphrey 1998). The TSP walks a team through launching and developing a product. While the TSP uses the four generic phases of requirements, design, implementation, and test, its emphasis is on multiple product versions and interleaved development activities. The TSP applies to teams of two to 20 hardware and software engineers who are PSP trained.

The TSP is introduced with a three-day launch workshop where the engineers establish their goals, select their personal roles, and define their processes. They make a quality plan, identify support needs, and produce a detailed development schedule. The TSP guides them through a risk assessment, describes how to track and assess their work, and suggests ways to report their status to management. After a team has completed one three-day launch workshop, a two-day relaunch workshop is adequate for each subsequent phase. They then integrate new team members, readjust role assignments, and reassess plans. The launch and relaunch workshops are not training courses; they are vital parts of the project.

The PSP and TSP have been used on development projects and have produced substantial cost, schedule, and quality improvements. In general, once engineers are PSP trained, they have one-fifth to one-tenth as many unit-test defects as before, and their integration, systems, acceptance, and usage defects are 20 to 100 or more times lower. One company, for example, found that PSP training reduced system-test time from two to three months to three to five days (Ferguson et al. 1997; Hayes 1997; Humphrey 1996).

PSP QUALITY MEASUREMENTS

The principal process measures in software development are time, size, and defects. If one measures these precisely, then most other important measures can be derived. The way this is done in the PSP and TSP is as follows:

1. The development process is defined at several levels of detail.

2. At the lowest level, the process steps are reduced to individual engineering activities. Examples include the detailed design for a program module, coding that module, or compiling the module until it compiles with no errors.

3. PSP-trained engineers track and record their activities for each process step. They track their time in minutes, count and record the defects they inject and remove, and measure the size product they produce.

While this level of detail might seem intrusive, the PSP shows engineers that such data are not difficult to gather. Engineers also find they need these data to plan their work and improve their performance. The data help engineers understand their personal abilities and where and how they can improve. Consider the problem of a track team. Without a measured track and a stopwatch it would be hard to decide which events to enter or how to practice. For software engineers, the PSP provides the equivalent of a measured track and a stopwatch.

Finally, PSP data are the property of the engineers. While managers need data at a team level, they do not need to see the engineers' personal data. With the composite team data on time, size, and defects for every process phase, managers can analyze the quality of the process used and assess the defect content of the finished products.

A SOFTWARE QUALITY STRATEGY

To help manage quality, measures of the defect content of one's work are needed. It is also necessary to judge the number of defects remaining in the products produced.

The PSP/TSP quality strategy. The PSP/TSP quality strategy is illustrated by the example of a large IBM program shown in Figure 2 (Kaplan, Clark, and Tang 1994). The correlation between development and usage defects was 0.964 for release one. For release two, the correlation was also high at 0.878. Thus, the number of defects found in development test indicates the likely number of defects remaining after test. Therefore, to significantly reduce usage defects engineers must remove defects before development test. They can only do this by using a disciplined personal process. The PSP shows engineers how to remove defects at the earliest possible time, generally before the first compile.

TSP quality data. While several industrial groups are using the TSP, the first completed project was from a team at Embry Riddle Aeronautical University (ERAU). An overall quality measure showed that they removed 99.4 percent of the defects before system test. The team's defect-removal profile is shown in Figure 3. The vertical scale on the left shows the defect density in defects per KLOC. The horizontal scale gives the development phases: detailed level design review, code review, compile, unit test, integration test, and system test.

In the PSP and TSP, the code review is done before any testing and even before the first compile. The engineers do these design and code reviews on their own code. After they have cleaned up their programs, peer reviews or inspections are more effective at finding and removing more sophisticated problems. Testing will then be even more effective.

While the curve in Figure 3 looks good, there were problems. An effective design review would have found at least two or three times as many defects as were found in unit test. The curve in Figure 3 indicates there were design-review problems with at least some of the components.

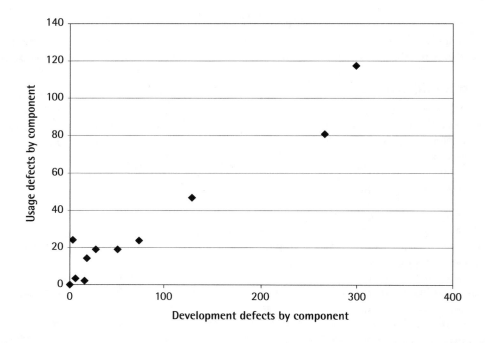

Figure 2   Development vs. usage defects: IBM Release 1 (r=0.9644).

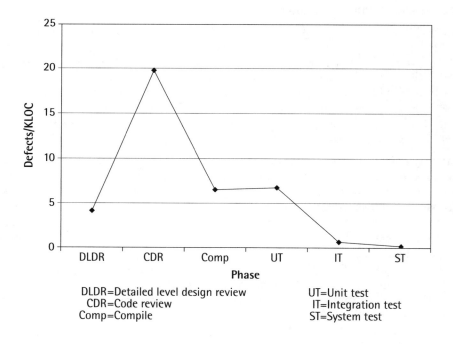

Figure 3   Defects/KLOC by phase.

THE QUALITY PROFILE

By examining the large volume of PSP data, the profile of a process that should consistently produce high-quality programs can be developed.

Some PSP Quality Data

Based on data from 2386 programs written in PSP courses, the engineers took 15,534 hours to develop programs of 308,023 LOC. They found 22,644 defects. Figure 4 shows how many defects were injected and removed per hour in each process phase. By examining the data on their personal work, engineers can estimate the number of defects they have injected and judge how long it would take them to remove these defects.

For example, engineers inject an average of 1.76 defects per hour in detailed design and remove 2.96 defects per hour in detailed level design review. Thus, for every hour of design, an engineer should plan on at least 0.59 hours of design review. Similarly, for every hour of coding, they will need an average of 0.64 hours of code review. From their personal data, engineers can then estimate how long it should take to remove the defects. Note that these are averages, and there is considerable variation among engineers.

By reviewing their defect data, engineers can see the benefits of careful practices. For example, while compiling engineers inject an average of 0.60 defects per hour and while in test they inject an average of 0.38 defects per hour. Clearly, when engineers rush to get through compiling and testing, they make a lot of mistakes. When PSP-trained engineers start injecting large numbers of defects in compiling and testing, they know they need to stop and think or take a break. By watching their personal data, the PSP helps engineers better manage their work.

The PSP course data also show the value of spending adequate time in design. As shown in Figure 5, engineers have fewer test defects in their programs when they spend more time in design. Here, the bars at the front of the figure show the percentage of programs with various unit-test defect densities. These front bars are for the case where the engineers spend enough design and design-review time.

In this figure, the front bars show when engineers spent as much or more time in design as they spent in coding. For design review, they spent more than 50 percent of design time. The back bars are for programs where engineers spent more time in coding than in designing, and where they had an inadequate amount of design-review time. As one can see from the figure, product quality is worse with poor practices. For example, with good practices (the front bars), about 46 percent of the programs had no unit-test defects. With poor practices, only about 18 percent had no defects. Most of the poor-practice programs had 20 or more unit-test defects per KLOC.

PSP phase	Injected/ hour	Removed/ hour	Removed/ Injected
Detailed level design	1.76	0.10	0.05
Detailed level design review	0.11	2.96	27.91
Code	4.20	0.51	0.10
Code review	0.11	6.52	59.78
Compile	0.60	9.48	15.84
Test	0.38	2.21	5.82

Figure 4   Defects injection and removal rates.

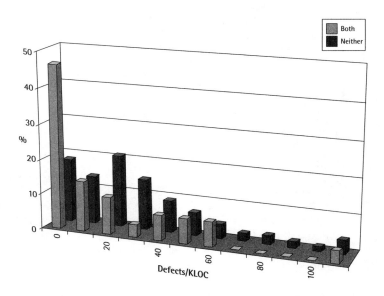

Figure 5   Unit-test defects vs. practices.

As one might expect, the situation is much the same for code reviews and compile defects. When code-review times are greater than 50 percent of coding time, compile defects are lower. With adequate code-review times, about 35 percent of the programs have zero to 10 compile defects per KLOC, and with little or no code review time only 9 percent do. In this no-review case, the largest number of programs have more than 100 defects per KLOC in compile.

Profile Values

Based on these PSP data one can establish process limits and a quality profile. Design time should be greater than 100 percent of coding time, design-review time should be greater than 50 percent of design time, and code-review time should be greater than 50 percent of coding time. Also, compile defects should be less than 10 per KLOC, and unit-test defects should be less than five per KLOC. When a factor meets or exceeds these criteria, that profile dimension is at the edge of the bull's eye. When the criteria are not met, say 25 percent design-review time instead of 50 percent, that dimension would be half way to the center of the bull's eye. These criteria are summarized in Figure 6. Every organization should gather its own data and set its own profile values based on its people, methods, tools, application areas, and experience.

Figure 7 shows an example of how these profiles are calculated. The data for this program component are as follows:

LOC:	336
Design time:	7.6 hours
Design-review time	1.25 hours
Coding time	8.9 hours
Code-review time	3.9 hours
Compile defects	3
Unit-test defects	4

Next, the profile dimensions are calculated as follows:

Design/code time = 7.6/8.9 = 0.85 < 1.0, so Design profile = 0.85/1.0 = 0.85
Design review/design time = 1.25/7.6 = 0.16 < 0.5, so
    Design-review profile = 0.16/0.5 = 0.33
Code review/code time = 3.9/8.9 = 0.44 < 0.5, so Code-review profile = 0.44/0.5 = 0.88
Unit-test defects per KLOC = 1000*4/336 = 11.9 > 5.0, so
    Unit-test profile = 2*5.0/(11.9+5.0) = 0.61
Compile defects per KLOC = 1000*3/336 = 8.93 < 10.0, so Compile profile = 1.0

While this component had three profile dimensions near 1.0, two were poor. Not surprisingly, this component had a defect found in integration testing.

Dimension	Meaning
Design/Code	The ratio detailed to coding time. When engineers do not take the time to produce a thorough design, they generally make more design errors. To reduce this risk, design time should equal at least 100% of coding time.
Code-review time	The time spent in code review, compared with coding time. By doing a personal code review before they compile, engineers can find a large percentage of their defects. A thorough code review should take 50% or more of coding time.
Compile defects/KLOC	The defects per KLOC found in compile. Even with good review times and rates, the review could still have missed many defects. For quality products, compile defects should be less than 10 defects/KLOC.
Design-review time	Detailed design-review time related to detailed design. A thorough detailed design review should take 50% or more of the time spent in detailed design. Anything less generally indicates an inadequate review.
Unit-test defects/KLOC	The defects per KLOC found in unit test. The number of defects found in unit test is one of the best indicators of the number that will be found later. When the unit test defects/KLOC exceed 5, subsequent problems are likely.

Figure 6 Quality profile dimensions.

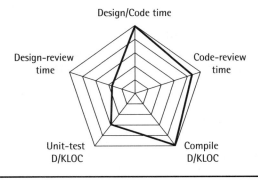

Figure 7 Component E quality profile.

Interpreting the Quality Profile

In reading the profiles, several guidelines can help identify potentially troublesome components.

- If engineers do not spend enough time during the design phase, they are probably designing while they are coding. As can be seen from Figure 4, they then introduce more than twice as many defects per hour as they would during a thorough design phase. The profile indicates this problem by a low value for design/code time.

- Since engineers inject defects during design, they must spend enough time reviewing these designs or they will not find the defects. This problem is indicated by a low value for design-review time.

- Even when engineers spend enough time doing a design review, they may not do an effective review. Merely looking at the design for a long time, for example, will not result in finding defects. Engineers must use sound review methods to find both the sophisticated and the simple design problems. Poor design-review methods are generally indicated by a high number of unit-test defects per KLOC (a profile value near the center).

- If engineers do not spend enough time reviewing their code before compiling it, they will likely leave defects to be found later. The profile indicates this problem with a low value for code-review time.

- Even when engineers spend enough time doing a code review, they may not do the review properly. This problem is generally indicated by a high number of compile defects per KLOC (a profile value near the center).

Note that profile values near the center indicate poor quality practices and suggest that the component will have defects found in later testing or use.

A QUALITY PROFILE ANALYSIS

The TSP is still in development, but it has already been used by about 30 teams, including three student teams. The quality profiles for one student team at ERAU are shown in Figure 8. This team removed 99.4 percent of development defects before they started system test. Before reading the next paragraphs, try to identify the components that had defects in either system test or integration test or will likely have defects found in use. Note that several defects were found in integration test and system test of this 5090 LOC subsystem. In several months of experimental use, no further defects have been found.

Interpreting the Profiles

The ERAU quality profiles can be read as follows:

Component A. While this engineer did not do an adequate design or design review, she had a low number of unit-test defects. While there is a risk of later defects, it is not a high risk.

Component B. This engineer spent slightly less time than optimum in design, design review, and code review, but the low numbers of compile and unit-test defects indicate low risk.

Component C. Here, while design time was low and the unit-test defects were slightly higher than desired, the design-review time was adequate. This is a moderate risk component.

Component D. In this case, the engineer spent an inadequate amount of design-review time and found an excessive number of unit-test defects. While code-review time was low, the low compile defects indicate there are likely few, if any, remaining coding errors. This component actually had an integration defect and likely has further undetected defects.

Component E. This component also had low design-review time and an excessive number of unit-test defects. It had an integration defect and could have further problems. This is the component used in the example in Figure 7.

Component F. This component is much like E only not as bad. It had one defect in system test.

Component G. This component looks good in all respects.

Component H. This component looks risky. While adequate time was spent in both design and code review, the excessive numbers of compile and unit-test defects are a concern. This component did not have defects in integration or system test, but it appears likely to have defects in later testing or use.

Component I. This component clearly has the worst of all 11 profiles. While it had low unit-test defects, it had an excessive number of compile defects and an inadequate amount of design and design-review time. This component had an integration defect and seems likely to have more defects.

Component J. The principal risk here is that there were an excessive number of unit-test defects. While this component had no integration or system-test defects, it is exposed.

Component K. This is another good-looking profile. This component had no integration or system-test defects.

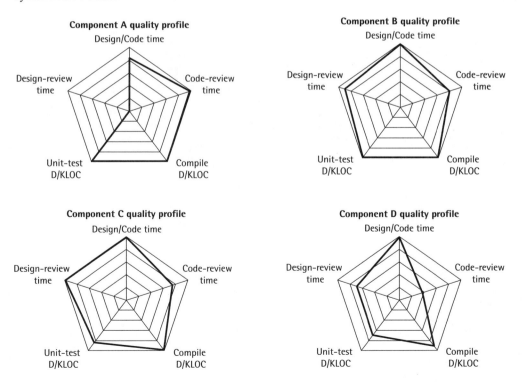

Figure 8   ERAU quality profiles.

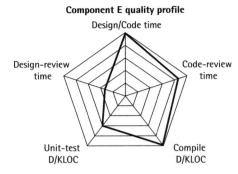

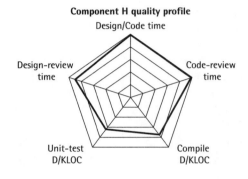

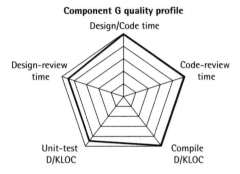

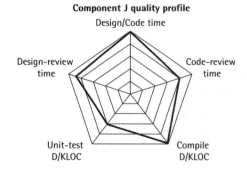

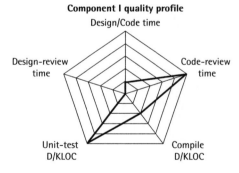

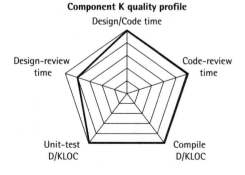

Figure 8   ERAU quality profiles (continued).

CONCLUSIONS

With TSP data, engineers can determine which components are most likely to have defects before they even start integration and system testing. By thoroughly inspecting and reworking these defect-prone components before integrating or system testing them, development teams can save substantial test time and produce higher quality products.

These results can best be understood by considering data. First, before PSP training, most experienced engineers inject between 80 and 125 defects per KLOC. They will find about half of the remaining defects in each subsequent compile and test phase. Thus, with the Galileo spacecraft, if one assumes that JPL used excellent engineers who injected only 80 defects per KLOC, that would be 1760 defects, of which about 880 would be found in compile, 440 in unit testing, and 220 in integration test. This would leave about 220 defects at system-test entry. In more than six years of testing they found 196 of these defects. Even though the mission was a success, it seems likely that the product still had a few remaining defects. To achieve this level of quality for a small 22,000 LOC product, however, JPL had to test for more than six years.

With the PSP, engineers remove most of their defects before integration or system test. Through a combination of sound design practices and careful reviews, they consistently produce products with fewer than 0.2 system-test defects per KLOC and essentially none in later use. With PSP training, the JPL engineers would then have had four or five defects to find in system test, and they could have completed testing in a few weeks instead of six years.

When engineers know how to measure their work they can obtain much useful quality information. The quality profile is one example of what one can learn about product quality, even before integration test entry. When engineers gather and use process data, they can manage product quality, save test time, cut development costs, and shorten schedules.

ACKNOWLEDGMENTS

Several people kindly reviewed the draft of this article and made helpful suggestions. I particularly thank Alan Koch, Mark Paulk, and Bill Peterson. I also thank the anonymous reviewers for this journal. Their perceptive comments were most helpful. Dr. Iraj Hirmanpoor, Dr. Soheil Khajenoori, and the student team at Embry Riddle Aeronautical University also deserve special thanks. They have provided strong support and a useful test environment for the early PSP and TSP work.

REFERENCES

Ferguson, Pat, Watts S. Humphrey, Soheil Khajenoori, Susan Macke, and Annette Matvya. 1997. Introducing the personal software process: Three industry case studies. *IEEE Computer* 30, no. 5: 24-31.

Hayes, Will. 1997. The personal software process: An empirical study of the impact of PSP on individual engineers. Carnegie Mellon University Software Engineering Institute technical report No. CMU/SEI-97-TR-001.

Humphrey, Watts S. 1995. *A discipline for software engineering*. Reading, MA: Addison-Wesley.

———. 1996. Using a defined and measured personal software process. *IEEE Software* (May): 77-88.

———. 1997. *Introduction to the personal software process*. Reading, Mass.: Addison-Wesley.

———. 1998. Three dimensions of process improvement, part 3: The team process. *Crosstalk*. (April): 14–17.

Kaplan, Craig, Ralph Clark, and Victor Tang. 1994. *Secrets of software quality: 40 innovations from IBM*. New York: McGraw-Hill.

Leveson, Nancy G. 1995. *Safeware: System safety and computers*. Reading, MA: Addison-Wesley.

Nikora, Allen P. 1991. Error discovery rate by severity category and time to repair software failures for three JPL flight projects. Software product assurance section. Jet Propulsion Laboratory, Pasadena, CA. (November 5).

Perrow, Charles. 1984. *Normal accidents: Living with high-risk technologies.* New York: Basic Books.

BIOGRAPHY

Watts S. Humphrey joined the Software Engineering Institute (SEI) of Carnegie Mellon University after his retirement from IBM in 1986. While at SEI, he established the process program, led the initial development of the software capability maturity model, and introduced the concepts of software process assessment and software capability evaluation.

While at IBM, Humphrey held various technical executive positions, including the management of all IBM commercial software development. This included the first 19 releases of OS/360. Most recently, he was IBM's director of programming quality and process.

Humphrey has a master's degree in physics from the Illinois Institute of Technology and an MBA from the University of Chicago. He is an SEI Fellow, a member of ACM, an IEEE Fellow, and a past member of the Malcolm Baldrige National Quality Award board of examiners. He has published six books, which include *A Discipline for Software Engineering, Managing Technical People: Innovation, Teamwork, and the Software Process,* and *Introduction to the Personal Software Process.* He was awarded the 1993 Aerospace Software Engineering Award presented by the American Institute of Aeronautics and Astronautics. Humphrey holds five U.S. patents.

Choice and Application of a Software Quality Model

Dave Miller

*T*his paper provides advice on choosing and adapting a software quality model for an organization. Several well-known models are examined to show that they generally agree on the elements that constitute software quality. A software development organization should choose the software quality model which best matches the needs of its customers. The development organization can adapt its processes to ensure these quality elements are specified and implemented.

Key words: organizational goals, product characteristics, quality attributes, quality factors, technical specifications

INTRODUCTION

Does your organization know what constitutes quality in software or which aspects of software quality are most important to your customers? Software developers spend considerable time discussing quality. Though customers and managers worry about quality of software, and most organizations have software quality groups, there is seldom formal agreement about how to measure the elements that constitute the quality of software products.

This paper provides advice on choosing and adapting a software quality model for an organization. Several well-known models are examined to show that they generally agree on the elements that constitute software quality. Assumptions underlying this paper are:

- Only by defining measurable elements of "software quality" can an organization systematically assess the quality of its software and set specific quality goals

- To be useful for setting goals, software quality elements must have clear definitions

- By specifically addressing quality elements in requirement specifications, design practices, and testing, an organization can systematically ensure its software products will meet those goals

WHAT IS SOFTWARE QUALITY?

Ask "what is software quality?" and answers will range from "the result of following a well-defined software lifecycle methodology" to "the result of thorough testing" to "good reliability," to "the functionality needed by users." Developers usually add "adaptable to other platforms and environments," "degree to which code can be reused," and "easy to read and maintain." Customers may add "configurable" and "easy to install." This paper only deals with what Rai, Song, and Troutt (1998) refer to as "technical" aspects of software quality as opposed to "managerial" (how to manage software quality efforts), "organizational" (how an organization deals with software quality), and "economic" aspects.

MODELS FOR SOFTWARE QUALITY

The elements which describe the quality of a piece of software are usually referred to as **"quality factors,"** and collectively they are usually referred to as a **"software quality model."** Discussed below are six well-known software quality models. Each has advantages and disadvantages. None completely subsumes any of the others. Additional models exist, but are generally similar. ISO 9000 (1997) and the Capability Maturity Model (CMM), though often referred to as "quality models," focus on processes rather than quality software.

Boehm's Model

Barry Boehm (1976) organizes software quality attributes in the hierarchy shown in Figure 1.

Cavano & McCall's Model

The "GE model" or "military model" for software quality, shown in Figure 2, resulted from studies done for the USAF by Cavano and McCall in 1978. Cavano and McCall categorize quality factors under three phases of the product lifecycle.

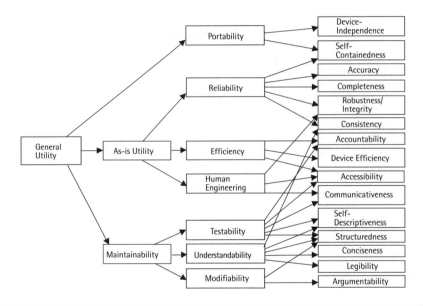

Figure 1   Boehm's software quality attributes.

Product Operations	Correctness	Satisfies specifications and fulfills user's mission objectives
	Reliability	Can be expected to perform its intended function with required precision
	Efficiency	Computing resources and code required by a program to perform a function
	Integrity	Access to software or data software or data by unauthorized persons can be controlled
	Usability	Effort to learn, operate, prepare input, and interpret output

Figure 2   Cavano and McCall's Model.

Product Revision	Maintainability	Effort to locate and fix an error
	Testability	Effort to test a program to ensure it performs its intended function
	Flexibility	Effort to modify a program
Product Transition	Portability	Effort to transfer a program from one hardware configuration and/or software system environment to another
	Reusability	Program can be used in other applications
	Interoperability	Effort to couple one system with another

Figure 2   Cavano and McCall's Model. (continued).

FURPS+

Hewlett Packard's FURPS+ model for software quality (Grady, 1992), dating from the mid-1980s, is organized quite differently from either Cavano and McCall's model or Boehm's model (Figure 3). It provides five general categories of quality attributes.

Functionality	Feature Set, Capabilities, Generality, Security
Usability	Human Factors, Aesthetics, Consistency, Documentation
Reliability	Frequency/Severity of Failure, Recoverability, Predictability, Accuracy, Mean Time to Failure
Performance	Speed, Efficiency, Resource Consumption, Throughput, Response Time
Supportability	Testability, Extensibility, Adaptability, Maintainability, Compatibility, Configurability, Serviceability, Installability, Localizability

Figure 3   FURPS+ model.

Garvin and Plsek's "Dimensions of Quality"

David Garvin (1988) and Paul Plsek (1987) discuss nine primary "dimensions" which define quality in general, in the spirit of W. Edwards Deming's teachings. Garvin and Plsek intend the "dimensions" to apply to many different products, including software (Figure 4).

Dimension	Meaning
Performance	Primary product or service characteristics
Features	Secondary operating characteristics, added touches
Conformance	Degree to which a product's design and operating characteristics meet preestablished standards
Reliability	Extent of failure free operation over time
Durability	Amount of use before replacement is preferable to repair
Serviceability	Resolution of problems and complaints
Aesthetics	Characteristics relating to the senses, such as color, fragrance, fit, or finish
Perceived Quality	Inferences about other dimensions; reputation
Response	Characteristics of the human-to-human interface like timeliness, courtesy, professionalism, and so on

Figure 4   Dimensions of Quality Model.

ISO 9126

ISO 9126 combines FURPS+ with aspects of other models (Figure 5). Citations make it clear that its authors were aware of FURPS+, Boehm's model, and Cavano and McCall's model. ISO 9126 is linked with test and development methods such as ISO 12119, ISO 14598-5, and ISO 12207, 12207.0, 12207.1, and 12207.2. A team is improving ties between these lifecycle processes and also with ISO 9000, IEEE Std 1074, and IEEE Std 1498. Geoff Dromey's articles (1995, 1996) suggest how ISO 9126 may be applied within an organization.

ISO 9126 Category	ISO 9126 Subcategory	ISO 9126 Definition
Functionality	Suitability	Presence and appropriateness of a set of functions for specified tasks
	Accuracy	Provision of right or agreed results or effects
	Interoperability	Ability to interact with specified systems
	Compliance	Adheres to application related standards or conventions or regulations in laws and similar prescriptions
	Security	Prevents unauthorized access, whether accidental or deliberate, to programs and data
Reliability	Maturity	Frequency of failure by faults in the software
	Fault Tolerance	Maintains a specified level of performance in cases of software faults or of infringement of its specified interface
	Recoverability	Capability to re-establish its level of performance and recover the data directly affected in case of a failure, and time and effort needed for it
Usability	Understandability	Users' effort for recognizing the logical concept and its applicability
	Learnability	Users' effort for learning its application (for example, operation control, input, output)
	Operability	Users' effort for operation and operation control
Efficiency	Time behavior	Response and processing times, and throughput rates
	Resource behavior	Amount of resources used and the duration of such use
Maintainability	Changeability	Effort needed for modification, fault removal, or for environmental change
	Analyzability	Effort needed for diagnosis of deficiencies or causes of failures, or for identification of parts to be modified
	Stability	Risk of unexpected effect of modifications
	Testability	Effort needed for validating the modified software
Portability	Adaptability	Opportunity for adaptation to different specified environments
	Installability	Effort needed to install the software in a specified environment
	Conformance	Adheres to standards or conventions relating to portability
	Replaceability	Opportunity and effort of using it in the place of specified other software in the environment of that software

Figure 5   ISO 9126 Model.

SEI Model

The Software Engineering Institute approaches software quality from another angle (Barbacci 1995), organizing software attributes and other concerns under a set of engineering disciplines. In another SEI publication, Paulk (1999) states, "Although not explicitly stated in Software CMM version 1.1, the definition of quality evolves as an organization moves up the maturity levels."

Performance Engineering	Concerns	Latency	Response window, precedence, jitter, criticality
		Throughput	Observation interval, processing rate, criticality
		Capacity	Utilization, schedule utilization, spare capacity
		Modes	
	Factors	Demand	Arrival pattern, execution time
		System	Type of resource, software services, resource allocation
	Methods	Synthesis	
		Analysis	Scheduling theory, queuing theory, formal methods
Dependability Engineering	Attributes (concerns)		Availability, reliability, safety, confidentiality, integrity, maintainability
	Impairments (factors)		Faults, errors, failures
	Means (methods)		Fault prevention, fault tolerance, fault removal, fault forecasting
Security Engineering	Concerns		Confidentity, integrity, availability
	Factors	Interface	Authentication, encryption, auditing and analysis
		Internal	Access control, auditing and logging, kernalization
	Methods	Synthesis	Process models, security models, secure protocols
		Analysis	Formal methods, penetration analysis, covert-channel analysis
Safety Engineering	Concerns		Interaction complexity, coupling strength
	Factors		Hazard, mishap
	Methods	Hazard identification	Brainstorming, consensus building, hazard and operability analysis
		Hazard analysis	Fault tree analysis, event tree analysis, failure modes and effects
		Implementation methodologies	Formal methods, transformations, version management
		Implementation mechanisms	Locking, lockouts, interlocks

Figure 6 SEI Model.

COMPARING THE MODELS

The models have some flaws, and they need more complete definitions to be useful. For instance, definitions for quality factors are often terse, without practical examples or guidelines. How does one write requirements for "stability" or "replaceability?" How does one test for "interoperability" or "analyzability?" Factors overlap. For instance, in ISO 9126, average developers may not distinguish between arcane distinctions: "interoperability," "adaptability," and "configurability" seem nearly identical. So are "understandability," "learnability," and "operability." "Recoverability" and "fault tolerance" overlap with "stability." Some factors seem unverifiable (Pressman 1992; Jarvis 1997). For instance, "consistency" and "usability" are subjective measures. Garvin and Plsek's "Dimensions of Quality" are much too general without being supplemented by software-specific guidelines.

The models do not agree on terminology or even on what factors should be included. "Supportability" in one model appears to be nearly synonymous with "maintainability" in another model. Scopes of definitions vary: one model may deal with "maintainability" as an aspect of "supportability," while another model discusses "maintainability" without including "supportability." ISO 9126 subcategories of "replaceability," "fault tolerance," "learnability," "stability," and "conformance" are not in other models. Is "replaceability" actually a quality concern, even though it is an indicator of portability? Similarly, The SEI model provides no factors in the categories of "usability" or "portability." Boehm's model includes coding style: "self-descriptiveness," "structuredness," "conciseness," "legibility," and "self-containedness" may lead to higher quality, but are they quality attributes?

None of the models consider cost or time to market. Such tradeoffs are mentioned often in the literature (Rai, Song, and Troutt would argue these are "economic" elements, while quality factors are "technical"). Similarly, none of the quality models address tradeoffs between quality factors, such as those in texts by Shumskas (1992), Glass (1992), and McConnell (1993), and there is little basis for quantative assessment of tradeoffs (Liu 1998). ISO software standards and guides are still being refined and do not (yet) tie quality factors specifically into development processes. Alan Gilles (1997) nearly—but not quite—bridges quality models with development processes.

WHICH SOFTWARE QUALITY MODEL TO PICK?

Organizations may be tempted to create their own software quality models and definitions. You may try to combine all these models, but beware: as Boehm (1981) explains, the more detailed the guidelines, the less the guidelines will be used. If your revenue is primarily associated with hardware, you may use hardware terminology and metrics (MTBF, MTBSS, availability, cost of quality). Your contracts may dictate which quality model to use.

I recommend you choose only one of the models discussed here. Consider how widely-accepted the model is: Boehm's model is well-known, but it is not apparent how widely or well it has been implemented. Despite the growing body of SEI literature, it is not clear if the SEI quality model has been tested. Cavano and McCall's model has been used for two decades on government software contracts. Garvin's and Plsek's "dimensions" are well-known, yet it is not clear how to adapt them for software. FURPS+ and ISO 9126 are widely-used. Given a choice between these two similar models, consider using the international standard—ISO 9126. How well can the model be adapted for testing? Some texts urge readers to choose a software quality definition or model and then to implement it in development and test practices. However, achieving that implementation will not be simple. None of the models offer a clear mapping of quality factors into test methods. How well can the model be combined into the development model or lifecycle model used by the organization?

It may not be worthwhile spending time selecting a software quality model if your organization does not follow development or test processes. (Why spell out quality goals systematically, if they will not be used systematically?) There is no guaranteed payoff for implementing a software quality model, and the literature does not contain case studies or guidelines, but if Garvin and Plsek are right, the most effective way of achieving customer satisfaction is to address quality elements systematically throughout the product lifecycle.

ROAD MAP FOR MAKING USE OF A SOFTWARE QUALITY MODEL

Step 1. Define your organization's needs and goals for software quality. If you do not know what your organization needs in terms of quality, you should not waste time on a software quality model. Answer the following questions:
- What are your customers' quality priorities?
- Do you have processes in place to monitor customer preferences?
- How do your customers feel about your products and services versus those of your competitors?
- Do you have special needs such as regulations or safety concerns?
- Do you have contractual or legal requirements to use a particular model?

Step 2. Identify which quality elements are most important to your business goals.

Step 3. Choose a model based on elements you selected in Step 2.

Step 4. Develop details and examples to explain the software quality factors which are most important to your organization. These will help communicate priorities to your teams.

Step 5. Build the quality factors and the quality model into your development and test methodologies. SEI technical reports (Kazman 1994 and 1998) may be useful.

Step 6. If you have accomplished the steps above, you have organized a software development, test, and quality process which systematically addresses the software quality elements which match your organization's strategic goals. But things change, so periodically recalibrate with your staff and customers to ensure agreement on goals and priorities.

REFERENCES

Barbacci, M., T. H. Longstaff, M. H. Klein, and C. B. Weinstock. 1995. *Quality attributes.* Pittsburgh, PA: Carnegie Mellon U., Software Engineering Institute, CMU/SEI-95-TR-021.

Boehm, B. W. 1981. *Software engineering economics.* Upper Saddle River, NJ: Prentice Hall.

Boehm, B. W., J. R. Brown, and M. Lipow. 1976. Quantitative evaluation of software quality. In *Proceedings, 2nd international conference on software engineering,* 592–605. Long Beach, CA: IEEE Computer Society.

Cavano, J. P., and J. A. McCall. 1978. A framework for the measurement of software quality. In *Proceedings of the software quality and assurance workshop,* 133–139. Los Angeles, CA: ACM Special Interest Group on Measurement and Evaluation,.

Dromey, R. G. 1995. A model for software product quality. *IEEE Transactions on Software Engineering* 21:146–162.

———. 1996. Cornering the chimera, *IEEE Software.* Jan. 1996, 33–43.

Garvin, D. A. 1988. *Managing quality: The strategic and competitive edge.* NY: The Free Press.

Gillies, A. C. 1997. *Software quality: Theory and management.* 2nd ed. London: International Thomson Computer Press.

Glass, R. L. 1992. *Building quality software.* Englewood Cliffs, NJ: Prentice-Hall.

Grady, R. B. 1992. *Practical software metrics for project management and process control.* Englewood Cliffs, NJ: Prentice-Hall.

ISO 9000-3. 1997. *Quality management and quality assurance.* International Standards Association.

ISO/IEC 9126. 1991. *Quality characteristics and guidelines for their use.* International Standards Association.

Jarvis, A., and V. Crandall. 1997. *Inroads to software quality: "How to" guide and toolkit.* Upper Saddle River, NJ: Prentice Hall.

Kazman, R., and L. Bass. 1994. *Toward deriving software architectures from quality sttributes.* CMU/SEI-94-TR-10.

Kazman, R. et al. 1998. *The architecture tradeoff analysis method.* CMU/SEI-98-TR-008.

Liu, X. F. 1998. A quantitative approach for assessing the priorities of software quality requirements. *Journal of Systems and Software* 42:105–113.

McConnell, S. 1993. *Code complete: Practical handbook of software construction.* Redmond, WA: Microsoft Press.

Paulk, M. C. 1999. Evolution of quality in the software CMM. *Software Quality* 2, 1, 3.

Plsek, P. E. 1987. Defining quality at the marketing/development interface. *Quality Progress,* June 1987, 28–36.

Pressman, R. S. 1992. *Software engineering: A practitioner's approach.* 3rd ed. New York: McGraw-Hill.

Rai, A., H. Song, and M. Troutt. 1998. Software quality assurance: An analytical survey and research prioritization. *Journal of Systems and Software,* Jan. 1998, 67–83.

Shumskas, A. F. 1992. Software risk mitigation. In *Total Quality Management for Software,* G. G. Schulmeyer and J. I. McManus (eds.), 218–19. New York: Van Nostrand Reinhold.

BIOGRAPHY

Dave Miller has managed quality and test organizations at Motorola's DigiCable business unit for the last nine years. He is responsible for product qualification and system test for digital cable television systems, and leads cross-functional teams that address quality issues. His degrees include a master's in information science from Drexel University and a PhD in English from Duke University. Before joining Motorola, he managed system test groups, design documentation groups, and technical writing groups for Contel and GTE satellite organizations, and worked as a senior systems analyst for Planning Analysis Corporation. Dave can be reached at Motorola, DigiCable, 101 Tournament Drive, Horsham, Pennsylvania, 19044, or by e-mail at dmiller@gi.com .

CHAPTER 1.3

Risk Management Supporting Quality Management of Software Acquisition Projects

Gerhard Getto, DaimlerChrysler AG

*C*hallenges to traditional business practices prompt a need for change in organization, business processes, and information technology. Since business process reengineering and software acquisition projects are complex and the process maturity on the acquirer's side is often very low, such projects are risky. Using risk management as a driver for the software acquisition process means quality assurance activities must focus on the most critical aspects. Risk management has been found to be an excellent mechanism for that purpose if it is carried out systematically and continuously. As organizational aspects are particularly crucial in complex software acquisition projects, the focus of this article lies on project and risk management organization and organizational risks. Also, experiences regarding risk management in general are discussed.

Key words: business process reengineering, critical success factor model, ERP (enterprise resource planning) system, project goal description, project quality management, roles in risk management

INTRODUCTION

Car manufacturers face a variety of challenges, such as worldwide competition, globalization, and new products and markets. There is a need for change in organization, business processes, information technology, and supporting software systems. Business processes have to be optimized to reduce product development time, shorten customer order lead time, and reduce manufacturing lead time. This allows changes to be made to customer orders at short notice, speeds up the confirmation of delivery date with sign-up of the order, and reduces costs. The main objective for information technology is to provide cost-efficient solutions that support future processes. Complex software acquisition projects are initiated to eliminate redundant software applications and databases, migrate to state-of-the-art hardware and software platforms, and make use of best-practice software solutions.

Software acquisition is a critical concern for businesses all over the world since the impact of software on business processes is increasing tremendously. U.S. enterprises alone spend more than $250 billion per year acquiring software products and services. There is a risk of failure in every acquisition project. Many of the mistakes that cause acquired software not to meet performance, schedule, and cost requirements include process-specific issues such as unrealistic time estimates, costs and manpower requirements, or suppliers and/or buyers who do not have adequate technical expertise (Moreau 1998). There are a number of risks in software acquisition projects due to their complexity and the fact that the process maturity on the acquirer's side is often much lower than on the supplier's side.

The awareness of the necessity of a mature software acquisition process is quite new. For example, the Software Engineering Institute's Software Acquisition Capability Maturity Model (SA-CMM) (Ferguson et al. 1996) was published in 1996, whereas the first version of CMM for software (Paulk et al. 1993) was available in 1984. The importance of risk management in software acquisition projects is illustrated by the fact that it is one of the key process areas of SA-CMM. The European Commission sponsored the development of a risk management-driven software acquisition method called Euromethod (1996) and a best-practice library for managing software acquisition processes (ISPL 1999), which takes advantage of the experiences of using Euromethod in a range of acquisitions. An evaluation of existing software acquisition approaches can be found in Getto (1999).

This article presents experiences gained in establishing quality and risk management at DaimlerChrysler AG along these lines of thought. As organizational aspects are particularly crucial in complex software acquisition projects, the focus of this article lies on project and risk management organization and organizational risks. A methodological view of this risk management process can be found in Getto and Landes (1999). A business process reengineering project currently under way at DaimlerChrysler is used as a sample project to back these arguments.

THE ACQUISITION PROJECT

The reference project aims at reorganizing the complete logistics chain in the passenger car division at DaimlerChrysler in Germany. The newly defined logistics processes are to be supported by a software system largely consisting of an enterprise resource planning (ERP) package with only minor organization-specific adaptations. Since the diversified demands made on car manufacturers are not being met by the available standard software, an ERP automotive software package must be developed. This is done by a leading ERP supplier in joint ventures with car manufacturers and their suppliers.

Because of the cross-sectional nature of logistics processes, a variety of departments are impacted, such as development units, production plants, DP departments, marketing, and so on. Moreover, the logistics chain is active in various DaimlerChrysler plants within Germany. Consequently, all of these departments and plants would have to be represented in the project for an integrated and consistent solution to be developed. Therefore, the reference project is extremely complex with respect to the project size and the project organization.

There is, however, little that is unique to the business segment in question. Indeed, these insights are shared because of the commonalities in software acquisition projects across business segments and application areas that make these problems and proposed solutions of general interest.

PROJECT QUALITY MANAGEMENT
A Success Factor Model in Software Acquisition Projects

Traditionally, quality assurance has focused primarily on the project's results: the products, the software developed, and the associated documentation. Sometimes the development and management processes within a project are also objects for quality assurance—then called process improvement. In this case, the quality assurance group takes a look at the project development and management techniques, configuration and change management, and so on to improve the effectiveness and efficiency of these processes.

A wider scope is required, however, for quality management. Product and process quality are key success factors in complex projects, but they are not the only ones. Consider a model of project success factors that are clustered in accordance with the following principles (see Figure 1). The figure merely includes examples:

- The central success factors are the customers and their goals, needs, and requirements.
- Products developed in the project have to fulfill these needs.
- To develop first-rate products, there must be well-established, effective, and efficient development and management processes. (This article addresses only development and management processes within a project. A wider scope including organizational issues is covered in ISO/IEC 12207 [1995]).
- To run effective and efficient processes, one needs adequate resources.
- The project context describes constraints, such as company standards, or context information, such as interrelated projects.

Project quality management in software acquisition projects is defined as the planning, carrying out, and controlling of activities to ensure the realization of the aforementioned success factors within a project. Even though quality management is a major responsibility of the project manager, in complex projects he or she does not have the time to do all of these activities alone and should establish a quality management group. It is essential that the project manager feel responsible for quality management and work with the quality management group closely. This model could be used at different points of the project, for example, to define goals, plan quality assurance activities, and identify risks.

Project Organization Supports Project Quality

The reference project is divided into 16 subprojects, which are logically arranged in a matrix organization. The work areas in one dimension of the matrix focus on eight

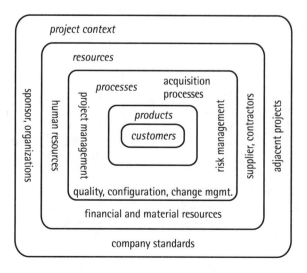

Figure 1　Model of project success factors.

specific subprocesses of the logistics chain, while the teams in the orthogonal dimension are charged with tasks affecting the following subprocesses:

- Risk and quality management
- Project controlling
- Process integration
- System integration
- Training and marketing
- Business cases and cost/benefit analysis
- Roll out
- Competence center ERP system

In addition to the steering committee, which consists of top executives from the organizations involved, a so-called strategy team including middle management was organized. It develops and maintains the business strategy; makes decision recommendations regarding the impact of the project results on the organization; and is the strategic counterpart to the ERP provider, the link to multiproject management, and the first escalation step of the decision path.

The following examples show that this project organization supports project quality as defined in the project success factor model (see Figure 1).

- Customer and user interests are considered in various ways, as user departments participate in all of the subprojects, strategy teams, and steering committees. Business cases and cost/benefit analyses ensure customer and sponsors' interests as well.
- To ensure excellent product quality, standard quality assurance techniques, such as document reviews and testing, are used. Risk and quality management, process integration, and system integration subprojects play a major role here. For example, the consistency and integration of logistics chain subprocesses are guaranteed by the process integration group through defining requirements and guidelines for documents, reviewing process documents, developing concepts, and solving problems together with the logistics chain subprojects.
- Processes such as project, risk, and quality management are described, executed, and controlled by a project controlling and risk and quality management subproject where the ERP provider participates.
- Financial, material, and human resources are acquired and managed by the project leader. User departments and ERP provider consultants participate in every logistics chain subproject. "Not enough people with know-how about user domains and ERP systems" was one of the risks identified for the project. Therefore, the development process of the ERP provider was used as a first version and improved upon later.
- The complex project framework results in many activities, such as system migration and rollout planning and execution, definition and building of an ERP competence center, and the integration with other ERP projects that are effected by specific subprojects.

Risk Management As a Key Factor of Quality Management

One consequence of this wider quality management scope (see Figure 1), however, can be an enormous increase in quality management activities, making it more difficult to carry out quality management effectively and efficiently (Getto 1998). Effectiveness means being able to concentrate on the "right" quality management activities; efficiency means implementing them with the least effort necessary.

Consider four instruments for the definition and prioritization of quality management activities: 1) project planning; 2) quality planning; 3) problem management; and 4) risk management. Project planning and quality planning take activities that can be planned, such as product quality assurance activities, into account. In contrast, there are a variety of project situations where one has to react to an unplanned situation. Problem management is therefore extremely dynamic and reactive. But can project management be more proactive? This is where risk management contributes.

To avoid problems, it is important to know the project risks. A risk is defined as the possibility of loss (Dorofee et al. 1996). If risks are not handled, they can become problems and lead to losses. Risk management includes all of the activities connected with the identification, analysis, and control of risks before they become problems. So risk management is a proactive discipline.

Risk management, if carried out systematically, is a key element in focusing quality management activities on aspects that are most critical for the project's success. In this sense, risk management is a key factor and driver of quality management (Getto and Landes 1999). The combination of risk management and quality management is not mere coincidence, but rather, in experience, greatly beneficial. For reasons of simplicity, the remainder of this article will focus on the risk management aspects covered by the quality and risk management group.

SYSTEMATIC RISK MANAGEMENT

The Risk Management Process in General

Over the last few years, several generic approaches for managing software risks have been presented in the literature (for example, Boehm 1991; Charette 1989; Dorofee et al. 1996; Hall 1998). In the reference project, the Riskit method (Kontio 1997) was used as the basis for the risk management process (see Figure 2). As it turned out (Kontio, Getto, and Landes 1998), the method must be adapted not only to the specific project organization, but also to the quality management approach (Getto and Landes 1999).

Riskit distinguishes two phases: an initialization phase and a risk analysis cycle. The initialization phase lays the groundwork for carrying out risk management activities. This basically means obtaining the commitment of the project management or project steering authorities to perform risk management in a project.

The risk analysis cycle focuses on the continual identification of new risks and on revisiting known risks, analyzing their impact on the project's goals, and defining and performing risk control activities. Since goal orientation is among the method's core principles, the risk analysis cycle also encompasses continuous feedback to and review of project goals.

Risk Management Implementation in the Acquisition Project

Risk Management Initialization. As the first major activity in the initialization phase, the risk management mandate that defines the scope and frequency of risk management must be determined. It recognizes the stakeholders and answers the questions why, what, when, who, how, and for whom risk management is to be implemented. Moreover, the risk management mandate includes an agreement with the project management or project steering authorities on which methods, techniques, and tools will be used for the risk management activities, who is responsible for risk management, and

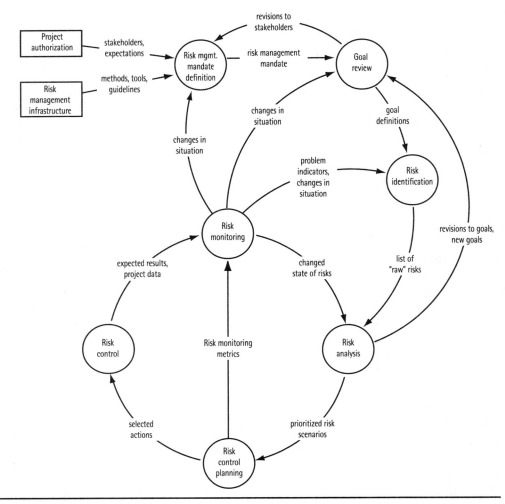

Figure 2   Riskit risk management process.

which scope of risks will be considered. In the reference project, it was decided that a risk management cycle for identifying, analyzing, controlling, and monitoring risks had to be executed every month. Furthermore, because of limited resources, attention should be restricted primarily to a small set of high-priority risks. Finally, responsibilities within the process were defined and assigned to different people or groups.

Centralized and decentralized risk management. Since limited resources are a problem in almost every project, and extra time must be invested in quality management or risk management, it is accepted by most of the people only if it is deployed effectively and efficiently.

Some projects choose a centralized risk management approach where risks are only discussed in project management meetings. Thus, only few resources are consumed. The disadvantage is that risk management is unsystematic and partially ineffective; many risks are not discovered since detailed knowledge on potential risks may reside outside this group. Furthermore, people tend to discuss problems after the fact rather than risks beforehand.

Conversely, if risk management is to be carried out in a decentralized fashion, for instance, at subproject level, there are two possible outcomes. Risk management may be performed with reduced efforts, as identification of risks and risk control are not the major concerns of the subprojects. This again leads to low effectiveness. The other possibility is that almost all project members are involved, and additional effort for coordinating decentralized activities is required. In that case, efficiency tends to be decreased.

The "overseer" approach (Getto and Landes 1999) aims at an appropriate combination of centralized and decentralized risk management activities. The risk management group, and overseers in particular, ensure effectiveness if they have know-how and experiences about risk management best practice and drive the risk management process. To ensure efficiency, they should take particular care that available resources are used optimally. A means of improving efficiency used in the sample project is to have risk and quality management activities carried out by the same group and to use risks to drive quality management.

Roles and Activities in the Risk Management Process

Because of the project's complexity, the risk management group is not able to be familiar with the relevant aspects. Thus, different roles and tasks within the risk management process are defined (Getto and Landes 1999). The columns in Figure 3 show these roles; the rows refer to the main risk management activities.

- **Project managers.** Project managers are responsible for the definition of the risk management mandate and are supported by the risk management experts. Their second task is risk identification, as they have the most comprehensive knowledge about external risks and are responsible for the goal review.

- **Subproject members.** The subproject members play the most important role in risk identification, since they know the most about internal project risks.

- **Project management.** Every potential high-level risk is discussed in project management meetings. If the risk is accepted as a high-level risk, a risk owner who is responsible for analyzing and describing the risk and defining risk-control actions is defined.

- **Risk owner.** If necessary, the risk owner, supported by the risk overseer, performs a detailed risk analysis. The risk owner is also in charge of executing risk-control actions.

- **Project management supporting group.** Risk-control actions are tracked by the project management supporting group as a normal project management activity.

- **Risk management group.** The risk management group is responsible for driving the whole risk management process. Furthermore, they assign risk overseers to every high-level risk, administrate risks, and present the risk status in management meetings.

- **Risk overseer.** Often risk owners are not members of the quality management group. Therefore, a member of the quality management group is selected as a so-called risk overseer for each high priority risk. The overseer of a risk serves as an interface between the quality management group and the risk owner. On one hand, he or she keeps the risk owner informed of the current state of discussion within the group. On the other hand, the overseer advises the risk owner as to which control actions might be appropriate and then reports back to the group on the control actions the risk owner has decided to take and the outcome of the actions implemented thus far.

Activity	Project manager	Project mgmt. group	Project mgmt. support	Subprojects	Risk mgmt. group	Overseer	Risk owner
Risk management initialization phase							
Risk management mandate definition	R				D		
Risk management training					R	D	
Review project goals	R			P	D	P	
Risk analysis cycle							
Risk identification	R			R	P	D	
Risk prioritization		R			D		
Assignment of risk owner		R			D		
Assignment of risk overseer					R, D		
Risk analysis				P		P	R, D
Documentation of high-level risks				P		R, D	P
Risk control planning						P	R, D
Risk controlling						P	R, D
Risk control action tracking			R, D			P	P
Risk monitoring						R, D	P
Risk maintenance					R, D		
Status present in management meetings					R, D		

Key: R = the role is responsible for the activity   D = the role drives the activity
P = the role participates in the activity

Figure 3   Roles and activities in the risk management process.

Risk Analysis Cycle

The goal of the risk identification step is to produce a comprehensive list of the reasonable risks of the project. The first risk identification step is the most important, as many risks will be identified for the project lifetime from the viewpoints of different stakeholders. As it is essential to obtain information from outside sources (at least at the beginning of the project), interviews with a group of project-internal and project-external people were carried out. To gather representative information, the interview partners were chosen from complementary pairs (see Figure 4).

Structured interview techniques with open questions were used; for example, the respondents were asked about the goals and expectations of the interview partner and his or her organization with respect to the project, which results must be achieved for the project to be deemed successful, and the success factors and success probability of the project.

During the first risk management cycle, risks were identified for every area of the project success factor model (see Figure 1). In summary, in addition to the identified

• Experts	as well as	management people
• People from factories	as well as	people from central departments
• People from IT and administration	as well as	people from user departments
• People from development departments	as well as	people from production departments
• Project decision-makers	as well as	project subproject members

Figure 4   Stakeholders for the first risk identification.

risks, a variety of useful information was gathered on goals, expectations, and success factors from the respondents' points-of-view.

Risk identification within the second and successive risk management cycles is affected solely by the subprojects and the project leader. They identify risks every month, supported by risk overseers. In addition to interviews, group-oriented techniques were used, such as "structured brainstorming," based on questions derived from the success factor model (see Figure 1) and checklists.

During risk analysis, risks are grouped, filtered, and prioritized. The projects use predefined risk clusters for grouping and a two-dimensional ranking grid for assigning priorities.

To a large extent, risk control planning and risk control are accomplished outside the risk management group. During risk identification, a risk owner is assigned to each high-priority risk. The risk owner is responsible for taking appropriate actions to control the particular risk. Ownership of a risk also includes the obligation to decide which control actions to take. It is common for the project manager to be the risk owner for many of the identified risks in a project, but there are usually some other risk owners, too. For example, the quality manager for review of an important but risk-prone document.

In the acquisition project, risk monitoring means two things: tracking risks and presenting risk reports to management groups. The second activity is often considered a kind of tracking from the viewpoint of management groups, since it gives this group the chance to actively intervene.

Defined risk-control actions are documented and tracked as a normal activity within project management meetings, guaranteeing that risk management is an active task within project management mechanisms. A second kind of tracking is a periodic meeting between risk owners and their overseers to check the status of the entire risk, not only the risk-control actions. The risk overseer is in charge of documenting the changes in the risk information sheet.

EXAMPLES OF RISKS

Description of Risks

The definition of a risk should include at least two components: a description of the current condition that may lead to the loss and a description of the loss or consequence (Kontio 1997), as shown in the following examples:

- Risk *"different organizational models."* In addition to the reference project, a number of related projects also aim at the introduction of ERP software. If there is insufficient coordination of these overlapping ERP acquisition projects, there will be separate and incompatible organizational models, poor process integration, and different IT platforms.

- Risk *"inflexibility of ERP software."* Business processes must be flexible and responsive to changing circumstances. If the ERP software cannot be adapted easily and cheaply, automation will produce inflexible business processes and potentially higher costs for adaptation.

High-priority risks are documented in a template, which is a customization of the risk description sheet in (Dorofee et al. 1996). Three high-priority risks in this project and the corresponding risk-management responses are detailed next.

Risk "Unclear Project Goals"

At project start only high-level goals were defined. They were not prioritized and not measurable. In the first risk-analysis cycle, some interview partners stated that the goals were unclear and could lead to discussions, conflicts, and schedule overruns. On the other hand, interview partners were also questioned about specific goals and expectations. The results showed some conflicts with existing project goals and different goals and expectations from the view of different stakeholders. Therefore, a risk "unclear project goals" was identified.

The risk and quality management subproject executed the following risk controlling activities:

- *Analyzing project documents to find hidden goals.* The results were merged with the outcome of the interview, clustered, and hierarchically structured into three levels. At the highest level were the existing project goals, as they had already been communicated to external departments and top management, plus one new high-level goal. The project management team discussed goals conflicts and forwarded the results.
- *Determining the contribution of the most important subprojects to project goals.* For example, managers answered the following questions: "Which high-level goal is important for your subproject?" "To which high-level goal does your subproject supply a substantial contribution?" "Which contributions and goals does your subproject have?" This increased the goal transparency and the number of goals to more than 100.
- *Prioritizing goals on the second level of the goal hierarchy.* Seventeen high priority goals were concretely described, using the following attributes: name, type (product, process), category (measurable, assessable), textual description, stakeholders, metrics, values, range of acceptance, time of achievement, and current status. These goals were communicated externally, for example, by a poster.
- *Deriving concrete operative goals for the ongoing year.*

Risk "Cooperation in Development Partnership"

DaimlerChrysler management considered an ERP automotive standard solution beneficial. The ERP provider and DaimlerChrysler are strong partners driving the development of the logistics part of such software. Both companies decided to implement a joint venture, which caused some risks, for example, complex know-how transfer processes or conflicting interests such as the realization of existing concepts versus generally accepted concepts.

Since highly integrated project organization and integrated project management processes are critical success factors for a development partnership, activities similar to the following were carried out:

- A development partnership contract was signed
- The ERP supplier was integrated in the project management team, strategy team, and steering committee

- ERP software training was carried out for project members
- ERP supplier consultants supported every logistics chain subproject, thereby ensuring information transfer from DaimlerChrysler to the ERP supplier's development group
- Participation of project members drives the development of standard concepts in ERP user groups
- Workshops with project participants and ERP software developers were executed to discuss major concepts
- ERP's software customizing process was used, and joint project and documentation reviews were performed

Risk "DaimlerChrysler Post-Merger Integration"

When DaimlerChrysler was created from the merger of its two predecessor corporations, an integration process toward a truly global company began. Therefore, many post-merger integration teams are coordinating this process. Post-merger activities and decisions are accorded higher priority than projects. As some of the post-merger issues have an impact on ongoing projects, there was a risk that the logistics processes defined there and processes defined in the project would not match.

This necessitated some controlling actions:

- Discussions with key players were required; presentation of the project at top management level was a must
- Attempts were made to achieve a high-value position in the new IT project portfolio of DaimlerChrysler
- The project manager and some logistics chain subproject leaders participated in the relevant post-merger integration teams
- Chrysler stakeholders were integrated into the project and steering committees
- Participation in the logistics process benchmarking activities of the post-merger integration teams became essential
- Integration of joint logistics target processes together with the post-merger integration teams was carried out

LESSONS LEARNED

During the execution of risk management in this and other complex software acquisition projects, many lessons were learned. A few are worth mentioning.

Critical Success Factors for Risk Management Processes

- **Risk management should start before the projects starts.** Starting risk management before the project start has two main benefits. First, project managers can take known risks into account when planning resources, budgets, and schedules. Second, the awareness of risk management is increased and the resources required to execute an effective and efficient risk management process are provided.
- **The risk management process must be systematic and continuous.** Although every project manager uses risk management, it is often deployed intuitively instead of systematically. When an unsystematic risk management approach is used, not every important risk is identified and the controlling actions are not as effective as when a systematic approach is deployed. Continuous risk management is essential, as risks change through the controlling actions and events taken, new risks arise, and existing risks can be closed.

- **Both creativity and structure contribute to effective, efficient risk management.** Since people have to invest extra time in risk management, this effort will be acceptable only if it is effectively and efficiently deployed. A combination of creative and analytic techniques is best suited for identifying risks. In an initial step, a creative technique, such as structured interviews with individuals or structured brainstorming within a workshop, should be used. Later, a project-specific questionnaire, which is derived from generic checklists, for instance Carr et al. (1993), is helpful to ensure important risks are not overlooked.

- **Inclusion of all relevant stakeholders is crucial.** The first identification and analysis cycle is crucial since many of the identified risks remain relevant throughout the project's lifetime. All project stakeholders must be included in risk identification. In this phase, interviews with a representative group of internal project members and external stakeholders should be conducted to identify risks.

- **The risk management process needs drivers to work properly.** Since people in a project are normally busy with other things, a group should be set up to ensure a continued treatment of risks. Therefore, a risk management group and, in particular, the overseers drawn from that group, are essential for the proper functioning of the process. Of course, the project manager must also view risk management as crucial to the project's success.

- **Risk and project management processes must be integrated.** Since, on the one hand, the risk management process had some decentralized components and, on the other, the project teams are located within one building, thus ensuring that communication is intensive, it was important to make sure there was no duplicate work in discussing and managing identified risks. The solution came through integrating risk and project management processes at two points. First, an identified risk was presented in the project management meeting within one week after it was first mentioned. This group prioritized the risk and assigned a risk owner for high-level risks. Second, controlling activities as defined or assigned were documented by the project office and tracked automatically.

Other Observations

- **Risk management changes the culture of the project.** People become more aware of risks. They no longer consider a risk merely as a danger but come to regard it as normal and its explicit recognition as a chance to avoid problems. The author's experience is that risk management is an important success factor in complex projects.

- **Risk management improves project quality.** Every known and controllable risk reduces the probability of project failure with regard to costs, time schedule, product quality, or other project quality success factors (Figure 1) and, therefore, improves project quality.

- **Overseers must be critical and troublesome.** People try to live in harmony and do not normally think too much about risks. Many people only become active when risks have already turned into problems. A special task of the overseer is to raise the awareness for risks and the benefits of risk management. A risk paradox is that the participants in software acquisition projects often have strong incentive at the early stages of an activity to downplay or hide risks, even though the possible consequences of this behavior should give them strong incentives to detect and disclose risks (Schmidt et al. 1999). Therefore, he or she sometimes must be critical and troublesome. To ensure the effectiveness of risk management, the right people have to be selected for this job.

- **Quantification of risk impacts is difficult in complex software acquisition projects.** Most risk management approaches rely on risk estimation approaches, such as the expected value calculations of Boehm (1991). Such calculations (that is, risk = probability × loss) in complex software acquisition projects are often difficult to perform with quantitative precision. Their value must then be in more qualitative uses, such as rank ordering of risks for prioritization.

- **Goals and stakeholder concepts require commitment to use.** Two of the key concepts of the Riskit method are goal and stakeholder orientation, which are helpful for a systematic risk management approach. In practice there are difficulties with these concepts. At the beginning of the projects the goals were at a very high level and of little practical use. When goals were explicitly defined (measurable or assessable) many risk owners did not want to analyze concrete impacts on goals and stakeholders because of considerable investment of time required.

CONCLUSIONS

Especially in strategic software acquisition projects within an organization, risk and quality management are becoming increasingly important in collaboration. Because of the inherent complexity of these projects, however, quality management cannot address the quality of the products only, but must also consider aspects such as the processes, resources, and constraints that the project must obey.

The project organization has to consider these factors, quality supporting subprojects have to be defined, and the necessary resources have to be made available. Quality assurance activities must be focused on areas that are most critical for the success of the project. An excellent means of identifying these critical areas and of deriving appropriate controlling actions (which can be viewed as quality assurance activities) is systematic risk management. To be systematic, effective, and efficient, a risk management method must be tailored to the context in which it is applied. Experiences gained in a business process reengineering project that is currently under way at DaimlerChrysler have shown that the risk management process in particular must be adapted to the constraints imposed by the project organization. To implement an effective and efficient process, some critical success factors, such as identifying risks before project start, including all relevant stakeholders, and defining roles and drivers, must be considered. Risk identification must be performed at both the project and subproject levels, and the risk analysis and controlling is primarily shared between the risk owner and a so-called risk overseer. Risk management executed in this way changes the culture of the project and improves project quality.

Risk management should be viewed as a key contributor to quality management, as there are other areas that may benefit from effective and efficient risk management. Risk management allows one to act proactively before difficulties turn into real problems.

ACKNOWLEDGMENTS

The author would like to thank Guenther Pauler, the project head of the reference project, and Hartwig Wortmann, the head of the risk and quality management subproject, for supporting the described risk management process and allowing publication of some risk examples. Several project results, such as the business case written by Holger Spiegel, gave some important incitements, especially the need for changing business processes. In addition, many thanks to several people for reviewing this article, especially Dieter Landes. The comments of the reviewers for this journal were particularly helpful.

REFERENCES

Boehm, B. W. 1991. Press software risk management: Principles and practices. *IEEE Software* 8 (1): 32–41.

Carr, M. J., S. L. Konda, I. A. Monarch, F. C. Ulrich, and C. F. Walker. 1993. *Taxonomy-based risk management identification* (SEI-93-TR-006). Pittsburgh: Software Engineering Institute, Carnegie Mellon University.

Charette, R. N. 1989. *Software engineering risk analysis and management.* New York: McGraw-Hill.

Dorofee, A. J., J. A. Walker, C. F. Alberts, R. P. Higuera, T. J. Murray, and R. J. Williams. 1996. *Continuous risk management guidebook.* Pittsburgh: Software Engineering Institute, Carnegie Mellon University.

Euromethod. 1996. Version 1 of URL document www.fast.de/euromethod .

Ferguson, J. R., J. Cooper, M. Fallat, M. Fisher, A. Guido, J. Marciniak, J. Matejceck, and R. Webster. 1996. *Software acquisition capability maturity model (SA-CMM^{sm}) version 1.01* (CMU/SEI-96-TR-020). Pittsburgh: Software Engineering Institute, Carnegie Mellon University.

Getto, G. 1998. Qualitätsmanagement in komplexen softwareprojekten der Daimler-Benz AG. In *Proceedings of the 3rd kongress software qualitätsmanagement "made in Germany,"* Köln.

———. 1999. Evaluation von prozessen und methoden für softwarebeschaffung und management von auftragnehmern. In *Proceedings of the 4th kongress software qualitätsmanagement "made in Germany,"* Köln.

Getto, G., and D. Landes. 1999. Systematic risk management as a key factor in the management of project quality. In *Proceedings of the 6th european conference on software quality (ECSQ),* Vienna.

———. 1999. Risk management in complex project organizations: A godfather-driven approach. In *Proceedings of the Project Management Institute (PMI) Conference 99,* Philadelphia.

Hall, E. 1998. *Managing risks, methods for software systems development.* New York: Addison-Wesley.

ISO/IEC 12207: *Information Technology—software lifecycle processes.* 1995. Geneva, Switzerland: International Organization for Standardization.

ISPL (Information Service Procurement Library). 1999. *Managing risks and planning deliverables.* Hague, The Netherlands: ten Hagen & Stam.

Kontio, J. 1997. *The Riskit method for software risk management, version 1.00* (CS-TR-3782/UMIACS-TR-97-38). College Park, MD: University of Maryland.

Kontio, J., G. Getto, and D. Landes. 1998. Experiences in improving risk management processes using the concepts of the Riskit method. In *Proceedings of the 6th international symposium on the foundations of software engineering (FSE-6),* Orlando.

Moreau, N. P. 1998. Software acquisition strategies—A look at current practices. In *Proceedings of the 52nd annual quality congress,* Philadelphia.

Paulk M. C., B. Curtis, M. B. Chrissis, and C. V. Weber. 1993. *Capability maturity model for software, version 1.1* (CMU/SEI-93-TR-25). Pittsburgh: Software Engineering Institute, Carnegie Mellon University.

Schmidt C., P. Dart, L. Johnston, L.Sterling, and P. Thorne. 1999. *Disincentives for communicating risk: A risk paradox.* Information and Software Technolog 41 (7): 403-411.

BIOGRAPHY

Gerhard Getto is a manager at DaimlerChrysler Research and Technology in Ulm, Germany. His research interests are methods and experiences about management process in information technology (IT) risk management, quality management, software acquisition, and supplier management.

Getto has a degree in mathematics from the University of Stuttgart, Germany. He has 19 years of experience in the IT area. During this time he was active in software development, system implementation worldwide, business process analysis, information management, project management, quality management, risk management, and research. He has published papers in the areas of risk management, quality management, and software acquisition. Getto can be reached at DaimlerChrysler AG, P. O. Box 23 60, D-89013 Ulm, Germany, or by e-mail at gerhard.getto@DaimlerChrysler.com .

PART TWO

Quality Management

Consider the range of concerns that quality professionals must address. These concerns are both objective (in software) and subjective (among humans). Framing quality as "the degree to which the requirements of the user are satisfied" leads to the further elaboration that the requirements might be both explicit (specifications) and implicit (expectations). Note, too, that speaking of a "degree" of satisfaction means considering tradeoffs and shades of gray between wholly acceptable and wholly unacceptable.

As software ranges farther into uses with possible impact on public health and safety, its quality may also became the concern of regulatory agencies. More recently, a new set of stakeholders has entered the circle of those to whom practitioners must communicate the quality message: the investors who must choose to finance development efforts.

The interests of potential investors and of potential customers could be quite different. Correspondingly, development and quality activities are often addressed to these different audiences in different ways. Investors are keen to understand commercial opportunity, potential competitors, and the likelihood that a firm has the technical, marketing, and organizational capabilities to do what it says.

John Elliott addresses **"Achieving Customer Satisfaction through Requirements Understanding."** He shows how such satisfaction depends on a deep understanding of business needs and associated user requirements, as well as the ability to communicate those requirements to the system developer. In the end, customer satisfaction and confidence depend upon the level of system assurance offered throughout the system development lifecycle. If requirements are not properly understood, there are penalties in the form of poor customer-supplier relationships, unnecessary rework, and overruns in cost and time.

"People Management and Development Process" reports on the efforts of a geographically distributed and culturally diverse development organization to attract and retain good workers. Evangelisti, Peciola, and Zotti share an approach to motivating and developing the all-important human resource that is the key success factor for any business. Through job analysis, individual competence assessment and improvement, and a career advancement and reward system, their organization has decreased turnover and increased personal satisfaction.

CHAPTER 2.1

Achieving Customer Satisfaction Using Evolutionary Processes

**John Elliott, Systems and Software Engineering Center,
U. K. Defence Evaluation and Research Agency**

*A*chieving and measuring customer satisfaction is a key aim in systems development. Widespread customer satisfaction, however, is not normally attained, largely because of inadequate understanding of requirements and quality-related issues. This lack of understanding is a function of the semantic gap between customers and developers during system evolution. A universal customer-oriented evolutionary lifecycle process is required to support the through-life attainment of customer satisfaction by minimizing barriers to any quest for common understanding, for example, of need, requirements, process, and product quality.

This article describes a process improvement case study and an associated experiment to explore how to achieve customer satisfaction using a through-life requirements-driven evolutionary process. A customer satisfaction reference model was developed to derive the idealized requirements for such a customer-oriented process. An experiment was undertaken to examine the cost effectiveness and customer-friendly attributes of the Dynamic Systems Development Method (DSDM) that was chosen as a candidate for evaluation as a customer-oriented process. The overall progress toward a customer-oriented process requirement, together with some positive observations about DSDM, was considered an effective study result. The study's lessons learned provide information to help further customer satisfaction studies.

Key words: customer satisfaction, Dynamic Systems Development Method (DSDM), evolutionary development, process evaluation, process improvement, product quality, system measurement

INTRODUCTION

One goal of businesses is to achieve a continuous and high level of customer satisfaction in the delivery of services and/or products. Such satisfaction is believed to be the basis of long-term profitability and growth. In the realm of computer-based system products, customer satisfaction is dependent on how system development projects evolve to build operational product systems that satisfy perceived and actual customer needs and associated system requirements.

Ultimately, successful customer satisfaction depends on the depth of "through-life" understanding of the business need, user requirements and product quality assurance for a future system, and the ability of customers and developers to communicate and negotiate these understandings. In particular, customer satisfaction and confidence depends on the level of system assurance offered throughout the system development lifecycle that the resulting product will be fit for its purpose. Furthermore, requirement-understanding problems inevitably lead to poor customer-supplier relationships, unnecessary reworks, and overruns. In fact, great gains to both customers and developers are available with improved understanding of requirements and quality issues. Achieving these gains stimulates the vision of this customer-oriented process case study.

This article describes a process improvement case study and associated experiment whose main thrust was to improve customer satisfaction using a new style of evolutionary lifecycle process. This process will pay due regard to requirement issues and other quality-related aspects.

TECHNICAL CONTEXT FOR CASE STUDY

Process improvement case studies are difficult to design and implement, and thus, it is important to provide a technical context for interpreting their findings. Hence, this section sets the scene for a customer satisfaction study that presents a particularly challenging area. This case study was initiated as a learning exercise to help understand the scope for process improvements to achieve customer satisfaction. As indicated, the case-study plan included undertaking a detailed process experiment to try to determine the impact of any new process. Fully objective arguments, based around detailed measurements, were not expected given the practice limitations of process experiments and the challenge of measuring customer satisfaction.

One key aspect of the quality perspective concerns the customer and supplier agreeing on a required level of quality to be achieved within defined and understood cost and time constraints. Additionally, the quality level must be defined and be subject to some agreed upon measurement to monitor attainment.

The case study and experimentation, however, were planned and designed carefully to maximize the potential for qualitative assessment. This involved adopting a systematic method of study and making appropriate use of all qualitative and quantitative evidence in arguing if "hypothesized" new process benefits appear (or are likely) to arise based on a single application project. In addition, the study sought to predict the business-related impact across many types of projects. Following are the case-study steps:

Pre-Experiment

1. Identify key concepts for understanding and identifying software development variables that may be postulated to influence customer satisfaction; define a customer reference model.
2. Use these variables to derive the characteristics (requirements) for a new customer-oriented process.
3. Select a candidate process to be the focus for a detailed process experiment.

Conduct Experiment

4. Design the process experiment to test a series of defined hypotheses concerning the expected impact the new process should have on customer satisfaction and associated variables.
5. Generate evidence by applying the new process to a single development situation, by fulfilling any defined experimental requirements, such as controls, data collection, and so on.

6. Generate equivalent evidence by postulating the use of existing or old processes to the same single development situation, still fulfilling relevant experimental requirements.

7. Analyze and assemble the generated evidence to be used in an assessment to test the likely satisfaction of the defined hypotheses.

8. Using the evidence and analysis, assess through argument whether each hypothesis is likely to be satisfied based on the single application project experience.

Post-Experiment

9. Determine, through argument, the likely impact of the candidate, or similar process, on improving customer satisfaction across many project types.

10. Determine the technological and business lessons learned by the experiment.

11. Provide the study conclusions accounting for the experiment and its limitations.

Overall, this article presents the philosophy, strategy, and approach taken to improve customer satisfaction through process design. Detailed experimental results can be found in Raynor-Smith and Elliott (1999). Raynor-Smith and Elliott is also available on the European Software Systems Initiative's (ESSI's) Web site (ESSI 2000), which also contains the results of many European process improvement experiments (PIEs). This article is referring to the Requirements Engineering through Joint Interactive Object-Oriented Consultation Experiment (REJOICE) PIE. The remainder of this article presents the rationale and results associated with the main case-study stages: pre-experiment, experiment design, and execution.

PRE-EXPERIMENT: CUSTOMER SATISFACTION CONCEPTS

Concept Overview

Customer satisfaction depends on many factors associated with the business need, the development project, and resultant system product quality. Ultimately customers are looking for added value within a defined time frame at an affordable price; hence, the customer priority is for an overall *successful business*. The system supplier perspective is to deliver a system within agreed cost plans to satisfy customer requirements, thus contributing to the supplier's profit and reputation; hence, the supplier priority is for a *successful project*. These different perspectives are typically controlled through inflexible and formal contract management arrangements in the pursuit of a successful project for both customer and supplier. The cornerstone to such success involves a rigorous and long-term approach to quality.

Quality may be loosely inferred to mean "satisfying requirements" embracing the provision of added capability (that is, improved business function and performance) and any associated trustworthiness or integrity (that is, continuously performs as intended without harmful side effects on business services). One key aspect of the quality perspective concerns the customer and supplier agreeing on a required level of quality to be achieved within defined and understood cost and time constraints. Additionally, the quality level must be defined and be subject to some agreed upon measurement to monitor attainment.

The remaining development project consideration is the level of risk and uncertainty associated with attaining the required and agreed upon quality level; the risk perspective depends on the available knowledge of the project constraints and their implications. Hence, both customers and suppliers must understand the risk each is taking within their quality level agreement. In practice, the notion of risk sharing between customers and suppliers is a difficult area that influences the nature of any supporting legally binding contractual arrangements. In summary, both customers and suppliers must plan and implement compatible quality and risk strategies for the development project. These strategies must be reflected in any contractual agreements.

Returning to quality within the customer satisfaction arena, customers must be assured that defined and measurable final *product quality* attributes demonstrate that their defined needs and associated requirements are satisfied. Achieving defined product quality depends on "getting the system requirements right" and then "building the product right" to meet these requirements. Measuring product quality requires considering various external and internal system product attributes; external attributes include product functionality and performance (such as speed, reliability, maintainability, safety, security, and so on), whereas internal attributes include its architectural structure, portability, and so on. Authors such as Fenton and Pfleeger (1997) and Gillies (1992) describe and review different quality models, including that developed for the ISO 9126 standard (1992).

Defining and achieving product quality is not easy within traditional contracting processes that tend to encourage the communication of requirements through formal documents and review activities. This inflexible and formal approach is often the reason customer and supplier teams are not effective in achieving continuous levels of understanding, which is sometimes colored by a culture of disrespect and mistrust.

Model of Customer Satisfaction and Its Components

The customer satisfaction problem domain depends on four key dimensions:

- **Business need:** The need for new business strategy and change, operations, and usability.
- **System requirements:** The user/system product definition including quality and risk levels and process criteria and constraints, such as interoperability with existing systems, time scales, and costs.
- **Confidence in the quality:** The capability of the development and assurance processes and the competence of people, both with attendant risks.
- **Product quality:** Confidence, demonstration, arguments, and evidence about quality and fitness.

These dimensions are the basis of a customer satisfaction model. Figure 1 shows the essential relationships between these dimensions and the influence on customer satisfaction.

Of significance is the distinction between the need-related business criteria and the requirements-related technical criteria. Also, while these dimensions are fundamental to achieving customer satisfaction, there are other viewpoints of project success that also must be considered (see Garrity and Saunders 1998).

The following viewpoints, as shown in Figure 1, complement the customer satisfaction model's dimensions and are necessary for defining a *customer-oriented process:*

- **Understanding.** Both customers and developers fully understand the business need and requirements throughout an evolutionary-oriented development lifecycle.
- **Teamwork.** Customers and developers work toward the same project goals within a trusting and respectful partnership based on effective communication, decision making, and action.

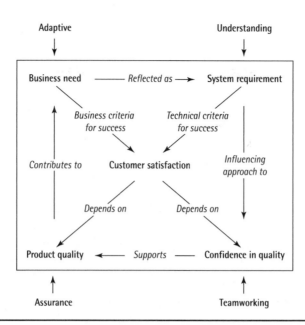

Figure 1   Dimensions and viewpoints of customer satisfaction.

- **Assurance.** The confidence that the resulting product meets the required level of quality and is fit for its purpose within accepted risk levels (derived from "fit for purpose" arguments and supporting evidence involving assessments and measurements about process criteria and product criteria).

- **Adaptability.** The inevitable changes in the customer's business needs and perception about the system requirements must be accommodated in the delivered system.

These dimensions and viewpoints regarding customer satisfaction constitute a framework reference model (customer satisfaction model) that can be used to design and/or evaluate future development processes.

PRE-EXPERIMENT: CUSTOMER-ORIENTED PROCESSES REQUIREMENTS

One case-study aim has been to define a strategy for designing or selecting and implementing a customer-oriented process. This process is to be based on the fundamental understanding embodied in the customer satisfaction model. The process strategy will aim to enhance the level of customer satisfaction through improved customer-developer communication and interaction with an emphasis on through-life requirements and product quality understanding.

Idealized Customer-Oriented Process Requirements

Based on the concepts described, Figure 2 shows the ideal requirements that must be considered when designing a new approach to customer satisfaction.

These idealized process requirements are the basis of whether existing development lifecycle strategies are customer friendly. See example lifecycles in Somerville (1996), McConnell (1996), and Pressman (1997). Also, they provide insights about the characteristics of the techniques to support such a process requirement. The next sections briefly describe the result of this case study's review (Elliott 1998) of current lifecycles and supporting techniques.

Type	Requirements
Through-life Understanding/Evolution	• *Through-life* treatment of system requirements and business need; this will focus attention on the ultimate project goals and success criteria.
	• Need to embrace the whole system *evolution* lifecycle; this will ensure that systems are not viewed as totally new but rather as add-ons or modifications to existing, albeit larger, systems.
	• Need to ensure that customers get operational systems as a series of *increments* to meet shorter-term priority needs; this will enable customers to get useful employable systems as a series of incremental deliveries formed within a well-founded overarching business system architecture.
	• Must be *fast* to react to changing customer perspectives about system requirements; this helps customers quickly see the impact of their desired changes.
	• Enable executable system prototypes to be *visible* and allow user play back; this enables the customer team to see the evolving product in concrete terms and respond accordingly.
	• Must be able to *roll* the current system solution both forward and backward; this helps the speed at which changes (using new or old perspectives) can be played back.
Adaptability	• Need to be *flexible* to changing customer needs and perspectives; this will encourage effective contracting and working arrangements to be in place that are based on the premise that such change is inevitable and technical agreements must change.
	• Must manage the customer needs and requirements and their *satisfaction* through a flexible yet controllable approach to system planning and its execution; this will focus both parties on the theme of customer satisfaction and project success by ongoing requirements and quality understanding.
Teamworking/communication	• Need for customer-supplier teams to work in *partnership;* this will enable both parties with separate overall business aims to share a more focused and explicit common project goal within a trusted contractual and working relationship that involves more risk and information sharing and joint decision making.
	• Needs effective *communication/interfacing* between customer and supplier teams; this enables a common and shared understanding about the business need, system requirements, and the development processes and products.
	• Need customers and suppliers to be regularly *interactive* about key business and development changes affecting the partnership; this enables an ongoing approach to holism, learning, and adaptability throughout system evolution.
	• Need frequent customer *feedback* on design concepts and system increments prior to final acceptance and in-service use; this will ensure that customers declare timely change based on business use perspectives.
	• Appropriate processes, methods, and tools must be *universally* understandable and accessible to those involved in the customer and developer teams.
Assurance management	• Need to enable the risk and quality levels to be defined and agreed; this leads to different needs for process, project, and people management.
	• Must provide effective demonstration and control mechanisms to decide about system *fitness;* this will enable customers and suppliers to understand any arguments based on evidence about risks and fitness prior to operational use.

Figure 2   Idealized customer-oriented process requirements.

Customer-Oriented Processes and Current Lifecycle Models

The main lifecycle variant labels are: Waterfall, V-model, Spiral, evolutionary prototyping, incremental/staged delivery, design to schedule, design to tools, commercial off the shelf, and evolutionary delivery. These variants differ in their attempt at imposing different engineering structures for project management purposes based on implicit premises about flexibility and degrees of change, speed of delivery, reuse and integration, and system delivery strategies.

The overall conclusion is that these lifecycle variants only partially address the requirements for a customer-oriented lifecycle process, and a new approach is required to fully encompass customer orientation. The main lifecycles tend to be sequential, static, and prescriptive in nature, and assume all projects need the same process structure. No lifecycle adequately represents the real-world dynamic activities between customer and developer, partly because of their variability and complexity.

Customer-Oriented Lifecycle Techniques

The major techniques must support and facilitate the goals for customer satisfaction through more attention to requirement understanding and product quality related aspects. These techniques cover the following process areas:

- **Business analysis.** As in business process reengineering (BPR) (MacDonald 1995) to guide the way in which the customer's real needs are articulated and understood.

- **Communication and interaction.** Such as embodied in Joint Application Development (JAD) (Bell and Wood-Harper 1998) and Rapid Application Development (RAD) (McConnell 1996; Martin 1991) to assist stakeholder communication, negotiation, and exploration.

- **Requirements understanding, management, and engineering.** For example, formalized approaches to capture, model, analyze, and prioritize any statement of requirements, and to support their management to allow change management and traceability, and so on.

- **Design.** To use modeling representations that maximize the scope of "playing back" the evolving requirements to the customer, as models or partial/executing prototypes (that is, includes the use of object-based or reuse-oriented design methodologies).

- **Measurement.** Such as that of a system's fitness derived from arguments and associated evidence using measurements (of project, process, and product) where possible.

- **Project, process, quality, and risk management.** Such as to control and monitor project and product success with reference to quality assurance process and process assessment, for example, ISO's software process improvement and determination (SPICE) model and the Software Engineering Institute's Capability Maturity Model (CMM).

The aim is to populate a customer-oriented lifecycle with a set of relevant techniques, selected from a customer-oriented toolkit, to address the previously listed process areas. This review showed that many techniques, albeit not optimal, may be used within any future customer-oriented process.

PRE-EXPERIMENT: CANDIDATE CUSTOMER-ORIENTED PROCESS

The candidate customer-oriented lifecycle process was based on selecting an approach that exhibited customer-friendly characteristics, consistent with those in Figure 2. In essence, any selected process, and associated techniques, must provide an effective understanding (by customers and developers) of initial and changing needs and requirements. Furthermore, the process should provide through-life assurances through improved visibility and demonstration of defined processes and products. In this way, these techniques must also address accomplishing and preserving product quality throughout the product lifecycle.

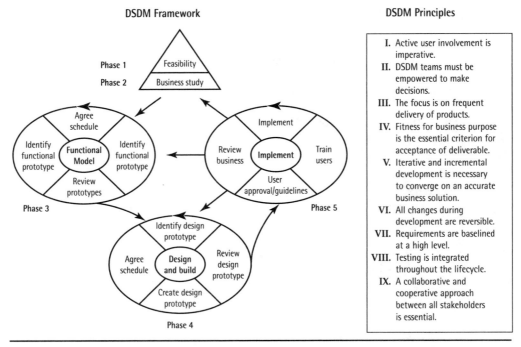

DSDM Framework

DSDM Principles

I. Active user involvement is imperative.
II. DSDM teams must be empowered to make decisions.
III. The focus is on frequent delivery of products.
IV. Fitness for business purpose is the essential criterion for acceptance of deliverable.
V. Iterative and incremental development is necessary to converge on an accurate business solution.
VI. All changes during development are reversible.
VII. Requirements are baselined at a high level.
VIII. Testing is integrated throughout the lifecycle.
IX. A collaborative and cooperative approach between all stakeholders is essential.

Figure 3   DSDM-based customer-oriented lifecycle process framework and principles.

As embodied in the customer satisfaction model and the derived process requirements, the process must support team-working partnerships, and also be responsive (and adaptive) to a customer's desire for change. A final consideration is that a new customer-oriented approach must be widely applicable and geared toward the nonsoftware specialists, needing no special tools, knowledge, or equipment. This will enhance the ability of customers and developers to adapt, and benefit from, the new approach. Were all these aspects effectively implemented, the resultant systems should be delivered on time and to cost, and actually meeting the customer's needs.

The candidate customer-oriented lifecycle process has been based on a minor adaptation (Raynor-Smith 1998) of the Dynamic Systems Development Method (DSDM 1996; Stapleton 1997) framework. DSDM offers a generic lifecycle framework that is geared to being more flexible, faster reacting, and dynamic involving joint customer-developer working. Figure 3 shows the five DSDM-based customer-oriented lifecycle process phases. The proposed process adaptations to DSDM, as used within the REJOICE process improvement experiment, combine and refine phase 1 and 2 activities.

The DSDM phases are:

- **Phase 1: Feasibility study.** An assessment is made as to whether the DSDM approach is correct for the anticipated project. (This is not a conventional form of feasibility.)

- **Phase 2: Business study.** Provides the foundations on which all subsequent work is based and provides an understanding of the business and technical constraints. (This study is intended to be relatively short with the aim to describe a first-cut high-level requirement.)

- **Phase 3: Functional model.** This activity is broadly equivalent to a functional specification but expressed using an executable prototype with some documentation support.

- **Phase 4: Design and build.** This activity is refining the functionality to reflect nonfunctional and other quality/integrity requirements; the detailed designs are as executable prototypes but with improving quality attributes, supported by essential documentation.

- **Phase 5: Implement.** This activity is applying the product within a series of systems trials ultimately being accepted in the operational environment.

The essence of this approach is for the customer and developer to work in *partnership* ensuring that the *needs and requirements* are understood by all throughout a development lifecycle. The system is allowed to evolve in terms of refining prototypes resulting in useable increments. The strategy is to be flexible and *adaptive* to changing requirements and to progressively build quality into the evolving product. The *customer-development interactions* occur throughout allowing for learning, feedback, and adapting to influence development directions.

The risk of the flexibility offered must be countered through the application of sufficient management, quality, and product assurance practices incorporating process and product checks with sufficient traceable documentation. For DSDM to be truly customer friendly, there must be a particular implementation focus on ensuring that *project* (process, people, and product) *assurances* are evident, as well as providing enough visibility to give the customer confidence in the evolving software system. This assurance aspect is an issue for the process experiment.

Finally, the DSDM approach to some extent depends on effective modeling approaches and tool-sets in order to provide regular product quality demonstration and thus gain the desired customer satisfaction benefits.

PROCESS EXPERIMENT: DESIGN AND RESULTS

An experiment was undertaken to examine the effectiveness of the proposed DSDM-based approach to customer satisfaction together with associated understanding about requirements and quality. This activity was a European Union (EU)-funded PIE, referred to as REJOICE, ESSI Project 23893. The purpose of the PIE was to demonstrate whether the new customer-oriented process could provide the business benefits sought as improvement goals. There are various elements to the experiment, including business context, improvement goals, proposed process, experimental considerations, results and assessment, and experimental limitations.

Business Context

The experiment was set in the U.K. Defence Evaluation and Research Agency's (DERA's) System and Software Engineering Center (SEC). The SEC is an autonomous development and consultancy business that largely serves the defense system businesses within DERA and the U. K. Ministry of Defence. The SEC is associated with a wide range of systems for high-technology research, system requirements and design modeling, tool development, and operational activities. The SEC operates within a highly controlled business management culture (based on the ISO 9000 series), and its activities are regularly subjected to process assessments (for example, ISO, CMM, SPICE). The SEC has a "maturing" software culture supported by its DERA Software Practices. The DERA practices incorporate an in-built measurement system.

Improvement Goals

The SEC is striving to achieve the highest levels of CMM maturity (currently achieving level 3 in some areas) for all its activities supported by the use of SPICE to develop excellence in particular process domains. There were a number of improvement areas identified from various process assessments. These included those concerned with customer relations and ensuring that the SEC meets customer needs and requirements. The relevant customer-related goals to be satisfied through an improved approach to requirements understanding and product quality were:

- More customer satisfaction (20 percent)
- No extra effort on requirements activities
- A decrease in requirements-generated problems (15 percent)

The SEC aim was to realize the quantified benefits over many projects to improve business benefits. As only one single (sample) application of the process is involved, this case study, through its experimentation, can only assess the likelihood that the benefits should be achieved by adopting the new process. In addition, the qualitative lessons learned from exploring the use of the new DSDM-based process within the SEC's project environment are of importance. Assessing whether the business goals may be met across many projects depends on the combination of the qualitative lessons and the evidence from the sample project applications. These issues have affected the approach taken to the experimental design and the subsequent case-study assessment.

Proposed Process

The customer-oriented lifecycle process, an adaptation of DSDM, was applied within specific development projects. The adaptation was to combine phases 1 and 2 of DSDM into a single phase, "User Requirements Study." This was to remove the DSDM suitability analysis (less important to the REJOICE goals than to rapid application development objectives) and to increase the focus on the feasibility and definition of user requirements against a real, and rigorously studied, strategic need for business change. Hence, this new phase focuses on the communication, understanding, elicitation, and high-level capture of business needs and requirements.

Before the adapted DSDM lifecycle process (referred to as the REJOICE process) can be fully applied, further DSDM tailoring considerations (the subject of experiment 1) must be addressed:

- **How can the flexible proposed process be used and integrated within a high-control business and quality management culture?** Integration involves interfacing the proposed lifecycle processes into established project, risk, and quality management practices. This will involve identifying the tailoring issues surrounding the introduction of a customer-oriented approach into established software practices and local cultures.

- **Given the inherently flexible DSDM-based lifecycle process, what level of detail should be defined within any relevant process standards?**

- **How does one define the exact process incorporating methods and tools to apply to a specific project?**

It should be stressed that the new customer-oriented process represents a major shift in development culture, a major issue for the REJOICE experiment. In support of the new process, a set of specific methods and tools were selected from which the experiment process details were selected. There was an emphasis on business analysis (such as BPR), interaction management and facilitation (such as JAD), design methodology (such as object orientation), and requirements management support (such as procedures and tools).

Experimental Considerations

The experimentation was designed to explore the issues associated with the introduction, definition, tailoring, and application of the new DSDM-based REJOICE process. The experiment was divided into four parts:

- **Experiment 1.** Defining, tailoring, and introducing the new customer-oriented REJOICE
- **Experiment 2.** Partial application of the REJOICE process to the development of a requirements modeling tool
- **Experiment 3.** Applying and measuring the impact of the REJOICE process during the development of a DERA intranet-based CMM self-assessment tool
- **Experiment 4.** Comparing the REJOICE process with the existing traditional development process during the development of a DERA intranet-based CMM self-assessment tool

Experiments 1 and 2 were focusing on an important learning activity to assess the impact of standardizing and adopting all or part of the radical REJOICE process approach. Experiments 3 and 4 were the main activities for assessing the impact of the new process on projects and on the whole development business activity. These experiments involved the following project development context: a project duration of 12 weeks; a team of three full-time development staff members; a customer team of two staff members; and a final system of 40,000 lines of Java code, (in addition to reusing an estimated 60,000 lines of "equivalent Java" code of off-the-shelf libraries). The impact of scaling up the conclusions on larger or other types of projects was assessed and reported in the lessons learned section. Finally, the reference to the existing traditional processes represents a V-model lifecycle approach as set out in Mazza et al. (1994), the basis of the standard SEC software practices.

Each experiment had its own detailed design that included specific hypotheses to be tested and an associated measurement scheme, each of which was generally linked to the improvement goals. Overall, the measurement strategy included maximizing the use of qualitative observations backed up by arguments based on valuable experience identifying the issues, in addition to collecting selected yet limited quantitative measures. The data collection involved a combination of surveys, interviews, project resource extracts, and tracking what processes were being implemented. The major experimental part was the application of the new process to be applied to two tool development projects. Each project had specific and well-informed customer teams; one project was a requirement modeling tool and the other was a CMM assessment support tool.

The definition of measures applicable to experiments 3 and 4 to study the effectiveness of the new lifecycle and supporting techniques focused on its cost effectiveness using criteria concerning customer satisfaction, identifying need, communication/interaction, and requirements control. The outline measurement scheme to examine the new process is shown in Figure 4. More details for all experiments are described in Raynor-Smith and Elliott (1999).

Experimental Results

The main results of the four experiments are detailed in the REJOICE Final Report (Raynor-Smith and Elliott 1999). These are presented in the form of arguments about the validity of various customer-oriented process hypotheses supported by detailed qualitative and quantitative evidence.

Goal	Area for measurement	Generic metrics
Increase (20%) in satisfying customer needs	**Customer satisfaction** • Meeting need and requirements • Confidence in product **Product quality and effectiveness** • Product quality claimed • Demonstration of quality	**Customer metrics** • Degree of satisfaction of need • Degree of confidence in product quality **Product metrics** • No. of requirements satisfied and not satisfied • No. of new and changed requirements satisfied • No. of models, prototype releases, and demonstrations delivered for validation • No. of requirement defects found during customer use of software deliveries (prototypes, demonstration, and trials)
No change in cost of requirements activity	**Requirements efficiency** • Process cost • People impact (interactions)	**Process metrics** • Number of, and effort spent in, interactions for requirements clarification and negotiation, demonstration (models and prototypes), collating and responding to feedback (that is, rework) about models and prototypes, (interaction profile) • Effort spent in the equivalent requirements, design and build stages of projects, (lifecycle effort profile)
Decrease (15%) in problems due to poor requirements understanding	**Requirements efficiency** • Requirement defects • Process cost impact	**Product metrics** • No. of changes to requirements **Process metrics** • Effort spent responding to feedback and associated reworking

FIGURE 4. Goal-oriented measurement approach.

The overall results are briefly summarized in Figures 5 and 6. Figure 5 shows qualitative results from the experience of all four experiments, and this is followed by a selected set of quantitative results on experiments 3 and 4 in Figure 6. The qualitative results are formed from capturing the experimental experience, and this represents an important background for the quantitative analysis and the derivation of case-study lessons.

These qualitative results expose the potential strengths and weaknesses of the REJOICE process. The main issues raised are the controllability of the process and the resultant product quality. Other key uncertainties include project implementation techniques and incorporating the new process into a quality management environment. The detailed quantitative assessment in Figure 6 allows some further judgments against the business goals as set for the experimentation.

The collective qualitative and quantitative evidence from these experiments provides the basis for deriving the lessons that have been learned within the REJOICE process improvement experiment in terms of the technological and business impact of the new DSDM-based REJOICE process. This article also adds the research lessons from developing customer satisfaction understandings for future process design or evaluation. Prior to presenting the lessons learned, readers are reminded about some experimental limitations.

Experimental Limitations

The experiment ultimately aimed at a comparison between the old and new approaches. An ideal comparison could have been made if there were two teams working in parallel, each using the old and new process. This was not feasible, so it was only possible to estimate the resources that would have been used for the traditional process, using data collected from similar developments and expert peer reviews. Clearly those comparative results are open to some interpretation, but the REJOICE team is confident about the general implications.

Experiment	Main results
Experiment 1 Defining, tailoring, and introducing the customer-oriented process	• Successive levels of tailoring are involved; they are difficult to clearly define. • The DSDM-based customer-oriented framework is loosely defined and requires further refinement and instantiation to be employable. • The new DSDM-based process does not fit easily with existing quality systems. • Detailed DSDM-based processes cannot be fully prescribed because of the highly iterative processes involved that are dependent on actual product development progress. • Detailed project planning cannot be achieved: plans must stay at a high level or they will lag behind the actual development.
Experiment 2 Applying and measuring the impact of the new customer-oriented process: requirement tool project	• The pragmatic use of DSDM-based principles leads to a fit for purpose product. • High-level user requirements are difficult to resolve and manage contractually. • The use of prototyping techniques is very effective. • The contract requirements would not have been met if traditional processes had been used.
Experiment 3 Applying and measuring the impact of the new customer-oriented REJOICE process: CMM assessment tool project	• There was good buy-in by the development team. • There were high levels of user involvement. • There was a high level of user satisfaction with the final product. • The users sometimes resented the demands on their time. • The team focus on achieving a final fit product means that documentation/testing suffers unless control is exercised; this may be a problem for longer-term customer satisfaction. • Any organizational and cultural changes to accommodate REJOICE processes are nontrivial. • It was difficult to control and plan prototyping. • It was difficult to monitor project progress with traditional management techniques. • The development team was not used to empowerment and perceived a lack of direction and management prior to customer interactions.
Experiment 4 Comparing the new customer-oriented REJOICE process with the existing traditional development process	• It is difficult to exactly compare results (some aggregate comparisons are possible as in Figure 6) with traditional methods because of nonequivalence with stages in the V-model and variants. • Customer surveys provided evidence of improved satisfaction. • The REJOICE process was found to be more efficient than traditional methods in terms of required functionality achieved for developer effort. • If the development project had followed the existing traditional process, it may have led to the development of a different tool, not considering real business need. • The longer-term customer satisfaction advantages are more difficult to assess as they depend on the scale and type of projects. • The REJOICE process developed products may be more difficult to maintain and evolve.

FIGURE 5. Qualitative experimental results by experiment.

REJOICE was unable to realistically test and explore the full effectiveness of the DSDM-based REJOICE process as the result of typical business project constraints. REJOICE includes the use of JAD workshops that were not fully used even though some equivalent facilitated workshops had been undertaken outside the REJOICE process. This raises the issue of when a development project lifecycle process such as REJOICE actually starts to be used in solving a business requirements problem. More information could have been gained about the process if a more complex and larger baseline project had been possible. This might, however, have led to more experimental difficulties. REJOICE was limited to producing a single software product increment. Also, the main baseline part of the REJOICE experiments had minimal complications in terms of contractual arrangements, normally a project constraint affecting the lifecycle process selection and implementation. Furthermore, REJOICE used business and development tools as the subjects for experimentation rather than mainstream business or embedded engineering systems.

Goal	Main quantitative results (with arguments)
Increase (20%) in satisfying customer needs	**Customer metrics** • 38% improvement in satisfaction of need • 23% improvement in confidence about the product quality • While the reliance on sensitive scoring techniques was necessary, it seems conclusive that the REJOICE process leads to satisfaction benefits. **Product metrics** • All user requirements were satisfied. • There were eight customer feedback sessions in the 12-week duration project. • Only two of the original 38 user requirements were changed; more detailed system specification details arose in feedback sessions. • No final requirements defects were identified as the feedback/iterations had refined specification, and consequent enhanced requirement and quality understanding.
No change in costs of requirements activity	**Process metrics** • The customer interactions (that is, eight times) used 16% of total project effort for requirements clarification and negotiation and demonstration (models and prototypes), collating feedback about requirements, and prototypes. • Overall the development effort for the REJOICE process was 10% less than for a traditional lifecycle model as in (Mazza et al. 1994). • A comparison of phase efforts for the REJOICE process with the traditional (V-model) process is: % effort by phase REJOICE process Traditional process Requirements 46% 13% Design 13% 19% Build and test 41% 68% • The REJOICE process used 46% in the equivalent requirements stage of projects compared with 13% for the traditional process. This extra effort includes 16% of customer interaction and 15% in responding to the changes/feedback; hence 15% of the remaining requirements effort was actually creating the specifications, models, and prototypes. The 15% of traditional process effort was spent on absolute minimal customer interaction. • The cost of creating requirements including minimal effort on clarification was about the same effort in both processes. However, the big difference is that the REJOICE customer interaction was up-front early in the lifecycle thus saving on later reworking efforts. The traditional process used similar reworking effort levels, possibly more costly as the reworking of requirements problems would have occurred later in the lifecycle. • This rework impact is evidence from the build and test effort being 41% in REJOICE compared with 68% in the traditional processes.
Decrease (15%) in problems due to poor requirements understanding	**Product metrics** • As described against the customer satisfaction goal, only 5% of high-level user requirements changed. • The REJOICE process resulted in 50% fewer changes to requirement baselines as the requirements were allowed to change more freely than in the traditional approaches that tend to freeze requirements documents. **Process metrics** • As indicated when considering the requirement activity cost, the amount of reworking occurred in the more extensive requirements part of the REJOICE process. This amounted to four iterations. This is about 50% more reworks than the traditional process for the requirements phase. The REJOCE process, however, did not have any requirement-led problems within its design and build and test phases, whereas the traditional process would probably have had at least the two changes reported to have dealt with later in the cycle. • It is not possible to indicate whether 15% fewer problems arose, but it would seem reasonable that this improvement is achievable, or even improved upon, given the requirements iterations involved in the REJOICE process.

FIGURE 6. Goal–related quantitative experimental results.

The use of the REJOICE process within more complex projects could be the subject of a further process improvement study. In hindsight, the original project proposal and the subsequent experimentation framework were rather ambitious. Ordinarily, the measurement of process improvement is plagued with statistical difficulties, but REJOICE has endeavored to measure the impact of the radical DSDM-based approach affecting "soft," "longer term," and "wider business" issues such as customer satisfaction.

POST EXPERIMENT: LESSONS LEARNED

This section assesses the impact of this customer satisfaction case study in terms of its research on customer satisfaction and related aspects. Subsequently, from the REJOICE experimentation, the impact of the new DSDM-based candidate process in relation to technological, project, and business viewpoints is assessed. These lessons are intended to assist future researchers, experimenters, or developers in the customer satisfaction area.

Research Viewpoint

This viewpoint assesses the potential contribution of the initial customer satisfaction analysis and associated framework reference model, and of the derived customer-oriented process requirements. The lessons are:

- Understanding the influences on customer satisfaction is central to achieving effective customer-oriented process design and execution.

- Customer satisfaction is more than opinion gathering, as it depends on perceptions derived from objective-based arguments and associated evidence based on the real demonstration of achieved satisfaction of need, requirements, and product quality assurances.

- The customer satisfaction reference model provides a structured vehicle for further study and elaboration, particularly in deriving a set of measurable and relevant attributes about the variables that influence satisfaction and a product's fitness for purpose.

- The customer research added more weight and context for selecting DSDM as a candidate customer-oriented process. It was possible to determine the critical experimental hypotheses to be tested from a theoretical analysis of the attributes of DSDM and its supporting techniques compared with the derived customer-oriented process requirements. This scope for theoretical analysis can ease the burden and justification of future "fit for purpose" method selection.

Technological Viewpoint

This viewpoint assesses the impact of the new candidate process in relation to current software practices and their evolution. The lessons are:

- Adoption by the SEC of a new evolutionary yet controlled lifecycle approach (where appropriate to the projects) is expected to lead to improved customer satisfaction.

- DSDM offers a useful set of concepts (sensible principles, flexible requirements philosophy, strong user and end-product focus) that will advance the SEC best practices.

- DSDM is not only suitable for "RAD type" projects, but its concepts can be integrated, in full or in part, into more traditional lifecycle approaches.

- The integration of the DSDM-based process within a traditional ISO 9000 quality controlled software development operation is nontrivial, unless DSDM is used to do RAD developments only.

- Commonly available tools generally support the basic DSDM-based REJOICE process, although more model-based tools are needed that facilitate effective user-modeling interaction (to study requirements and acceptance testing issues).

Overall, the technological lessons about the DSDM-based REJOICE processes are fundamental. More radical software lifecycles are designed to improve customer-developer relations. These require new ways of thinking about project control and tool-based cultures. There is clear evidence that the REJOICE process is sufficiently mature and does indeed enhance customer satisfaction, assuming that a joint product-focused management approach is taken by both customers and developers. In short, the REJOICE process offers clear claimed benefits when used in part or in full, but there are a number of nontrivial project and quality management issues to overcome.

Project Viewpoint

This viewpoint assesses the impact of the new candidate process on a variety of projects of different scale and type. This assessment is derived by a reasoned approach. These project results will impact the subsequent business viewpoint. The lessons about the wider use of the DSDM-based REJOICE process are:

- DSDM is not suitable for all types of projects; it cannot be used in whole for embedded systems or where system assurance must be very high.

- Some of the DSDM ideas (such as to achieve understanding, team-working, and adaptability) may be useful in all projects types, even higher assurance systems.

- As the project size and complexity increase, there are potential implementation difficulties to be overcome (that is, maintaining a high level of customer interaction, more complex prototyping tasks, more stringent nonfunctional aspects in the design and build stages, less able to fully demonstrate the product quality in a realistic operational setting, and so on).

The implications of different projects are assessed against the REJOICE business goals:

- **Customer satisfaction.** The degree of improvement will depend on the full or partial use of DSDM activities. If full use, greater gains are likely in smaller projects as the implementation issues are less difficult (for example, up to 40 percent gains in satisfaction possible) compared to larger projects where some gain should always be achieved, albeit 10 percent to 20 percent. The problems will be when the stakeholders do not want to be involved and when difficulties in understanding or agreements arise. If partial use, all projects where improved levels of customer participation are achievable will provide satisfaction gains of at least 10 percent.

- **Requirement costs and problems.** The same assessment applies as for customer satisfaction. The only difference is that the requirement costs are dependent on effective iteration and feedback through sufficient demonstration and customer interaction. If the quality, rather than the amount, of interaction is suspect then the requirements efficiencies as observed in the REJOICE experiment will not apply.

In essence, software businesses will do well to use some of the DSDM techniques on all projects and there will always be some gain. This will be at least a 10 percent improvement in customer satisfaction, and reduce project costs based on requirement efficiencies by a very small gain (for more complex or embedded system projects) or up to 20 percent savings (for smaller projects).

Business Viewpoint

This assessment has considered the impact of the new candidate process in relation to business goals and activities. The lessons are:

- Derived from the previous project viewpoint, customer satisfaction and the attendant advantages are likely to be achieved by using the DSDM-based REJOICE process.

- Derived from the previous project viewpoint, the REJOICE process is likely to provide cost-saving gains in the efficiency of requirements-based activities, depending on project complexity and associated implementation issues. There is evidence that this may even reduce total project costs as less requirement problems arise too late in the lifecycle process.

- The REJOICE process requires a cooperative product-focused management approach.

- Definition and management of contractual boundaries will be challenging.

- Cultural changes may be difficult to manage.

- Consider applying DSDM techniques to smaller projects until confidence is gained.

- A REJOICE-type process will increase business opportunities through improved customer relations.

Overall, many software businesses should benefit from the DSDM-based REJOICE concepts, process, and techniques in terms of customer satisfaction and requirements efficiencies. The degree of success, however, will depend on the organization and customer culture, the appropriate application to suitably complex projects, and an effective use of available software technologies. In short, the REJOICE process framework is well founded, but its success depends on the management of people and technical resources during any development project implementation.

SUMMARY

This article describes a customer satisfaction process improvement case study that also includes an EU-funded process improvement experiment, REJOICE. The article describes the underpinnings and development of a customer and requirements focused lifecycle process that provided the key rationale for selecting a candidate process, the DSDM-based REJOICE process. The underpinning arises from the evolving development of an innovative customer satisfaction reference model that also provides a structured basis for future system measurement. This model can be used to derive the requirements for designing, evaluating, or selecting a customer-oriented lifecycle process.

The REJOICE experiment has focused on the business impact of the selected DSDM-based process improvement geared to improve customer satisfaction; the business goals include improved customer satisfaction and cost-effective requirements management. The experimental findings support the main hypothesis that the flexible process should yield the business benefits suggested; however, a careful approach to process introduction and quality control is required as a new cultural approach to customer-supplier partnerships is critical. If implemented well, both customers and suppliers should reap major benefits.

Acknowledgments and Disclaimers

The author would like to acknowledge the European Commission for funding the process improvement experiment, REJOICE, Project 23893, supplemented by internal Defence Evaluation and Research Agency funding on the general concepts underpinning requirements understanding. Furthermore, the author would like to thank the dedication of the REJOICE team, in particular that of Peter Raynor-Smith for his major contribution. In addition, thanks to the Euro-SPI '99 committee that selected the original conference paper "Achieving Customer Satisfaction through Requirements Understanding" for further publication; the original paper has been revised and updated for *SQP*.

The views expressed in this article are entirely those of the author and do not represent the views, policy, or understanding of any other person or official body. Further details can be requested from the Defence Evaluation and Research Agency (DERA Malvern), Systems and Software Engineering Center.

REFERENCES

Bell, S., and T. Wood-Harper. 1998. *Rapid information systems development—System development in an imperfect world*. 2nd ed. New York: McGraw-Hill.

DSDM Consortium. 1996. *DSDM manual*. Farnham, U. K.: Tesseract Publishing.

Elliott, J. J. 1998. REJOICE framework report, version 1.0., U. K. DERA Report.

ESSI VASIE. 2000. See URL www.cordis.lu/esprit/src/stessi.htm .

Fenton, N. E., and S. L. Pfleeger. 1997. *Software metrics*. 2nd ed. Boston: Thomson Computer Press.

Garrity, E. J., and G. L. Saunders. 1998. *Information systems success measurement*. Hershey, PA: IDEA Group.

Gillies, A. 1992. *Software quality—theory and management*. New York: Chapman and Hall.

International Organization for Standardization (ISO). 1992. *ISO 912—software product evaluation*. Geneva, Switzerland: International Organization for Standardization.

MacDonald, J. 1995. *Understanding business process reengineering*. London: Hodder & Stoughton.

Martin, J. 1991. *Rapid application development*. New York: Macmillan.

Mazza, C. et al. 1994. *Software engineering standards*. Upper Saddle River, N. J.: Prentice-Hall.

McConnell, S. 1996. *Rapid development*. Redmond, Wash.: Microsoft Press.

Pressman, R. S. 1997. *Software engineering—a practitioner's approach*. New York: McGraw-Hill.

Raynor-Smith, P. M. 1998. REJOICE Process. U. K. DERA Report.

Raynor-Smith, P. M., and J. J. Elliott. 1999. REJOICE final report, version 1.0. U. K. DERA Report.

Somerville, I. 1996. *Software engineering*. Reading, MA: Addison-Wesley.

Stapleton, J. 1997. *Dynamic systems development method*. Reading, MA: Addison-Wesley.

BIOGRAPHY

John Elliott is a technical manager within the U.K. Defence Evaluation and Research Agency's Systems (DERA) and Software Engineering Center. He has a master's degree in information systems engineering and is a member of the British Computer Society. Elliott has a strong background as a statistician as well as a system/software engineer. He is currently leading systems and software research activities (including process improvement studies). His technical areas embrace systems and software assurance, including systems thinking, product quality, measurement, critical systems, and risk management. He has spent more than 20 years specializing in advanced system and software engineering.

Elliott has extensive knowledge of system and software lifecycle processes and associated standards. He has experience as a manager, developer, consultant, and assessor of software-based systems in a variety of defense and nondefense domains. Prior to joining DERA in 1997, Elliott led two separate software assurance groups at U.K. consultancy companies and was involved in systems assessments and state-of-the-art research programs in safety critical systems. Elliott can be reached by phone at 44 1684-895161 or by e-mail at jjelliott@dera.gov.uk .

CHAPTER 2.2

People Management and Development Process

Giovanni Evangelisti, Emilia Peciola,
and Cosimo Zotti, Ericsson Telecommunications SpA

*T**his article reports the results of a project run in Ericsson Telecommunicazioni Italia, Research and Development—Global Product Center. The process described is an innovative way to handle human resources in order to have motivated people, realize an effective job staffing, and prepare the organization for the future. The process was launched in May 1998, and this article reports preliminary feedback on its application based on data collected from a questionnaire measuring people satisfaction distributed to all staff members in December 1998.*

Key words: career paths, competencies, human resources, individual assessment, job descriptions, personnel development, roles and responsibilities

INTRODUCTION

"The only rule I have in management is to ensure that I have good people—real good people—and that I grow good people, and that I provide an environment where good people can produce."

(CURTIS, KRASNER, AND ISCOE 1988)

In the last 20 years software organizations have concentrated on improving their capabilities, working actively on processes and technologies. But this is not enough to keep ahead of continuous change: Software systems are more complex, competition is stronger, and customer demands are greater, aiming at lower costs and higher quality.

In the 1990s, many software organizations discovered that improved processes and technologies are not enough, and that a third component, people, plays an important role (see Figure 1).

Ericsson Telecomunicazioni Italia, Research and Development, Global Product Center Division (TEI R&D-GPC), was originally the research center of the Italian branch of Ericsson. It was created 25 years ago and during the 1990s grew from fewer than 50 people to about 600 people. Its mission changed during this growth, and the company's initial goal of being a center of technological excellence became the prop for releasing successful products.

The current organization is quite complex, distributed over four geographical sites and striving toward product responsibilities. The technological focus is kept both on software (SW) and on hardware (HW), but to drive the organization, strong managerial attention toward employees, projects, and products is needed.

TEI R&D-GPC today is a good example of a workplace where people with different attitudes work side-by-side, exploiting diversity to generate cooperation—people with technical skills working together with managerial people. But diversity easily generates fear when one's future is uncertain.

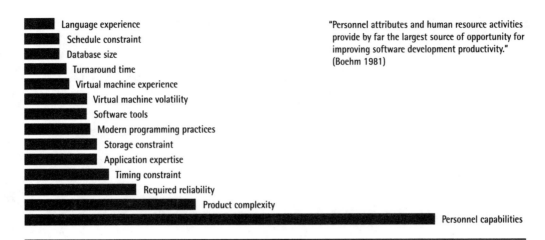

Figure 1   Factors impacting productivity.

Since top management strongly believes that knowledge is the best antidote for fear, in the beginning of 1998 the focus on transparency sharpened, as well as the desire to create an environment where one can easily relate with the organizational structure and needs, the early knowledge of organizational events can reduce surprise and anxiety, and one's career is the consequence of discovering one's talents rather than of giving them up.

The organization's goal is "to attract, develop, motivate, organize, and retain the best people talented in the areas that fit with TEI R&D-GPC business goals." This article reports the results of an initiative that began two years ago that aimed to increase internal transparency by defining the basic net of processes and procedures for people management. Talented people are not caught by this net, but GPC believes it is useful in retaining them. In fact, the company's target people have a good sense of belonging, and these types of people like to work where the "rule of law" is perceived.

People are attracted by money, but GPC does not believe an organization can attract the best people just with high salaries. The company believes it can gain a competitive advantage when people perceive a service-oriented environment.

People processes are the fundamental part of this service environment. Employees want to build a specific development path, have access to interfaces to ask questions, be supported in changing jobs, have opportunities to speak with the managers, receive more information, and improve the quality of their lives (and working hours gain importance as free time decreases and will decrease even more).

They expect attention to be paid not only to managerial roles, as each individual, independently from his or her activities, wants to feel that the workplace can offer the best development conditions.

To meet these demands, the company initiated a project from February to May 1998. The goal of this project was to define a process for innovatively managing human resources. Two people worked full time with the support of a reference group of 15 line managers who met once a month.

REASONS FOR, AND GOALS OF, THE PROJECT

Prior to beginning this project, people satisfaction and motivation were low. The results of a questionnaire distributed in early 1996 showed that people's dissatisfactions stemmed from:

- Failures in planning development programs
- A low level of feedback on performed activities
- Partially defined training programs
- No possibility for job rotation
- Unclear criteria for development opportunities and rewards

Management practices were not formalized and interconnected, and the only processes regularly executed were competence development and potential evaluation.

The actions toward employees often were not related, with lack of causal ties between them and risks of inconsistencies toward the individuals. Managers were not supported enough by the organization in their interwork with their people. Career development of technical people was not emphasized enough and their job changes were seldom planned and prepared through appropriate training. In this context, the level of service provided by the organization was perceived by employees as low.

Following is a scale of levels in caring people management services:

- **Physical environment.** An environment suitable and equipped for work is provided.

- **Regulatory environment.** The rules that are valid in this work environment are communicated.

- **Processes and services.** Support practices are made available so as to reduce sources of distraction and worry.

- **Relations environment.** Relations between individuals are facilitated and the distance between private life and work is reduced.

The company scarcely reached the second level, as even the knowledge of many existing rules was not sufficiently diffused. The goals of the action program were:

- To establish practices well suited to pay more attention to the expectations of employees in their interwork with the organization
- To focus on technical roles and ensure them the same dignity as managerial roles

In the beginning of 1998, the design of the people management and development process (PMDP) was a sign that GPC's management cared about people issues and wanted technical people to be motivated as well as excellent.

To achieve the second goal, toward the end of 1998, a new method for classifying employee contributions through roles was introduced. Roles were classified into three ladders (that is, areas of contribution) with different organizational goals:

- **Professional.** The responsibility consists in the provision of professional performance.

- **Solution manager.** The responsibility consists in pursuing short- and mid-term objectives, making decisions, negotiating, and exploiting resources.

- **Organization manager.** The responsibility mainly consists in managing resources such as company assets and pursuing strategic objectives.

Ladders were structured into levels, and equal development possibilities and recognition were assured to roles belonging to a certain level, independently from the specific ladder. The levels allowed a transparent comparison between roles belonging to different ladders.

COMPETENCE MODEL AND ROLE CLASSIFICATION

The competence model used in the organization for competence management is shown in Figure 2. The activities of the company are modeled in "company processes" (for example, the product management process, provisioning process, marketing process, sales process, accounting process, human resources process, and so on). The company processes are composed of job families, and job families of roles.

Job families used in TEI R&D-GPC are: administration support/secretary; finance/control/treasury; general management; human resources; marketing; product management; provisioning management; provisioning support; change and innovation; function test; HW design; SW design; systems engineering; systems management; and systems test.

At any time, each employee has a single role associated with him or her. The roles are characterized by:

- A list of tasks and responsibilities
- A "reference competence radar" (competence chart)
- A "specialization"

Specialization is the basic competence (for example, HW, FW, open SW, and so on) common to a number of roles and is the element used in the operative planning to take basic staffing agreements between a project and the different line organizations, as the resolution provided by job families is not sharp enough.

Roles are classified into the three ladders mentioned previously (professional, solution manager, and organization manager) according to the specific organizational goals. The classification of roles within the ladders is shown in Figure 3. This classification is also a model for competence development and a model to capture the present reality of the organization.

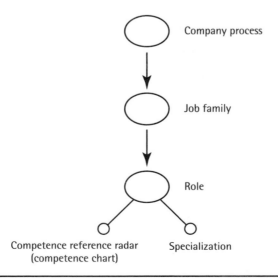

Figure 2   The competence model.

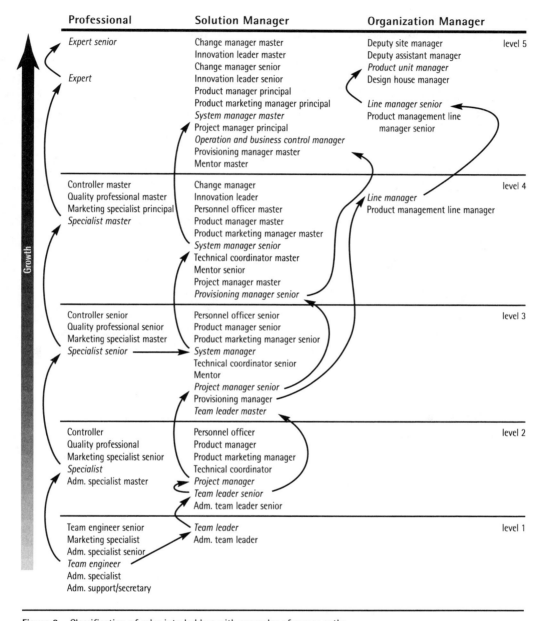

Figure 3 Classification of roles into ladders with examples of career paths.

The large number of roles does not stem from the goal of creating a specific role for each individual: Many roles are empty and purely represent development possibilities; few roles contain most of the employees (in particular, the technical roles of the professional ladder, such as team engineer, specialist, and so on). In the table each member of the organization must find his or her present role and the roles he or she will cover along his or her career.

In Figure 3 some possible movements between roles are shown as examples of career paths. These movements also show that the classification of roles into ladders does not prevent transitions between ladders; rather, the classification facilitates the identification of ladder-specific competencies and attitudes that are crucial in role changes along the individual career path.

Declinations (base, senior, master, principal) associated to the same role permit the recognition of different levels of competence and contribution. Note that for simplicity, in the professional ladder, only the types of roles are shown; the characterization of the job family (for example, HW, SW, and so on) that the role belongs to is omitted. Also, it is possible to reach the highest level of recognition (level 5) in each of the three ladders.

PMDP DESCRIPTION

- The PMDP process encompasses all of the company's activities that are aimed at finding and motivating the right people.
- Hiring and purely administrative activities are not included in this process.
- The process architecture is shown in Figure 4. It consists of eight subprocesses and their information interfaces.

Following are the key issues of each subprocess.

Competence Planning (CPL)

The competence planning subprocess aims to:

- Have a clear picture of the company processes, job families, competence groups, and roles requested by the division for the next year (definition of a human resources plan)
- Define the reference competence radar for each role
- Provide an indication of the competence gap (role numerical gap) existing within TEI R&D-GPC between current year's end role staffing and next year's role numerical needs

Management needs this picture to perform the activities requested to close the competence gap.

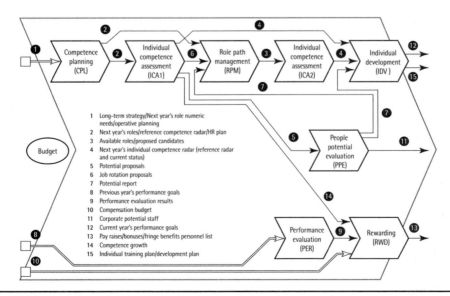

Figure 4   PMDP architecture.

Individual Competence Assessment Phase 1 (ICA1)

The individual competence assessment subprocess is devoted to assessing the qualifications of the people working at TEI R&D-GPC to create a reference frame for effectively managing these competencies. The individual competence assessment aims to:

- Create a clear picture of each employee's competencies
- Identify candidates for open positions so as to improve people motivation and effective staffing
- Identify candidates for people potential evaluation in order to manage them appropriately
- Evaluate the competence growth of each person with the purpose of recognizing his or her professional efforts during the last year

Role Path Management (RPM)

The competence growth of TEI R&D-GPC personnel is supported by job rotation activities defined in this process. The role path management subprocess aims to:

- Define the possible paths from each role within T Division
- Provide job rotation proposals based on the needs coming from competence planning and the candidates coming from individual competence assessment (first run)

Individual Competence Assessment Phase 2 (ICA2)

To secure the company with critical and strategic competencies, each role in the organization must be covered by employees with an adequate competence profile. The individual competence assessment (phase 2) subprocess is devoted to evaluating and selecting candidates for job rotation identified in the RPM subprocess. ICA2 aims to:

- Assess the competence level of candidates for job rotation in order to select the most suitable people for the jobs to be staffed
- Identify the people willing to move to other sites or divisions for overstaffed roles

Individual Development (IDV)

To ensure that all people are qualified to perform their assignment, each level of the organization must identify the competence required to perform critical tasks and the training needs within each line. This ensures that each person receives the necessary training. The individual development subprocess aims to:

- Identify an adequate competence development plan for each person
- Identify a consistent training program for each person
- Define performance goals for T Division first- and second-level managers

People Potential Evaluation (PPE)

The organization wants to identify and value people who are suitable to assume key roles in the future so as to improve. To achieve this goal, the first step is to identify people whose potential has some unexpressed dimensions. The people potential evaluation subprocess aims to:

- Evaluate the technical and managerial potential of the candidates proposed in the list coming from the individual competence assessment (first run).
- Identify which candidates can be considered potentially suitable to assume, in the short and medium term, key roles within TEI R&D-GPC, TEI, and Ericsson corporate.

Performance Evaluation (PER)

To reward first- and second-level managers based on their contribution to results and values, it is necessary to provide objective performance evaluation results. The purpose of PER is to produce these objective results as input to the rewarding subprocess. The performance evaluation subprocess aims to:

- Assess the performances of first- and second-level managers
- Summarize the evaluation of first- and second-level managers' performances in a performance evaluation result

Rewarding (RWD)

The purpose of the rewarding subprocess is to reward all employees based on their contribution to results and values for the organization. The rewarding subprocess aims to:

- Compensate employees with pay raises and promotions
- Compensate teams with bonuses

DESCRIPTION OF PROCESS–TIME RELATIONSHIP

This section is devoted to the relationship between PMDP subprocesses and time. The relationship is illustrated in Figure 5, "PMDP subprocesses–timetable" and Figure 6, "PMDP subprocesses–time relationship."

In Figure 5 a two-year period is shown to provide an idea of process periodicity and time periods between subsequent process executions. Figure 6 considers a time frame of three years and shows which information is needed from the previous year and which information is passed on to the next year. The positions of the arrows show the time of year in which the action is executed.

Estimation of Next Year's Competence Needs

At the end of January, the CPL process is able to produce the first rough estimate the next year's competence needs (that is, the role numerical needs for the next year). This information is composed of two different types of data: new possible roles that should be introduced in TEI R&D-GPC and numeric gap information for each role. The first competence-needs estimate allows the activation of the "core step" for achieving overall PMDP goals: the individual interview.

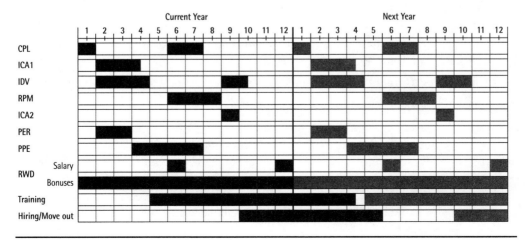

Figure 5   PMDP subprocesses–timetable.

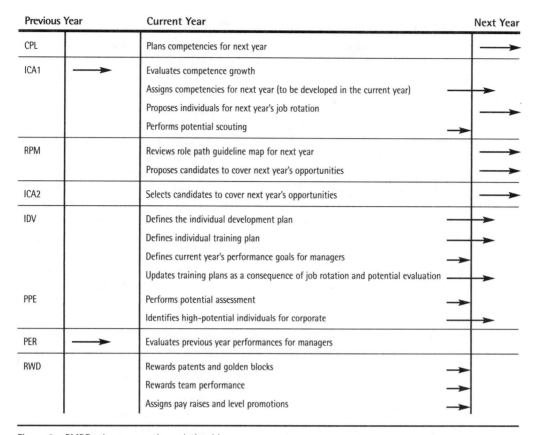

Previous Year		Current Year		Next Year
CPL		Plans competencies for next year		→
ICA1	→	Evaluates competence growth		
		Assigns competencies for next year (to be developed in the current year)	→	
		Proposes individuals for next year's job rotation		→
		Performs potential scouting	→	
RPM		Reviews role path guideline map for next year		→
		Proposes candidates to cover next year's opportunities		→
ICA2		Selects candidates to cover next year's opportunities		→
IDV		Defines the individual development plan		→
		Defines individual training plan		→
		Defines current year's performance goals for managers	→	
		Updates training plans as a consequence of job rotation and potential evaluation		→
PPE		Performs potential assessment	→	
		Identifies high-potential individuals for corporate		→
PER	→	Evaluates previous year performances for managers		
RWD		Rewards patents and golden blocks	→	
		Rewards team performance	→	
		Assigns pay raises and level promotions	→	

Figure 6   PMDP subprocesses–time relationship.

Individual interview. In February and March, line managers individually interview their staff members. In the same period, second-level managers are interviewed by first-level managers and by the director of TEI R&D-GPC. The interviews activate different PMDP subprocesses: ICA1, IDV, and PER. First of all, the ICA1 deals with the competence assessment and competence growth evaluation of each person. In addition, the ICA1 performs potential scouting (that is, identifies people suitable for potential evaluation) and identifies possible proposals for job rotation.

The individual interview also activates the IDV in which the development plan and the training plan for each person are produced. The IDV identifies individual performance goals for first- and second-level managers. It is worthwhile to note that the IDV also includes some work that line managers do after completing the individual interviews (for example, final training definition), and therefore, this subprocess is supposed to end later than ICA1, which terminates with the end of the interviews. The scope of the PER is limited to first- and second-level managers. It is activated during the individual interview and has the objective of evaluating managers' performances by assessing the achievement of the individual goals defined in the previous year's IDV.

Potential evaluation. In April, PPE starts. It aims at evaluating the potential of the candidates proposed by the ICA1. The potential assessment identifies employees who are suitable to assume key roles within the organization. The output of the PPE is formalized in a "potential report."

Definition of Next Year's Competence Needs

In July, CPL is able to produce a new and elaborate version of the human resource plan. This document contains information that is relevant for the RPM.

Job rotation. From June to August RPM performs two kinds of activities. The first is the periodic review of the guidelines that define the possible role paths in the T Division. The second is related to job rotation. In case the gap for a specific role is positive, the RPM identifies the most suitable people, among those individuated by ICA1, for that specific role and forwards to ICA2 a list of job-rotation proposals (that is, an ordered list of people who should be interviewed to verify their suitability for the new job). In case the gap for a specific role is negative (that is, indicates a reduction for a specific role), the RPM, after exploiting all the possibilities to apply job rotation for the involved people, forwards to ICA2 only a numeric indication of the people to be moved to other divisions or sites. Once RPM has completed the compilation of the job-rotation proposals (respectively, in case of layoff, the numeric indications) for the lines, the line managers start a new cycle of interviews.

Individual interviews for job rotation. In September, the new cycle of interviews activates ICA2 and IDV. ICA2 aims at assessing the competence level of candidates for job rotation in order to select the most suitable people for the unstaffed roles. It is worthwhile to note that IDV is activated during the second cycle of interviews in order to redefine, if necessary, the training and development plan of the people who are going to rotate their jobs. Another reason for activating IDV in September is the completion of PPE. The indications of the potential report may determine some changes in the training and development plan of the people involved in the potential evaluation.

Compensation. The RWD aims at compensating people with pay raises and promotions and teams with bonuses. For pay raises and promotions, the subprocess is activated twice a year—in June and December. Bonuses (for example, patent and "golden block" awards, team rewards) are processed throughout the year.

PROCESS EXECUTION AND PRELIMINARY RESULTS

The process was launched in May 1998 and presented to all staff members. A copy was also placed on the company intranet. Three-hundred-and-forty-three individuals in TEI R&D-GPC have been involved in subprocess execution, and positive feedback has been received by most employees during the interviews, as well as some improvement proposals. Regarding potential evaluation, at the end of the interviews, 68 candidates were proposed for the assessment; however, the capacity of the process limited the formal assessment to 30.

In December 1998 the same employee satisfaction survey used in 1996 was run again and the results are considered very promising. In fact, compared with the results obtained in 1996, the survey general index increased 24 percent. Detailed results pertaining to some of the survey's modules are listed in Figure 7.

The results show that the communication generated by this initiative paid off and also boosted the perception of practices that were already in place. Another important parameter to be reported relates to the turnover registered in the last six months. In fact, just 2 percent of the staff left the company and another 2 percent asked to be rotated to other divisions.

Survey Modules	% of increase
Work task	10%
Development opportunities	51%
Information	21%
Culture and climate	33%

Figure 7   Survey results.

CONCLUSIONS

The actions concerning people management performed during 1998 in Ericsson Italy were of two types:

1. Through the PMDP, people were informed that more attention was going to be devoted to them, particularly by improving services (in terms of processes) that concerned their interwork with the company (competence development, career path, potential evaluation, and so on).

2. More importance was given to technical roles and the same dignity of managerial roles was recognized to them.

These long-term actions were chosen rather than more direct actions on salaries or bonuses because dissatisfaction was not acute and turnover was normal (less than 5 percent).

Dissatisfaction seemed to stem from the type of interwork between the individuals and the company rather than from specific claims about salary. The PMDP project, in addition to communication and cultural shift, produced a process description including an overview of the whole process and a detailed description of each subprocess.

Before, the potential assessment was run by consultants and scarcely documented. In addition, there was the form to fill out during interviews and corporate or company descriptions of people procedures whose applicability to the organization was uncertain.

The introduction of PMDP together with the new transparent classification of roles into ladders had a strong impact on the organization's culture:

- People have become the subject of a process as it was for any other important company asset and goal as technology, quality, time (through project), and so on. This sounds like a statement of recognition.

- The existence of a process provides certainty, as it creates a known and visible reference for everybody and a shared starting point for discussions and improvements.

- The career picture provided by ladders defines the present point of balance in the shift affecting leadership models and says that a single managerial view cannot garrison the different competition edges of a company, recognizing value to each type of contribution that is needed.

In the beginning of 1999 a project to implement People-CMM model (Curtis, Hefley, and Miller 1995) was started and a revision of PMDP was necessary to align the process to the new model. Because of People-CMM, more than 100 improvement actions were planned and 15 of them concerned changes to PMDP. The overall architecture of PMDP, however, could be kept and no additional process was introduced. Changes affected only the methods used in the processes and the interwork between processes. PMDP proved to be a strong infrastructure, robust enough to incorporate the new requirements.

REFERENCES

Argyris, C., and D. A. Schon. 1978. *Organizational learning: A theory of action perspective.* Reading, MA: Addison-Wesley.

Boehm, B. 1981. *Software engineering economics.* Upper Saddle River, N. J.: Prentice-Hall.

Curtis, B., H. Krasner, and N. Iscoe. 1988. A field study of the software design process for large systems. *Communication of the ACM* 31, 11: 1268–1287.

Curtis, B., W. E. Hefley, and S. Miller. 1995. *People capability maturity model.* Pittsburgh: Software Engineering Institute, Carnegie Mellon University.

Drucker, P. F. 1999. *Management challenges for the 21st century.* New York: Harperbusiness.

Grant, R. M. 1991. The resource-based theory of competitive advantage: Implications for strategy formulation. *California Management Review* (spring).

Hammer, M., and S. A. Stanton. 1995. *The reengineering revolution.* New York: HarperCollins.

Lawler, E. E. III. 1994. From job-based to competency-based organizations. *Engineering Management Review* (fall).

Prahalad, C. K., and G. Hamel. 1990. The core competence of the corporation. *Harvard Business Review* (May/June).

Weick, K., and E. Weick. 1969. *The social psychology of organizing.* Reading, MA: Addison-Wesley.

BIOGRAPHIES

Giovanni Evangelisti graduated with a degree in electronic engineering from the University of Genoa in 1972. He joined Ericsson in 1974 and worked as a systems engineer and system coordinator. He then worked as line manager and was responsible for central units in the Research and Development Division of Ericsson Italy, with a special focus on improving people management processes. He can be reached by e-mail at giovanni.evangelisti@tei.ericsson.se .

Emilia Peciola graduated in 1984 from the University of Pisa with a degree in computer science. She joined Ericsson in 1985 and worked as a software designer and software technical coordinator. Since 1996, she moved to managerial assignments, leading software departments. She is currently leader of the project office and chair of the Software Technology Committee for software innovation in Ericsson Italy's Research and Development Division.

Cosimo Zotti graduated with a degree in electronic engineering from the University of Naples in 1986. He joined Ericsson in 1992 after working as a software designer and as a project leader in Italtel and ARE. At Ericsson he was engaged in process development and improvement with a special focus on requirements management and people management. He is currently change manager in the Research and Development Division. He can be reached by e-mail at Cosimo.Zotti@ex1.tei.ericsson.se .

PART THREE

Software Processes

In his 1979 classic *Quality Is Free*, Phil Crosby introduced what he called the "Quality Management Maturity Grid." He described a five-stage progression beginning with "Uncertainty"—the confused and uncommitted stage—and passing through "Awakening" and then "Enlightenment" and "Wisdom," finally becoming fully realized in the stage of "Certainty."

Crosby saw the grid as a means of projecting a commonly accepted view of an organization's status, as well as a source of direction for what needs to be done next. He characterized the maturation as it was manifest in several categories, including management understanding and attitude, quality organization status, and problem handling techniques.

Some report the paradox of an apparent worsening of quality during the early phases of maturation, but it is not that quality is worsening, it is rather that one's awareness (initially naïve) is more closely approximating reality. While the actual cost of quality is dramatically decreasing across the maturity stages, the greater maturity is also bringing a more realistic understanding of the cost. In the end, the reported and actual figures coincide. "Certainty" has been achieved.

Jeff Tian surveys and compares **"Risk Identification Techniques for Defect Reduction and Quality Improvement."** Each technique is briefly described and illustrated with practical application examples. The techniques are compared using several criteria including simplicity, accuracy and stability of results, ease of result interpretation, and utility in guiding defect reduction and quality improvement activities. The recommended life-cycle approach integrates these quality analysis and improvement activities into the existing development process and can be tailored by practitioners to fit their own application environment.

How does one get management to understand and support quality initiatives? Speak the language of management—money. In **"Cost of Software Quality: Justifying Software Process Improvement to Managers,"** Dan Houston applies to software processes a technique already widely accepted in the manufacturing and service industries. He shares data on costs of software quality that have proven a strong indication of financial return on investment in process improvement

"Defect Prevention: The Road Less Traveled" describes the experiences of one organization that chose to move beyond after-the-fact corrective actions. Craig Smith relates the importance of management commitment, training in problem-solving techniques, and the integration of defect prevention into other software development processes. He elaborates on representative defect prevention methods: defect cause analysis, effective process design, and project postmortems. Among the results was a twenty-fold reduction in post-release defects as well as markedly reduced cost overruns, decreased cycle times, and improved overall customer satisfaction.

Risk Identification Techniques for Defect Reduction and Quality Improvement

Jeff Tian, Department of Computer Science and Engineering, Southern Methodist University

*T*his article surveys and compares risk identification techniques that can be used for defect reduction and quality improvement. Each technique is briefly described and illustrated with practical examples from industrial or governmental projects. The techniques are compared using several criteria, including simplicity, accuracy, and stability of results; ease of result interpretation; and utility in guiding defect reduction and quality improvement activities. The author also recommends an integrated lifecycle approach so these techniques can be used throughout the software development process for quality assessment and improvement.

Key words: defects and software metrics, learning algorithms, pattern matching, quality improvement, risk identification, statistical analysis techniques

INTRODUCTION

Software must be as defect-free as practical. A *defect* generally refers to a problem in the software, which may lead to undesirable consequences for both the software development organization and the software users. The potential for such undesirable consequences, including schedule delays, cost overruns, and highly defective software products, is usually referred to as *risk*. Various statistical and learning algorithm-based techniques have been developed to identify and reduce such risks.

In software, a defect generally results in fixes to several modules or product components, and those fixes may also be propagated to related product releases. The author uses the term *defect fix*, denoted as DF, to refer to the action of identifying and correcting a localized problem. It is also used to measure product quality in this article. DF can be identified with specific modules; therefore, it can be used to analyze software quality at both the module level and the product level.

Defect distribution is highly uneven for most software products, regardless of their size, functionality, implementation language, and other characteristics. A lot of empirical evidence has accumulated over the years to support the so-called 80:20 rule, which states that 20 percent of the software components are responsible for 80 percent of the problems. Figure 1 shows a typical defect distribution for a commercial software product studied in Tian and Troster (1998), where only 19.2 percent (248) of the modules have more than 2 DF (DF > 2), but they represent 84 percent (1989) of the total DF.

Because of the uneven defect distribution among software modules, there is a great need for risk identification techniques so actions can be focused on those potentially high-defect modules for effective quality improvement. To measure and characterize these high-defect modules, various software metrics can be used to capture information about software design, code, size, change, and so on (Fenton and Pfleeger 1996). Once the measurement data are collected from existing project databases or calculated using

Module with DF=	0	1	2	3	4	5	6	7	8	9	10~19	20~37	all
# of modules	771	174	102	63	31	29	23	25	16	7	50	14	1295
% of modules	58.8%	13.4%	7.9%	4.9%	2.4%	2.2%	1.8%	1.9%	1.2%	0.5%	3.9%	1.1%	100%
DF sum (DF x #)	0	174	204	189	124	145	138	175	128	63	673	417	2367
% of total DF	0%	7.4%	8.6%	8.0%	5.2%	6.1%	5.8%	7.4%	5.0%	2.7%	28.4%	17.6%	100%

Figure 1   Distribution of DF for a commercial product.

measurement tools, various techniques can be employed to analyze the data to identify high-defect modules. Like other statistical techniques, these risk identification techniques cannot establish proof of a causal relationship. They can, however, provide strong evidence that there may be a causal relationship in an observed effect. By extracting the characteristics of existing high-defect modules, these analyses can help software professionals identify new modules demonstrating similar measurement characteristics and take early actions to reduce risks or prevent potential problems.

The author next briefly surveys risk identification techniques and illustrates their use through practical examples from industrial and governmental projects. Data, models, and analysis results presented in this article are extracted from several commercial (IBM) software products studied in Khoshgoftaar and Szabo (1996); Tian (1995); Tian and Troster (1998), governmental (NASA) projects studied in Porter and Selby (1990); Briand, Basili, and Hetmanski (1993), as well as software systems used in aerospace, medical, and telecommunication industries studied in Munson and Khoshgoftaar (1992); Khoshgoftaar et al. (1996). The article concludes with a comparison of these techniques and the author's recommendation for an integrated lifecycle approach where selected techniques can be used effectively through software development for defect reduction and quality improvement.

TRADITIONAL STATISTICAL ANALYSIS TECHNIQUES

Various traditional statistical analysis techniques (Venables and Ripley 1994) can be used to understand the general relations between defects and other software measurement data. These statistical relations and the general understanding can be used to a limited degree to identify high-defect modules.

Correlation Analysis

The statistical correlation between two random variables x and y can be captured by the (linear) correlation coefficient $c(x, y)$, which ranges between -1 and 1. A positive correlation indicates that the two variables are generally moving in the same direction (that is, a larger x is usually accompanied by a larger y), while a negative correlation indicates the opposite. The closer to 1 the absolute value $|c(x,y)|$ is, the more tightly correlated x and y are. Because software measurement data are often skewed, such as in Figure 1, where many modules contain few DF while a few modules contain many, rank correlations are often calculated in addition to the linear correlations.

If the observed defects are highly correlated to a software metric, one can then identify those modules with larger (or smaller, if negatively correlated) values of the given metric as high-defect modules. However, DF-metric correlations are generally low (Card and Glass 1990; Fenton and Pfleeger 1996), which limits one's ability to predict high-defect modules based on metrics data. For example, the highest DF-metric correlation is 0.731, between DF and changed source instructions or changed lines of code (CSI), for the product LS studied in Tian and Troster (1998).

Linear Regression Models

Linear regression models express a selected random variable y, referred to as the dependent variable, as a linear combination of n other random variables, $x_1, x_2, ..., x_n$, referred to as independent variables, in the form of: $y = \alpha_0 + \alpha_1 x_1 + \alpha_2 x_2 + ... + \alpha_n x_n + \varepsilon$, where ε is the error term, and parameters $\alpha_0, \alpha_1, ..., \alpha_n$ can be estimated from the observation data. Because of the data skew, logarithmic transformation of data can also be used, yielding a log-linear regression.

When regression models are fitted to defect and metrics data, DF can be expressed as a linear or log-linear function of other metrics. The correlation coefficient between the observed defects and the fitted linear or log-linear models (the square root of the corresponding multiple R-squared value) can be interpreted in similar ways as for DF-metric correlations. These corrections are 0.767 and 0.789, respectively, for the product LS studied in Tian and Troster (1998)—only slightly higher than correlations between DF and the individual metrics. Similar patterns were also observed in studies of other products. In general, linear or log-linear regression models suffer from similar shortcoming as correlation analysis models and do not perform well in predicting high-defect modules. In addition, parameter estimates for these models are usually unstable owing to high correlation in the metrics data.

Other Traditional Statistical Models and General Observations

Various other traditional statistical analysis techniques, such as nonlinear regression models, generalized additive models, logistic regression models, and so on (Venables and Ripley 1994), can also be used to identify high-defect modules. However, they suffer from similar limitations as models described previously. Data from the majority of low-defect modules dominate these statistical results, which contain little information about high-defect modules. To overcome these limitations, alternative analysis techniques need to be used.

NEW TECHNIQUES FOR RISK IDENTIFICATION

Recently, new techniques have been developed and used for risk identification purposes, including classification and analysis techniques based on statistical analysis, learning, and pattern matching. The author next surveys these techniques and illustrates how they can be used to identify high-defect modules.

Principal Component Analysis and Discriminate Analysis

Principal component analysis and discriminant analysis are useful statistical techniques for multivariate data (Venables and Ripley 1994). The former reduces multivariate data into a few orthogonal dimensions, while the latter classifies these data points into several mutually exclusive groups. These analysis techniques are especially useful when there are a large number of correlated variables in the collected data. Software metrics data fit into this scenario, where many closely related metrics exist to measure design, size, and complexity of the data and control structures in the code (thus, the measurement results are correlated, too).

The principal components are formed by linear combinations of the original data variables to form an orthogonal set of variables that are statistically uncorrelated. If the original data with n variables are linearly independent (that is, none of the variables can be expressed as linear combinations of other variables), then their covariance matrix, Σ, an $n \times n$ matrix, can be expressed as its eigendecomposition, $\Sigma = C^T \Lambda C$, where Λ is a diagonal matrix with eigenvalues λ_i, $i = 1, 2, ..., n$, in decreasing order (representing decreasing importance). Figure 2 gives the first four principal components (pc1 ~ pc4) for the product NS studied in Tian and Troster (1998) where the original data contain 11 variables (for 11 different metrics for modules in NS). Among the principal components, pc1 ~ pc4 explain 88 percent of the total variance. As a result, the original data can be reduced to these four principal components without much loss of information.

Once a few important principal components are extracted, they can be used in various models to identify high-defect modules. For example, selected principal components were used with discriminant analysis to classify software modules into *fault-prone* and *other* for software systems used in aerospace, medical, and telecommunication industries (Munson and Khoshgoftaar 1992; Khoshgoftaar et al. 1996). The models using principal components have several advantages over similar models using the original (raw) data: They are simpler because fewer independent variables are used, and the parameter estimates are more stable because of the orthogonality among the principal components.

Discriminant analysis is a statistical analysis technique that classifies multivariate data points or entities, such as software modules characterized by different metrics, into mutually exclusive groups. This classification is done by using a discriminant function to assign data points to one of the groups while minimizing within-group differences. For example, a discriminant function defined on selected principal components was derived to separate fault-prone software modules from the rest for telecommunication software developed by Nortel (Khoshgoftaar et al. 1996). These applications have yielded fairly accurate results for grouping modules in the current project, with a misclassification rate at about 1 percent, and for predictions into the future, with misclassification at 22.6 percent or 31.1 percent for the two models used in Khoshgoftaar et al. (1996).

Artificial Neural Networks and Learning Algorithms

Artificial neural networks are based on learning algorithms inspired by biological neural networks and can be used to solve challenging problems, including pattern classification, categorization, approximation, and so on (Jain, Mao, and Mohiuddin 1996). Processing of an individual neuron is depicted in Figure 3, with:

$$h = \sum_{i=1}^{n} w_i x_i \quad \text{and } y = g(h)$$

where $x_1, x_2, ..., x_n$ are the input, $w_1, w_2, ..., w_n$ the input weights, g the activation function, and y the output. The commonly used activation functions include threshold, piecewise linear, sigmoid, and Gaussian. Sigmoid function depicted in Figure 3 and used in Khoshgoftaar and Szabo (1996) is defined by:

$$g(x) = \frac{1}{1+e^{-\beta x}}$$

An artificial neural network is formed by connecting individual neurons in a specific network architecture.

	pc1	pc2	pc3	pc4
eigenvalue λ_i	2.352	1.296	1.042	0.711
% of variance	55.3%	16.8%	10.8%	5.1%
cumulative % of variance	55.3%	72.1%	82.9%	88.0%

Figure 2   Principal components for a commercial product.

When an artificial neural network is applied to a given data set, an iterative learning procedure is followed to minimize the network error, or the difference between the predicted and actual output. This can be achieved by following various learning algorithms to adjust the weights at individual neurons. One of the most widely used such algorithms is backward propagation, summarized in Figure 4.

Recently, artificial neural network models were used in Khoshgoftaar and Szabo (1996) to identify high-defect modules for some system software (Kernel.1, Kernel.2, and Kernel.3) developed by IBM. Both the raw data and the principal component data from Kernel.1 were used as input to the models, starting with a small number (20) of hidden layer neurons and gradually adding more neurons until the models converge. Forty hidden-layer neurons were needed for the model with raw data as input to converge, while only 24 were needed for the principal component data. In addition, as shown in Figure 5, once they were applied to Kernel.2 and Kernel.3, the model based on principal components significantly outperformed the one based on raw data. The combination of principal component analysis and neural networks also outperformed linear regression models (Khoshgoftaar et al. 1996). This combination offers an effective and efficient alternative to identifying high-defect modules for quality improvement.

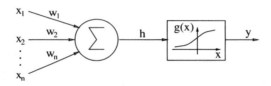

Figure 3 Processing model of a neuron.

0. *Initialization:* Initialize the weights to small random values.
1. *Overall control:* Repeat steps 2 – 6 until the error in the output layer is below a prespecified threshold or a maximum number of iterations is reached.
2. Randomly choose an input.
3. Propagate the signal forward through the network.
4. Compute the errors in the output layer.
5. Compute the deltas for the preceding layers by propagating the errors backward.
6. Update the weights based on these deltas.

Figure 4 Backward propagation algorithm for artificial neural networks.

System	Model data	Output error			
		mean	std#dev	min.	max.
Kernel.2	Raw	11.4	6.6	0.19	32.8
	principal components	7.1	5.6	0.05	42.8
Kernel.3	Raw	11.0	6.3	0.12	31.6
	principal components	4.7	4.1	0.02	26.2

Figure 5 Predicting defects using artificial neural networks.

Data Partitions and Tree-Based Modeling

In general, different modules of a large software system may possess quite different characteristics because of the diverse functionalities, program sources, and evolution paths. Sometimes it is not the particular values but specific ranges that have practical significance. Arguably, such data are more properly handled if they are partitioned and analyzed separately to accommodate for the qualitative differences among the partitioned subsets. In this way, high-defect modules with different characteristics for different partitions can be identified, and different actions can be carried out to correct the problems.

Tree-based modeling (Clark and Pregibon 1993) is a statistical analysis technique that handles data partitions and related analysis. The model construction involves the data set being recursively partitioned, using split conditions defined on selected predictors (or independent variables), into smaller subsets with increasing homogeneity of response (or dependent variable) values. The binary partitioning algorithm, supported by the commercial software tool S-Plus™, is summarized in Figure 6. Each data subset associated with a tree node is uniquely described by the path and associated split conditions from the root to it. The results presented in such forms are natural to the decision process and, consequently, are easy to interpret and easy to use. The characterization of individual nodes and associated data subsets can also help one understand subsets of high-defect modules, and therefore, can be used to guide remedial actions focused on identified modules and on modules demonstrating similar characteristics in related products.

Tree-based models were first used to analyze data from NASA Software Engineering Laboratory, where various software metrics data were used to predict project effort and to identify high-risk areas for focused remedial actions (Porter and Selby 1990). Recently, the technique was used to identify high-defect modules for several commercial

---

0. *Initialization.* Create a list of data sets to be partitioned, referred to as Slist, and put the complete data set as the singleton element in Slist. Select the size and homogeneity thresholds T_s and T_h for the algorithm.

1. *Overall control.* Remove a data set S from Slist and execute step 2. Repeat this until Slist becomes empty.

2. *Size test.* If $|S| < T_s$, stop; otherwise, execute steps 3 through 6. $|S|$ is the size (or the number of data points) of data set S.

3. *Defining binary partition.* Using a numerical predictor p and a cutoff value c, S can be partitioned into two subsets S_1 with $p < c$, and subset S_2 with $p \geq c$. A binary grouping of the categories (or levels) of a categorical predictor can also yield a binary partition.

4. *Computing predicted response and prediction deviance for S, S_1, and S_2.* The predicted value $v(S)$ for the response for a set S is the average over the set, that is, $v(S) = \frac{1}{|S|} \sum_{i \in s} (v_i)$; and the prediction deviance $D(S)$ is $D(S) = \sum_{i \in s} (v_i - v(S))^2$.

   where v_i is the response value for data point i.

5. *Selecting optimal partition.* Among all the possible partitions, the one that minimizes the deviance of the partitioned subsets is selected, that is, the partition with minimized $D(S_1) + D(S_2)$ is selected.

6. *Homogeneity test:* If $\left(1 - \frac{D(S_1)\ 1\ D(S_2)}{D(S)}\right) \leq T_h$, stop; otherwise, append S_1 and S_2 to *Slist*.

Figure 6 Algorithm for tree-based model construction.

software products (Tian and Troster 1998). Figure 7 shows a tree-based model constructed for NS, one of these products, relating DF to 11 other design, size, and complexity metrics defined in Card and Glass (1990) and Fenton and Pfleeger (1996). The specific metrics selected by the tree construction algorithm include:

- HLSC, or high-level structural complexity, a design complexity metric reflecting the number of external function calls
- MLSC, or module-level structural complexity, a design complexity metric reflecting the number of internal function calls within the module
- McCabe, or McCabe's cyclomatic complexity, a program complexity metric defined to be the number of independent control flow paths for a given program

The subsets with extremely high DF can be easily identified as those associated with leaf nodes "rlll" and "rr"' in Figure 7. Each node is labeled by the series of decisions, "l" for a left branching, "r" for a right branching, from the tree root to the specific node. Figure 8 summarizes the data subsets associated with these nodes, characterized by the chains of split conditions. The identification of these high-defect modules and their characterization can lead to focused remedial actions directed at such modules. These and other results were used by the development teams to guide their selective software inspection effort for cost-effective quality assurance and improvement.

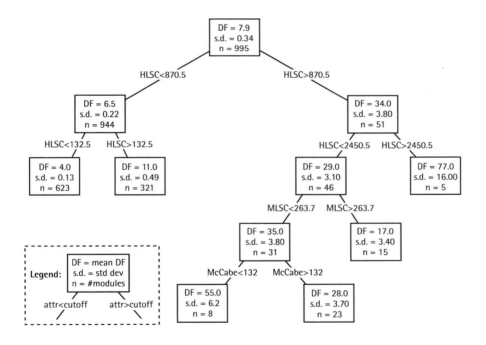

Figure 7   Tree-based defect model for a commercial product.

node:	split conditions/subset characteristics	#modules	predicted-DF	std-dev
rlll:	870.5 < HLSC < 2450.5, MLSC < 263.7, McCabe < 132	8	55.0	6.2
rr:	HLSC > 2450.5	5	77.0	16.0

Figure 8   Characterizing high-defect modules for a commercial product.

Pattern Matching and Optimal Set Reduction

In the previously mentioned tree-based models, each data subset can be uniquely described by a set of split conditions. Therefore, the data subset can be viewed as to follow a unique "pattern." Many commonly defined patterns in practical applications do not have to be mutually exclusive, however, and can be used in combination and in parallel to identify problematic areas. This kind of analysis can be carried out using a pattern matching technique called optimal set reduction (Briand, Basili, and Hetmanski 1993).

The model construction for optimal set reduction can be summarized by the recursive algorithm in Figure 9. The *pattern* for a subset is defined by a condition on an explanatory (independent) variable, similar to the split conditions in tree-based models. The *entropy* is defined on the dependent variable values, capturing the uniformity of a subset. For example, for a subset of data, S, all mildly changed modules (subset S_1, characterized by the pattern: $1 \le CSI \le 10$, where CSI is the changed lines of code) are likely to have high defects (DF > 5, which defines the high-defect class). All modules with high data content (subset S_2, characterized by the pattern: operand-count > 50) are also likely to have high defects. Then, S_1 and S_2 can be extracted from S in parallel, because of the low entropy for these subsets (most of these modules are high-defect modules). Notice that this kind of subset may overlap, yielding a general graph instead of a tree structure, as illustrated by Figure 10.

Optimal set reduction was recently used to analyze various project effort and metrics data from NASA Software Engineering Laboratory, and to identify high risk (high-effort) modules (Briand, Basili, and Hetmanski 1993). It performed better (with 92.11 percent accuracy) than other techniques, including classification trees, logistic regression without principal component, and logistic regression with principal component (with 83.33 percent, 76.56 percent, and 80 percent accuracy, respectively). In addition,

Step 1. Both the dependent (response) variable and the explanatory (predictor or independent) variables are discretized by using cluster analysis or some other method if they are continuous.

Step 2. Select all statistically significant subsets defined by a pattern whose entropy (or uniformity) is within a threshold of the minimal entropy.

Step 3. Step 2 is repeated until no significant gain can be made in entropy reduction.

Figure 9   Algorithm for optimal set reduction.

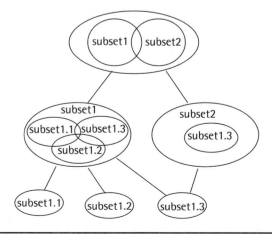

Figure 10   Example hierarchy for optimal set reduction.

the combination of patterns for high-risk modules were also identified by the modeling result, which can be used to guide focused remedial actions.

COMPARISONS AND RECOMMENDATIONS

The risk identification techniques are compared according to several criteria. The criteria, as well as how selected techniques can be integrated into the software development process, are addressed here.

Important Issues and Criteria for Comparison

- **Accuracy.** Accuracy of analysis results can be measured by the difference (error) between predicted and actual results. The standard deviation of error can be used to measure accuracy for models with numerical response (for example, defect count), and proportion of misclassification for those with categorical response (for example, high defect versus low defect). Since the data and applications are from diverse sources, only a qualitative comparison of result accuracy is possible here. In general, new techniques for risk identification perform better than traditional statistical techniques.

- **Simplicity.** Simplicity of the analysis technique has many ramifications. A simple technique is generally easy to understand, easy to use, easy to perform on a given set of data, and more likely to be supported by existing tools. Minimal training is needed for a software quality professional to learn and master the technique. Among the risk identification techniques, correlation and regression analyses are simple statistical techniques, while others are more complex, with artificial neural networks (multiple parallel, hidden neurons) and optimal set reduction (overlapping subsets extracted in parallel) among the most complex.

- **Early availability and stability.** There is a strong need for early modeling results, because problems found late in development are much harder and cost significantly more to fix. Ideally, models could be fitted to observations early and remain fairly stable so that timely and consistent remedial actions can be applied. All the techniques discussed in this article can be used early, but their stability differs considerably: Linear regression models are usually highly unstable because of high correlation in the metrics data, while models using principal component analysis are much more stable. On the other hand, techniques depending on data ranges (for example, tree-based modeling and optimal set reduction) are more likely to be stable than those depending on numerical values (for example, traditional statistical models).

- **Ease of result interpretation.** Ease of result interpretation plays an important role in model applications. A good understanding of the analysis results is a precondition to follow-up actions. For example, tree-based models present results in a form similar to decision trees commonly used in project management. Thus, the results are easy to interpret and easy to use. At the other extreme, artificial neuron networks employ multiple hidden layer neurons and give the result as if from a "black box," making result interpretation hard.

- **Constructive information and guidance for quality improvement.** Tree-based models and optimal set reduction can characterize identified high-defect modules by their split conditions or patterns defined by certain metrics values or ranges. Such constructive information can be used to guide quality improvement activities. For example, if the identified high-defect subset of modules are characterized by numerous changes and high data contents, this information can be used in several ways: to minimize change for such modules, to reduce data contents by restructuring the modules, or to take extra precautions and quality assurance steps toward these modules.

- **Availability of tool support.** Availability of tool support also has a significant influence on the practical applications of specific techniques. Traditional statistical analysis techniques are supported by many statistical packages. Some modern statistical packages also support principal component analysis, discriminant analysis, and tree-based modeling. Special tools are needed, however, to support artificial neural networks (several such tools are available) and optimal set reduction (a tool developed at the University of Maryland).

Summary of Comparison

Figure 11 summarizes the comparison of the risk identification techniques. Notice that principal component analysis is not listed as a separate entry, but rather included as part of discriminant analysis.

Like any other analysis techniques, the risk identification techniques are only a tool to provide evidence or symptoms of existing problems. The ultimate responsibility to use the analysis results and to make changes lies with the development teams and their managers. Tree-based modeling seems to combine many good qualities appropriate for this kind of application: It is conceptually simple and is supported by a commercial tool S-Plus. It provides accurate and stable results and excellent constructive information, both in a consistent and uniform structure (tree) intuitive to the decision process. Therefore, tree-based modeling is an excellent candidate that can be used effectively to solicit changes and remedial actions from developers and managers. The analysis results and remedial action plans can often be cross-validated by other techniques, taking advantage of their individual strengths.

Future Integration into the Software Development Lifecycle

To facilitate practical applications of selected risk identification techniques, the analysis and follow-up activities need to be integrated into and carried out throughout the existing software development process. Such an integrated approach can be used to track quality changes and to identify and characterize problem areas for focused remedial actions. This approach can be implemented in several stages. Initially, the analyses can be handled off-line by a dedicated quality analyst to minimize disruption to existing processes and to provide timely feedback. Thereafter, the analysis activities can be gradually automated, so minimal effort is needed by the project teams to produce analysis results for remedial actions.

Analysis technique	Accuracy	Simplicity	Stability	Interpretation	Guidance	Tool support
Correlation	poor	simplest	fair	easiest	fair	wide
Regression	poor	simple	poor	moderate	poor	wide
Discriminant	good	moderate	excellent	moderate	fair	moderate
Neural networks	good	complex	fair	hard	poor	moderate
Tree-based modeling	good	moderate	good	easy	excellent	moderate
Optimal set reduction	good	complex	fair	moderate	excellent	limited

Figure 11   Comparison of risk identification techniques.

All the data and examples presented previously are based on software artifacts, such as defects and metrics data associated with specific software modules. Similar risk identification techniques, however, can also be applied to process or activity-based data. For example, tree-based modeling was used to link test results (successful versus failed executions) to various timing and input state information for several IBM software products (Tian 1995). The modeling results were used to identify clusters of test executions associated with abnormally high failures for focused remedial actions, which lead to significantly higher quality for these products as compared to earlier products. Similar analyses can also be performed on inspection data typically gathered in the earlier phases of software development. Each inspection can be treated as a data point, with all the circumstantial information associated with the inspection, such as components inspected, inspection method used, inspectors, and time spent, as predictors, to build similar tree-based models to identify high-defect areas for focused quality improvement.

CONCLUSIONS AND PERSPECTIVES

Because of the highly uneven distribution of defects in software systems, there is a great need for effective risk identification techniques so high-defect modules or software components can be identified and characterized for effective defect removal and quality improvement. The survey of risk identification techniques presented in this article brings together information from diverse sources to offer a common starting point for software quality professionals. The comparison of techniques can help them choose appropriate techniques for their individual applications. The recommended lifecycle approach integrates these quality analysis and improvement activities into the existing development process, and can be tailored by professionals to fit their own application environment.

As an immediate follow up to this work, the author will apply existing risk identification techniques to additional industrial software projects, to further validate and quantitatively evaluate the applicability and effectiveness of these techniques, and possibly develop more effective new ones. He also plans to package application experience from diverse sources, and to provide more useful guidance to the selection and tailoring of specific techniques for specific applications. All these will help advance the state of practice in industry, leading to a state where high-defect software modules can be identified early, easily, and accurately by software quality professionals for effective quality improvement.

ACKNOWLEDGMENT

This work is supported in part by NSF CAREER award CCR-9733588, Nortel Networks, and IBM Toronto Lab. The author wishes to thank the anonymous reviewers for their comments and suggestions.

REFERENCES

Briand, L. C., V. R. Basili, and C. J. Hetmanski. 1993. Developing interpretable models with optimal set reduction for identifying high-risk software components. *IEEE Trans. on Software Engineering* 19, no. 11:1028–1044.

Card, D. N., and R. L. Glass. 1990. *Measuring software design quality.* Englewood Cliffs, N. J.: Prentice Hall.

Clark, L. A., and D. Pregibon. 1993. Tree-based models. In *Statistical models in S*, J. M. Chambers and T. J. Hastie, eds. London: Chapman & Hall.

Fenton, N., and S. L. Pfleeger. 1996. *Software metrics: A rigorous and practical approach.* 2nd ed. Boston: PWS Publishing.

Jain, A. K., J. Mao, and K. M. Mohiuddin. 1996. Artificial neural networks: A tutorial. *IEEE Computer* 29 no. 3:31–44.

Khoshgoftaar, T. M., E. B. Allen, K. S. Kalaichelvan, and N. Goel. 1996. Early quality prediction: A case study in telecommunications. *IEEE Software* 13, no. 1:65–71.

Khoshgoftaar, T. M., and R. M. Szabo. 1996. Using neural networks to predict software faults during testing. *IEEE Trans. on Reliability* 45, no. 3:456–462.

Munson, J. C., and T. M. Khoshgoftaar. 1992. The detection of fault-prone programs. *IEEE Trans. on Software Engineering* 18, no. 5:423–433.

Porter, A. A., and R. W. Selby. 1990. Empirically guided software development using metric-based classification trees. *IEEE Software* 7, no. 2:46–54.

Tian, J. 1995. Integrating time domain and input domain analyses of software reliability using tree-based models. *IEEE Trans. on Software Engineering* 21, 12:945–958.

Tian, J., and J. Troster. 1998. A comparison of measurement and defect characteristics of new and legacy software systems. *Journal of Systems and Software* 44, no. 2:135–146.

Venables, W. N., and B. D. Ripley. 1994. *Modern applied statistics with S-plus.* New York: Springer-Verlag.

BIOGRPAHY

Jeff (Jianhui) Tian received a bachelor's degree in electrical engineering from Xi'an Jiaotong University in 1982, a master's degree in engineering science from Harvard University in 1986, and a doctorate in computer science from the University of Maryland in 1992. He worked for IBM Software Solutions Toronto Laboratory between 1992 and 1995 as a software quality and process analyst. Since 1995, he has been an assistant professor of computer science and engineering at Southern Methodist University in Dallas. His current research interests include software testing, measurement, reliability, safety, complexity, and telecommunication software and systems. Tian is a member of IEEE and ACM. He can be reached at Southern Methodist University, Dallas, TX, 75275, or by e-mail at tian@seas.smu.edu .

CHAPTER 3.2

Cost of Software Quality: Justifying Software Process Improvement to Managers

Dan Houston, Honeywell, Inc. and Department of Industrial and Management Systems Engineering, Arizona State University

*S*oftware process improvement advocates may have a hard time convincing senior managers of the need for process investments. The cost of quality (CoQ) technique, developed to show managers the financial benefits of process improvements, has been widely used in manufacturing and service industries for several decades. Only recently has it been applied to software development, and the results are demonstrating substantial opportunities for software organizations. These results indicate that software quality costs can be reduced dramatically through long-term process improvement programs. This article reviews the CoQ concept, examines cost of software quality data from the open literature, discusses application of the CoQ technique to software, and illustrates the technique with an application example.

Key words: cost of quality (CoQ), cost of software quality (CoSQ), CoSQ chart, software process improvement, SPI

INTRODUCTION

Software process improvement (SPI) advocates sometimes have a hard sell when it comes to convincing senior managers of the need for process investments. The economic benefits of SPI have begun to appear in the literature in recent years. These studies usually report SPI benefits in terms of productivity gains, improved product quality, reduced cycle time, total cost and effort savings, or return on investment (ROI). These metrics, however, present difficulties for immature organizations. The ROI measure is easily misinterpreted (Herbsleb et al. 1994; Brodman and Johnson 1995), and the other metrics require comparisons across multiple projects, which may not be comparable.

Managers want to know that money spent on better development practices will yield good returns, and to be convinced of that, they want to see numbers that show an impact on the bottom line. This is what motivated J. M. Juran to develop the cost of quality (CoQ) technique more than 40 years ago. The CoQ technique has been successfully applied to manufacturing and service industries. Not only does it address the impact of SPI on development costs, it is relatively easy to implement and measure. In recent years, a few software organizations have applied this technique, and the published results have been good news for those interested in software processes.

CoQ: A REVIEW OF THE CONCEPT

The basis for CoQ is the accounting of two kinds of costs: those incurred because of a lack of quality (nonconformance) and those incurred in the achievement of quality (conformance). Costs due to a lack of quality are further divided into costs of internal failures and costs of external failures. Costs of achieving quality are divided into appraisal costs and defect-prevention costs. Figure 1 illustrates this breakdown, and Figure 2 provides definitions of the four CoQ categories with typical costs of software quality. Prevention costs are in both the development cycle and organizationwide activities, such as process definition and metrics collection and analysis.

Conformance costs and nonconformance costs ordinarily exhibit an inverse relationship: as the investment in achieving quality increases, the costs due to lack of quality decrease. This relationship and its effect on the total cost of quality (TCoQ) are normally shown as a set of two-dimensional curves that plot costs against time or a measure of quality (see Figure 3). The quality measure is usually a defect rate, such as the number of defects per manufactured piece. In traditional CoQ models, the TCoQ has a point of diminishing returns, a minimum prior to achieving 100 percent of the quality measure. Manufacturing experience has shown that increased attention to defect prevention leads to reduced appraisal costs.

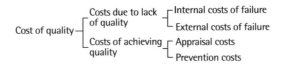

Figure 1   Cost of quality breakdown.

Category	Definition	Typical costs of software
Internal failures	Quality failures detected prior to product shipment	Defect management, rework, retesting
External failures	Quality failures detected after product shipment	Technical support, complaint investigation, defect notification, remedial upgrades and fixes
Appraisal	Discovering the condition of the product	Testing and associated activities, product quality audits
Prevention	Efforts to ensure product quality	Software quality assurance administration, inspections, process studies and improvements, metrics collection and analysis

Figure 2   Definition of cost of quality categories.

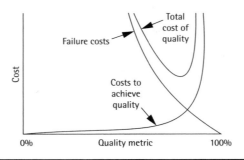

Figure 3   Cost of quality model.

COST OF SOFTWARE QUALITY: THE DATA

While the costs of software quality assurance and process improvement have been a topic of concern for more than 20 years and the CoQ categories have been used broadly in discussions of software quality, little data have been available in the open literature for discussing the cost of software quality (CoSQ). A Price Waterhouse study (1988), Knox's model (1993), and the Raytheon studies (Dion 1993; Haley 1996) reveal trends in software quality costs.

The Price Waterhouse study analyzed the costs and benefits of software quality standards from a survey of 19 U. K. software suppliers. The study estimated the cost of a quality control effort (prevention and appraisal costs) to be 23 percent to 34 percent of development effort. The study also estimated failure costs at 15 percent of development effort for a total cost of software quality (TCoSQ) of 38 percent to 49 percent of development effort. Note that this study excluded the costs of unit testing and associated rework because the suppliers could not separate these costs. With increases in the estimates to account for this oversight, the study suggests that TCoSQ in a software organization with a quality system can range from 40 percent to 55 percent of development costs, with a conformance costs to nonconformance costs ratio from 1.5 to 2.

Because of the limited data available on CoSQ, Knox used the emerging CoQ model developed in manufacturing environments and extended it across the Software Engineering Institute's Capability Maturity Model (SEI CMM) (Paulk et al. 1993) to produce a theoretical CoSQ model (see Figure 4). The SEI CMM specifies practices of software organizations according to five levels of process maturity (see Figure 5).

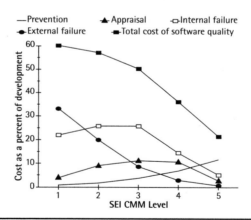

Figure 4   Knox's theoretical model for cost of software quality (Knox 1993).

SEI CMM level		Description
1	Initial	Software processes are undefined and depend on individual efforts.
2	Repeatable	Basic project and configuration management enable repeatability.
3	Defined	Processes are documented, standardized, and integrated into the organization.
4	Managed	Process and product quality are managed using detailed measures.
5	Optimizing	Continuous process improvement is enabled by quantitative process feedback.

Figure 5   Levels in the Software Engineering Institute's capability maturity model.

Starting with the TCoSQ at 60 percent of development costs (based on two industry figures) for CMM level 1 organizations, Knox used manufacturing experience to hypothesize that CMM level 5 organizations can cut this CoSQ by about 67 percent. He then rationalized the four component costs at each CMM level. His model suggests that for level 3 organizations, CoSQ is about half of development costs.

The same year that Knox's paper appeared, Dion (1993) used the CoQ model to interpret the results of quality initiatives undertaken at Raytheon Electronic Systems (RES). Recently Haley (1996) updated this study. The CoSQ results are shown in Figure 6. (Appraisal and prevention costs were shown separately in the Dion paper, but not in the Haley paper.)

Starting at CMM level 1, RES introduced a software process improvement program in August 1988. Using the results of tracking 15 projects, it achieved CMM level 3 practices in a little more than three years. Their results agree well with Knox's model: In the level 1 stage, RES's CoSQ fluctuated between 55 percent and 67 percent of total development costs, and by the time of reaching level 3 process maturity, its CoSQ had dropped to approximately 40 percent of total project cost. At last report, this organization's TCoSQ was approximately 15 percent of development costs, and the rework due to both internal and external failures had been reduced to less than 10 percent of development costs.

The figures obtained from the data in the Price Waterhouse study generally agree with a period late in 1990 when RES was approaching CMM level 3: RES's TCoSQ was about 45 percent of development, and its ratio of conformance to nonconformance costs was 1.5. Turning to Knox's model, it predicted that a CMM level 3 organization would have a TCoSQ of 50 percent, but with a conformance-to-nonconformance cost ratio of 0.5. It appears that Knox's model is a fair predictor of TCoSQ for maturing software organizations, but actual conformance costs are much higher and nonconformance costs much lower than what the model predicts.

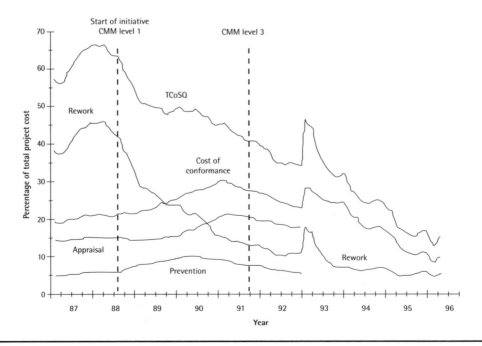

Figure 6   Cost of software quality for 15 projects at Raytheon Electronic Systems (Dion 1993 and Haley 1996).

Typical manufacturing CoQ, ranging from 5 percent to 25 percent of company sales, contrasts significantly with CoSQ (Plunkett and Dale 1990). From the previous data, one can expect CoSQ, with the present state of software engineering practice, to range from 20 percent to 70 percent of development costs. Even accounting for the margin between production costs and sales, CoSQ appears to be roughly twice manufacturing CoQ. Also, the optimum manufacturing CoQ often ranges from 95 percent to 100 percent of conformance to quality standards (as in measurements and failures). The open literature lacks data for CoSQ as a function of conformance to quality standards or metrics, but the rework figures in the data suggest that software producers have yet to reach such an optimum.

CONSIDERATIONS FOR APPLYING CoSQ

Many sources discuss implementation of CoQ reporting and its use in a quality improvement program (for example, Crosby 1988, Juran and Gryna 1980, Groocock 1974, and Evans and Lindsay 1993). Several points can be made with regard to measuring and using CoQ information specifically for software development organizations. These include initiating a CoSQ effort, accounting and gathering the quality cost data, gathering the quality metrics, and presenting the results.

Initiating the CoSQ Effort

Convincing management of the value of tracking CoSQ is often the first hurdle encountered in using this technique. Initially, estimates of quality costs may suffice for several reasons:

- The largest CoSQ costs usually can be estimated from time and activity reports, so the expense of data gathering is limited until its value is demonstrated
- Curtis and Statz (1996) point out that a controlled, scientific study is unlikely and that incomplete data can suffice in beginning a software cost benefit analysis
- The published data indicate that the quality cost difference between an improved and unimproved organization is large
- The main purpose of the initial CoSQ effort is to show the opportunity for cost savings

Accounting

Gathering quality cost data assumes that costs have been accounted using task categories, which can be summed into the four major categories of quality costs. Some software organizations track costs in a manner amenable to quality costing, but others do not. In the latter case, a preliminary step of defining and installing such a chart of accounts is required. A sample of a quality-costs chart is provided in Figure 7. The quality categories in a software organization's chart of accounts must be tailored to reflect its software process. To realize the full benefit of CoSQ, it must also allow for the addition of process-improvement tasks.

Ideally, quality costs can be taken directly from departmental accounting reports. Otherwise, it may be necessary to resort to basic accounting and engineering records, such as schedules, time reports, defect reports, and purchasing records. In the worst cases, one may fall back on interviews with members of the software organization to construct estimates of each quality cost category.

One of the pitfalls of a CoSQ program is "controversial cost categories" (Gryna 1988). Usually the question is about which costs are normal operating costs and which are quality costs. An example would be the cost of producing a project-management

1 Prevention costs
  1.1 Requirements
    1.1.1 Marketing research for customer/user quality needs
    1.1.2 Customer/user quality surveys
    1.1.3 Product quality risk management
    1.1.4 Prototyping for customer review
    1.1.5 User requirements/specification reviews/inspections
  1.2 Organization and project
    1.2.1 Process-maturity evaluation
    1.2.2 Process improvement
    1.2.3 Project quality planning
    1.2.4 Project process validation
    1.2.5 Quality assessment of development platform and tools
    1.2.6 Platform and tools development for quality
    1.2.7 Developer quality training
    1.2.8 Quality metrics data collection
    1.2.9 Design for quality: software component reuse
    1.2.10 Formal inspections/peer reviews
    1.2.11 Project configuration management
    1.2.12 Supplier capability assessment
  1.3 Reuse library
    1.3.1 Salaries
    1.3.2 Expenses
    1.3.3 Training
    1.3.4 Platform and tools
  1.4 Configuration management
    1.4.1 Salaries
    1.4.2 Expenses
    1.4.3 Training
    1.4.4 Platform and tools
  1.5 Software process improvement/ software quality assurance (SQA) administration
    1.5.1 Salaries
    1.5.2 Administrative expenses
    1.5.3 Software process and standards definition and publication
    1.5.4 Metrology: data maintenance, analysis, and reporting
    1.5.5 Quality program planning
    1.5.6 Quality performance reporting
    1.5.7 Quality education/training
2 Appraisal costs
  2.1 Supplied product qualification and testing
  2.2 Project appraisal costs
    2.2.1 Verification and validation activities
    2.2.2 Testing: planning, platforms, setup, test data generation, test execution and logging, reporting, test data evaluation
    2.2.3 Product quality audits
    2.2.4 SQA process compliance audits
  2.3 External appraisals
    2.3.1 Field-performance trials
    2.3.2 Special product evaluations
3 Internal failure costs
  3.1 Product design defect costs
    3.1.1 Causal analysis and reporting
    3.1.2 Design corrective action
    3.1.3 Rework and retest due to design corrective action
    3.1.4 Work products wasted due to design changes
  3.2 Purchased product defect cost
    3.2.1 Defect-analysis cost
    3.2.2 Cost of obtaining product fix
    3.2.3 Cost of defect workarounds
    3.2.4 Rework for defects
  3.3 Implementation defect costs
    3.3.1 Defect measurement and reporting
    3.3.2 Defect fixing
    3.3.3 Causal analysis and reporting
    3.3.4 Project process corrective action
    3.3.5 Inspection of rework
    3.3.6 Retest and integration
4 External failure costs
  4.1 Technical and field support for responding to defect complaints
  4.2 Product returned due to defect
  4.3 Maintenance and release due to defects
  4.4 Defect fixes and notifications
  4.5 Upgrade due to defect
  4.6 Service-agreement claims (warranty expense reports)
  4.7 Liability claims (insurance and legal reports)
  4.8 Penalties (product contract reports)
  4.9 Costs to maintain customer/user goodwill due to dissatisfaction (sales reports)
  4.10 Lost sales/market share due to quality problems (field salesperson reports)

Sources of quality cost data: ordinarily quality cost data for the majority of categories would be obtained from salary and expense reports. Exceptions are in the external failure category and are shown in parentheses.

Figure 7 A sample CoSQ chart (adopted from Campanella 1990).
Adapted from: Principles of Quality Costs: Principles, Implementation, and Use by Jack Campanella. 1990. Milwaukee: ASQC Quality Press.

plan. While this plan is produced to help manage a project's expenses and schedule, it also influences product and process quality. Here, it is helpful to keep in mind the following points:

- The trend among quality specialists has been to view quality costs as those incurred to directly prevent, appraise, and address the failures of poor quality.

- Arguments over controversial categories have been known to sabotage CoQ programs.

- The largest quality costs are those that are most easily discerned, such as reviews, software quality assurance, testing, and rework. Therefore, it is often safe to exclude controversial categories without unduly affecting the TCoSQ.

- Consistency throughout a CoSQ program is more important than thorough inclusion of quality costs because consistency allows for clear identification of improvements and candidates for improvement.

Concerns may also arise as to how to categorize quality costs. Again, consistency is important. For example, in Figure 7 the costs associated with formal inspections (peer reviews) are treated as prevention costs rather than appraisal costs. This is a matter of interpretation, depending on when a work product is considered ready for appraisal. Although manufacturing inspections are conducted on pieces after they are produced, in software production, inspections may be incorporated in the production process per the peer reviews key process area for the SEI CMM level 3. For documentation, this means that a document is not complete until it has undergone a peer review and been revised. The same is true for code, especially when code inspections precede unit testing, which is clearly an appraisal activity. Thus, peer reviews, including formal inspections, can be considered prevention activities when performed prior to product test phases.

An alternative means of categorizing software quality costs is shown in Figure 8. The development engineering organization at Honeywell Industrial Automation and Control recently began using this table as part of a scheme for charging time to the organization's software projects. The table lists an activity-based work breakdown structure and indicates which quality cost categories may be applied to each activity.

Project charge codes

Codes for charging time to project activities are 10 characters: TTPPPPANNQ

TT	= Two characters for process type, for example SW for software
PPPP	= Four characters that designate a project
ANN	= Three characters that designate the activity in the WBS, such as A01
Q	= One character that designates the category relative to quality costs.

The value of Q is one of the following:
- D Initial development of work products
- P Defect prevention activities
- T Initial test of work product
- R Product rework
- M Miscellaneous/other

Software WBS activities/CoSQ modifiers

The chart at right indicates what types of categories with regard to quality costs may be used for each WBS activity. For example, in requirements development, initial development of a requirements document would be D, validation of requirements with a customer would be P, and reworking a requirements document would be R.

		D	P	T	R	M
A01	Project management planning					•
A02	Requirements development/validation	•	•		•	
A03	Product concept development	•	•		•	
A04	Requirements analysis	•	•		•	
A05	Functional concept development	•	•		•	
A06	Define architecture	•	•		•	
A07	Test-plan development			•	•	
A08	Software configuration management (SCM) planning					•
A09	Detailed functional specification	•	•		•	
A10	Detailed design, code, debug	•	•		•	
A11	Unit testing			•	•	
A12	Integration testing			•	•	
A13	System test scripts			•	•	
A14	System test specification			•	•	
A15	User information development	•	•		•	
A16	User evaluation		•			
A17	Final test			•	•	
A18	Beta test			•	•	
A19	Project plan maintenance and updates					•
A20	Project tracking and metrics					•
A21	Software quality assurance		•			
A22	Subcontract management					•
A23	SCM builds	•	•		•	
	Other SCM functions					•
A24	Requirements and change management					•
A25	Establish/maintain development environment					•
A26	Miscellaneous activities					•

Figure 8   A software project charge scheme using an activity-based WBS with CoSQ modifiers.

Quality Metrics Collection

Regarding quality measures, CoQ has been used primarily with a fundamental approach to quality, that is defect rates (manufacturing) or service-problem reports (service industries) rather than broader approaches that would take into account factors such as usability, testability, maintainability, and so on. The fundamental approach has the advantages of straightforward measurement and ease of understanding. It also allows comparison of dissimilar products. Furthermore, if failure costs are collected in a defect-tracking system, the most expensive defects can be identified for root-cause analysis (Mandeville 1990). This discussion recognizes that most software producers take a fundamental approach to quality, concentrating on defect measurement, prevention, and removal.

Defect density is a good metric to begin measuring CoSQ improvements. Specifically, CoSQ can be plotted against defect density at the completion of system testing. This metric may be obtained from defect reports during alpha and beta tests and for a time period, say six months, following product release. Better yet, it may be generated statistically based on post-release defect reports for previous products from the same organization. Stoddard and Hedstrom (1995) offer an example of this approach using Bayesian statistics in a defect-prediction model. External failure costs can be estimated from the defects-at-release metric.

CoSQ Presentation

Juran and Gryna (1980) suggest that the relationships that have the greatest impact on management are:

- Quality costs as a percent of sales
- Quality costs compared to profit
- Quality costs compared to the magnitude of the current problem

The technique used by Knox and by Dion, showing CoSQ as a percent of total development costs, is appropriate to software for several reasons. First, sales and profit may not have a direct relationship to the actual cost of a software product since software pricing is often dictated by market forces. Second, all but a small percentage of software development costs can be measured in labor hours, so the costs can be readily shown in either hours or dollars. Third, the state of the art in software development is such that comparing quality costs to development costs illustrates the magnitude of the current problem.

Though quality costs as a percent of development costs can show significant effects of process improvements (as in the case of Raytheon), it does not show the optimum cost of quality. The optimum can be seen when quality costs are shown as absolute costs against a quality measure. Plotting CoSQ costs against a quality measure such as defect density provides the CoSQ curve and reveals trends in an organization's quality processes.

AN EXAMPLE OF AN INITIAL CoSQ EFFORT

The Building Solutions Centre Europe (BSCE) in Maintal, Germany, is a facility of the Home and Building Control Division of Honeywell. BSCE has 80 employees who work in marketing, engineering, distribution, and support of advanced building-control systems. Until 1995, the software development group at BSCE was experiencing many of the problems endemic to immature software organizations: schedule slippages; budget overruns; customer satisfaction issues; crisis management; and poor planning, tracking, and estimating. In 1995, the BSCE quality manager, Franz Kern, suggested that the software projects measure their quality costs while the organization planned for a set of process improvements designed to prevent software defects.

During 1995, BSCE defined and reviewed a set of software quality goals, put more effort into project planning and tracking, introduced design and code reviews, and began testing in earlier project phases. At the same time, the organization was implementing SEI CMM level 2 key practices. By 1996, the process improvements were being practiced. The organization was assessed at SEI level 2 in December 1996.

In early 1997, CoSQ data for the two prior years were collected. Quality costs data were collected from time reports, project expense reports, and BSCE expense reports. The costs were classified using the categories shown in Figure 9. The software workload for both 1995 and 1996 included four to five medium-size projects (four person-months to three person-years) and 12 to 20 small projects (six person-weeks to three person-months). Two person-weeks were required to gather, analyze, and create a presentation of the CoSQ data. In early 1998, the figures for 1997 were collected. Figure 10 shows the CoSQ results for 1995, 1996, and 1997.

The TCoSQ for 1995 was 58 percent of total development costs, comparable to previous data for CMM level 1 organizations. Quality costs have been cut in half over the three-year period, which is better than the trend in the previous data. Most of the savings have been in rework costs. The 1997 rework costs (17 percent of total development costs), however, as well as the ratio of conformance costs to nonconformance costs (0.86), indicate room for continued improvement and savings.

An anomaly in these data is that between 1995 and 1996, costs in all categories went down. This is explained by the fact that prevention costs in 1995 were extraordinarily high. That was the year BSCE began its software process improvement program. Consequently, it expended much effort in creating new procedures and guidelines and training the organization in using them. The prevention costs increased from 1996 to 1997 as more emphasis was placed on code reviews and inspections.

Prevention	Testing	Rework
• Software quality assurance	• Unit testing	• Maintenance due to internal defects
• Design reviews	• System integration testing	• Maintenance due to external defects
• Code inspections and walkthroughs	• Beta testing	• Defect report administration
• Early developer test phases • Planning of test concepts (prior to test planning)		• Defect related portion of customer support by the technical assistance center

Figure 9   Building Solutions Centre Europe (BSCE) cost of software quality categories for 1995–96.

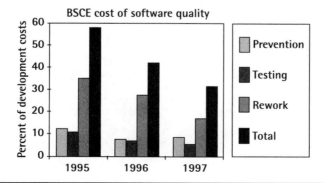

Figure 10   Building Solutions Center Europe (BSCE) cost of software quality indicating the benefits of process improvements.

The CoSQ data have proved useful to BSCE. First, they were used as a motivational vehicle when presented to the software organization to show employees how their efforts were contributing to the center's financial results. Second, to demonstrate the benefits of software process improvements to senior managers, the CoSQ data were also presented to the director of engineering, the vice president of the Home and Building Control Division for Europe, and the president of Honeywell Europe. Third, it has given BSCE management a lifecycle view of software products. For example, the maintenance costs of one product were found to be about the same as the product's revenue. This observation prompted a reassessment of the product's role in BSCE's business.

Software process improvement has become an important activity at BSCE, and CoSQ data have become a barometer for measuring its successes.

CONCLUSIONS

Software process improvement advocates must often justify to senior managers the expense of introducing and institutionalizing new practices. Industry data indicate that process improvements not only provide increased quality and reduced development schedules, but also provide the most opportunities for savings in development costs. Measuring CoSQ before and after improvement initiatives provides data that can convince management of the financial benefits of such initiatives. Particularly for immature organizations and those undertaking process-improvement programs for the first time, CoSQ is a useful technique because it can be employed for a relatively small cost.

REFERENCES

Brodman, J. G., and D. L. Johnson. 1995. Return on investment (ROI) from software process improvement as measured by U.S. industry. *Software Process Improvement and Practice* 1, no. 1: 35–47.

Crosby, P. B. 1988. *Quality without tears.* New York: McGraw-Hill.

Curtis, B., and J. Statz. 1966. Building the cost-benefit case for software process improvement. In *Proceedings of SEPG '96.* Pittsburgh: Software Engineering Institute, Carnegie Mellon University.

Dion, R. 1993. Process improvement and the corporate balance sheet. *IEEE Software* 10 (July): 28–35.

Evans, J. R., and W. M. Lindsay. 1993. *The Management and control of quality,* 2nd ed. St. Paul, Minn.: West Publishing.

Groocock, J. M. 1974. *The cost of quality.* London: Pitman House.

Gryna, F. M. 1988. Quality costs. In *Juran's quality control handbook.* 4th ed. F. M. Gryna and J. M. Juran, eds. New York: McGraw-Hill.

Haley, T. J. 1996. Software process improvement at Raytheon. *IEEE Software* 13 (November): 33–41.

Herbsleb, J., A. Carleton, J. Rozum, J. Siegel, and D. Zubrow. 1994. *Benefits of CMM-based software process improvement: Initial results* (CMU/SEI-94-TR-013). Pittsburgh: Software Engineering Institute, Carnegie Mellon University.

Juran, J. M., and F. M. Gryna. 1980. *Quality planning and analysis.* 2nd ed. New York: McGraw-Hill.

Knox, S. T. 1993. Modeling the cost of software quality. *Digital Technical Journal* 5, no. 4: 9–16.

Mandeville, W. A. 1990. Software costs of quality. *IEEE Journal on Selected Areas in Communications* 8, no. 2: 315–318.

Paulk, M. C., B. Curtis, M. B. Chrissis, and C. V. Weber. 1993. *Capability maturity model for software, version 1.1* (CMU/SEI-93-TR-25). Pittsburgh: Software Engineering Institute, Carnegie Mellon University.

Plunkett, J. J., and B. G. Dale. 1990. Quality costing. *Managing Quality.* New York: Philip Allan.

Price Waterhouse. 1988. *Software quality standards: The costs and benefits.* London: Price Waterhouse Management Consultants.

Stoddard, R., and J. Hedstrom. 1995. A Bayesian approach to deriving parameter values for a software defect predictive model. In *Proceedings of the sixth annual conference on applications of software measurement.* Orlando, FL: Software Quality Engineering.

Biography

Dan Houston is a software engineer at Honeywell Industrial Automation and Control in Phoenix, Ariz. He is a doctoral candidate in industrial engineering at Arizona State University. His current research efforts focus on software development economics and risk factors and on modeling and simulation of software development processes. He may be contacted by e-mail at dan.houston@iac.honeywell.com .

Defect Prevention: The Road Less Traveled

Craig Smith, Motorola, Arlington Heights, Illinois

*T*his paper chronicles progress toward a defect prevention culture at Motorola software development organizations, Arlington Heights, Illinois. It also draws from software standards and technical references with defect prevention ideas to provide a framework for those seeking to develop or enhance defect prevention activities in their software development organization.

Key words: continuous improvement, defect cause analysis, preventive actions, process improvement, project management

INTRODUCTION

The Arlington Heights facility of the Network Systems Group (NSG) designs, develops, markets, and services cellular systems, networks, and infrastructure equipment for use worldwide. Major NSG facilities are located in England, Ireland, Texas, and the Chicago, Illinois area. This paper will focus on software development activities at the Arlington Heights, Illinois facility which was formerly known as the Cellular Infrastructure Group.

In the early 1990's NSG embarked on a software development improvement program that resulted in a tenfold reduction in customer-found defects and significant improvement in customer satisfaction scores. These achievements were driven largely by two initiatives: the adoption of the Software Engineering Institute Capability Maturity Model (SEI CMM) as the model to guide software process improvement, and the implementation of Fagan inspections to improve defect detection methods.

By 1996, quality improvement gains within NSG had leveled off in many organizations dictating the need for new quality strategies including attention to defect prevention (DP). Major topics covered in the paper include:

- Overview of the two standards influencing Motorola quality programs and defect prevention: the Motorola Corporate Quality System Review (QSR) Guidelines, and the SEI CMM—the key process area

- A description of fundamental DP program components such as DP education

- An overview of three representative DP methods used: defect cause analysis, effective process design, and project postmortems

- A discussion of the distinctive characteristics of one NSG organization with an SEI CMM qualified DP program

- An evaluation of DP program status within NSG: lessons learned and results achieved

Figure 1 provides an overview of the basic components of a defect prevention program (DPP).

The "Inputs" to DPP provide the information drivers for the program; they can include quality goals, defect problem reports, and any metrics that will aid in determining the types and causes of defects occurring. The "Controls" provide a framework

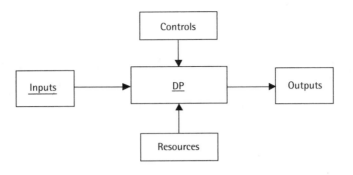

Figure 1   Basic components of a defect prevention program (DPP).

for program operations in the form of policies, plans, description of methods used, and procedures which describe how the various aspects of the DPP operate. The "Resources" include people assigned to perform DP activities and software tools providing enhanced capability to operate an effective DP program. Fundamental to the success of the program are the various forms "Outputs" in including defect root causes and recommendations for process improvement. These outputs typically feed into a separate process improvement or technology change function which will be briefly discussed later in the paper.

This paper will emphasize the future thinking aspects of prevention, not just after-the-fact correction of defects. C. Michael Taylor, in a *Quality Progress* article on prevention, stated a key question asked by a company president after a costly quality problem occurred, "What could we have done to prevent the problem before it actually happened?" (Taylor, 1998). Ideas from this paper will help answer this question. Let's review the two standards influencing DP program development within NSG.

A FRAMEWORK FOR DEFECT PREVENTION

Motorola Corporate Quality System Review (QSR) Guidelines

Every two years, Motorola business units receive a quality systems assessment by a team composed of personnel from other Motorola locations. Sections one through nine of this assessment standard, the QSR Guidelines, outline generic requirements for an organization's quality system. Section 1.10 provides an excellent framework for defect prevention and opens with this question: "Are there programs in place with sufficient resources assigned to support a culture of problem prevention in order to achieve best-in-class satisfaction for customers?" (Motorola, 1998). This QSR section suggests the following DP program qualities:

- Many successful examples of problem prevention
- A structured corrective action process in place
- Use of lessons learned across the organization
- Proactive process variation reduction

While the QSR Guidelines provide sound overall principles of defect prevention, the CMM's Defect Prevention key process area offers software development specific criteria.

The SEI Capability Maturity Model (CMM) DP Key Process Area

The following components from the CMM's DP key process area provide a useful framework, used by several organizations at our Motorola location, with which to guide their program development (Paulk 1993):

- Written DP policy statement
- Evidence of software project level DP planning and activities
- Regular defect cause analysis meetings
- A DP link to the organization's software processes
- Key goal: common causes of defects are prioritized and systematically eliminated

Organizations should heed one caution when using the CMM to guide DP program development: A full-blown DP program should contain many more DP methods than just the defect cause analysis and project kickoff meetings that receive primary emphasis in the CMM.

Using the guidance found in these two standards and other references, software organizations can construct the framework of their DP programs. This next section describes five necessary components of such a program.

DEFECT PREVENTION PROGRAM KEY COMPONENTS

DP Policy

A good starting point to DP program development is to draft a brief policy describing the basic philosophies of the prevention program, such as program scope, management responsibilities, and training requirements. Several of our Motorola organizations have embedded their DP policy within an overall software development policy document. Once the policy is in place, other components can be addressed as follows.

DP Education and Training

One of the major sections of the Motorola QSR guidelines focuses on problem solving as a key ingredient to an effective quality improvement program. For years it has been a company philosophy that a large percentage of employees be trained in basic problem-solving skills. For this reason, Motorola's internal training organization, Motorola University, offers a number of courses in individual and team problem-solving.

As a supplement to Motorola University, several Arlington Heights location courses were developed to support quality improvement and defect prevention activities. One such course, Problem Solving Techniques, provides an overview of basic tools for problem-solving including brainstorming, cause-and-effect diagrams, Pareto Charts, and control charts. As part of the course, students are given a copy of *The Memory Jogger II* (Brassard and Ritter 1994). Not only does this reference provide a concise explanation of 20 problem-solving techniques, but it explains the classic plan–do–check–act (PDCA) problem-solving model.

Craig Kaplan, a co-author of *Secrets of Software Quality,* reports on IBM's success in defect prevention at the Santa Teresa Labs in San Jose, California. Kaplan says a key factor contributing to prevention effectiveness was the fact that about half of all the employees at this huge lab received DP training (Kaplan 1995).

Once employees are trained in basic problem-solving skills they are ready to participate on quality improvement teams, which are heavily emphasized within Motorola. An individual employee with a tool kit of problem-solving methods is more likely to take the initiative to investigate a problem and recommend a solution.

Integration of DP Into Other Processes

Defect prevention activities do not stand alone; they are integrated into the software development lifecycle and the processes that support software development. A critical factor in the success of our site's CMM Level Five organization's (hereafter referred to as "the GSM group") DP program was its integration into the other processes of software development (Gutowski 1998). By making DP part of the culture and not an add-on activity, prevention became a way of life for software developers. Software engineers are more likely to perform activities that are part of the normal lifecycle rather than special events.

Using the SEI CMM model as a framework, here are potential links between DP and other key processes within an organization:

- Recommended DP process changes referred to a process change management function, usually administered by a Software Engineering Process Group
- Approved DP process changes integrated into the organization's standard software processes as defined in the Organization Process Definition key process area
- Metrics necessary to determine high frequency defects and major quality problems provided by a Quantitative Process Management function
- Software Quality Assurance conducts DP process verifications

DP Action Tracking

An effective DP program will generate many recommendations for quality improvement which must be documented and tracked through implementation and closure—in effect, a closed loop corrective action system. Our software organizations use several different action tracking software tools to aid this process. The requirements for an effective action tracking system include the following key points:

- Action tracking system documented in a structured process
- Actions are prioritized by management or teams using defined criteria
- Each action has an owner
- Actions taken are preventive, not just containment and quick fixes
- Prevention results are shared with other organizations

Management Oversight

No small part of the success of a DP program rests on management attention to this important quality program element. Management oversight should be exercised in at least two levels—senior management and project management.

At least quarterly, senior management should review the status of the DP program by looking at such indicators as the number of DP actions successfully implemented during the period and the backlog of DP actions. This level of management may be involved in the prioritizing of DP actions, especially those with high dollar implementation costs. Quality improvement topics, including DP actions, are part of monthly quality program reviews in several of our software development organizations.

Some elements of the DP program must be integrated into each software project by such means as software development phase reviews and postmortems, discussed next in the DP methods section. Project managers must think prevention by ensuring that development teams are aware of the common defects likely to occur in each development phase and the steps to take that will prevent these defects. Several of our organizations conduct software development phase kickoff meetings and defect awareness is a common topic.

This section has reviewed five components of a mature DP program. Other topics that should be considered include resource planning and the flow-down of successful DP methods to key suppliers and software subcontractors, as applicable.

A mature DP program may include the use of 10 or more DP methods. The next section addresses three methods used at our Arlington Heights location.

REPRESENTATIVE DP METHODS

Defect Cause Analysis

Probably the most commonly used prevention method is Defect Cause Analysis (DCA). Section Six of the Motorola QSR guidelines, dealing with problem-solving and preventive actions, contains evaluation factors useful for an organization as it conducts DCA:

- Employees trained in prevention and problem solving
- Quality data used to prioritize and drive problem-solving efforts
- Problem solving is timely and effective (such as, permanent corrective action demonstrated)
- Prevention efforts demonstrate process variation reduction

Typically organizations conduct most DCA as part of teams, frequently called process improvement teams. Our GSM group uses key drivers of customer satisfaction as a determining factor as to what quality problems to tackle. For example, a key driver of customer satisfaction is a very low level of customer-found software defects. Members of the systems test group conducted an escaped defect analysis of customer-found defects to determine which ones should be caught in systems testing. They completed a Pareto analysis by both product functional area and by test phase of possible detection. From these charts, further analysis of selected customer-found problems uncovered the need to revise some test methods with emphasis on improved regression testing.

The availability of quality metrics is fundamental to DCA success. The following metrics are typically used by our organizations to aid in defect cause analysis:

- Customer-found defects
- Inspection and test defect count by type (for example, logic error) and by development phase (for example, design)
- Recurring defects escaping detection during a software phase and found later

Those desiring to review an excellent reference on DCA program operation should consult David Card's IEEE Software article on this subject (Card 1998). Some key points in this article that warrant mentioning include the importance of the DCA being conducted by practitioners familiar with the process and product area, not an outside team, and the need to concentrate on a few systemic defect areas, not the whole range of quality problems that an organization may be facing.

Effective Process Design

In the early 1990s our Motorola location adopted the IEEE Std 1074, IEEE Standard for Developing Software Lifecycle Processes, as our process architecture standard (IEEE 1995). Evolving from this adoption came local process descriptions and definitions.

A number of organizations created process templates requiring each of the procedures documenting the software development lifecycle processes to contain the following information:

- Overall scope and objectives of the process
- Process entry criteria
- Task descriptions
- Interfaces to other processes
- Invocations of other processes (for example, an inspection for a created software work product)
- Reference to a software work product template for quality requirements and other details
- Process control mechanisms (for example, escaped defect feedback to the process)
- Process exit criteria

Let us review the subject of effective process design (EPD) by addressing several of the more important process definition components listed above. Our less mature software organizations tend to view entry criteria for a process as merely a list of required inputs. For example, for a software design procedure, a required entry criteria might be: "Applicable Requirements Specification." One of our preventive minded organizations would state this entry criteria more rigorously: "Complete and properly inspected Requirements Specification with all defects found, resolved." Using the first entry criteria, an organization might be prone to accept an incomplete or uninspected Requirements Specification.

A second process definition criteria critical to the prevention of defects concerns the proper invocation of the inspection process. An Arlington Heights policy prescribes software work product verifications: requirements for formal inspections and less rigorous technical reviews. However, not all software work products created are covered in this policy. The less mature software organization tends not to define the type of verification required for work products, such as estimates not directly related to the production of software code.

Process control mechanisms are critical to lowering the defect rate. Several of our organizations have implemented control limits for aspects of the inspection process, such as an hourly review rate for code and documents. Management monitors these rates and takes action when inspections fall outside the optimum effectiveness rates derived from organization experience and outside sources. In addition, some processes performed by our GSM group call for orthogonal defect classification (ODC). ODC, which creates a defect-type process signature, enables improved process monitoring and is believed to be superior to traditional defect cause analysis (Bridge and Miller 1997).

Two references are worthy of note for EPD. The first is the SEI CMM's Organization Process Definition key process area. This guideline provides sound advice for development of process standards and the maintenance of process assets. In addition, the Process Management category of the 1998 Malcom Baldrige National Quality Award Criteria describes the ingredients of effective process design: a preventive orientation, continuous improvement, knowing process capability, and process error-proofing (NIST 1998).

Project Postmortems

NSG organizations employ both in-phase reviews and postmortems to assess the quality of development projects and provide an opportunity to review the project for what went right and what needs improvement. Suggested guidelines for post mortems include:

- Being conducted at key project milestones and critical events
- Being run by a subject matter expert or skilled meeting facilitator
- Emphasizing these key outcomes: 1) What are the problems and how can they be fixed? 2) What lessons were learned and how can they be disseminated?
- Judging postmortem effectiveness based on ability to apply lessons learned to future projects

A postmortem was held following the shipment of one of our important software releases. The postmortem generated: 19 strengths, two lessons learned for dissemination to other projects, and 38 improvement opportunities. The improvement opportunities were prioritized so that action would start on the most important, first. Among the opportunities was the need to redesign three error-prone processes and recommendations for introducing several new verifications. Perhaps the most innovative action resulting from this postmortem was the creation of a Motorola intranet Web page containing important information on software about to be released to the field. This new information proved to be an informative aid to the team preparing for field installations.

In regard to learning about mistakes, Tom DeMarco said, "We must begin by cataloging such failures and learning from their patterns. The postmortem plays a key role in this process" (DeMarco et al. 1996).

A QUALIFIED DP PROGRAM

Our GSM group attained SEI CMM Level 5 in the Fall of 1997. Let's look at three characteristics of this organization relevant to DP program success (Miller 1998):

- Using key drivers of customer satisfaction to direct quality improvement
- Employing a wide variety of DP methods
- Making continuous improvement part of everyone's job

NSG has been a leader within Motorola in the area of measurement of customer satisfaction. An outside market research firm surveys customers regularly. From this information, key drivers of customer satisfaction are derived. Our GSM group has utilized this information better than most of our other software organizations. As previously mentioned, customer satisfaction indicators are used to prioritize process improvements including defect prevention actions. GSM has linked key drivers of customer satisfaction, such as effective software testing, back to the processes that can impact the key driver.

Some of our software organizations can only point to a few DP methods in operation. Our GSM group has identified over 10 different methods including: phase reviews, postmortems, escaped defect analysis, orthogonal defect classification, and inspection metrics analysis. It is important to employ a variety of DP methods to ensure that prevention permeates the organization and is not just resident in a group or team here and there.

One estimate of GSM's attention to continuous improvement places the total organization's quality improvement effort at 10 percent of the total development time. Anyone in the organization can generate an "Unscheduled Improvement." The full-time quality organization is small because GSM has built a continuous improvement culture involving all employees (such as, everyone owns their own quality).

EVALUATION OF THE DP PROGRAM

This section evaluates NSG learning and results on the road less traveled toward a defect prevention culture. First, here are some lessons learned.

Process stability is fundamental to many DP activities. When many of our software organizations were CMM Level 1 or 2, one product group organized a team to conduct defect cause analysis studies. Several long and insightful reports were published. However, not much came of the conclusions because the software processes were changing and the conclusions became out-of-date. Many software experts suggest waiting until Level 3 before embarking very far on a DP program, and our experience bears this out.

However, organizations must not err in the other extreme by postponing DP activities because of the CMM Level 5 location of the DP key process area. One danger for a DP program is to look at DP as something to consider only as an organization nears Level 5. All software organizations do some defect prevention, and this effort should be recognized and built upon. Most likely, some defect cause analysis is occurring. Each organization should plan a progression of new DP methods to gradually achieve the requirements of the CMM or other selected standards. Preventive cultures take time to build; they cannot be suddenly turned on.

Make sure software engineers know the difference between detection, correction, and prevention. Mention defect prevention to some engineers and the first two thoughts that come to mind are inspections and defect cause analysis. Their thinking goes something like this: "Defects are present and we must find them" (detection), or "Defects have occurred and now its time to find the causes so they will not happen again" (correction). What is necessary is the additional perspective of preventing the defects before they even occur, using techniques such as software development phase kickoffs, where engineers are made aware of common defects that can occur and how they can be avoided.

Effective process design does not mean creating long and complex procedures. In the early 1990s our location developed a set of standard process specifications. Their acceptance was limited because of long length and bias to methods used by a large, then-dominant software organization (Smith 1997). Since that time, a new set of concise process standards was written that is much more usable and less prescriptive. Our GSM group employs concise process standards (for example, the low level design process description is three pages in length).

What have been the results of our quality improvement and defect prevention efforts? During the past few years, most organizations at our location can point to quality improvements in at least one or two areas, but not a progression of good results in most key quality measures. Our GSM group is the exception. Here are their results:

Quality Measure	*1994-98 Results*
1) Post release defects	20-fold reduction
2) Schedule overruns	5-fold reduction
3) Cycle time decrease	2-fold reduction
4) Overall customer satisfaction improvement	38% increase

CONCLUSION

We have reviewed progress at our Motorola location on the road less traveled toward a preventive culture. One of our organizations has maintained a steady course on this road for several years. Our remaining organizations have made inroads to a preventive culture, but much work remains. While we have become more aware of the components of a defect prevention program and its methods, attention is now focused on building a manage-by-data organization exhibiting quantitative practices of the SEI CMM Level 4 key process areas.

In *Quality Is Free*, a classic quality field book with a focus on defect prevention, Phil Crosby reports that some years ago, a company undertook an assessment to determine causes of poor quality products. One manager concluded, "The whole company is oriented to patching things up rather than preventing" (Crosby 1979). Hopefully, you have read this paper and gained useful ideas for building an effective DP program in your company and, perhaps, overcome the patch and rework oriented mentality all too common in the software industry today.

ACKNOWLEDGMENTS
My thanks to Motorola colleagues Don Gross and Neda Gutowski who reviewed drafts of this paper and advised on how to properly describe the features of an effective DP program.

REFERENCES
Brassard, Michael, and Diane Ritter. 1994. *The memory jogger II*. Methuen, MA: GOAL/QPC.

Bridge, Norman, and Corinne Miller. 1997. Orthogonal defect classification: Using defect data to improve software development. *Proceeding of the Seventh International Conference On Software Quality*, Montomery, AL.

Card, David N. 1998. Learning from our mistakes with defect causal analysis. *IEEE Software* 1:56–63.

Crosby, Philip B. 1979. *Quality is free*. New York: McGraw-Hill.

DeMarco, Tom, et al. 1996. A defined process for project postmortem review. *IEEE Software* 4:65–72.

Gutowski, Neda. 1998. An integrated software audit process model to drive continuous improvement. *Proceedings of the Pacific Northwest Software Quality Conference/8ICSQ*. Portland, OR.

IEEE. 1995. IEEE standard 1074 for developing software lifecycle processes. New York: Institute of Electrical and Electronics Engineers.

Kaplan, Craig, et al. 1995. *Secrets of software quality*. New York: McGraw-Hill.

Miller, Corinne. 1998. Sustaining a continuous improvement culture, *Software Engineering Process Group Proceeding SEPG 98*. Chicago, IL.

Motorola. 1998. Motorola corporate quality system review guidelines, Revision 5. Schaumburg, IL: Motorola Univ. Press. Available from: (847) 576-3142.

NIST. 1998. Malcom Baldrige National Quality Award, *1998 Criteria for Performance Excellence*. Gaithersburg, MD: National Institute of Standards and Technology (NIST).

Paulk, Mark, et al. 1995. *The capability maturity model: guidelines for improving the software process*. Reading, MA: Addison-Wesley.

Smith, Craig. 1997. Software development process standards: Challenges for process assurance. *Proceedings Third IEEE International Software Engineering Standards Symposium and Forum*. CA.

Taylor, C. Michael. 1998. Preventive vs. corrective action: The horse, the barn door, and the apple. *Quality Progress* 31, no. 3, March 1998: 66–71.

BIOGRAPHY

Craig Smith is currently a Senior Staff Engineer, Software Quality Assurance at Motorola in Schaumburg, Illinois. He has over twenty years of diversified experience in Quality Assurance and Information Technology, which included employment with General Dynamics and TRW prior to joining Motorola in January 1994. Smith earned the BS Degree in General Engineering from University of Illinois and completed graduate work completed at University of Illinois and California State University, San Bernardino. He has presented technical papers at ten professional conferences since 1996 including the fifth and ninth International Conferences on Software Quality, ASQ Quality Audit Division Conference, and two IEEE Computer Society conferences. Smith is an ASQ Certified Quality Engineer.

PART FOUR

Project Management

Some have suggested that a companion to the famous Statue of Liberty might well be a "Statue of Responsibility." Such a counterbalance would emphasize the complementary nature of freedom and accountability.

One sure mark of the maturing of the software quality profession would be software malpractice claims. Note that *malpractice* presumes an agreement on what constitutes *acceptable practice*, which is known as a "standard of care." Violating this standard crosses the line from the acceptable to the unacceptable.

Fortunately, many success factors for project management have been well established and are rather directly applicable to software development projects. What seems difficult to understand is why so much behavior that would be unacceptable in other settings is tolerated on many software-related projects.

"Initial Experiences in Software Process Modeling" shows how models of project management have offered opportunities for organizational learning and process improvement. Ray Madachy and Denton Tarbet describe how examining the models and simulated behavior has fostered communication among managers and helped them understand the key factors in complex scenarios. Knowledge of the interrelated technical and social factors has improved their planning and management processes in such areas as earned value techniques, productivity estimation, requirements volatility effects, and extrapolation of project tracking indicators.

Alan Weimer and Jack Munyan offer a **"Recipe for a Successful System: Human Elements in System Development."** The human—as opposed to technological—components are their key ingredients: adequate budget, business alignment, clear deliverables, end-user involvement, and appropriate training. Planning and change management are also essential, first to set the proper course and then to steer through the shifting winds and currents of a project. The authors conclude that good communication is essential to facilitate acceptance of even the most technically correct of systems.

Initial Experiences
in Software Process Modeling

Ray Madachy and Denton Tarbet,
Litton Guidance and Control Systems

*L*itton's Guidance and Control Systems (GCS) Division has been using system dynamics to create mostly small-scale models for investigating managerial process issues and supporting personnel training. At the project level, these include models for planning specific projects, studying Brooks' Law and hiring issues, an interactive earned value model, requirements volatility, and a detailed peer-review model. Insights provided by the models have supported decision making at different levels and helped galvanize process improvement efforts. The training applications have added spark in classes and improved overall learning.

Key words: Brooks' Law, COCOMO, earned value model, simulation, software quality management, training

INTRODUCTION

Litton GCS achieved CMM level 4 certification in 1998, and process simulation is being used to support continued improvements. The company has started some efforts in the areas of managerial training and project and organizational modeling. As a high maturity organization, existing process performance baselines provide leverage in developing and calibrating meaningful simulation models. Experimenting with these models has identified opportunities for process improvement, including the applicable ranges of conditions for improvement. Longitudinal results of these efforts will be reported in the future.

Software development is a dynamic and complex process, as there are many interacting factors throughout the lifecycle that impact the final cost, schedule, and quality. Unfortunately, these factors are rarely accounted for on software projects. Many organizations and their models gloss over process interactions and feedback effects, but these must be recognized to achieve greater improvements. GCS is attempting to bring simulation into the everyday fold.

Knowledge gleaned from a global perspective that considers these interactions can be represented in executable simulation models that serve as a common understanding of an organization's processes. Systems thinking, as a way to find and bring to light the structure of the organizational system that influences its dynamic behavior, together with system dynamics as a simulation methodology, provide critical skills to manage complex software development.

Models are also an excellent vehicle for learning efforts on both organizational and personal levels. Organizational learning in the context of a software process involves translating the common "mental model" of the process into a working simulation model that serves as a springboard for increased learning and improvement. Mental models must be made explicit to frame concerns and share knowledge among people on a team. Everyone then has the same picture of the process and its issues. Collective knowledge is put into the models as the team learns. Elaborated representations in the form of simulation models become the bases for process improvement.

For personal learning, GCS has been using models to demonstrate basic and advanced project management concepts through simulation. Student awareness is heightened when "games" like simulations are used, particularly when they participate. Visual dynamic graphs provide faster and easier remembered learning compared to the traditional lecture format. Exploration is encouraged through the ability to modify and replay the models.

A process modeling characterization matrix initially developed by Kellner is used to place the various GCS studies in Figure 1. See Kellner, Madachy, and Raffo (1999) for information regarding the characterization framework.

IMPLEMENTATION

The Software Engineering Process Group (SEPG) is responsible for organizational analysis and training, and model development. The SEPG and senior executives first confer on model purpose. Team techniques are then used to elicit process views and formulate explicit representations of the mental models into executable simulation models. The software director helps "sell" the analyses and results to other affected groups, thus improving intergroup coordination. Hard issues are dealt with using the model results as objective evidence. Previous hand waving is replaced with explicit quantitative models. The rest of this section provides a brief overview of some models developed at GCS. Each subsection describes a main application category.

Scope / Purpose	Portion of lifecycle	Development project	Multiple, concurrent projects	Long-term product evolution	Long-term organization
Strategic management				product-line reuse strategies	
Planning	stage-based cost/ schedule estimation	staffing project cost/ schedule/quality estimation	reuse costs		
Control and operational management	stage tracking	earned value tracking			
Process improvement and technology adoption	peer review and optimization	peer review effects on project	interproject reuse processes	product-line reuse processes	
Understanding		requirements volatility	core reuse dynamics		
Training and learning	managerial metrics training	managerial metrics training			

Figure 1 Characterization of initial Litton case studies.

Software Manager Training

Selected process management principles are demonstrated using live classroom simulations. Software managers and other designated leaders receive training from the SEPG in project management, software metrics, and other related subjects. Live simulations have been used in the training venues for students to better visualize metrics trends and to improve their control techniques via interactive situations.

Using the dynamic models has enlivened the training sessions and stirred thought-provoking discussions. Using the models in real-time also allows for quick simulation runs to explore issues brought up during discussion. For example, a posed question may be translated into model input and the simulation run for all to see the outcome. This often happens when presenting managerial subjects, as students propose specific scenarios that can be quickly evaluated through the simulation model.

The first models used for training purposes are an earned value model, Brooks' Law model, and a simple estimated productivity model. The earned value model is also used as a basis for actual project control and evaluating the impact of requirements volatility, and the Brooks' Law model is also used to determine optimal staffing for some real projects.

Earned value model. Earned value is an approach for monitoring performance against budgeted plans. Earned value refers to the dollar value of work accomplished, where the value of a given task is defined in a cost or schedule budget baseline. Value is earned after completing the budgeted milestones as work proceeds. Objective milestones consist of directly observable steps or events in the software process, and earned value is therefore a measure of progress against plan.

The earned value model has been used to: 1) demonstrate what earned value is; and 2) show how it can be used to manage a project using feedback. The model implements the basic formulas for cost performance index (CPI) and schedule performance index (SPI) using dynamic cost indicators. CPI represents cost efficiency against plan and SPI represents schedule efficiency against plan. See Figure 2 for the earned value model.

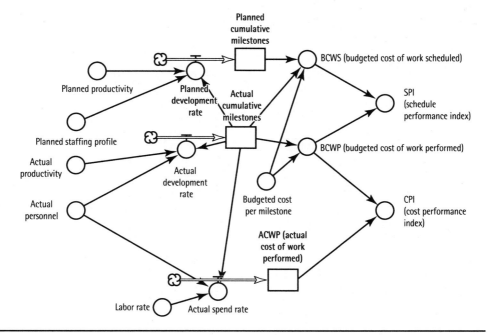

Figure 2   Earned value model.

The model is used to teach managers to spot trends early in order to affect control. This is done by monitoring the slope of earned value trends as opposed to current static values only. A classic example involves evaluating progress compared to planned completions. A quick glance at early trends to see whether task completion is behind may be deceiving. Figure 3 shows sample output from the model.

For example, a project that starts out solving easy problems quickly creates an illusion of early overall completion. Whereas the slope of the progress line, also borne out in the dynamic CPI/SPI curves, clearly shows a worsening negative trend. A partial simulation of two comparative projects is shown to students for discussion before completing the simulation. Many people fail to consider the changing slopes of the initial progress trends, and erroneously choose which project will perform best.

Part of the training involves managers interacting with project simulations as they are running. This is often called "flight simulation" analogously. The earned value model is used for hands-on practice in this manner. For example, simulated CPI and SPI trends are monitored by an individual who can control certain parameters during the run. Typically the simulation is slowed down or paused so individuals can react in time by varying sliders. In the earned value simulation, managers can control the staffing levels interactively as the simulation progresses. See Figure 4 for a sample flight simulation interface to the earned value model.

Brooks' Law model. In the early software engineering classic *The Mythical Man-Month*, Fred Brooks (1975) stated: "Adding manpower to a late software project makes it later."

His explanation for the law was the additional linear overhead needed for training new people and the nonlinear communication overhead (a function of the square of the number of people). These effects have been widely accepted and observed by others. The simple model in Figure 5 describes the situation and will be used to test the law.

The model is conceived around the following basic assumptions:

- New personnel require training by experienced personnel to come up to speed
- More people on a project entail more communication overhead
- On average, experienced personnel are more productive than new personnel

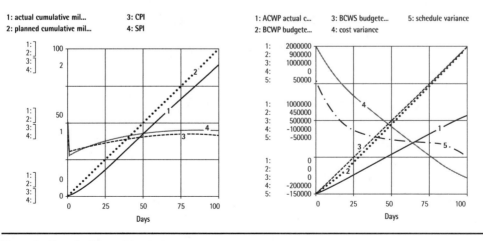

Figure 3   Earned value model output.

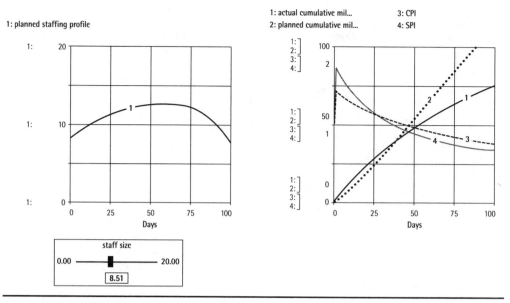

Figure 4   Flight simulation interface for earned value model.

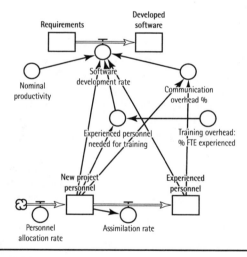

Figure 5   Simple Brooks' Law model.

It is built on two connected flow chains representing software development and personnel. The software development chain assumes a level of *requirements* that need to be implemented. The requirements are transformed into *developed software* at the *software development rate*. The level of developed software represents progress made on implementing the requirements. Project completion is when developed software equals the initial requirements. Software size is measured in function points, and the development rate is in function points per person-day.

The software development rate is determined by the levels of personnel in the system: *new project personnel* who come onto the project at the *personnel allocation rate,* and *experienced personnel* who have been assimilated (trained) into the project at the *assimilation rate.*

The model is a high-level depiction of a level-of-effort project, and it will be exercised by adding more people via the personnel allocation rate. This will allow for tracking the software development rate over time and assessing the final completion time to develop the requirements under different hiring conditions.

As time progresses, the number of requirements decreases since it represents requirements still left to implement. These requirements are processed over time at the software development rate and become developed software, so requirements decline as developed software rises. The software development rate is constrained by several factors: the nominal productivity of a person, the communication overhead percent, and the number of personnel. The effective number of personnel equals the new project personnel plus the experienced personnel minus the amount of experienced personnel needed for training the new people. The communication overhead percent is expressed as a nonlinear function of the total number of personnel that need to communicate. The experienced personnel needed for training is the training overhead percentage as a fraction of a full-time equivalent experienced personnel. The default of .25 indicates one-quarter of an experienced person is needed to train a new person until he or she is fully assimilated.

The bottom structure for the personnel chain models the assimilation of new project personnel at an average rate of 20 days. In essence, a new person is trained by one fourth of an experienced person for an average of 20 days until he or she becomes experienced in the project.

The *nominal productivity* is set to one, with the productivities of new and experienced personnel set to .8 × *nominal productivity* and 1.2 × *nominal productivity*, respectively, as a first-order approximation.

Sample results. The default steady state behavior of the model shows a final completion time of 274 days to develop 500 function points with a constant staff of 20 experienced personnel. Experimental runs are then performed to optimize the schedule finish. The first perturbation run injects an instantaneous pulse of five new people at the 100th day, and on the next run 10 people are added at the 100th day. Figure 6A is a sensitivity plot of the corresponding software development rates for the default condition and the two perturbation runs.

With an extra five people (curve no. 2), the development rate nose dives, then recovers after a few weeks to slightly overtake the default rate, and actually finishes sooner at 271 days. When 10 people are added, however, the overall project suffers (curve no. 3). The initial productivity loss takes longer to stabilize, the final productivity is lower with the larger staff, and the schedule time elongates to 296 days. The plunge and smooth recovery seen on both are the training effect. The extra staff gains in the first case are greater than the communication losses, but going from 20 to 30 people in the second case entails a larger communication overhead compared to the potential productivity gain of having more people.

Project application. The Brooks' Law model was applied to an actual GCS project in order to trade off some staffing alternatives. For a project already behind schedule with about four months to go, the following options were considered:

- **Case 1:** Do nothing to current staff. Let staff members work for four months at same rate.
- **Case 2:** Add nine people in one week. Incur training losses and extra communication overhead.

After some minor calibrations to the model to reflect the project, the following results were obtained.

Scenario	Cost	Schedule
Case 1	1870 person-days	85 days
Case 2	2930 person-days	96 days

Figure 6B shows the productivity trends for these two cases. Adding people in this case clearly added more cost and schedule time to the project, and was decided against.

The model shows how the law holds only under certain conditions, since there is a tradeoff between the number of added people and the time in the lifecycle. There is a threshold of new people that can be added until the schedule suffers. A specific addition of people may be tolerable if injected early enough. Conversely, the project time determines how many can be effectively added.

Based on the insight provided, Brooks' Law can be clarified. *Adding manpower to a late software project makes it later if too much is added too late.* That is when the additional overhead is greater than productivity gains due to the extra staff. See Madachy and Boehm (2000) for more details.

Estimated productivity. A simple model of estimated productivity has been developed, which represents the ongoing estimate of the productivity to be achieved at project completion. It combines an estimate-to-complete (EAC) with a size stability indicator (estimate of the final size). Tracking this indicator includes periodic updates to the EAC accounting for actuals to date and monitoring of size stability. The model demonstrates how to combine these dynamic trends in order to track estimated productivity and stay on top of the project. Figure 7 shows sample output from the model.

1: Software development rate – no extra hiring
2: Software development rate – add five people on the 100th day
3: Software development rate – add ten people on the 100th day

1: Software development rate – no extra hiring
2: Software development rate – with adding nine people in one week

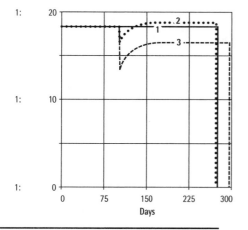

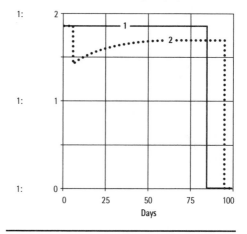

Figure 6A Sensitivity of software development rate to varying personnel allocation pulses.

Figure 6B Brooks' Law tradeoff on GCS project.

Project Planning and Control

A new project is being used as a pilot for dynamic planning and control to raise the visibility of certain planning issues and to monitor the project. The critical project is a large integrated system development with incremental releases. Major elements of the system dynamics model include incremental development, Brooks' Law effects, hiring delays, earned value, and requirements volatility.

A first-cut baseline of the project staffing dynamics and schedule milestones was derived with the COCOMO cost model. The Costar cost-estimation tool was used to develop a baseline staffing profile for the planned increments using a sophisticated incremental version of COCOMO. The profile was then translated into manpower addition and transfer rates to achieve the desired staffing, and used as a basis for exploring requirements volatility and hiring issues.

The COCOMO model assumes breakage from requirements changes is constant throughout the project, but different behavior is expected on this particular project. Because of software dependency on unprecedented hardware development and other factors, most breakage is expected during integration. This indicates a model clash between static COCOMO and assumed actual breakage patterns.

Figure 8 shows the nominal staffing profile with estimated requirements volatility coincident with increment integration points, whereby the volatility is modeled independently of the staffing profile (the numbers have been slightly modified to mask actual project data and preserve anonymity). Past organizational data and expert judgment were used to estimate the magnitudes of volatility. It makes clear that some replanning and risk mitigation is necessary, and the model will be used to evaluate different decisions.

Several other dynamic effects are also being explored on this project. A Brooks' Law model is used to determine optimal staffing-up rates and team sizes. An earned value model is connected with the actual and planned task completions to predict and monitor earned value trends like CPI and SPI.

The earned value model was modified to incorporate requirements volatility. The delayed effect on CPI and SPI of unbudgeted requirements changes has been demonstrated during senior management reviews of selected projects, including this one. The public visualization has been used to improve communication between software engineering and project control personnel.

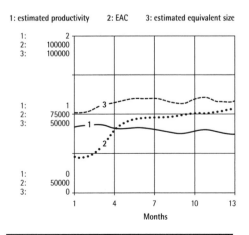

Figure 7   Estimated productivity.

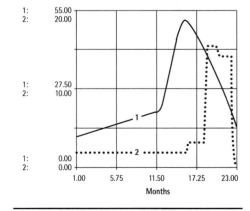

Figure 8   Project model initial staffing profile and expected requirements volatility.

Brooks' Law and Hiring

GCS is also using the Brooks' Law model to support hiring and project-transfer decisions. The model shows under what circumstances hiring people on a late project will help and those when it will not. Effort is increased in every case, and schedule time can be recouped only under certain conditions. In particular, there are losses due to training new staff and communication overhead. If the teams are relatively small and hiring does not continue very late, then schedule performance can be slightly improved. This is a multiattribute problem that system dynamics provides insight for.

Hiring policies have also been analyzed. Despite project plans and aggressive recruiting, bringing on new hires entails months of delays. The average hiring delay is slightly greater than two months for an individual, though business management virtually never accounted for these effects. After the simulation results were presented, management started producing more realistic and conservative hiring plans.

Project Contention Model

A model of resource switching was motivated by reactive behavior on the part of executive management whereby senior people were juggled between projects to fix short-term problems per customer whims. The software engineering department wanted to demonstrate that the practice was counterproductive in terms of cost and schedule performance. Both projects suffered learning-curve and communication overhead drains that overwhelmed any gains on the initial "troubled" project. Additionally, the juggled individuals experienced losses due to the multiple context switching. Their net output is much less when attempting to work on several tasks at once compared to a single task.

The model is shown in Figure 9. One key to the model is expressing the learning curve as a function of volume (that is, tasks produced) rather than time per se.

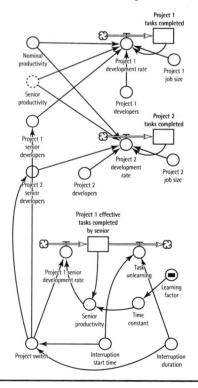

Figure 9   Project contention model diagram.

See Raccoon (1996) for a detailed discussion of software learning curves. When there are interruptions and context switching between projects, then an individual going back to a project requires longer than the interruption time to reach previous productivity levels.

A Delphi-poll and other queries were used to gauge the learning-curve losses. It was estimated that two to three weeks are needed after a one-week break to get back into the productive mode of the original project. Added together, the respective losses and gains for the involved projects produced a net loss compared to not hot-switching personnel. More important, the anticipated schedule slips were directly correlated to customer (dis)satisfaction. These results were shown to the executives who could not disagree with the conclusions, and they have changed their corresponding policies. Figure 10 shows sample output.

The effects of working on multiple tasks has also been quantified by Weinberg (1992). He developed a table of relative productivity versus the number of tasks that validates the results found in the Litton GCS model, and is a good lesson for software organizations to keep in mind.

Peer-Review Model

An inspection model was initially developed at Litton's Data System Division (DSD) in conjunction with the University of Southern California to answer the research question: What are the dynamic project effects of performing inspections? It has now been modified at GCS to model other types of peer reviews, particularly walkthroughs. The model portion for the product and error chains is shown in Figure 11A.

The dynamic model serves to examine the effects of peer-review practices on cost, schedule, and quality throughout the lifecycle. It uses system dynamics to model the interrelated flows of tasks, errors, and personnel throughout different development phases and is calibrated to industrial data. Details on the original model are in Madachy (1996).

The original inspection model was calibrated to data at DSD. GCS walk-through data were used to parameterize the model, and scenarios were run to quantify the expected cost and schedule impacts of peer reviews. The experimentation has helped solidify plans for peer reviews on specific projects. On others, it was shown that performing additional peer reviews may not be worthwhile. The model has also helped educate executives and developers alike on the importance of peer reviews, and provided motivation to optimize the peer-review processes.

The model is general enough that it required no structural changes to handle other peer-review types besides inspections. The following calibration parameters were determined for each project based on existing GCS baseline data as refined for specific projects:

- Nominal productivity
- Review efficiency
- Design defect density
- Code defect density
- Average design defect amplification

Project-specific parameters include:

- Job size
- COCOMO effort parameter
- Schedule constraint

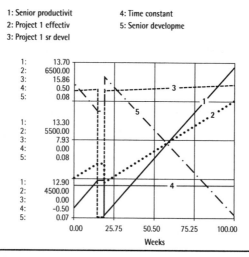

Figure 10   Project contention model results.

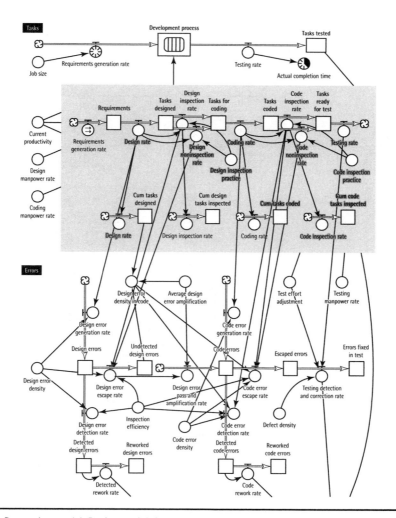

Figure 11A   Peer review model: Product and defect chains.

The following parameters represent management decisions regarding scheduled processes for each project:

- Design walk-through practice (percent of design packages reviewed)
- Code walk-through practice (percent of code reviewed)

An illustration of data used to calibrate the defect introduction rates, detection rates, and review efficiencies for the peer review model is shown in Figure 11B. The data have been sanitized from some actual project data. All data come from the defect-finding mechanisms listed in the left column, and the review efficiencies are calculated accordingly.

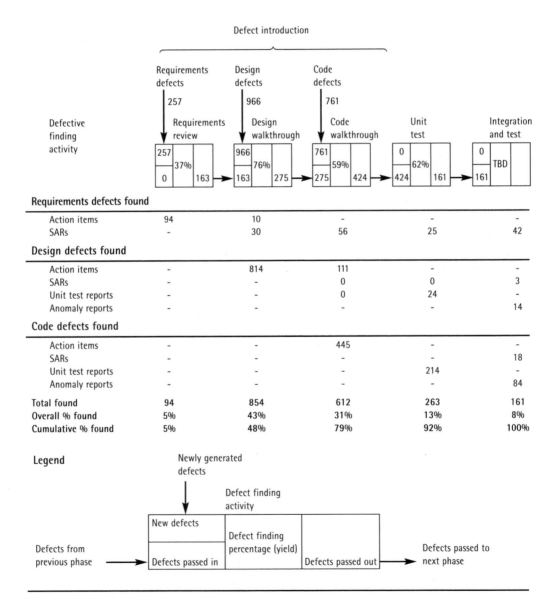

Requirements defects found

	Requirements review	Design walkthrough	Code walkthrough	Unit test	Integration and test
Action items	94	10	-	-	-
SARs	-	30	56	25	42

Design defects found

Action items	-	814	111	-	-
SARs	-	-	0	0	3
Unit test reports	-	-	0	24	-
Anomaly reports	-	-	-	-	14

Code defects found

Action items	-	-	445	-	-
SARs	-	-	-	-	18
Unit test reports	-	-	-	214	-
Anomaly reports	-	-	-	-	84
Total found	94	854	612	263	161
Overall % found	5%	43%	31%	13%	8%
Cumulative % found	5%	48%	79%	92%	100%

Figure 11B   Sample defect calibration data.

Core Software Reuse Model

Product line reuse is a major risk item. GCS has several product lines, one of which has a team developing reusable components for multiple projects. The core software is shared among projects within the product line. Unfortunately, the planned reuse levels are rarely met on a project. It is not known whether current reuse practices involving the core software library are economical. Changes to the core library by one project often adversely affect other projects. These side effects create new problems that often lead to cost and schedule overruns. Experience indicates a conflict with business development policies, which presume significant cost savings.

The observed effects are due to increasing software entropy. A software system that undergoes continuous change will grow in complexity and become more disorganized over time. This phenomenon is often attributed to conventional software architectures, whereby the entropy increases when interfaces are changed for tactical reasons. Generally the software lifetimes are much shorter than commonly expected. At Litton, this problem was exacerbated by the fact that more than a dozen projects use the core-reuse library simultaneously. Changes from a single project ripple into problems on other projects.

A product-line reuse model is being developed to analyze the dynamics of core software reuse. The effort is currently in the conception and data-collection phases. Some past trend data serve as reference behavior for the model in terms of the core dynamics. To parameterize the model, reuse process data are currently being collected and analyzed, and the collection is also being automated.

Based on the eventual findings, an architecture team will investigate ways to improve reusability across projects over longer periods. Conversely, reuse criteria and reuse planning processes will be revamped. Figure 12 shows a high-level model of the situation.

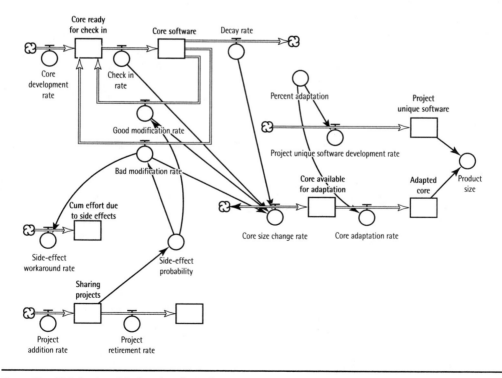

Figure 12   High-level model of product-line software reuse.

CONCLUSIONS

System dynamics simulation is well suited to exploring process issues. Even small models are highly valuable for providing insight into dynamic trends. In fact, smaller is better when presenting results to people not familiar with process modeling or simulation. The models are also well received as training vehicles for a fun and interactive learning experience. Simulation has proved to be a real "utility" player for the organization in that it can play different roles and attack many types of problems. It supports learning at the organizational and individual levels.

An important thrust of the modeling work has been multiproject in nature, where studies look at specific well-defined problems. Rather than producing a complex model of the entire organization at this time, Litton GCS has been using system dynamics for partitioned focused studies on common issues and problems in its environment. This provides individual lessons that collectively have improved management's vision and actions.

There are important advantages to using simulation in the classroom. It can be used to impart information in a more meaningful and dynamic way compared to traditional methods. Some principles are better visualized through time-based simulations. Live demonstrations also keep up the interest of the student audience as opposed to strict lecture, and interactivity serves to drill in the learning experience. Not all lessons can be enhanced by demonstrating management principles through live simulations. Whether to use live simulation should be considered on a per-case basis.

REFERENCES

Brooks, F. 1975. *The mythical man-month.* Reading, MA: Addison-Wesley.

Kellner, M., R. Madachy, and D. Raffo. 1999. Software process simulation modeling: Why? What? How? *Journal of Systems and Software* (Spring).

Madachy, R. 1996. System dynamics modeling of an inspection-based process. In *Proceedings of the eighteenth international conference on software engineering.* Berlin: IEEE Computer Society Press.

Madachy, R., and B. Boehm. Forthcoming. *Software process dynamics.* Washington, D. C.: IEEE Computer Society Press.

Raccoon, L. 1996. A learning curve primer for software engineers. Software Engineering Notes, *ACM Sigsoft* (January).

Weinberg, G. 1992. *Quality software management,* vol. 1: Systems thinking. Dorset House Publishing.

BIOGRAPHIES

Dr. Raymond Madachy is a managing principal at C-bridge Internet Solutions serving as professor and chief software process architect. Previously he was manager of the Software Engineering Process Group at Litton Guidance and Control Systems when this work was done. Litton GCS achieved CMM level 4 during his tenure there. He is also an adjunct assistant professor in the Computer Science Department at the University of Southern California teaching graduate-level software engineering. He has published more than 40 articles and is currently writing a book, *Software Process Dynamics,* with Dr. Barry Boehm. He is a co-author of the soon-to-be released book *Software Cost Estimation with COCOMO II.*

Madachy received his doctorate in industrial and systems engineering at USC, has a master's degree in systems science from the University of California, San Diego, and a bachelor's degree in mechanical engineering from the University of Dayton. He can be reached by e-mail at rmadachy@c-bridge.com .

Dr. Denton Tarbet is the director of software engineering at Litton Guidance and Control Systems. Previously he managed systems engineering at Edwards Air Force Base, was director of the Computer Science Center at Tektronix, was vice president of engineering at Hydro-Aire, and has had other management and consulting positions for embedded real-time software development. He teaches seminars in configuration management, project management, and quality assurance. He received a doctorate in systems engineering from the University of Houston, a master's degree in operations research from the University of Houston, and a bachelor's degree from Truman University. He can be reached by e-mail at tarbetd@littongcs.com .

CHAPTER 4.2

Recipe for a Successful System: Human Elements in System Development

Alan L. Weimer and R. Jack Munyan,
University of Tampa

*S*ystems development efforts frequently fail because of a lack of attention to "people" issues. Technological innovation and improvement alone will not guarantee a system's success. The authors present a checklist of 13 elements that must be present in a successful system development effort. All elements must be present for a development effort to succeed; failed systems typically omit one or more of these elements. Survey results indicate that current systems development efforts are neglecting many of the elements in the list, especially the human elements.

Key words: end users, information systems (IS), interpersonal techniques, organizational behavior, quality management, software processes

INTRODUCTION

The global competitiveness that has emerged in the last decade has dramatically changed the way businesses operate. Companies must look beyond their national borders for business strategy and must gain a competitive advantage by finding ways to differentiate their products or services from others. A company must provide its customers with the products and services they want, in the right place, at the right time, in the right quantity, and at the right price.

One of the most important means to this end is possessing high-quality information. The best information systems provide people with the information they need to perform their jobs better, whether that job is producing widgets or predicting the best long-term allocation of company resources. Companies can no longer afford to tolerate mediocre or inefficient information systems. Timely, strategic information and supporting software processes are primary factors for creating or maintaining a competitive advantage.

The technology available for information systems can meet the demands of a global marketplace. Companies have the ability to collect, process, and disseminate information globally, rapidly, and in a variety of formats and languages. Seamlessly integrated systems can generate information on demand from a local, national, or global perspective. Current application-development tools are higher quality, easier to use, and enable systems to be developed faster than ever before.

Businesses have not been slow to embrace new technology. Companies are quickly acquiring parallel processors, distributed processors, greater processing speeds, faster networks, wireless communications, data warehouses, CASE development tools, object-oriented databases, and so on. But despite technological improvements, companies still wind up with information systems that never provide a meaningful return on investment, either monetarily or operationally.

How do systems development efforts miss their mark? The problems often exist from conception. Frequently a system automating an outmoded manual system does not redesign the processes; it simply reproduces existing redundancies and inefficiencies. More commonly, new systems depart so radically from the way users are accustomed to operating (either changing processes or making them unnecessarily complicated) that users cannot adapt. The authors have personally been called in to salvage a number of systems development efforts in business and government organizations. These systems were typically way over budget, stalled in a development phase, or far astray from their original requirements. In all cases, the technology was not at fault; the problem was a lack of attention to crucial elements in the systems development effort.

PROBLEM STATEMENT:
DISSATISFACTION OF END USERS

In an attempt to ascertain the status of current systems development efforts and whether specific elements in systems development are being ignored, the authors conducted an informal survey of 75 experienced information systems (IS) professionals and end users from business and government organizations. The survey asked a variety of questions about their systems development efforts and how well the resulting systems satisfied their needs. The IS personnel averaged more than 14 years' experience, and the end users—three-quarters of whom had participated in development efforts—averaged almost nine years of work with automated systems. The questions (and the answers received) in the survey are listed in Appendix 1.

The systems in this survey did not receive positive reviews. While most participants felt their computer systems were beneficial, more than half expressed reservations about the systems, and about one-fifth felt the systems *hindered* their work. A system may be a hindrance because it is poorly designed (difficult or awkward to use), slow, or prone to breakdown, but it may still provide help in performing the job. For example, if one is using an over-designed, slow-responding order-entry package that requires navigating through eight screens to complete an order, one might despise its inefficiency but still prefer it to having no order-entry system at all.

In this survey, 78 percent of the end users and 38 percent of the IS personnel felt that their system only partially met its goals. Although this was a small sample, the high-negative percentages are disturbing. If the percentages extrapolate to the thousands of new systems development efforts under way, the figures suggest that information developers and implementers are not meeting their commitment to quality and to user needs.

End users responded with higher negatives (indicating dissatisfaction with the system or lack of a crucial element in system development) to every question in the survey. While this survey did not control for variations across organizations and systems, the spread between IS and end-user responses suggests that the elements of systems development efforts that lead to user satisfaction and acceptance are being neglected.

Technology Elements versus Human Elements

Information systems developers have always emphasized the technology elements of system development, since this is a technology-driven enterprise. The technical components of a system—development tools, database structures, programming languages, hardware, software, network environments—are the developer's building blocks; without them, the system would not exist. But technology is a tool to be applied to human endeavors. No matter how sophisticated a system's technology, the criteria by which it is ultimately judged is whether it improves people's performance and thus improves the company's bottom line. People operate systems and generate the data that become organizational knowledge. Businesses that expect to implement successful, world-class information systems must devote as much time, money, and attention to the human elements of system development as to the technology.

By human elements, the authors mean activities involving the people who support and use the system. Human elements include management support; clear communication of system goals; end-user involvement in design and testing; and careful, complete implementation planning. Unless a system improves and streamlines a company's operational paradigms, it will not contribute to the company's success in today's competitive environment (Pegels 1994). New technology can enable reengineered systems, but without end user input and management and end-user support, it may simply reproduce inefficient processes—and never overcome the resistance to change in an organization.

The people surveyed were asked about their experience with some of the human elements in systems development, such as communication of objectives, training, documentation, implementation, budget, and management sponsorship. A majority of both end users and IS personnel felt that management assigned more importance to technology than to people issues. For almost every human element, between one-quarter to more than half of those surveyed said attention was inadequate.

Through more than two decades of designing, developing, implementing, and studying information systems, the authors have seen again and again how important human elements are in technological and organizational change. Most people want stability rather than change, and most people resist change if it is perceived as threatening or burdensome. But when a new system streamlines an individual's work and makes him or her feel more productive and valuable to the organization, change is welcomed, accepted, and implemented. The human elements in systems development efforts involve users at all levels of the organization in producing a system that meets shared goals. If information systems developers do not try to engage and empower their user community with new systems, no amount of sophisticated technology will provide the organizational benefits that were originally envisioned. Jack Welch, CEO of General Electric, stated this phenomenon concisely:

"If you aren't thinking all of the time about making every person more valuable, you don't have a chance."
(BENNIS AND MISCHE 1995)

This has never been truer than now, as downsized corporations place more and more responsibility on the remaining employees.

RECIPE FOR SUCCESS

The authors have distilled their experience and observations into a list of essential elements for a successful computer system implementation called the "Recipe for a Successful System." The framework (or pot) in which all the recipe's ingredients are mixed is a resolve to develop and implement an information system that aids the organization in its goals of successful global competition and differentiation. The human elements of systems development are primary components of the recipe. The recipe requires investing in workers' skills and providing a workplace that encourages people to further develop their skills.

This list is intended as an easy-to-remember, generic guide to success. Systems development is usually presented in terms of phases, charts, timelines, and responsibility matrices. In the welter of detail, the larger goals and imperatives of a development effort are often overlooked or forgotten. The list will ensure that a system stays on track. Like a successful recipe, *all* ingredients must be present to achieve the intended results.

Recipe for a Successful System

1. **Adequate budget.** Senior management must appropriate enough money to support the entire lifecycle, including implementation issues such as training, documentation, and conversion. If people do not have the money, or if they think they can shortchange a systems development effort by lopping off part of it, all their effort will be wasted. *A high percentage of both IS personnel and end users (41 percent and 50 percent, respectively) in the survey felt that the budget was inadequate.*

2. **Alignment with business goals.** State the strategic objectives of the system as related to the organization's business goals, and make the strategic objectives known to everyone involved in the systems development and implementation effort. The strategic objectives must be clear and understandable. Do not keep people in the dark about the larger purpose of their work. *More than 20 percent of both survey groups felt that their organization's strategic goals were not considered in system planning.*

3. **Clear and concise deliverables.** If the required deliverables cannot be stated simply and concisely, they are not proper ingredients for the stew. The expected deliverables must be expressed early in the systems development lifecycle. A system that lacks a clear, defined scope will be mush rather than stew. *In the survey, 20 percent of the IS personnel and 40 percent of the end users were never informed of the system goals and objectives.*

4. **End-user involvement.** The people who will use the system must be involved from beginning to end. Top-down control without bottom-up involvement is a recipe for disaster. End-user knowledge is valuable; it should not be ignored. User participation helps create user motivation and commitment, and this leads to system success. User involvement in a systems development effort is also an important opportunity for self-development, which benefits the system, the employee, and the organization. *All IS participants surveyed worked with users and 75 percent of end users were currently or had been involved in development efforts. Their involvement, however, was overwhelmingly limited to testing. Users need to be involved in requirements gathering and design throughout the development and implementation processes.*

5. **Adequate training.** It has never made sense that companies invest so much money in information systems development, and when the system is finally implemented, most people do not know how to use it. People must be trained in new skills, and their skills must be constantly updated and upgraded. A company cannot rely on informal conversations among employees to spread knowledge of new technology. Training is not an expense; it is an investment in human resources. It is a mistake to allow economic pressures to force companies to reduce or eliminate these vital and necessary expenses (Bennis and Mische 1995). *Training was inadequate for 30 percent of the IS personnel and 50 percent of the end-users surveyed.*

These five ingredients form the main stock of the system. Each is essential to a successful systems development effort. The following extra ingredients and condiments can also be added:

6. **Executive sponsorship.** Change is hard. People, especially middle managers, will resist a new system unless it is strongly supported by top management and all layers underneath. Only top management can drive a true commitment to change in a company. The executive sponsorship must be direct (it cannot be delegated) and reiterated, both to managers and workers. *Executive sponsorship is increasingly common, but 22 percent of IS personnel and 25 percent of end users said it was not present.*

7. **Change management.** If people are changing the way they do their jobs, they must be prepared for the change psychologically and professionally. Companies must sell their employees on change by showing employees how changes will benefit them. When change is prepared for and introduced gradually, it does not make people insecure and resentful; it turns them into advocates. The goal is to present change as empowering rather than threatening. *User dissatisfaction, lack of communication of system goals, and lack of training are strong signs that change management is not effectively implemented in a development effort.*

8. **Effective software project management.** Systems development and implementation efforts do not run themselves. There must be an experienced project manager with a history of success. *While almost all IS professionals reported that project management was used, only half of the users were aware of a project manager.*

9. **Leadership.** This ingredient is like a spice that sharpens the flavors of everything else; without it, the stew will be flat and compromised in quality. Leadership keeps everyone on track, cares about (and fights for) doing things right, and inspires others to make an extra effort. Leadership is an intangible, but it is a key ingredient in every successful system. Ideally there will be leadership on both the systems development and user side. *The project manager, technical lead, or user lead can provide leadership. Without leadership, a project easily slips into delays and mediocrity. A project manager who monitors progress toward deliverables is not a substitute for leadership.*

10. **Thorough implementation plan.** As the last phase of system development, implementation is frequently rushed and poorly planned. Implementation is often seen by developers as the last, rather tedious transition that must be performed after the interesting work is over. This is unfortunate, because implementation is one of the most crucial phases of systems development. Implementation is show time. It requires putting the finishing garnish on the stew and serving it to the customers (users). A botched implementation can destroy all the goodwill built up for a system and make implacable enemies out of users. *In the survey, 45 percent of users said inadequate time was allotted for conversion, training, and debugging, and 22 percent of IS professionals felt time was inadequate.*

11. **Technical and end-user documentation.** Documentation is a marketing tool (it continues to sell people on the system); a learning tool for users and new technical personnel; and a reference guide for users, support, and development after the system is in use. Documentation captures the components and workings of the real system (in contrast to the designed system). The development effort should be documented as work progresses, not after the fact. If documentation is left until later, it will never be done. Without documentation, a system does not truly belong to the company. If a crucial programmer (or user) leaves, no one else may be able to duplicate that person's system knowledge. *One-third of users had never seen end-user documentation.*

12. **Development methodology.** There are many variations of the systems development lifecycle. It does not matter which variation people choose, as long as they choose one and follow it.

13. **Rapid development tools.** The new development technology enables systems to be developed faster and obtain user feedback more quickly. Rapid development tools cost more up front but pay for themselves many times over in time saved later and in making mistakes visible to both developers and users. Systems requiring a tremendous amount of rework because of mistakes can fall so far behind schedule that they lose most or all of their utility. *Survey results confirm that development methodologies and rapid development tools are widely used.* Methodology and tools are essential to an efficiently managed development effort. User involvement throughout the lifecycle and active participation in feedback sessions will ensure that the methodology and tools are used effectively.

None of these ingredients is new, but using them in combination will ensure a successful system. This recipe has resulted in many successful automated computer implementations and has been used to repair and recommend changes to systems that were on the brink of failure. Although it seems simple, this recipe is not widely practiced.

Importance of Human Elements

In addition to asking whether their development efforts used the ingredients in the authors' recipe, the survey asked participants to rate their importance. The responses of end users and IS professionals were almost exactly alike. This is good news. The two groups appear to understand each other's role in the systems development effort and appear to be merging in their perception of the factors that contribute to a successful system.

The most striking results of this survey are that for both IS professionals and end users, the items ranked as highest priority are the same items that are used the least. *The lists of most important and least-used items are mirror images of each other.* In order of their importance and absence in development efforts, the items are:

1. Adequate training
2. Managing change
3. Adequate budget
4. Thorough plan for conversion
5. End-user involvement
6. Clear and concise deliverables/strategic objectives/technical and end-user documentation (tie)
7. Project management
8. Development methodology/rapid design tools/leadership (tie)
9. Executive sponsorship

These results are provocative and suggest areas for future research to clarify the results. End users and IS departments seem to agree on the importance of people issues in theory; however, IS departments apparently do not focus on them in practice. Overall, the users of these systems were a lot less satisfied with IS products than the IS development staff itself.

Although the technical aspects of systems development (the "how," such as rapid design tools and project management) were on the bottom half of the list, this does not mean they are unimportant. On the contrary, their low positions may simply be because they are taken for granted. As participants noted, systems development managers traditionally consider technology and tools to be the most important elements in development efforts and make strenuous efforts to include them.

Survey respondents may have ranked human element items as most important precisely because they are not included. The real question that emerges from the survey is: Why are both users and IS professionals saying that training, change management, adequate budget, and conversion activities are not present in systems development efforts? The survey suggests areas in which there are gaps in current software implementations. Since, according to the authors' recipe, all ingredients must be present for a successful system, these omissions may be significant contributors to the decidedly mixed reviews that participants gave their automated systems.

CONCLUSION

The survey responses reinforce the authors' personal experiences of the top priorities for systems development and strongly support use of the recipe they have developed. The highest-ranked items all directly affect how people interact with the system. The human elements are clearly on people's minds as most important, perhaps in part because they are most neglected. It is these factors that most affect user satisfaction with end systems. The omissions suggest why users rank their systems, even those in which they have participated in the development cycle, much lower than the developers themselves.

Three areas emerge as particularly significant in development efforts: budget, conversion issues, and communication.

- **Budget.** Software development managers must be realistic about budget and plan for the project end. An inadequate budget affects all areas of a development effort, but will most influence what management perceives as extras, such as change management, development tasks that affect or require end-user involvement, and conversion issues. The technology is paid for at the beginning. When time and money become scarce at the end of a project, conversion issues in particular are often skimmed or skipped.

  In preparing a project budget, management should always plan for the worst and separately monitor the budget for each phase. No phase can be skipped or skimped. It is not acceptable, for example, to abbreviate system test because the project has run out of time and money. Projects that cut short crucial phases or activities invariably wind up spending more money on piecemeal fixes, rework, and protracted user-acceptance testing.

- **Conversion issues.** Conversion issues include testing, debugging, cutover plan, training, and user and support documentation. These activities directly affect user perception and acceptance of the delivered product. Conversion issues cannot be omitted or shortchanged. All too frequently systems development efforts expend most their time and budget in design and coding activities, and then rush into production a system that is full of bugs and for which users are inadequately prepared. The result may be user dissatisfaction, complaints, and revolt against a basically sound system.

  Systems development efforts should include a core group of users who become part of the development effort from start to finish. The users can assume lead roles in testing, conversion, and implementation. Core users who are vested in the system will carry their commitment and increased system and development knowledge back to the user community. Such users facilitate system acceptance within the user group and become invaluable liaisons to development and support in troubleshooting as a new system settles into production.

- **Communication.** Communication issues are also often neglected, and yet they lay the groundwork for a successful development effort. Management statement of system objectives, clear deliverables, and documentation are all part of the communication of system goals. Consistent, continuous communication to both end users and IS personnel will knit the groups together in common under-standing of the development effort and give them a shared sense of purpose.

  Systems development efforts often announce the start of a new systems effort, then come back nine months later with the finished product. Communication can be as simple as including user representatives in all development reviews and project meetings. Rapid development tools enable prototyping for user reviews and give users direct feedback on how their ideas are being incorporated. Communication must be two-way; users want to know what is going on, and they must feel that development is listening to them.

Interrelationship of Elements

The lack of attention IS professionals are giving to people issues may be due to factors such as poor project management, absence of leadership, or passive sponsorship. These factors can affect budget and communication issues. Communication issues can affect budget. Budget can affect conversion issues. Omitting any element can affect others. Most end users and many IS professionals are not aware of how the various components of a system development effort interrelate. A systems development effort mixes many ingredients. Each factor, but especially those involving people and communication, works to make every other factor a success. Systems development is a dynamic system of interdependent relationships.

The "Recipe for a Successful System" will keep systems development focused on the human rationale that is the beginning and end of all information systems. Systems development efforts are improving, but have a long way to go. People must work to narrow the gap between priorities and practice. Successful systems emerge from a shared consensus of users, managers, and developers. A development effort must draw people in rather than shutting them out, becoming a positive agent for change in employees and the organization. The way for software development managers to ensure that a new system produces improvement in processes is to involve the people who are directly and indirectly responsible for system results, from end users to top management.

REFERENCES

Bennis, Warren, and Michael A. Mische. 1995. *The 21st century organization: Reinventing through reengineering.* San Diego: Pfeiffer and Company.

Munyan, R. Jack, and Gordon Couturier. 1996. Integrating the client/server environment: A case study. In *Reengineering: systems integration success.* Edited by Michael A. Mische. Boston and New York: Auerbach.

Pegels, C. Carl. 1994. *Total quality management: A survey of its important aspects.* Danvers, MA: Boyd and Fraser.

BIOGRAPHIES

Alan L. Weimer is director of the MBA program at the University of Tampa in Tampa, Florida. He is also a lecturer and coordinator of the strategic analysis program (SAP) for the University of Tampa. Weimer has more than 20 years' experience as an information systems manager and consultant. He can be reached at the University of Tampa, Tampa, FL 33606 or by e-mail at weimer@alpha.utampa.edu .

R. Jack Munyan is ex-chair and professor emeritus of computer information systems at the University of Tampa in Tampa, Florida.

Appendix I   Survey Results (answers are in bold).

Question	End Users		IS Professionals	
	Yes	No	Yes	No
1. Are you an end user?				
2. Are you an information systems professional?				
3. Have you used computers for more than one year?				
4. If 'yes', how many years?				
5. Do you consider the computer applications you use appropriate to complete your job duties effectively and efficiently?	37	7		
6. Are the computer systems you use a benefit to you in accomplishing your job duties?	41	3		
7. Are the computer systems you use a hindrance to you in accomplishing your job duties?	10	34		
8. Are the computer systems you use a benefit to you in accomplishing your job duties?	40	4		
9. Do you feel the computer systems you use fall somewhere between appropriate/beneficial and inappropriate/hindrance?	26	16		
10. Do you or your department work with the people who design, develop, and implement computer applications: currently or in the past?	35	8		
11. If you or your department **currently** are involved with any of the following activities related to computer application development, or have been involved in these activities in the past, check the appropriate box and indicate current or past: • Initial requirements definition • Analysis • Design • Development • Testing • Implementation	34 (22 testing only; 12 require- ments; 2 analysis; 5 imple- mentation)	7		
12. Do you or your department maintain the computer applications after implementation?	23	18		
13. If you or your department **currently** work with users on any of the following activities related to computer application development, or have worked with users on these activities in the **past**, check the appropriate box and indicate current or past: • Initial requirements definition • Analysis • Design • Development • Testing • Implementation			31 (27 testing; 20 require- ments; 8 imple- mentation)	0
14. Do you or your department maintain the computer applications after implementation?			24	7
15. Do you feel that the effort to build and implement appropriate computer systems was sponsored by management?	33	10	26	5
16. Was the budget adequate for the entire project?	18	22	18	13
17. Was training adequate for: • Technical staff? • End users?	24 (tech) 20 (user)	16 (tech) 22 (user)	21 (tech) 21 (user)	10 (tech) 10 (user)
18. Was end-user documentation available?	29	14	24	2
19. Was project management used?	22	13	29	2
20. Did the technology being applied (e.g., computer type, operating system, network, software, etc.) take precedence over the people involved?	22	17	20	11

Appendix I   *(continued).*

Question	End Users		IS Professionals	
	Yes	No	Yes	No
21. Before putting the system on-line, was adequate time allotted for the following: • Conversion from old systems • Training in the new • Debugging	23	20	24	7
22. Were the goals and objectives of the new system explained: • Verbally • In writing • Clearly	24	18	25	6
23. Do the computer applications you work with meet the goals and objectives: • Fully • Partially	22 full	19 partial	15 full	16 partial
24. Were the future goals, needs, and growth of the organization considered in implementing your applications?	30	11	25	6
25. Does your system function together with other systems?	26	17	30	1
26. If your system is separate, do you feel isolated from other people in your organization?	10	26	30	1
27. Do you consider your systems to be quality systems?	27	15	27	4
28. Do you feel that the systems you use provide your organization with a competitive advantage in the marketplace?	22	19	22	9
29. In the following list of items, check the "should be used" box if you believe that the item **should be** included in a well-developed and appropriate computer system. Check the "was used" box if you believe that the item should be included in a well-developed and appropriate computer system. Check the "was used" box if the item was actually used in system sponsorship/development effort that you are familiar with. If you do not know whether the item was used, check "unknown if used."	**All items were "should be used." In order of "used" in system development efforts (combined scores):** 1. Development methodology 2. Rapid design tools/executive sponsorship/project management (tie) 3. Clear and concise deliverables 4. Technical and end-user documentation 5. Strategic objectives 6. End-user involvement 7. Thorough plan for conversion 8. Adequate budget 9. Managing change 10. Adequate training			
30. Please review the preceding list and rate the five items that you consider most important in the development of a new computer application. **The results are in order of most votes received for most important (combined scores):**	1. Adequate training 2. Managing change 3. Adequate budget 4. Thorough plan for conversion 5. End-user involvement 6. Clear and concise deliverables/strategic objectives/technical and end user documentation (tie) 7. Project management 8. Development methodology/rapid design tools/leadership (tie) 9. Executive sponsorship			

PART FIVE

Measurement

A key principle of the quality profession is reliance on data, on verifiable factual information. How many quality engineers, auditors, or process-improvement advisors would gain credence by saying "I just don't have a good feeling about this"? By contrast, the professional ideal is to provide a factual basis for any judgments, to offer objective evidence for findings or recommendations. Professionals seek to be data-driven in their decisions.

William Florac and Anita Carleton assert that statistical process thinking must be employed to understand the stability and capability of software development processes. Their **"Using Statistical Process Control to Measure Software Processes"** describes the basis for characterizing current performance and establishing a foundation for process improvement. It provides an introduction to the key concepts of variation, assignable causes, process capability, and control charts. Numerous practical examples—and warnings—are offered.

Another experience-based contribution comes from Denis Meredith, who provides insights into **"Managing with Metrics: Theory into Practice."** The two-year project about which he reports saw an evolution in the project team's efforts to use a variety of measures in order to provide insight and to support decision-making at various levels within the project. These measures began with cost and schedule concerns, evolved mid-project into metrics for project management and software development as well as procurement and installation, and finally focused on production measurements. The author concludes with a six-step action plan for those putting project metrics into practice.

In **"Experiences Implementing a Software Project Measurement Methodology,"** Beth Layman and Sharon Rohde draw on three years of implementing a process of using quantitative data to manage software projects. This process provides project managers with insight to support decision-making and influence project outcomes through selection and tracking of success factors. Measurements are successively scrutinized through estimation, feasibility analysis, and performance analysis. Practical guidance is offered on how to start such a process.

Using Statistical Process Control to Measure Software Processes

William A. Florac and Anita D. Carleton,
Software Engineering Institute, Pittsburgh, PA

*T*he demand for increased efficiency and effectiveness of our software processes places measurement demands beyond those traditionally practiced by the software engineering community. Statistical and process thinking principles lead to the use of statistical process control methods to determine consistency and capability of the many processes used to develop software. This paper presents several arguments and illustrations suggesting that the software community examine the use of control charts to measure the stability and capability of software processes as a basis for process improvement.

Key words: control charts, process capability, process improvement, stability, variation

INTRODUCTION

Over the past decade, the concepts, methods, and practices associated with process management and continual improvement have gained wide acceptance in the software community. These concepts, methods, and practices embody a way of thinking, a way of acting, and a way of understanding the data generated by processes that collectively result in improved quality, increased productivity, and competitive products. The acceptance of this "process thinking" approach has motivated many to start measuring software processes that are responsive to questions relating to process performance. In that vein, traditional software measurement and analysis methods of measuring "planned versus actual" are not sufficient for measuring or predicting process performance. We believe the time has come to marry, if you will, the "process thinking" with the "statistical thinking" when measuring software process behavior.

STATISTICAL AND PROCESS THINKING

"Statistical thinking" embraces three principles (Britz et al. 1997):

- All work occurs in a system of interconnected processes
- Variation exists in all processes
- Understanding and reducing variation are keys to success

"Process thinking" stems from W. Edwards Deming's approach to process management (Deming 1986):

- Focus on the processes to improve quality and productivity
- Managers must focus on fixing processes, not blaming people
- Management action uses data from the process to guide decisions
- Recognize that variation is present in all processes and that it is an opportunity for improvement

When we combine these principles we develop a capability to understand the "reliability" of human processes, establish bounds on management expectations, understand patterns and causes of variations, and to validate metric analysis used to forecast and plan our software development activities (Keller 1999). Since software engineering is a human-intensive activity, Keller contends that humans will fail; the issues are which and how often root causes can be eliminated or minimized. Establishing bounds on management expectations entails distinguishing variations due to people problems from variations that are process problems—fixing the wrong problem could be catastrophic. It is also critical to realize which variations are signals requiring action versus just noise in the process. Understanding patterns and causes of variations enables us to understand which parameters represent stability and what "stable" means in a particular environment. Using measurement analysis for forecasting and planning are paramount because repeatability and predictability of processes are key to effective forecasting and planning.

If we examine the basis for these "process thinking" and "statistical thinking" concepts, we find that they are founded on the principles of statistical process control. These principles hold that by establishing and sustaining stable levels of variability, processes will yield predictable results. We can then say that the processes are under statistical control. Controlled processes are stable processes, and stable processes enable you to predict results. This in turn enables you to prepare achievable plans, meet cost estimates and scheduling commitments, and deliver required product functionality and quality with acceptable and reasonable consistency. If a controlled process is not capable of meeting customer requirements or other business objectives, the process must be improved or retargeted.

When we relate these notions of process and statistical thinking to the operational process level, we realize that a key concern of process management is that of process performance—how is the process performing now (effectiveness, efficiency), and how can it be expected to perform in the future? In the context of obtaining quantified answers to these questions, we can address this issue by decomposing the question of process performance into three parts.

PROCESS PERFORMANCE

First we should be concerned about process performance in terms of compliance—is the process being executed properly, are the personnel trained, are the right tools available, and so on. For if the process is not in compliance, we know there is little chance of performing satisfactorily.

If a process is compliant, then we ask, Is the process performance (execution) reasonably consistent over time? Is the effort, cost, elapsed time, delivery, and quality consumed and produced by executing the process consistent? Realizing that variation exists in all processes, is the variation in process performance predictable?

Finally, if the process performance is consistent, we ask the question, Is the process performing satisfactorily? Is it meeting the needs of interdependent processes and/or of the needs of the customers? Is it effective and efficient?

Historically, software organizations have addressed the question of compliance by conducting assessments which compare the organizations' software process against a standard (for example, the Capability Maturity Model). Such an assessment provides a picture of the process status at a point in time and indicates the organization's capacity to execute various software processes according to the standard's criteria. However, it does not follow that the process is executed consistently or efficiently merely because the assessment results satisfied all the criteria.

The questions of process consistency, effectiveness, and efficiency require measurement of process behavior as it is being executed over some reasonable time period. Other disciplines have addressed this issue by using statistical process control methods, specifically, Shewhart control charts. They have come to realize that control charts, or more appropriately, process behavior charts, provide the basis for making process decisions and predicting process behavior.

Successful use by other disciplines suggest it is time to examine how statistical process control techniques can help to address our software process issues. In so doing, we find that Shewhart's control charts provide a statistical method for distinguishing between variation caused by normal process operation and variation caused by anomalies in the process. Additionally, Shewhart's control charts provide an operational definition for determining process stability or consistency and predictability as well as quantitatively establishing process capability to meet criteria for process effectiveness and efficiency.

We use the term "software process" to refer not just to an organization's overall software process, but to any process or subprocess used by a software project or organization. In fact, a good case can be made that it is only at subprocess levels that true process management and improvement can take place. Thus, we view the concept of software process as applying to any identifiable activity that is undertaken to produce or support a software product or service. This includes planning, estimating, designing, coding, testing, inspecting, reviewing, measuring, and controlling, as well as the subtasks and activities that comprise these undertakings.

PROCESS PERFORMANCE VARIATION AND STABILITY

The basis for control charts is recognition of two types of variation—common cause variation and assignable cause variation.

Common cause variation is variation in process performance due to normal or inherent interaction among the process components (people, machines, material, environment, and methods). Common cause variation of process performance is characterized by a stable and consistent pattern over time, as illustrated in Figure 1. Variation in process performance due to common cause is thus random, but will vary within predictable bounds. When a process is stable, the random variations that we see all come from a constant system of chance causes. The variation in process performance is predictable, and unexpected results are extremely rare.

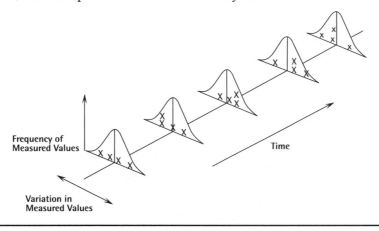

Figure 1   The concept of controlled variation.
Source: Wheeler, Donald J., and David S. Chambers. *Understanding Statistical Process Control,* Knoxville, TN: SPC Press, 1992.

The key word in the previous paragraph is "predictable." Predictable is synonymous with "in control."

The other type of variation in process performance is due to assignable causes. Assignable cause variation has marked impacts on product characteristics and other measures of process performance.[1] These impacts create significant changes in the patterns of variation. This is illustrated in Figure 2. Assignable cause variations arise from events that are not part of the normal process. They represent sudden or persistent abnormal changes to one or more of the process components. These changes can be in things such as inputs to the process, the environment, the process steps themselves, or the way in which the process steps are executed. Examples of assignable causes of variation include shifts in the quality of raw materials, inadequately trained people, changes to work environments, tool failures, altered methods, failures to follow the process, and so forth.

When all assignable causes have been removed and prevented from recurring in the future so that only a single, constant system of chance causes remains, we have a stable and predictable process.

Stability of a process with respect to any given attribute is determined by measuring the attribute and tracking the results over time. If one or more measurements fall outside the range of chance variation, or if systematic patterns are apparent, the process may not be stable. We must then look for the assignable causes and remove any that we find if we want to achieve a stable and predictable state of operation.

When a process is stable, 99+% of process performance variation will fall within 3 sigma of the mean or average of the variation. When the process variation falls outside of the 3 sigma limits, the variation is very likely caused by an anomaly in the process.

When a process is stable, or nearly so, the 3 sigma limits determine the amount of variation that is normal or natural to the process. This is the "voice of the process" or the process telling us what it is capable of doing. This may or may not be satisfactory to the customer if it is, it is "capable," if it is not, the process must be changed since we know that the remaining variation is due to the process itself.

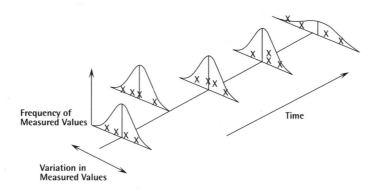

Figure 2   The concept of uncontrolled or assignable cause variation [Wheeler 92].
Source: Wheeler, Donald J., and David S. Chambers. *Understanding Statistical Process Control*, Knoxville, TN: SPC Press, 1992.

---

[1] *Assignable causes are sometimes called special causes, a term introduced by W. Edwards Deming.*

THREE IMPORTANT FACTORS

Before we look at an example, there are three important notions that should be discussed:

- The importance of operational definitions
- Homogeneity
- Issues of rational subgrouping

The need for operational definitions is fundamental to any measurement activity. It is not enough to identify your measures. You must also be able to define your measures in such a way as to tell others exactly how each measure is obtained so that they can collect and interpret the values correctly.

The primary issue is not whether a definition for a measure is correct, but that everyone understands, completely, what the measured values represent. Only then can we expect people to collect values consistently and have others interpret and apply the results to reach valid conclusions.

Communicating clear and unambiguous definitions is not easy. Having structured methods for identifying all the rules that are used to make and record measurements can be very helpful in ensuring that important information does not go unmentioned. When designing methods for defining measures, you should keep in mind that things that do not matter to one user are often important to another. This means that measurement definitions—and structures for recording the definitions—often become larger and more encompassing than the definitions most organizations have traditionally used. This is all the more reason to have a well-organized approach. Definition deals with details, and structured methods help ensure that all details get identified, addressed, and recorded. They also help you deal with people who believe that attention to detail is no longer their responsibility.

Operational definitions must satisfy two important criteria:

- **Communication.** If someone uses the definition as a basis for measuring or describing a measurement result, will others know precisely what has been measured, how it was measured, and what has been included and excluded?

- **Repeatability**. Could others, armed with the definition, repeat the measurements and get essentially the same results?

These criteria are closely related. In fact, if you can't communicate exactly what was done to collect a set of data, you are in no position to tell someone else how to do it. Far too many organizations propose measurement definitions without first determining what users of the data will need to know about the measured values in order to use them intelligently. It is no surprise, then, that measurements are often collected inconsistently and at odds with users' needs. When it comes to implementation, rules such as, "Count all noncomment, nonblank source statements" or "Count open problems" are open to far too many interpretations to provide repeatable results.

Although communicating measurement definitions in clear, unambiguous terms requires effort, there is good news as well. When someone can describe exactly what has been collected, it is easy to turn the process around and say, "Please do that again." Moreover, you can give the description to someone else and say, "Please use this as your definition, but with these changes." In short, when we can communicate clearly what we have measured, we have little trouble creating repeatable rules for collecting future data.

Next, the notions of homogeneity and rational subgrouping need to be understood and addressed. Homogeneity and rational subgrouping go hand in hand. Because of the non-repetitive nature of software product development processes, some believe it is difficult to achieve homogeneity with software data. The idea is to understand the theoretical issues and, at the same time, work within some practical guidelines. We need to understand what conditions are necessary to consider the data homogeneous. When more than two data values are placed in a subgroup, we are making a judgement that these values are measurements taken under essentially the same conditions, and that any difference between them is due to natural or common variation. The primary purpose of homogeneity is to limit the amount of variability within the subgroup data. One way to satisfy the homogeneity principle is to measure the subgroup variables within a reasonably short time period. Whether we are talking about producing widgets or software products, the issue of homogeneity of subgroup data is a judgement call that must be made by one with extensive knowledge of the process being measured.

The principle of homogeneously subgrouped data is important when we consider the idea of rational subgrouping. That is, when we want to estimate process variability, we try to group the data so that assignable causes are more likely to occur between subgroups than within them. Control limits become wider and control charts less sensitive to assignable causes when containing non-homogeneous data. Creating rational subgroups that minimize variation within subgroups always takes precedence over issues of subgroup size.

USING CONTROL CHARTS

Now let's examine how control charts can be used to investigate process stability and lead to process improvement.

There are a number of different kinds of control charts applicable to software process measurement (Florac & Carleton 1999). In software environments, measurements often occur only as individual values. As a result, there may be a preference to using the individuals and moving range (XmR) charts to examine the time-sequenced behavior of process data. For example, Figure 3 shows an XmR control chart for the number of reported but unresolved problems backlogged over the first 30 weeks of system testing. The chart indicates that the problem resolution process is stable, and that it is averaging about 20 backlogged problems (the center line, CL, equals 20.4) with an average change in backlog of 4.35 problems from week to week. The upper control limit (UCL) for backlogged problems is about 32, and the lower control limit (LCL) is

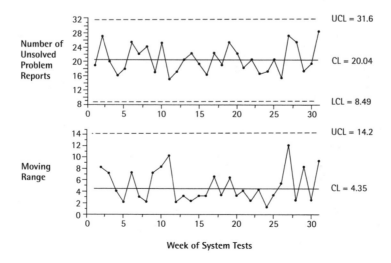

Figure 3   Control chart for the backlog of unresolved problems.

Source: Florac, W., and A. Carleton, *Measuring the Software Process: Statistical Process Control for Software Process Improvement,* Addison-Wesley, May 1999.

about 8. If future backlogs were to exceed these limits or show other forms of nonrandom behavior, it would be likely that the process has become unstable. The causes should then be investigated. For instance, if the upper limit is exceeded at any point, this could be a signal that there are problems in the problem-resolution process. Perhaps a particularly thorny defect is consuming resources, causing problems to pile up. If so, corrective action must be taken if the process is to be returned to its original (characteristic) behavior.

We must be careful not to misinterpret the limits on the individual observations and moving ranges that are shown in the control chart. These limits are estimates for the limits of the process based on measurements of the process performance. The process limits together with the center lines are sometimes referred to as the "voice of the process."

The performance indicated by the voice of the process is not necessarily the performance that needs to be provided to meet the customer's requirements (the voice of the customer). If the variability and location of the measured results are such that the process, albeit stable, does not meet the customer requirement or specification (for example, produces too many nonconforming products), the process must be improved. This means reducing the process performance variability, moving the average, or both.

AVOIDING PITFALLS

When analyzing process performance data, you must be concerned that you have identified all sources of variation in the process. If a conscious effort is not made to account for the potential sources of variation, you may inadvertently hide or obscure variation that will help you improve the process. Even worse, you may mislead yourself and others with a faulty analysis. When data are aggregated, you will be particularly susceptible to overlooked or hidden sources of variation. Overly aggregated data come about in many ways, but the most common causes are:

- Inadequately formulated operational definitions of product and process measures
- Inadequate description and recording of context information
- Lack of traceability from data back to the context from whence it originated
- Working with data whose elements are combinations (mixtures) of values from non homogeneous sources or different cause systems

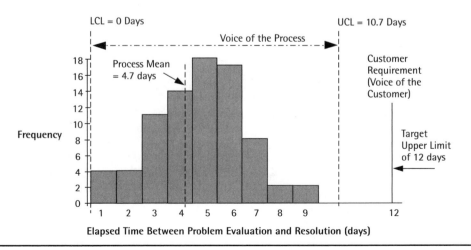

Figure 4   Frequency histogram reflecting voice of the process and voice of the customer.

Source: Florac, W., and A. Carleton, *Measuring the Software Process: Statistical Process Control for Software Process Improvement*, Addison-Wesley, May 1999.

Overly aggregated data easily lead to:

- Difficulty in identifying instabilities in process performance
- Difficulty in tracking instabilities to assignable causes
- Using results from unstable processes to draw inferences or make predictions about capability or performance
- Anomalous process behavior patterns

The following example illustrates several of these points. The top two rows in Figure 5 show the numbers of defects found during design inspections for 21 components of a new system. Each component is believed to possess the same area of opportunity in terms of the potential for defects to occur and be found. The numbers of defects of each type found in each component are shown in the bottom eight rows of Figure 5.

XmR charts that were constructed for the total number of defects found in each component show no signs of instability from component to component (see Figure 6). Based on this cursory examination, it would appear that the combined process of design and inspection was stable and under control.

It is important to know whether or not the component design process is in control for the different types of defects found. Therefore, XmR charts were constructed by plotting the number of defects for each type in the sequence in which the components were completed. The control charts for these individual values are shown in Figure 7. Here we see that the disaggregated data for the numbers of defects found suggests unstable conditions in seven of the eight control charts. Several points are out of bounds, and one chart shows a run of eight points below the center line. The charts for individuals show that as many as eight different components may have been associated with the instabilities. This suggests that reasons for the unusual variations be sought. If reasons are found, actions can be taken to fix the problems that caused the unusual variations.

Note that when assignable causes are found and the corresponding points are removed from calculating the process control limits, the control limits will become narrower, and the performance of the process will be more predictable for each defect type.

This example shows that a single control chart of aggregated data, as in Figure 6, may be ineffective for identifying instabilities or for pointing to potential opportunities for improvement unless the aggregated data is demonstrably stable as well. The more

Component	1	2	3	4	5	6	7	8	9	10	11	12	13	14	15	16	17	18	19	20	21	Totals
Defects	12	16	18	32	22	16	23	35	15	27	16	25	20	26	20	23	23	36	22	27	17	471
Defect Type	Number of Defects per Type per Component																					
Function	3	5	4	4	4	3	3	20	4	11	2	3	3	5	3	7	4	5	5	15	2	115
Interface	2	2	4	4	3	4	2	3	3	4	2	3	5	3	3	3	2	16	6	2	4	80
Timing	1	1	0	1	1	0	2	1	0	0	2	0	1	1	1	1	1	0	1	0	0	15
Algorithm	0	0	1	14	2	0	0	0	0	0	0	1	5	2	7	6	5	1	2	0	1	47
Checking	1	1	5	1	7	1	1	2	0	1	6	3	1	12	1	0	2	4	3	5	2	59
Assignment	0	2	0	4	1	2	1	3	2	3	2	8	1	0	2	1	2	1	0	1	1	37
Build/Pkg.	3	1	1	2	1	0	0	4	3	6	1	0	2	1	1	1	3	2	2	2	1	37
Document	2	4	3	2	3	6	14	2	3	2	1	7	2	2	2	4	4	7	3	2	6	81

Figure 5 Defects found in design review of software components.

Source: Florac, W., and A. Carleton, *Measuring the Software Process: Statistical Process Control for Software Process Improvement*, Addison-Wesley, May 1999.

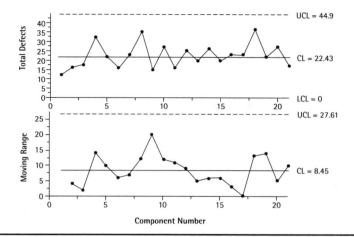

Figure 6   Control chart for total defects found in design review.

Source: Florac, W., and A. Carleton, *Measuring the Software Process: Statistical Process Control for Software Process Improvement,* Addison-Wesley, May 1999.

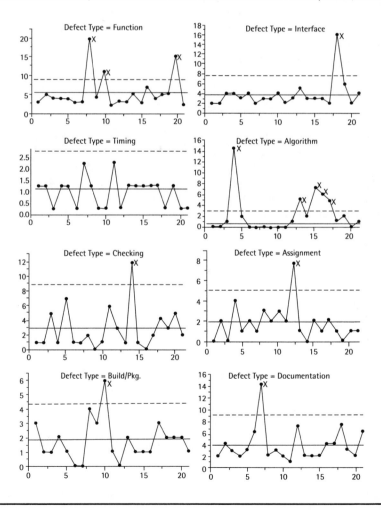

Figure 7   Control charts for each defect type.

Source: Florac, W., and A. Carleton, *Measuring the Software Process: Statistical Process Control for Software Process Improvement,* Addison-Wesley, May 1999.

sources of nonconformity that are combined on one chart, the greater the likelihood that the chart will appear to be in control (Wheeler and Chambers 1992). Thus, although charts such as the one in Figure 6 may provide a useful record of what is happening, they are not very useful for improving a process. Due to the smoothing produced by aggregating the effects of several sources of error, control charts for the total number of defects can easily fail to identify both the timing of instabilities and the potential sources of assignable causes. Figure 8 shows the control chart for total defects when the assignable causes have been removed from the process. Note the improvement in process performance compared to that reflected in the control chart in Figure 6.

Control charts can be used to serve many different purposes. Control charts can be helpful for monitoring processes from release to release to compare overall performance. They can be used for making process adjustments to ensure that stability is maintained for a process on a daily or weekly basis. Most importantly, control charts may be used for continuous improvement of a process that is stable and capable. It is important to keep in mind however, that the control charts provide the most value to the people or team where the process knowledge resides.

Management can also help set the example of how not to use the control charts. While the control charts can be used to improve personal performance, management should not misuse this tool or the data. Management has to remember that the old saw "we will continue the beatings until morale improves" comes into play whenever measurements are used as part of the "beating." Clearly, dysfunctional behavior is likely to occur if employees perceive that measurements are being used in this way (Austin 1996).

SUMMARY

There is evidence that Shewhart's control charts can play a significant role in measuring process performance consistency and process predictability (Paulk 1999). Those that have been successful have come to recognize it is extremely important to: 1) understand the concepts of variation, data homogeneity, common cause systems, and rational subgrouping, and 2) fully understand the process and subprocesses being measured. Furthermore, they have used the control charts to measure process performance at the

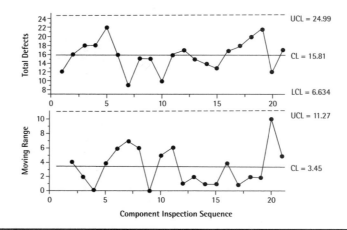

Figure 8   Revised control chart for total defects found.

Source: Florac, W., and A. Carleton, *Measuring the Software Process: Statistical Process Control for Software Process Improvement,* Addison-Wesley, May 1999.

subprocess (and lower) level realizing that there is far too much variation in the overall process to be helpful in identifying possible actions for improvement.

These software organizations have come to appreciate the value added when control charts are used to provide engineers and managers with quantitative insights into the behavior of their software development processes. In many ways, the control chart is a form of instrumentation—like an oscilloscope, or a temperature probe, or a pressure gauge—it provides data to guide decisions and judgements by process knowledgeable software engineers and managers.

REFERENCES

Austin, Robert D. 1996. *Measuring and managing performance in organizations.* New York: Dorset House Publishing.

Britz, Galen, Don Emerling, Lynne Hare, Roger Hoeri, and Janice Shade. How to teach others to apply statistical thinking. *Quality Progress* (June 1997): 67–78.

Deming, W. Edwards. 1986. *Out of the crisis.* Cambridge, MA: MIT Center for Advanced Engineering Study.

Florac, William A., and Anita D. Carleton. 1999. *Measuring the software process: SPC for software process improvement.* Reading, MA: Addison-Wesley.

Grady, Robert B. 1992. *Practical software measurement for project management and process improvement.* Englewood Cliffs, NJ: Prentice Hall.

Humphrey, Watts S. 1989. *Managing the software process.* Reading, MA: Addison-Wesley.

Keller, Ted. 1999. Applying SPC techniques to software development—A management approach. In *Proceedings from the 1999 software engineering process group conference.* Atlanta, GA.

Paulk, Mark C. 1999. Practices of high maturity organizations. In *Proceedings of the 1999 software engineering process group conference.* Atlanta, GA.

Wheeler, Donald J., and David S. Chambers. 1992. *Understanding statistical process control.* Knoxville, TN: SPC Press.

Wheeler, Donald J., and Sheila R. Poling. 1998. *Building continual improvement: A guide for business.* Knoxville, TN: SPC Press.

CHAPTER 5.2

Managing with Metrics: Theory into Practice

Denis C. Meredith, Meredith Consulting

*M*uch has been written about using metrics to manage a software development project. The author has conducted training in the use of software metrics and has provided consulting advice to organizations starting their metrics programs. One of the sad facts of a consultant's life is that he or she rarely sees the results of the effort put into helping clients. Recently, the author has been providing consulting support to a project for more than two years where he has had the opportunity to observe the results of his advice. This article covers the evolution of the project team's efforts to use a variety of measures and metrics to provide insight and support decision making at various levels within the project.

The article begins with a brief description of the project referenced. The theoretical way to implement metrics is discussed briefly, followed by the evolution of the application of metrics on the particular project. A discussion of the success of the project team in using metrics follows, closing with an action plan for readers who want to apply the lessons of this article in their own organizations.

Key words: communications, measurement, process improvement, project tracking, quality measures, risk management

INTRODUCTION

The project that is used as an example in this article was a high-volume data capture operation using scanning, optical mark recognition, and optical character recognition with unresolved characters entered by keyers. The captured data were converted to ASCII text and transmitted to a government agency for analysis. Data capture operations were intended to be conducted over a short period of time (less than four months), which meant that things had to be almost completely right the first time—there would be little or no opportunity for maintenance releases. To reduce the risk associated with a single final delivery, the product was developed, delivered, and tested in increments, with each increment considered a release. In reality, there were a number of patches delivered during data capture, including both fixes and enhancements.

PROJECT MANAGEMENT WITH METRICS
The Textbook Approach

Most authors discussing the use of software metrics suggest an orderly and structured approach to the implementation and use of measures and metrics to support management of software development projects (Grady and Caswell 1992; Putnam and Myers 1987). The metrics process starts with identifying project aspects to be controlled and defining planned measures and metrics to support that control to be used for the duration of the project. While this seems like a logical approach, for this project the only predefined metrics were those required by the customer, specifically cost and schedule, and those required by the contractor.

The next step involves identifying and acquiring metrics support tools. There are a number of such tools available (for example, PSM Insight). This project used the available *MS Access* and *MS Excel* for data collection and analysis. The next two steps are training the staff members who are expected to provide the data and use the metrics followed by implementing the metrics effort. On this project the project team reversed those two steps, with implementation driven by management direction and training provided through a mixture of on-the-job (trial and error), personal tutoring, and mentoring. The final step is to review the results and take appropriate action. The project team made this a review step followed by a revise step.

The review was performed at two levels. The first review was by the data collector, who was also tasked with understanding the results and making changes to get the numbers to move in a desired direction. The second review level was at monthly metrics meetings, cost reviews, and project management reviews with company executives. As readers will see, these reviews resulted in an evolving set of metrics for the project. It should be clear that not all metrics used to support project management are directly related to product quality. In fact, most are related to project and process factors.

EARLY EFFORTS

Cost and Schedule

Because this was a government contract, certain basic cost and schedule metrics were required. For example, cost performance index (CPI), schedule performance index (SPI), and variance at completion (VAC) were carefully tracked and reported to management and to the customer. A positive approach to management of cost and schedule on this project was to push cost account management to the lowest possible level, making the issues of cost and schedule visible to those people who had the most impact on them, and making those people accountable. Other metrics required by corporate management were also collected and reported but, as it turned out, those metrics were not used much to manage the project.

Figure 1 demonstrates a tight control of cost and schedule. From a project point of view, this tight control resulted partly from the fact that the customer was willing to pay what it cost to keep up with a stream of changing requirements. However, it also reflects how making people accountable resulted in better control. This report among others was shown and discussed at the monthly cost reviews, which were attended by the customer.

MID-PROJECT

Project Management Metrics

Monthly metrics meetings were instituted at the request of the project manager. She believed that she could better understand and manage the project if there were some consistent metrics that could show the health of the project and indicate where decisions on her part could improve project performance. The early meetings were a learning experience for the project team.

- The project manager took risk management seriously. It turned out to be a chore to get risk owners to keep the risk database updated in spite of the program manager's demonstrated interest. E-mail and announcements at meetings were equally ineffective at eliciting responses. Finally, a staff member was asked to go to each risk owner periodically and ask for verbal status and updates, which he then used to update the risk database.

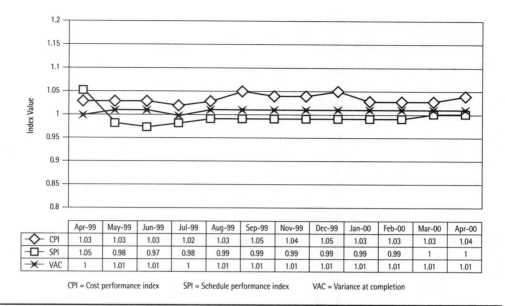

	Apr-99	May-99	Jun-99	Jul-99	Aug-99	Sep-99	Nov-99	Dec-99	Jan-00	Feb-00	Mar-00	Apr-00
CPI	1.03	1.03	1.03	1.02	1.03	1.05	1.04	1.05	1.03	1.03	1.03	1.04
SPI	1.05	0.98	0.97	0.98	0.99	0.99	0.99	0.99	0.99	0.99	1	1
VAC	1	1.01	1.01	1	1.01	1.01	1.01	1.01	1.01	1.01	1.01	1.01

CPI = Cost performance index   SPI = Schedule performance index   VAC = Variance at completion

Figure 1   Cost and schedule metrics.

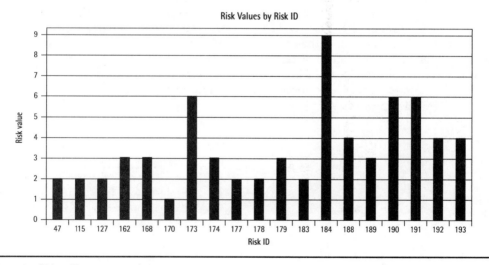

Figure 2   Risk management metrics.

A number of charts were developed (see Figure 2) to make the risks visible and in front of the project team regularly. Risk information was presented monthly at the cost reviews and metrics meetings, and weekly at the program manager's staff meeting. A different perspective was presented at each meeting so the attendees would understand the risks in the context of the particular meeting.

While the risk information, including mitigation plans, was available in the risk database and was thus accessible to the project team, presentation of the metrics helped put the individual risks into a project context. The project manager was able to look at the average risk and the number of risks open for each team and focus on supporting teams that needed it. As one would expect, the trend of the risks in aggregate was downward as the project progressed; there were occasional increases as the project progressed through the development, implementation, operational, and system disposition phases.

- Quality indices (discussed in more detail later and illustrated in Figure 3) were intended to give a quick look at how well the team was delivering software-related products.

- Activity in the areas of process, action items, and deviation requests was reported at the monthly metrics meeting. After a while, when it appeared that these activities were under control, the metrics were still collected and prepared but were not presented at the monthly meeting.

- Configuration management also reported various activities; some of these were later relegated to the prepared-but-not-presented section of the metrics meetings.

The risk management process required that each risk be given a score from one to three in the categories of *impact* and *probability*. The scores were then multiplied to yield a *risk value* for each risk. For the meetings, the risk values were displayed on a chart like the one shown in Figure 2, making it clear which risks needed to be followed most closely. In addition, the average risk value for each team was shown on a separate chart, as was the number of risks open for each team.

After a few metrics meetings, it became clear that there was no single chart, let alone a single metric, that would provide the program manager with a quick picture of the "goodness" of the software that was being delivered and the health of the project. As a result, a number of indices were generated and displayed early in the meeting together on a Kiviat chart like the one shown in Figure 3. (Not all indices were used at the same time, nor were they all used for the duration of the project.) The chart for "this month" was displayed on the same slide as the chart for "last month" so that any changes were apparent. These indices were intended to indicate not only software attributes but also project attributes.

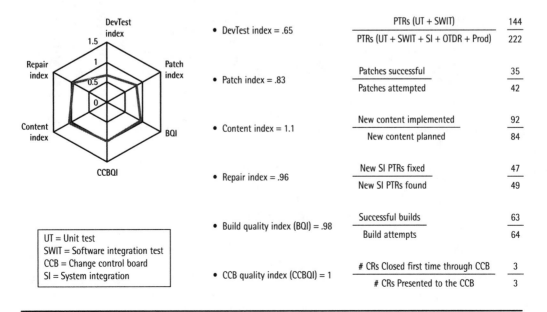

Figure 3   Program indices.

The development/test index showed how successful the development organization was at finding and fixing problems before promoting the product to system integration (SI). The patch index was used to show the organization's success was at delivering changes that did not roll over in the field. The content index was used to show how closely the project team met its planned delivery of incremental functionality.

Readers will notice that in this example the content index is greater than one. This means that more was ready than planned for a given release and was delivered ahead of time. The repair index shows what percentage of problems found in system integration were fixed prior to delivery.

The use of these indices prompted the question, "What must be done to bring the value to one?" leading to causal analysis of failures, leading to continuous improvement. As an example, it was observed that change requests (CRs) seemed to take a long time to be processed. Analysis showed that CRs were frequently rejected by the change control board (CCB), usually because of incomplete information. The CCB Quality Index was instituted to show the organization's progress in improving the handling of CRs so they would not be delayed because of CCB rejection.

Software Development Metrics

It was intended that this project would consist mostly of commercial-off-the-shelf (COTS) product integration, with only glue code being written by the project team. As it turned out, not all products did what their vendors promised they would do. So the project team wrote some additional code to implement the required but missing functionality, and in at least one instance, replaced a COTS product completely with bespoke code. Some products were replaced with others that more closely matched the application requirements. In any case, it was important to have a picture of the magnitude of development work required so requirements allocation was charted and displayed. This was a project where the customer did not have full control of the requirements (changes were sometimes made as a result of legislative action), so requirements change was considered important enough to be tracked and reported at the meetings.

Inspection efforts and results were recorded but did not have a place in the metrics meetings for a variety of reasons. Project-written code was tracked. Much emphasis was placed on problem tracking and reporting. Early graphic reports suggested that problem reports (called PTRs) were out of control. Investigation found that two things were distorting the reports. For one, there were a number of anomalies in the database because of mistakes in the data. For example, some PTRs had a status of closed, but a close date was never entered into the database. A concerted effort was made to clean up the data once these problems were identified, and the PTR management process was tightened to prevent recurrence of data problems.

The other distortion was caused by the fact that sometimes conscious decisions were made to take no action on a particular PTR, but the PTR was never closed. Again, once the problems were identified, procedures were instituted to assure that a status of "decided not to fix" was treated the same as "closed" for metrics purposes. The customer's auditor often attended the metrics meetings and paid particular attention to the project team's responsiveness to problems, and the PTR data were always given close scrutiny. The number of open PTRs and the PTR closure rate were taken as indicators of software readiness.

Wherever possible, the planned values for the metrics were displayed along with the actual metrics so the project manager could see if the activity was on track. In other instances, the trend was displayed with a view to understanding what it would take to make the numbers move in a desired direction.

Each development team reported on problems found after delivery of their products to SI with a view to eliminating those problems that the developers should have found before SI found them. The results were presented on a chart like the one shown in Figure 4. Each team was required to explain any unusual numbers and any changes from the last meeting, to describe what steps they had taken to improve the numbers, and describe the steps they planned to take to improve the results. The contents of this chart evolved over time; as particular problem types were found to contain larger numbers, the project team attempted to break them into separate categories to better focus on eliminating the root causes. Project knowledge, and project state knowledge, is required to properly interpret this chart. For example, 2-pass had zero to report at the time of the illustrated report because they had not started testing yet (see Figure 4). Data assurance was the most recently added subsystem and was relatively immature compared to most other subsystems, so it had a relatively high number of problems.

Hardware Procurement/Production/Installation Metrics

Part of the project was to procure, install, and maintain certain equipment at customer-procured sites (operation of the equipment and system was a separate contract with a different company). It was therefore important to know that those activities were proceeding as planned. Some equipment was built specifically for this project, so manufacturers' production data were collected and reported for that equipment for the appropriate periods. All metrics in this category except staffing were reported for only

Subsystem	Expect to find in SI		Should be found in UT or SWIT						Other*	Totals
	User IF	Misc. other only later tests	Functional	Development environment problems	Code delivery problems	Forms errors	System process	Misc. errors		
DRV	2		1					1		4
Imaging		2								2
Recognition		2								2
Workflow		6								6
Keying									1	1
Site										0
2-pass										0
Data assurance	1	3	11	12	10			10		47
Sys mgt		4			1				4	9
Totals	3	17	12	12	11	0	0	11	5	71

* Other = Non-repeatable, duplicates, new functionality (CR), against COTS product

A = Only detectable at later tests
B = Should be found in UT/SWIT
C = Other (see note above)

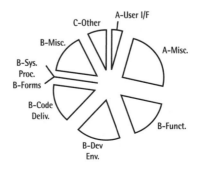

Figure 4 PTR causal analysis.

a short time (a few months). Staffing of support and maintenance activities was reported during operations but from a different view. Prior to data capture, staffing was interesting from the perspective of getting the right kinds of people on board in sufficient numbers to support data capture. Once operations began, things like attrition and attendance were of interest.

In preparation for the beginning of data capture, the equipment had to be ordered, shipped, delivered, and installed. Tracking these activities was important to managing the site preparation and installation effort. As one can see from Figure 5, the vendors performed very well, although the follow-on orders were not quite as timely because of the short timeframes involved between orders and delivery.

LATE PROJECT

Production Metrics

Use of the system is where the rubber meets the road. There were a number of factors used to indicate system success (that is, its ability to do the job for which it was designed). Some of these are shown on subsequent charts. Examples of metrics that were reported during this phase of the project are:

- Technical support: Number of problems, severity/priority, resolution level, causal analysis
- Throughput: Rates, accuracy, volume
- Environment control: Temperature, humidity, control limits
- Availability: Actual versus contract

Figure 6 shows the level at which trouble tickets (TT) were resolved for the month. There is a planned versus actual component to this metric. It was expected that the majority of TTs could be handled by the site support staff, that TTs would be opened at some rate, and that a single person could handle some other number of TTs within a given period of time. Any that could not be handled at the site would be elevated to central technical support (CTS); any that CTS could not handle would be elevated to development to fix the software. A small number were expected to be related to vendor-supplied equipment that would require something beyond normal maintenance. Staffing of on-site support, CTS, and development was based on the expected distribution of TT resolution; the chart in Figure 6 shows a distribution close to that which was expected.

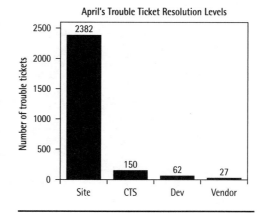

	Total Items	Late Items	% On Time	Items Damaged	% Damaged
Base orders	4,213	35	99.9	6	0.2
Follow-on orders					
Alterations	632	25	96.0	0	0.0
15th cluster	147	0	100.0	0	0.0

Figure 5   Procurement metrics.

Figure 6   Production problem resolution metrics.

Receipts and processing at each data capture center were plotted on the chart like the one shown in Figure 7, enabling the project team to check actual rates against expected receipts and required processing. As it turned out, the volume of forms was higher than predicted and arrived earlier than predicted; however, system processing capacity also turned out to be greater than required, so there was no out-of-control backlog buildup.

Figure 8 shows an example of the chart used to record temperature and humidity readings at specified locations in one of the data capture centers. Because the forms were to be scanned, it was particularly important to control humidity. (Temperature control was also important, but the tolerance of equipment is much greater than that of humans, so temperature was controlled more for comfort than for the equipment.)

The concern with humidity was that if the air (and consequently the paper) was too dry, static electricity could cause the paper to stick together and misfeed into the

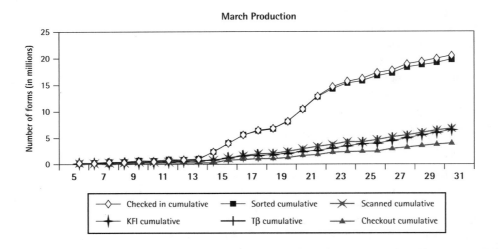

Figure 7   Processing metrics.

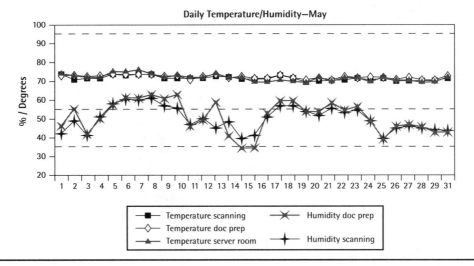

Figure 8   Environment control metrics.

scanners; if too damp, the paper could swell, causing it to jam the scanners and/or tear. Humidity was more difficult to control than expected because of the large openings at the loading docks where forms were offloaded from trucks. Large volumes of air could enter the buildings through these openings, often overloading the humidity control equipment. As it turned out, the paper and scanners were much less sensitive to humidity than expected, and processing proceeded with no adverse effect, even when humidity was outside the specified range.

There are two perspectives from which availability was viewed on this project. The first perspective was on an equipment basis. That is, the classic view including such factors as mean time between failures and mean time to repair on which the project team based its evaluation of the supplier. The second perspective is that of the ability of the system to meet its contractual requirements. The system was designed with sufficient redundancy in most components that even if several components were inoperative, the system could still meet 100 percent of the customers' requirements. Equipment reliability was better than expected. As a result of that and the fact that there was redundancy built into the system, system availability never fell below contractual requirements.

PROJECT MATURITY

The Light Goes On

Probably the most important lesson that the project team learned is that there is no single best metric or set of metrics that will be useful over the life of the project; the project's needs will change as it moves through its life, and it makes sense to change metrics when the team stops learning from the ones it has been working with. In some instances, metrics that were useful in one stage of the project were not applicable to other stages. In other instances, metrics were found not to be useful, interesting, or controllable, and were dropped. Finally, some aspects of the project were brought under control, as indicated by the metrics, and as a result those metrics were not presented at the metrics meetings any longer, although they were still tracked.

For some team members there was an epiphany when they discovered that these numbers they had to produce for the metrics meeting provided insight into how and what their teams were doing, and what they could do better.

Customer participation in the metrics meetings had many benefits. First, the meetings provided the customer visibility into the project's innards where they could see everything, both the good and the bad. Although there was a good working relationship with the customer, this transparency in communication strengthened that relationship. Second, their participation demonstrated that the project was in control and that the project manager could show that it was in control through metrics. Successful use of metrics on the project was driven by the project manager—without her support, metrics use on the project would have been not only unsuccessful but also nonexistent. From the project manager's perspective, the use of metrics on the project was so successful that when she was promoted to a position with authority over multiple projects, she introduced similar metrics programs on the other projects. Her successors as manager of the data capture project also valued the metrics program and continued to use and modify it for the life of the project.

ACTION PLAN

To put into practice what has been discussed in this article, one should:

1. **Desire to make better decisions.** When a manager is satisfied with the results of decisions made, then there is no reason to look for a better way. It is only when there is dissatisfaction with results that one may look for improvement.

2. **Recognize the value of metrics as tools.** Properly used, appropriate metrics can provide insight into project status, trends, and problems. When correct inferences are drawn, decisions can then be made with the intent of driving the metrics in a desired direction. Monitoring the metrics enables the manager to see if the decisions have had the desired effect.

3. **Get started.** Don't wait for a better time. The search for the perfect metric, or the perfect set of metrics, is fruitless. It is important to pick a few measures and metrics that look interesting and get started. Start with metrics that are repeatable (anyone counting gets the same result) and actionable (they represent things that are under one's control).

4. **Evaluate the value of the metrics chosen.** Attempt to drive the metrics in a desired direction and look at the results of decisions—did they help, hinder, or have no effect?

5. **Change as required.** If it happens that the data do not provide insight, guide decision-making, or lead to more questions, it makes sense to change the metrics that one collects and monitors.

6. **Repeat.** As the project progresses and as people learn more about how to use their metrics, both their needs and insight will change requiring that they continuously repeat steps 4 and 5.

ACKNOWLEDGMENTS

The charts, graphs, and numbers used in this article are examples only and may or may not reflect actual data values collected on the project. No inferences about the health or success of the project should be drawn from these data.

REFERENCES

Grady, Robert B., and Deborah L. Caswell. 1992. *Software metrics: Establishing a companywide program.* Englewood Cliffs, NJ: Prentice-Hall.

Putnam, Lawrence H., and Ware Myers. 1987. *Measures for excellence: Reliable software on time, within budget.* Englewood Cliffs, NJ: Prentice-Hall.

BIOGRAPHY

Denis C. Meredith is an independent consultant, concentrating in the areas of software testing and quality assurance; tools selection and implementation; and project selection, scheduling, and management. He has conducted testing, project management, metrics, and estimation seminars throughout the United States, Canada, Mexico, Europe, and Australia. His courses have been presented through the UCLA Extension, National Television University, and CSU Long Beach's Software Engineering Forum for Training. Meredith has served as program chair and program committee member for USPDI's International Conferences on Software Testing. He also serves on the editorial board for Software Quality Professional.

Meredith graduated from the U. S. Naval Academy with a bachelor of science degree and has completed graduate courses in business administration at Pennsylvania State University, where he also taught computer courses. Meredith can be reached by e-mail at DCMeredith@ACM.org.

Experiences Implementing a Software Project Measurement Methodology

Beth Layman, TeraQuest Metrics, Inc.
Sharon Rohde, Lockheed Martin Mission Systems

*T*his article discusses practical experiences gained after three years of implementing a proven software measurement process that emphasizes the use of quantitative data to manage software projects. The authors have helped commercial businesses and government agencies implement the process known as Practical Software Measurement: A Foundation for Objective Project Management (PSM). A brief description of the process, project measurement roadblocks to avoid, and advice for institutionalizing project measurement are discussed.

Key words: decision making, information needs, process improvement, project analysis, software measurement

INTRODUCTION

A software project manager's worst nightmare is having his or her project canceled. Unfortunately, studies have shown that as many as one in 10 software projects *are* canceled, often due to excessive cost or schedule overruns, unmanageable scope creep, or unmet technical objectives. Many software organizations measure schedule delays in years, not months or weeks. The industry is aware of the many contributors to this software project crisis: unrealistic estimates, poor planning, poor risk management, lack of information to support decision making, and so on. What can the industry do about it (Layman and Rhode 1998)?

There is a growing awareness in the software industry that measurement plays an important role in solving these problems. Measurement, when integrated into the overall project management process, provides the information necessary to identify and manage the issues inherent in software projects. Measurement at the project level can be used to objectively validate estimates and plans, track progress, and even anticipate potential problems such as schedule slippage and cost overruns. The goal of project-level measurement is to provide project managers with sufficient insight into the project to support decision making and positively influence project outcomes.

A few years ago, the U.S. Department of Defense, as a major acquirer of software, identified this software project crisis as a major problem and recognized that better use of quantitative techniques were needed on its programs. It initiated a program called Practical Software Measurement. *Practical Software Measurement: A Foundation for Objective Project Management (PSM)* (McGarry et al. 1998) is one of the program's primary products. It is a guidebook that presents a systematic measurement approach and explains techniques for using measurement to make project decisions in time to affect the outcome of a software project. PSM is unique in that it was developed by a working group of measurement experts from both government and industry, and has received endorsements throughout the international software measurement community.

One of the authors of this article helped write the guidebook and both authors are qualified PSM trainers. Both authors have been working to transition the *PSM* guidance to software-intensive commercial information technology, government, and aerospace software projects. This article provides an overview of the *PSM* guidance and then describes the lessons the authors have learned through their experiences implementing *PSM* during the last three years. These lessons should be useful to anyone implementing *PSM* or any other project measurement approach.

PSM OVERVIEW

PSM is a guidebook designed to help software project managers: 1) identify issues and objectives that are important to their project's success; 2) implement a measurement program focused on those issues; and 3) gain objective insight into those issues throughout the project's lifecycle. *PSM* represents a practical, easy-to-use set of best practices for software measurement. Because *PSM* presents a flexible measurement process versus a fixed set of software measures, it can be applied to virtually any software project. Information on how to obtain a complete copy of the *PSM* guidance is provided at the end of this article.

PSM characterizes the key elements or *principles* of a successful measurement program, then describes a comprehensive measurement process based on those principles. The process consists of three major activities, as shown in Figure 1. The first activity describes how to *tailor* the measurement program to address project-specific issues, risks, and objectives. The second activity describes a systematic process for *applying*, or using, measurement to gain insight into the project's issues and to aid in decision making. The third activity, *implementing* measurement, explains how to put measurement into practice within an organization. In addition to the process guidance, *PSM* includes detailed selection and specification guidelines for proven software measures, sample indicators, measurement case studies from real-life software projects, and guidance for putting measurement on contract.

DEVELOPING A MEASUREMENT PLAN

During the tailoring phase, measurement requirements for the project are identified. *PSM's* issue-driven approach stipulates that the project's unique issues and objectives drive the identification of measurement requirements. This is because the purpose of

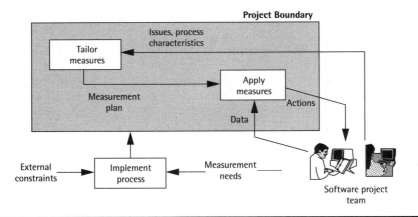

Figure 1   Software measurement activities (from McGarry et al. 1998).

measurement is, first and foremost, to help the project achieve its objectives, identify and track risks, satisfy constraints, and recognize problems early. *PSM* defines the following common types of project issues:

- Schedule and progress
- Resources and cost
- Growth and stability
- Product quality
- Development performance
- Technical adequacy

PSM emphasizes identifying project issues at the start of a project and then using the measurement process to provide insight into those issues. While some issues are common to most or all projects, each project typically has some unique issues. Examples of project-specific issues might be lack of available object-oriented expertise/resources or concerns about the implementation of a particular software package. Figure 2 shows an example of how project issues can be mapped to *PSM* common issues in order to further use the tailoring guidance to help identify useful measures and apply them.

Also, issue priority usually varies from project to project. Moreover, it is important to note that many of these issues are interrelated. For example, while an incremental development approach may help uncover or clarify requirements, it may also lead to more schedule slippage. Lack of available object-oriented expertise may not only contribute to additional costs and schedule delays but may also jeopardize software quality. The relationships between issues must be considered when prioritizing.

Once project-specific issues are identified and prioritized, measures can be selected that will provide insight into those issues. A measure is a quantification of an attribute of a software process or product. A variety of measures may be needed to provide insight into a single issue. Measurement selection will be driven by a number of factors including:

- The cost to collect the measure
- The availability of the measurement data
- The timeliness, accuracy, and validity of the measure
- The measures "fit" given relevant project/organizational characteristics

Figure 2   Example of the mapping of project-specific issues to PSM common issues.

For example, if requirements growth and stability is an issue, then a functional size measure will be needed to track it. The appropriate measure will depend on the nature of the project. Application domain and organizational history/experience will influence the choice of a functional size measure. Information technology organizations may already use function points. Contract software development organizations with a history of tight requirements management techniques, however, may be more comfortable using a requirements-counting schema. An important principle to consider at this stage of the tailoring process is whether the measures selected can realistically be integrated into the project's day-to-day operating procedures.

PSM provides a list of approximately 40 candidate measures. The measures identified in *PSM* are measures that have been used successfully by members of *PSM*'s technical working group, which is composed of measurement practitioners from more than 40 different software producing organizations. While this list of measures is by no means complete, it represents a starting place for identifying and specifying measurement requirements. For each measure identified, helpful information is included in the guidance such as data items and useful attributes to collect; recommended unit of measure, collection level, and reporting level; applicability to various domains; sample indicators; and so on.

The measurement plan documents the measurement requirements for the project, starting with the project's issues and ending with a complete specification of each measure selected. It does not have to be a lengthy document, but should document the following:

- Issues
- Measures (data elements to be collected, data definitions, data sources/tools, data collection level, data collection frequency, and access mechanisms)
- Aggregation strategy (how low-level data will be summarized)
- Frequency of analysis and reporting
- Reporting roles and responsibilities

APPLYING AND USING MEASUREMENT

Once a project gets under way, measurement data are regularly collected according to the measurement plan. Measurement tools, databases, and spreadsheets are often used to collect, store, and process raw measurement data. Once collected, the raw *data* are turned into *information*. As data are aggregated, compared, and analyzed within the context of recent project events, information emerges that can be used to help manage the project. *PSM* advocates using a flexible and dynamic analysis process that promotes the use of measurement as primarily an investigative activity. The key building blocks of this activity are indicators. An indicator is a measure or combination of measures that provides insight into a project issue. Indicators often compare actual project performance data to a plan or baseline and are often portrayed graphically.

One of the unique aspects of the *PSM* guidance is the detail provided regarding the measurement analysis process. *PSM* 3.1 describes three types of analysis that are performed on data:

1. **Estimation.** The development of targets based on historical data and project assumptions.
2. **Feasibility analysis.** The analysis of the feasibility of initial and subsequent project plans that use the estimates as a basis.
3. **Performance analysis.** The analysis of actual performance compared to project plans.

PSM also describes a four-step process that can be applied whenever data are analyzed: 1) identify the problem; 2) assess problem impact; 3) project possible outcomes; and 4) evaluate alternatives.

Finally, the importance of understanding the relationships between project issues and the data that represent them is stressed. *PSM* prescribes using an analysis model (see Figure 3), which shows how some indicators can serve as leading indicators for a particular issue, because they provide insight into something that contributes to the emergence of the issue. The plusses and minuses show whether an increase in the contributor results in an increase (+) or decrease (–) in the resulting issue. For example, an increase in functional size (due to requirements growth) can result in an increase in product size, and an increase in product size can result in an increase in the effort required to complete the project. Therefore, requirements growth could be viewed as a leading indicator of effort overruns; this means that this relationship and the possible resulting outcomes should be considered during the analysis process.

The last step in applying measurement on a project is to actually use the insight gained from measurement analysis to make decisions. This involves communicating the results of the analysis (current problems, impact, outcomes, and alternatives) to the decision makers and taking action. PSM provides guidance on how to clearly communicate results and how to track the results of actions taken.

Because new issues and problems can emerge at any time throughout a software project, *PSM* advocates that the measurement process implemented be flexible and responsive to change as the project evolves. This means revisiting the tailoring activities and modifying measurement plans as needed throughout the project lifecycle. The issues, measures, and analysis techniques must be changed over time to best meet the project's information needs.

LESSON LEARNED IMPLEMENTING PSM

The authors have provided training, conducted measurement planning workshops, and assisted with full-scale implementation of *PSM* on a number of projects—large and small—in both development and maintenance groups. The PSM process has received a very favorable response from the project teams they have worked with because the focus is on meeting their project's information needs versus meeting some requirement to provide "outsiders" with project data.

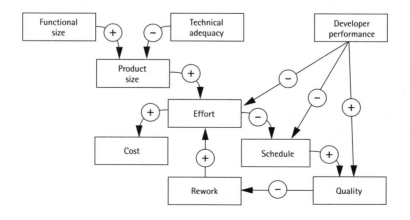

Figure 3   PSM's analysis model.

The authors have also encountered a number of difficulties. These potential problems must be understood and resolved before the process can be successfully deployed. The authors' experiences described in this section represent common or recurring implementation issues in the organizations they have consulted with.

Lesson 1: There Is Often a Disconnect between the Measures Currently Collected and the Issues "Real Projects" Face.

One way the authors help organizations implement *PSM* is through one- to two-day facilitated workshops. Using *PSM's* issue-driven approach, they typically lead project teams through an issue identification process early in the workshop. Here, they use brainstorming and project team synergy to identify existing project issues and constraints, and potential issues/risks that may affect future phases. Next, the authors identify the type of information that would provide insight into the highest priority issues. Only then do they look at data currently collected and measures/metrics requirements, if any. A disconnect between what is currently being measured and what information is needed to help the project address their issues often becomes apparent at this stage.

Many of the organizations the authors consult with already have measurement initiatives under way. Typically, a measurement group has been established, and that group has developed a required list of metrics that all projects are required to produce on a regularly scheduled basis. Project staff members often say that the required metrics are of no value to them. Also, because their project's process does not support, as a natural by-product, the collection of the data or the analysis (which should be an integral part of the project management and decision-making process), they often just meet the requirements without concern for data validity or accuracy (that is, fudged numbers).

Often, *PSM's* flexible-at-the-project-level, issue-driven approach is counter to existing measurement practices. This usually becomes apparent during the workshop—just as projects are starting to see that measurement might be of value in managing their projects and making real-time decisions, the measurement group begins raising objections about losing control of the measurement process. Another concern is losing the ability to capture common measures and compare status and performance across projects. While this seems like a big stumbling block, it usually is not. The concerns are usually overcome with one or more of the following:

- **Recognize that organizational reporting requirements are simply a subset of the project measurement process, and learn to make better use of what is required on the project.** If properly implemented, the measurement data collected can often be used to gain insight into a variety of different issues. The authors try to get everyone to realize that projects can provide a static set of graphs for organizational use while, at the same time, dynamically analyzing the same raw data and generating other graphs to get insight into their real-time issues.

- **Encourage the measurement group to look at the issues driving the organizational reporting requirements and streamline the requirements based on the highest priority organizational information needs.** Sometimes closer examination reveals that the required measures are not really being used to make organizational decisions or drive future estimates/plans, or the return on investment of collecting certain information is questionable. Sometimes, a more aggregated view of the data is all that is really needed (for example, planned and actual work effort by phase to use in future estimates versus detailed effort reporting by person, time period, and so on). Other times, it becomes clear that different measures for different types of projects are more appropriate (that is, function-point sizing for new development versus sizing based on change requests for maintenance).

- **Differentiate the information needed to make organizational decisions from information needed to provide senior management oversight into key projects.** If senior management wants oversight into key projects, this can usually be accomplished with regular project briefings where project-specific measures are presented. In fact, this approach is superior to the same-status-report-for-every-project approach, because it makes visible the things that are really impacting the project and forces management to help the project staff remove any real-time roadblocks. It does mean that senior managers may be slightly more taxed because they may now have to view different graphic indicators for each project.

- **Resolve to "walk first." Recognize that, without effective use of measurement at the project team level, the measurement program within an organization will be weak.** This is because most data used within a software-intensive organization come from the performance of project work. It is easier to get buy-in for collecting a common set of measures across projects after individuals buy in to the value of measurement.

The disconnect between organizational and project needs can be seen in the following example of the often-required schedule data. While monthly Gantt or schedule variance charts are often required for each project, they provide little insight into the cause of schedule slips and often do not indicate a problem until it is of major proportion. Once projects identify the nature of the schedule issue, simple work unit progress charts, like the one shown in Figure 4, can be used to augment or even replace the Gantt chart. Project leads can use these progress charts to pinpoint schedule problems long before they appear on a Gantt chart.

Lesson 2: Making People Need Measurement Is the Best First Step Toward Institutionalizing It.

The authors have learned that the best philosophy to adopt is this: Rather than fighting with logic the many and varied objections project teams may raise against project measurement, get them "hooked" on measurement instead. Measurement planning workshops are a good way to do this. The authors isolate the project team for one to two days, immerse them in *PSM*, change their perception of measurement, help them realize their need for information, and make them feel their "data deprivation." The authors show them how the information they need could be derived from their existing process,

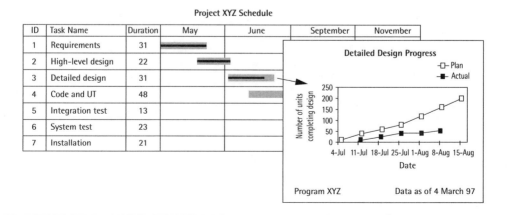

Figure 4   Organizational reporting requirements versus project information needs.

and show them how the information could be used during a project. This often transforms resistive types into chomping-at-the-bit advocates. A key to this transformation process is getting project teams to take ownership of their issues and recognize their responsibility for making visible the things that are happening on the project—things both within and outside their control.

Once people feel they need specific data or indicators, they find ways to use them. After they begin using them, they often find ways to build on what they have in order to meet other needs and build more measurement into their process. To get this cycle going and achieve real institutionalization (for example, where measurement is a natural by-product of the process and represents the "way we do things here"), startup assistance and ongoing consulting services are usually needed. This is where the measurement group can be of service. Many measurement groups the authors have encountered have traditionally "owned" the analysis of measurement data. They collect the data from the project and produce various charts and graphs. They interpret the data and often report results within the organization. With *PSM*, measurements are analyzed and used by the project team. The authors work with these measurement groups to help them transition from measurement "doers" into measurement "consultants." They offer their expertise to projects and help them build simple spreadsheets and collection systems to collect the data they need. They help project members learn how to generate graphs from spreadsheets. They share these simple tools across projects. And finally, they advise projects in the proper use of measurement and in this way, help establish true quantitative software project management within their organizations.

Many of the authors' clients with maintenance or sustaining projects have the recurring information need to make visible the impact of a "trickling resource drain." Typically the project staff is constantly being tagged for nonproject work, yet this drain is never assumed in project estimates nor is the impact of the drain quantified or even given visibility at the program management/customer level. A fixed staffing level is usually assumed. Project staff members identify the resource drain as a major issue, construct simple charts like the one in Figure 5 showing a gap between planned and actual staffing, and present it along with schedule data. Management and customers often say, "Wow—I had no idea!" and are willing to take corrective action to curb nonproject activities. A very simple measurement often helps solve a very big problem and gets project teams hooked on metrics.

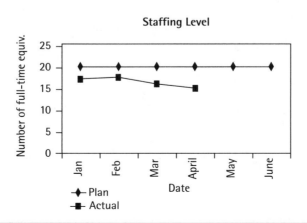

Figure 5 Meeting simple project-specific needs for resource drain.

Lesson 3: The Project Culture Will Impact the Implementation of Measurement.

One of the biggest roadblocks to implementing effective project measurement is the prevailing project culture, which is difficult and slow to change. Unfortunately, some organizations still suffer from one or both of the following:

- **Do not make bad news visible or be prepared to get blamed.** One workshop attendee lamented: "If this type of data become available, management will know where the project actually stands!" Of course, that is precisely what *PSM* is advocating—identify a problem as early as possible in order to fix the problem before it becomes catastrophic or unsolvable. Management that reacts negatively rather than constructively to less-than-stellar performance creates a culture that finds itself constantly in "crisis" mode. The authors have seen strong quality advocates and management consultants within developer organizations successfully alter this climate by educating and coaching management on the need to personally change from "blamers" to "helpers," but it is not a fast or easy transition.

- **Do not give customers insight into the development process—they do not understand these things.** *PSM* advocates sharing measurement information with the customer. This is particularly important when the customer is internal (MIS/IT) and/or when a single customer is paying the bill (MIS/IT or contractual situations). In these cases, customers play an important role in the project's success. Their inputs drive the development process and sometimes their decisions directly affect the project outcome. Because of this, they need to understand how the project is performing and why.

The bottom line is that both management and customers must be willing to listen and respond constructively to bad news. If this type of maturity is not present in an organization's current project culture and no attempt is being made to change it, measurement will only be useful within the project's limited scope of control.

OTHER SUGGESTIONS FOR GETTING STARTED

Based on their experiences with implementing *PSM* to date, the authors put forth the following additional suggestions for getting started with project measurement:

- **Market the approach.** Tie quantitative project management to current software process improvement efforts and show how measurement is integral to risk management, meeting project commitments, and improving process maturity. For example, the measurement approach described in *PSM* is consistent with, and can be easily linked to, ISO and Capability Maturity Model (CMM)-based improvement initiatives (CMM's repeatable level requires planning and tracking of project costs, schedule, effort, size, and quality). This type of marketing must occur continuously.

- **Provide education.** Ensure that all levels of the organization understand the benefits of measurement and are taught the basic measurement principles, steps, and techniques, such as those outlined in *PSM*. Management, in particular, needs to understand its special role in supporting the process and its responsibility to actively participate in analyzing/interpreting measurement results and taking corrective actions when needed. The authors have found that some managers do not understand how to properly analyze and interpret charts and graphs, so be sure to reinforce the use of a systematic analysis process like the one discussed in this article.

- **Conduct project planning workshops.** Consider measurement planning workshops as an alternative to traditional training courses to introduce people to project-level measurement concepts. This enables projects to develop their own measurement plan while learning the process.

- **Focus on a few measures.** For projects just starting to perform measurement, ensure that a *feasible* measurement plan is developed. This may translate into a very small subset of measures. Stress the notion that what one measures can change throughout the process as the project's issues evolve and as the project gains more experience with measurement.

CONCLUSION

The *PSM* guidance has served as a useful framework for introducing software organizations to the concept of an adaptable measurement approach that can be tailored to fit unique project needs. It has been used to establish measurement approaches on projects with little or no measurement, and has been used to hone comprehensive, formalized measurement programs. The authors hope that by introducing the *PSM* approach and that by sharing some of the implementation challenges they have encountered, readers will consider this approach to software project measurement and will be ready to deal with these common implementation difficulties.

Obtaining a Copy of the PSM Guidebook

At the time of this writing, version 3.1 of the PSM Guidebook (April 13, 1998) was available on the *PSM* Web site at www.psmsc.com and version 4 was under development.

ACKNOWLEDGMENTS

The authors of this article would like to acknowledge the other authors of *PSM*: John McGarry, Cheryl Jones, David Card, Betsy Bailey, Joseph Dean, Fred Hall, and George Stark; the PSM Support Center; and the many interesting (but unnamed!) projects and project team members whose experiences have served as input for the writing of this article.

REFERENCES

Layman, Beth, and Sharon Rohde. 1998. *Experiences implementing software measurement.* Presented at Pacific Northwest Software Quality Conference and the 8th International Conference on Software Quality, Portland, OR.

Layman, Beth. 1998. *Lesson learned implementing a best practice: Practical software measurement.* Presented at the Lockheed Martin Systems Engineering and Software Symposium, New Orleans, LA.

McGarry, Jack, et al. 1998. *Practical software measurement: A foundation for objective project management, version 3.1.* Available at www.psmsc.com .

BIOGRAPHIES

Beth Layman is a senior associate at TeraQuest Metrics, Inc. She has more than 20 years of software industry experience with a system development background and specialization in quality and process management. She provides consulting support to TeraQuest clients in the areas of software measurement, process improvement, and quality management. Prior to joining TeraQuest, Layman worked for Lockheed Martin and served as research director at the Quality Assurance Institute.

Layman is a CMM-based lead assessor, one of the principal authors of *Practical Software Measurement: A Foundation for Objective Project Management (PSM)*, and is an associate editor for *Software Quality Professional.* Layman can be contacted at TeraQuest Metrics, 5523 Cord Grass Ln., Melbourne Beach, FL 32951 or by e-mail at blayman@teraquest.com .

Sharon Rohde is a senior consultant at Lockheed Martin Mission Systems. She has more than eight years of experience in software engineering, program management, and applied engineering research and development, with three years specifically in software and systems engineering processes and measurement. Other areas of expertise include software methodologies, tools, testing, reuse, quality, and risk management. Prior to joining Lockheed Martin, Rohde developed and implemented a measurement plan for a major government agency and contributed to the Practical Software Measurement's Product Engineering Working Group. Rohde has authored journal articles dealing with systems engineering automation, risk management, and software reuse. She can be reached by e-mail at sharon.l.rohde@lmco.com .

PART SIX

Inspection and Testing

At least in name, inspection and testing are quality techniques recognizable from more traditional hardware-related concerns. There are, in fact, both valid and false analogies between these techniques as they have applied to hardware and how they add value in software development activities.

Inspection has almost a quarter-century track record as a quality assessment and assurance technique. Tom Gilb wants inspection to do more. He provides insights on **"Planning to Get the Most Out of Inspection"** by first surveying current practice and then providing a number of suggestions for improved performance. These range from strategy to planning to preparation, and address both entry and exit conditions. His case is that inspection needs to shift focus from cleanup to sampling, measurement, and defect prevention.

Yet another maturity model? Yes, this one addresses testing. Burnstein, Homyen, Suwanassart, Saxens, and Grom offer **"A Testing Maturity Model for Software Test Process Assessment and Improvement."** The main value of such an assessment is not so much to "score" an organization at a particular maturity level, but to serve as a guide for process improvement. The authors are also developing a framework of procedures, templates, and checklists to support integration of maturity models from various other specific software engineering concerns.

Mark Fewster and Dorothy Graham offer guidance on **"Choosing a Tool to Automate Software Testing."** Although the focus of their presentation is on testing tools, it offers a general process that should be applicable in tool selection for a wide range of quality applications. Tool selection is viewed as a project in its own right, with requirements specification and development of a business case for any purchase. The authors provide helpful insights into a range of constraints that might influence any such decision.

Planning to Get the Most Out of Inspection

Tom Gilb, Result Planning Limited

I *nspection, a proven technique for achieving quality and identifying process improvements, should be applied to documents throughout software development. The greatest
value from inspection can be gained through a proper understanding of its purposes and
benefits. Newer practices, such as sampling, should be incorporated into the more traditional
application of this technique. The full benefit of inspection can be found as it contributes to
measurement, exit control, and defect injection prevention.*

**Key words: defect detection, defect prevention, documentation, process improvement,
project management, return on investment, training**

INTRODUCTION

Inspection is a proven technique for achieving quality control of specifications and
identifying associated process improvements. In fact, Inspection can be applied to any
discipline that produces documents. It has been applied with excellent results to hardware engineering, management planning, and sales contract documentation.

Software Inspections are widely known within the software industry, but most
organizations do not make the most of them. This is because many people misunder-
stand and misinterpret Inspection. Often, they assume there is only one inspection
method—the 1976 IBM version (Fagan).

This article aims to provide some direction on getting the most value from
Inspections. It will also update readers on new practices, such as sampling. The author
assumes that readers are familiar with the basic Inspection process presented in the
book *Software Inspection* (Gilb and Graham 1993) (see Figure 1 for a simplified overview).
Readers who want to learn about Inspection in depth should see (Gilb and Graham
1993; and URL www.result-planning.com).

SOME BASIC DEFINITIONS

The author's process of *Inspection* (shown with a capital "I" to differentiate it from the
old inspection method) consists of two main processes: the defect detection process and
the defect prevention process. The defect detection process is concerned with document
quality, especially identifying and measuring defects in the documentation submitted
for Inspection and using this information to decide how best to proceed with the main
(product) document under inspection.

The defect prevention process is concerned with learning from the defects found
and suggesting ways of improving processes to prevent them from recurring. Note, the
process brainstorming component of the defect prevention process is not a costly,
in-depth examination of all defects; for each Inspection, it simply involves brainstorming
the reasons and preventive cures for several selected defects. The major part of the

defect prevention process involves in-depth process analysis, and it is actually carried out off-line from the normal day-to-day inspection of specific documents.

A *major defect* is a defect that, if not dealt with at the requirements or design stage, will probably have an order-of-magnitude or larger cost to find and fix when it reaches the testing or operational stages. On average, the find-and-fix cost for major defects is one workhour upstream but nine workhours downstream (Gilb and Graham 1993, 315).

A *page* is a logical page. It is defined as a unit of work on which Inspection is performed. A page must be defined as a quantity of noncommentary words (for example, 300 words).

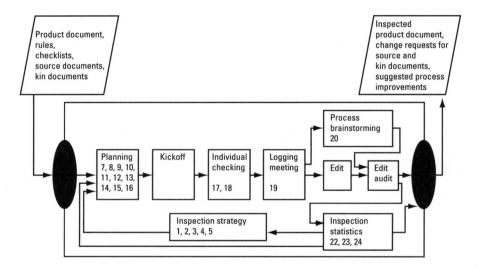

This diagram shows a simplified overview of the Inspection process. The numbers in the process boxes refer to the numbers of the key tips for improving Inspection. Some key tips could have appeared in several process boxes; for simplicity, each was put where it was considered to have its main impact.

The processes within Inspection are:

Inspection strategy: An organization has to understand its aims for Inspection. There has to be strong senior management support. Inspection strategy produces the tactics the organization must adopt to achieve its inspection goals.

Entry: The team leader ensures that the entry conditions for Inspection are met. This involves obtaining the product document, source documents, and kin documents, and checking them against the entry criteria.

Planning: The team leader produces the master plan for an Inspection. Basically, the team leader decides what material within the product document is to be inspected, what documents are to be included within the Inspection, what rules must be used, who is going to be on the Inspection team, and what their roles are. He or she also decides the optimum checking rate.

Kickoff: The team leader ensures the Inspection team understands its task.

Individual checking: The team members individually carry out their checking roles. They report to the team leader any serious problems they discover that might impact the Inspection process, for example, number of issues (potential defects) discovered is sufficiently large to consider abandoning the inspection.

Logging meeting: Inspection team members meet to report their issues and possibly carry out further group checking. There must not be discussion concerning the issues discovered—just logging of the issue (rule violation and position in the documentation).

Process brainstorming: The Inspection team brainstorms the causes and suggests preventive cures for several of the defects logged during the logging meeting.

Edit: The editor (usually the author) examines the logged issues, determines how to resolve them, and fixes the issues that are considered as defects.

Edit audit: The team leader audits the results of the edit process.

Exit: The team leader updates the database of Inspection statistics and decides whether the exit conditions are fulfilled.

Figure 1   Overview of the Inspection process.

BENEFITS AND CURRENT BEST PRACTICE

Given adequate management support, Inspection can quickly be turned from the initial chaos phase (20 or more major defects per page) to relative cleanliness (two or fewer major defects per page at exit) within a year (Gilb and Graham 1993). A good example is the experience of the British Aerospace Eurofighter Project. In software documentation, more than 20 defects per page were reduced to 1 to 1.5 defects per page within 18 months.

On one pass, the defect detection process can find up to 88 percent of existing major defects in a document (Gilb and Graham 1993, 23). This is important, but there is actually greater benefit achieved by the teaching effect of Inspection feedback. By attending Inspections, software engineers go through a rapid learning process, which typically reduces the number of defects they make in their subsequent work by two orders of magnitude within about five inspection experiences, and within a few weeks.

The defect detection process can and should be extended to support continuous process improvement by including the associated defect prevention process. The defect prevention process is capable of at least 50 percent (first year of project) to 70 percent (second or third year) defect cause reduction, and more than 90 percent in the longer term (Gilb and Graham 1993). It has also shown at least 13-to-1 return on investment (ROI) for the ratio of the downstream cost savings of engineering time (rework cost saved by using Inspection) compared to the operational cost of carrying out the Inspections (Gilb and Graham 1993; The Raytheon Report 1995; and Kaplan, Clark, and Tang 1994).

The defect prevention process is the model for the Software Engineering Institute's Capability Maturity Model (SEI CMM) level 5. Robert Mays worked with Ron Radice, who developed the CMM model at IBM. This model was the basis for the SEI model (Radice et al. 1999; Radice and Phillips 1988). Radice himself codeveloped Inspection with Michael Fagan (Kohli and Radice 1976).

Raytheon provides a good case study. In six years, from 1988 to 1994, using the defect detection process combined with the defect prevention process, Raytheon reduced rework costs from about 43 percent to between 5 percent and 10 percent, and, for process improvement, achieved ROI of 7.7-to-1. It improved software code generation productivity by a factor of 2.7-to-1, reduced negative deviation from budget and deadlines from 40 percent to near zero, and reduced defect density by about a factor of three (The Raytheon Report 1995).

Smaller software producers (30 to 60 programmers) have also experienced major business improvements as a result of using Inspection (Holland 1999). Further detailed costs and benefits can be found in (Gilb and Graham 1993; and URL www.result-planning.com).

IMPROVING INSPECTIONS

The following sections contain tips for improving the Inspection process and achieving the kinds of results cited previously. The tips are grouped under the part of the Inspection process they chiefly apply to. (Readers should keep in mind that some tips do cover a broader section of the process. See Figure 1, Overview of the Inspection process, and Figure 2, list of key tips, which shows the mapping of the key tips to the Inspection process.)

Inspection strategy

1. Do not misuse Inspection as a clean-up process. Use it to motivate, teach, measure, control quality, and improve your processes.
2. Use Inspection on any technical documentation.
3. Inspect upstream first.
4. Make sure there are excellent standards to identify defective practices.
5. Give inspection team leaders proper training, coaching after initial training, formal certification, statistical follow-up and, if necessary, remove their "license to inspect."

Entry conditions

6. Use serious entry conditions, for example, numeric quality of source documents.

Planning

7. Plan Inspections well using a master plan.
8. Plan Inspection to address the inspection purposes.
9. Inspect early and often while documents are still being written.
10. Use sampling to understand the quality level of a document.
11. Check against source and kin documents; check them for defects, too.
12. Check the significant portions of the material—avoid checking commentary.
13. Define a major defect as "possible larger costs downstream."
14. Check at an organization's optimum rates to find major defects.

15. Use the optimum number of people on a team to serve the current purpose of Inspection (for example, effectiveness, efficiency, and training).
16. Allocate special defect-searching roles to team members.

Individual checking

17. Use checking data (such as pages checked, majors found, time used, and checking rate) from individual checkers to decide whether it is worth holding a logging meeting.
18. Use the checkers' personal notes instead of proper meeting defect logs when the density of major issues is (nonexit level) high, or when there are many minor defects.

Logging meeting

19. At logging meetings, avoid discussions and avoid suggesting fixes.

Process brainstorming

20. Use the defect prevention process on Inspection itself for continuous improvement.

Exit conditions

21. Use serious exit conditions, for example, "maximum probable remaining major defects per page is 0.2 for exit."

Inspection statistics

22. Build or buy an automated software tool to process inspection basic data.
23. Put the inspection artifacts on a company Web site.
24. Measure the benefit from using Inspections.

Figure 2   List of key tips for improving the Inspection process.

Inspection Strategy

- **Don't misuse Inspection as a clean-up process. Use it to motivate, teach, measure, control quality, and improve processes.** Many people think Inspection is for cleaning up bad work, embedded faults, and other defects. The greatest payback, however, comes from the improved quality of future work. Ensure that the Inspection process fully supports the aspects of *teaching and continuous process improvement.*

  For continuous process improvement, integrate the defect prevention process into conventional inspections. The defect prevention process must be practiced early and should be fully integrated into inspection (see Gilb and Graham 1993, chapters 7 and 17 for details). CMM level 5 is too important to be put off until later—it needs to be done from the start.

- **Use Inspection on any technical documentation.** Most people think Inspection is about source code inspection. Once one realizes that Inspection is not a clean-up process, it makes sense to use it to measure and validate any technical documentation—even technical diagrams. Requirements and design documentation contribute 40 percent to 60 percent of code defects anyway (Pence and Hon 1993).

- **Inspect upstream first.** By the end of the 1970s, IBM and Inspection-method founder, Michael Fagan, recognized that defects, and thus the profitable use of Inspection, actually lie upstream in the requirements and design areas. Bellcore found that 44 percent of all defects were due to defects in requirements and design reaching the programmers (Pence and Hon 1993). Because systems development starts with contracts and management and marketing plans, the Inspection activity must start there, where the problems originate.

  One of the most misunderstood dictums from early inspections is "No managers present." This is wrong. Managers should only be excluded from Inspection that they would corrupt by their presence. They should not be excluded from Inspection of management-level documents, such as requirements or contracts. Nor should they be excluded if they are trying to experience the method with a view to supporting it. Having managers take part in Inspections is a great way to get their understanding and support. "No managers present" is a rule from the past when IBM was doing source code inspections.

- **Make sure there are excellent standards to identify defective practices.** Inspection requires that good work standards (Gilb and Graham 1993, 424) be in place. Standards provide the rules for the author when writing technical documents and for the Inspection process to subsequently check against. An example of a simple, powerful generic rule is "specifications must be unambiguous to the intended readership and testably clear." Violation of this rule is a defect.

  Standards must be built by hard experience; they must be brief and to the point, monitored for usefulness, and respected by the troops. They must not be built by outside consultants or dictated by management. They must be seen as the tool to enforce the necessary lessons of professional practice on the unwary or unwilling.

- **Give Inspection team leaders proper training, coaching after initial training, certification, statistical follow-up, and, if necessary, remove their "license" to inspect.** Proper training of team leaders takes about a week (half lectures and half practice). Experience shows that less than this is not adequate. Inspection team leader certification (an entry condition to an Inspection) should be similar in concept to that for pilots, drivers, and doctors—based on demonstrated competence after training. Note, at present there is no industry-recognized license or certification standard for Inspection.

  Team leaders who will not professionally carry out the job, even if it is because their supervisor wants them to cut corners, should have their "licenses" revoked. Professional Inspection team leadership must be taken seriously so checkers will take inspection seriously. Ensure that there are enough trained Inspection team leaders to support Inspections within an organization—at least 20 percent of all professionals. Some clients train all their engineers on a one-week team leader course.

Entry Conditions

- **Use serious entry conditions, such as minimum level of numeric quality of source documents.** Lack of discipline and lack of respect for entry conditions wastes time. One of the most important entry conditions is mandating the use of upstream source documents to help inspect a product document. It is a mistake to try to use the experts' memory abilities (instead of updated, inspection-exited source documents). It is also a mistake to use source documents with the usual uncontrolled, uninspected, unexited, 20-or-more major defects per page to check a product document. (The figure "20 or more" comes from the author's experience over several years. In fact, from 20 up to 150 major defects per page is not uncommon in environments where Inspection is new.)

It is not a good idea for the author to generate a product document using a poor quality source document. It is easy to check the state of a source document by using inexpensive sampling. A half-day or less on a few pages is a small price to pay to ensure the quality of a document. Another serious entry condition is carrying out a cursory check on the product document and returning it to the author if it has too many remaining defects. For example, if while planning the Inspection, the team leader performs a 15-minute cursory check that reveals a few major defects on a single page, it is time for a word with the author in private. If necessary, pretend the document was never seriously submitted. Do not waste the Inspection team's time to try to approve shoddy work.

In short, learn which entry conditions have to be set and take them seriously. Management needs to take a lead on this. It is often managers who are actually responsible for overriding the entry criteria. For example, carrying out an inspection is often mistakenly seen as fulfilling a quality process (regardless of the Inspection results). Managers have been known to demand that Inspections proceed even when a team leader has determined that the entry condition concerning majors per page is violated.

Planning

- **Plan Inspections well using a master plan.** Use a one-page master plan (the latest forms are on www.result-planning.com, or see slightly older ones in Gilb and Graham 1993, 401) rather than the conventional invitation. Document the many supporting documents needed, assign checkers special defect-searching roles, and carefully manage the rates of checking and the total checking time needed. Establish the formal purpose(s) of each specific Inspection—they do vary. Ensure a team numeric stretch goal is established and that there is a specific strategy to help attain it. A good master plan avoids senseless bureaucracy and lays the groundwork for intelligent Inspections.

- **Plan Inspection to address the Inspection purposes.** There are more than 20 distinct purposes for using Inspection, including document quality, removing defects, job training, motivation, helping a document author, improving productivity, and reducing maintenance costs (see Figure 3). Each Inspection will address several of these purposes to varying degrees. Be aware which purposes are valid for a specific Inspection and formally plan to address them (that is, by choosing checkers with relevant skills and giving them appropriate checking roles).

1. Reducing time to delivery	11. Training the team leader
2. Measuring document quality	12. Certifying the team leader
3. Measuring the quality of the process producing the document	13. Peer motivation
	14. Motivating the managers
4. Enabling estimation of the number of remaining defects	15. Helping the author
	16. Reinforcing conformance to standards
5. Identifying defects	17. Capturing and reusing expert knowledge (by use of rules and checklists)
6. Removing defects	
7. Preventing additional downstream defects being generated by removing existing defects	18. Reducing costs
	19. Team building
8. Improving the document production process	20. Fun—a social occasion
9. Improving the inspection process	
10. On-the-job training for the checkers	Note: This list is not necessarily complete.

Figure 3   Purposes for Inspection.

- **Inspect early and often while documents are still being written.** Leaving Inspection until after a large technical document is finished is a bad idea. If the process that generates the document is faulty, discover it early and fix it. This saves time and corrects bad processes before they cause too much damage. This is one form of sampling.
- **Use sampling to understand the quality level of a document.** It is neither necessary nor desirable to check all pages of long documents. Representative samples should provide enough information to decide whether a document is clean enough to exit at, for example, "0.2 major defects per page maximum remaining."

The main purpose of Inspection is *economic*—to reduce lead time and people costs caused by downstream defects. As in Harlan Mills' IBM "cleanroom" method (Mills and Linger 1987), defects should be cleaned up or avoided using disciplines such as Watts Humphrey's Personal Software Process (PSP) (1995), structured programming (Mills 1972; Mills and Linger 1987), defect prevention/continuous improvement (Gilb and Graham 1993), inspection, and verification. If all this works as it should, cleaning is unnecessary and sampling provides the information to decide if it is economically safe to release the document. Perfection is not required; it costs infinite resources and is dangerous as a guiding concept.

- **Check against source and kin documents; check them for defects, too.** Because of potentially poor quality control practices and craftsmanship, and because Inspection is imperfect on first pass (30 percent to 88 percent effective) (Gilb and Graham 1993, 23), one must focus on the major defects that still persist in source and kin documents. Source documents are input documents used as upstream engineering process inputs to produce the product document being evaluated for possible exit. Kin documents are documents derived from the same source documents as the product document. For example, a requirements document can be a source document and used to produce a design specification (a product document) that requires inspection. Associated kin documentation to consider including in the Inspection would be the testing specification.

Most people overfocus on the product document. In fact, the aim should be to find roughly 25 percent of the total defects external to the product document, mainly in source documents, even when they have exited with no more than one major defect per page.

- **Check the significant portions of the material—avoid checking commentary.** Most organizations waste time checking nonsignificant document areas. It is a waste of checker energy to check at optimum rates to uncover minor defects with no downstream savings. It is necessary to go at optimum rates to find the major defects but ensure that time is not wasted at those rates (one logical page of 300 noncommentary words checked per hour plus or minus 0.9 logical pages is the expected optimum checking rate range). The result of indiscriminate checking of trivia at an optimum rate could be 90 percent minor defects and 90 percent waste of time. It is equivalent to checking comments for 90 percent of the time instead of real code.

From practical experience, it pays to have a general specification rule that technical authors must distinguish between noncommentary and commentary text (or diagrams). Noncommentary (or "meat") text is text where any defects might translate into serious downstream costs (that is, major defects could be found). Commentary (or "fat") text can only contain minor defects and so is less important.

The distinction between "meat" and "fat" can be achieved, for example, by using italics for the *fat*. Some clients have even created Microsoft Word macros to count the volume of noncommentary text (nonitalics) and print the logical page count on the first page (Holland 1994; Holland 1999). Of course, the checker is allowed to scan and reference the commentary words but is not obliged to check them against all sources, rules, and checklists; it is not worth it.

- **Define a major defect as "possible larger costs downstream."** It does not matter if a defect is not precisely a nonconformance or if it is visible to a customer. If it could lead to significant costs if it escapes downstream, classify it as a major defect, and treat it with due respect.

Note major and minor after-the-checklist questions or rule statement. It is often useful to indicate super major or showstopper (a defect where the downstream effect could be an order of magnitude bigger than an average major, which is about nine hours downstream loss average) (Gilb and Graham 1993, 315). Super majors can be highlighted for management attention.

Concentrate on the major defects. This helps avoid the "90 percent minor syndrome" that often hampers Inspection. As mentioned previously, employees will waste time identifying 90 percent minor defects, unless strongly redirected. There are at least 18 different tactics that shift the focus from minor to major defects (see Figure 4). For example, using checklists can help people identify majors rather than minors. The checklist

1. Plan special roles with special role checklists that only ask questions directed at major defects.
2. Teach at kick-off meeting that the search for majors is primary.
3. Hand out checker procedures that define the fact that majors are the primary concern.
4. Use rule sets that for approximately 19 out of 20 rules are identifying major defects.
5. Limit rule sets and checklists to a maximum of one page. This has the effect of squeezing trivial ideas "off the page," as soon as higher priority major defect identification rules, task activities, and checklist questions are gradually identified.
6. Identify the probable classification of an issue identified in a checklist question next to the question itself as major or minor.
7. Ask checkers to do their own personal classification of major/minor during the checking activity.
8. Ask checkers to report (at the bottom of the inspection-plan form) how many issues they found during checking in the various severity categories. This is done orally with the team. Those who report numerous issues categorized as minors and few as majors will feel motivated to do better next time.
9. Have checkers always state orally "major" or "minor" when they report an issue to be logged at the "public" logging meeting. It's embarrassing to constantly cite "minor" when others are stating "major."
10. Calculate Inspection "return on time invested" based on major defects found, never on minors.
11. State numeric Inspection team process improvement objectives in terms of major defects per page and per hour. Never have it a team objective to get better at finding minor defects.
12. Never discuss the root causes of minor defects at the process brainstorming meeting. Only majors are worth discussing.
13. When time for logging is particularly short, report only major defects. If time permits, allow the reporting of minors and formally log them.
14. Report only a symbolic sample of minors, for example, on a single page. The rest, if checkers have notes of them, can be handed informally to the editor. They are simply not worth more formal treatment or priority.
15. If editing time is under pressure, only major defects might actually be fixed.
16. If edit audit has an overwhelming number of things to check, then the leader would take majors seriously and skim over the minors, perhaps looking at a sample only.
17. Report Inspection statistics to management based only on major defects.
18. Determine optimum rates of checking that ignore minors and use only majors found per hour per page as the basis for calculation of rates.

Note: This list is not necessarily complete.

Figure 4   List of tactics to encourage checkers to focus on major defects rather than minor ones.

contents should aim to detect majors and not minors. (Note: checklists are only allowed to help interpret the rules, which are an organization's official standards for writing a given document, and which define what constitutes defects.)

Another useful tactic is to log only majors at a meeting and calculate the ROI for Inspections only on the basis of the majors. This sends a clear message not to waste time on minor defects.

- **Check at an organization's optimum (coverage) checking rates to find major defects.** This is the big one. Most people, including many teachers of Inspection, manage to miss this point. Or worse, they recommend checking rates that are 10 times optimum speed (Kelly 1990; The Raytheon Report 1995). Optimum checking rate is not a reading rate. Checking in real Inspections involves checking a page against all related documents. This can involve up to 10 or 20 individual documents; these are source documents of large size, checklists, and standards. The requirement is to check a single product document line against many sources, and it takes time.

Adequate Inspection statistics can prove that an organization's employees have a clear, dramatic, and consistent optimum checking rate on specific document types. The expected optimum checking rate range is between 0.2 and 1.8 pages of 300 noncommentary words per checking hour. For example, at Raytheon it was about 20 plus or minus 10 lines per hour (0.3 pages) (Haley et al. 1995). Unfortunately, in spite of its own data, Raytheon suggested rates of about 100 to 250 lines per hour. This was probably because it had finite deadlines and did not understand sampling (see Figure 5).

As the checking speed moves toward an optimum speed for effectiveness of finding major defects, the curve for optimum checking rate moves dramatically upward in terms of major defects identified per logical page. The optimum may seem slow, but considering the amount of checking that has to be done, it is fast. The point is that there is a best speed at which to check, and an organization could easily be operating at only 1 percent of defect identification effectiveness if it fails to heed it.

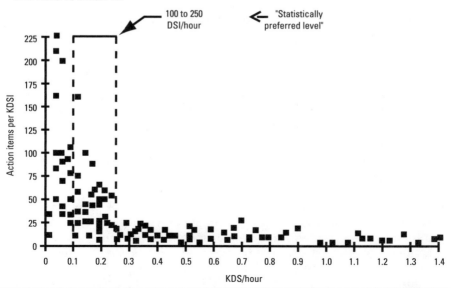

Figure 5   This figure is from the Raytheon Report (1995). It shows that their optimum checking rate is probably about 10 to 20 statements per hour for an individual checker.

Note that the optimum checking rate applies both to the checking carried out during the individual checking phase (also known as preparation) and to the optional checking carried out during the logging meeting. This second logging-meeting check will produce roughly an additional 15 percent defects (Gilb and Graham 1993, 86). In fact, there is no need to carry out this extra checking if the document is found to be clean enough to exit as a result of initial checking sampling, or if it is so polluted that a major rewrite is required anyway. It is only useful in clean-up mode.

- **Use an optimum number of people on a team to serve the current purpose of Inspection, for example, effectiveness, efficiency, and training.** For 13 years, one large U.S. telecommunications company had 12 to 15 people on each inspection team because each person "had" to be sent there to protect territorial interests. There seemed to be no motivation to cut these costs.

  The number of people needed on an inspection team is a function of the Inspection purposes. By measuring Inspection experiences, it has been established that best effectiveness at finding major defects uses four to six people; best efficiency (effect over cost) needs two to four people; and only 'teaching as a purpose' justifies larger numbers (Kelly 1990; Weller 1993). The results of varying team sizes should be monitored within an organization to discover the optimum for a given document type.

- **Allocate special defect-searching roles to people on the team.** Each person on an Inspection team should be finding different defects. Much like a coach on a ball team, the Inspection team leader should assign specialist roles to team members (for example, identify time and money risks, check against corporate standards for engineering documentation, and check security loopholes) when planning the inspection. Special role checklists help people know exactly what to look for.

Individual Checking

- **Use checking phase data that are collected at the beginning of a logging meeting or beforehand (such as pages checked, majors found, time used, and checking rate) from individual checkers to decide whether it is worth holding a logging meeting.** Older inspections plunge into the logging meeting without forethought and consequently waste time. A process of logging meeting entry evaluation must be carried out before holding a logging meeting. To do this, collect the data from the checkers about their checking rates and major issue density. (Note: to avoid personal conflict, issues—not defects—are logged during the logging meeting. An issue may or may not become a defect, as judged by the responsible product document editor later.) Based on this checking-phase data, make a series of decisions about the logging meeting and the rest of inspection. The most critical decision is whether a meeting is necessary. Other decisions include whether to log minors and whether to continue checking. Shutting down the rest of the inspection entirely is also a possibility.

- **Use the individual checkers' personal notes instead of proper meeting defect logs when the major-issue density is (nonexit level) high, or when there are many minor defects.** Checkers should not be required to use any particular method to make notes during the checking process. In practice, most checkers choose to mark the defective words on a paper document, using underlines, circles, or highlights. Some use electronic notes. It is important that they note, against the defective words, exactly which rule was broken (the issue). A note classifying subjective decisions as to severity (major or minor) of the issue is also required.

Whenever there are more issues than would be an allowable exit level, it is suggested that, with author agreement, the notes made during individual checking (sometimes known as "scratchings") be simply handed over to the author. This is better than pedantically logging all the issues. In such situations, authors must rewrite and resubmit their documents, and they might as well use the rough checking information to correct their work. The usual problem leading to a high defect density is that the author fails to take sources and rules sufficiently seriously.

Logging Meeting

- **At logging meetings, avoid discussions and suggesting fixes.** Inspection is not for talkers and quibblers—it is for professionals committed to making maximum, meaningful progress on the project. It is important to have a good time but not by detailed technical discussion, idle gossip, or insults.

Process Brainstorming

- **Use the defect prevention process on Inspection itself for continuous improvement.** Recognize that systematic continuous improvement of the inspection process is necessary. Initially, this is required not only to improve the Inspection process but also to learn to implement the correct Inspection process and tailor it to the organization.

Exit Conditions

- **Use serious exit conditions, such as "maximum probable remaining major defects per page is 0.2 for exit."** Exit conditions, if correctly formulated and taken seriously, can be crucial. It is wrong to have the customary vote to accept a document once the logged defects are fixed, because this ignores the known factor of the number of remaining unfound defects (a value that is computable and verifiable from past data and experience).

Remember that Inspection processes, like other testing processes, have a maximum effectiveness for a single pass in the range of 30 percent to 88 percent of existing defects. If the maximum probable remaining defect density is a high-quality low count, such as 0.2 majors per page, then it does not matter much if the detected defects are removed at this stage; the document is clean enough (economically speaking) to exit without fixing them. It is probably better to catch them later.

If defect density is high, for example, 20 or more majors per page (quite common), the undetected defects, at say 50 percent effectiveness, are more than enough to make exit uneconomical. If there are 10 majors remaining per page in a 100-page document, there are an expected $9 \times 10 \times 100$ hours of additional project work to clean them up by testing and discovery in the field. It costs an order of magnitude less to find them now. Admittedly, this situation is only the lesser of two evils. Ideally they should have been prevented in the first place using the defect prevention process rather than being cleaned up, even if at an earlier stage than test, using the defect detection process. Management must understand the large-scale economics of this and take action to make clear policy about the levels of major defects per page that will be allowed to escape (Gilb and Graham 1993, 430–431).

Inspection Statistics

- **Build or buy an automated software tool to process Inspection basic data.** Use automated software to capture data-summary data and to present trends and reports (Software Development Technologies 1997). Inspection generates a lot of useful data. It is vital that good computer support be given early, so the process owners and management take the data seriously and the early champions are not overwhelmed.

  The key distinction between Inspections and other review processes is the use of data to manage inspections. For example, the optimum checking rates must be established early and updated as they change, through continuous improvement. It also is vital to statistically see the consequences of inadequate exit levels (too many major defects floating downstream), which then must be caught with expensive testing processes.

- **Put Inspection artifacts on a company Web site.** If an organization has an intranet, all relevant Inspection artifacts, standards, experiences, statistics, and problems should be added as soon as possible.

- **Measure the benefit from using Inspections.** Inspection should always be highly profitable, for example, 10-to-1 ROI. If not, then it is time to adjust the Inspection process or to stop it. Benefits to be measured include rework costs, predictability, productivity, document quality, and ROI (Haley et al. 1995). Inspection profitability must be evaluated for each type of specification individually. In general, the upstream Inspections (requirements, contracts, bids) will be the most profitable.

SUMMARY

The art of Inspection has progressed considerably since it was first publicly documented by IBM. It has shifted focus from cleanup to sampling, measurement, exit control, and defect injection prevention. By taking the technical points that made inspection strong at IBM and elsewhere and combining them with the recent process improvements, inspection will continue to be a powerful software process tool. Ignoring the process improvements makes it likely that one will end up with a costly failure of a process.

ACKNOWLEDGMENT

Thanks are due to Lindsey Brodie for helping edit this article.

REFERENCES

Fagan, M. 1976. Design and code inspections to reduce errors in program development. *IBM Systems Journal* 15, no. 3: 182–211. (Reprinted in *IBM Systems Journal* 38, no. 2: 259–287 or see URL document www.almaden.ibm.com/journal.)

Gilb, T., and D. Graham. 1993. *Software inspection.* London: Addison-Wesley Longman.

Haley, T., B. Ireland, E. Wojtaszek, D. Nash, and R. Dion. 1995. *Raytheon electronic systems experience in software process improvement* (CMU/SEI-95-TR-017). Pittsburgh: Software Engineering Institute, Carnegie Mellon University (or see URL document www.sei.cmu.edu/products/publications/documents/95.reports/95.tr.017.html).

Holland, D. 1999. Document inspection as an agent of change. *Software Quality Professional* (December): 22–33. (See also chapter 5 of Jarvis and Hayes, eds. 1999. *Dare to be excellent.* Englewood Cliffs, NJ: Prentice Hall PTR.)

Holland, D. 1994. See URL document www.pimsl.com/inforserver/public/spi/index.hts/ .

Humphrey, W. 1995. *A discipline for software engineering*. New York: Addison-Wesley.

Kaplan, C., R. Clark, and V. Tang. 1994. *Secrets of software quality: 40 innovations from IBM*. New York: McGraw Hill.

Kelly, J. 1990. An analysis of Jet Propulsion Laboratory's two year experience with software inspections. In *Proceedings of the Minnowbrook workshop on software engineering*. Blue Lake, NY.

Kelly, J. 1990. An analysis of defect density found during software inspection. In *Proceedings of 15th annual software engineering workshop* (NASA SEL-90-006). Pasadena, CA: Jet Propulsion Labs.

Kohli, O. R., and R. A. Radice. 1976. Low-level design inspection specification. *IBM Technical Report* (TR 21.629). Armonk, NY: IBM.

Mills, H. D., and Linger, R. C. 1987. Cleanroom software engineering. *IEEE Software* (September): 19–25.

Mills, H. D. 1972. *Mathematical foundations for structured programming*. (FSC 71-6012). Bethesda, MD: IBM Corporation Federal Systems Division.

Pence, J. L. P., and S. E. Hon III. 1993. Building software quality into telecommunications network systems. *Quality Progress*. (October): 95–97.

Radice, R. A., J. T. Harding, P. E. Munnis, and R. W. Philips. 1999. A programming process study. *IBM System Journals* 2 and 3.

Radice, R. A., and R. W. Phillips. 1988. *Software engineering, an industrial approach*, vol. 1. Englewood Cliffs, N. J.: Prentice Hall.

Raytheon. 1995. *The Raytheon report*. URL document www.sei.cmu.edu/products/publications/documents/95.reports/95.tr.017.html . Also see URL document www.Result-Planning.com and www.stsc.hill.af.mil/SWTesting .

Software Development Technologies. 1997. Software Inspections Automation, Edward Kit, URL document www.stdcorp.com .

Weller, Ed. F. 1993. Lessons from three years of inspection data. *IEEE Software* (September): 38–45.

**CMM is a trademark of Carnegie Mellon University.

BIOGRAPHY

Tom Gilb has been an independent consultant since 1960. He is the author of several books, including *Principles of Software Engineering Management* (1988) and *Software Inspection* (1993, with Dorothy Graham). Gilb emigrated to Europe from his birthplace, California, in 1956 and joined IBM Norway in 1958. He spends approximately half his time working in the United States and half in Europe. Gilb can be contacted at Iver Holtersvei 2, N-1410 Kolbotn, Norway, or by e-mail at Gilb@ACM.org .

CHAPTER 6.2

A Testing Maturity Model for Software Test Process Assessment and Improvement

Ilene Burnstein, Ariya Homyen, Taratip Suwanassart, Gary Saxena,
and Rob Grom, Illinois Institute of Technology

*T*his article reports on the development of a testing maturity model (TMM) designed to support software development organizations in assessing and improving their software testing processes. The internal structure of the TMM is described, as well as the model framework of maturity goals, subgoals, and activities tasks and responsibilities that support the incremental growth of test process maturity. This article also addresses the TMM Assessment Model, which allows organizations to determine the current state of their testing processes and provides guidance for implementing actions to support improvements. Results from a trial evaluation of the TMM questionnaire in industry are discussed, and feedback received from the software industry regarding the TMM and maturity model integration issues is presented.

Key words: inspections, maturity models, process assessment, software processes, software quality management

INTRODUCTION

Software systems are becoming increasingly important in modern society. They have a strong impact on vital operations in domains such as the military, finance, and telecommunications. For this reason, it is imperative to address quality issues that relate to both the software development process and the software product. The authors' research focuses on process and its impact on quality issues. The authors are developing a testing maturity model (TMM) designed to assist software development organizations in evaluating and improving their testing processes (Burnstein, Suwanassart, and Carlson 1996a, 1996b, 1996c). The TMM complements the Capability Maturity Model (CMM) by specifically addressing those issues important to test managers, test specialists, and software quality professionals. Testing as defined in the TMM is applied in its broadest sense to encompass all software quality-related activities. The authors believe that applying the TMM maturity criteria will improve the testing process and have a positive impact on software quality, software engineering productivity, and cycle-time reduction efforts.

APPROACH TO MODEL DEVELOPMENT

The TMM is designed to support assessment and improvement drives from within an organization. It is to be used by:

- An internal assessment team to identify the current testing capability state
- Upper management to initiate a testing improvement program

- Software quality assurance engineers to develop and implement process improvement plans
- Development teams to improve testing effectiveness
- Users/clients to define their role in the testing process

There are several existing process evaluation and assessment models, including the Software Capability Maturity Model (SW-CMM) (Paulk et al. 1995, 1993a,1993b), ISO 9001 (Coallier 1994), BOOTSTRAP (Bicego and Kuvaja 1993), and SPICE (Paulk and Konrad 1994). None of these models, however, focuses primarily on the testing process. The widely used SW-CMM does not adequately address testing issues. For example, in the SW-CMM:

- The concept of testing maturity is not addressed
- Inadequate attention is paid to the role of high-quality testing as a process improvement mechanism
- Testing issues are not adequately addressed in the key process areas
- Quality-related issues such as testability, test adequacy criteria, test planning, and software certification are not satisfactorily addressed

Because of the important role of testing in software process and product quality and the limitations of existing process assessment models, the authors have focused their research on developing a TMM. The following components support their objectives:

- **A set of levels that define a testing maturity hierarchy.** Each level represents a stage in the evolution to a mature testing process. Movement to a higher level implies that lower-level practices continue to be in place.

- **A set of maturity goals and subgoals for each level (except level 1).** The maturity goals identify testing improvement goals that must be addressed to achieve maturity at that level. The subgoals define the scope, boundaries, and needed accomplishments for a particular level. There are also activities, tasks, and responsibilities (ATRs) associated with each maturity goal that are needed to support it.

- **An assessment model consisting of three components.** These components include: 1) a set of maturity goal-related questions designed to assess current test process maturity; 2) a set of guidelines designed to select and instruct the assessment team; and 3) an assessment procedure with steps to guide the assessment team through test process evaluation and improvement.

The general requirements for TMM development are as follows. The model must be acceptable to the software development community and be based on agreed-upon software engineering principles and practices. At the higher maturity levels it should be flexible enough to accommodate future best practices. The model must also allow for the development of testing process maturity in structured step-wise phases that follow natural process evolution. There must also be a support mechanism for test process assessment and improvement. To satisfy these requirements, the following four sources served as the principal inputs to TMM development:

1. **The CMM.** The SW-CMM is a comprehensive process evaluation and improvement model developed by the Software Engineering Institute that has been widely accepted and applied by the software industry (Paulk et al. 1995, 1993a, 1993b). Like the SW-CMM, the TMM uses the concept of maturity levels as a script for testing process evaluation and improvement. The TMM levels have a structural framework as do those in the SW-CMM. The authors have added a

component called "critical views" to their framework to formally include the key groups necessary for test process maturity growth. Both models require that all of the capabilities at each lower level be included in succeeding levels. To support the self-assessment process, the TMM also uses the questionnaire/interview evaluation approach of the SW-CMM. Besides these structural similarities, the TMM is visualized as a complement to the SW-CMM. This view is essential, since a mature testing process is dependent on general process maturity, and organizational investment in assessments can be optimized if assessments in several process areas can be carried out in parallel. TMM/SW-CMM relationships are discussed in more detail later.

The TMM reflects the evolutionary pattern of testing process maturity growth documented over the last several decades. This model design approach will expedite movement to higher levels of the TMM as it will allow organizations to achieve incremental test process improvement in a way that follows natural process evolution. Designers of the SW-CMM also considered historical evolution an important factor in process improvement model development. For example, concepts from Philip B. Crosby's quality management maturity grid, which describes five evolutionary stages in the adaptation of quality practices, were adjusted for the software process and used as input for developing the SW-CMM maturity levels (Paulk et al. 1995).

2. **Gelperin and Hetzel's Evolutionary Testing Model.** The authors used the historical model provided in a paper by Gelperin and Hetzel (1988) as the foundation for historical-level differentiation in the TMM. The Gelperin and Hetzel model describes phases and test goals for the 1950s through the 1990s. The initial period is described as "debugging oriented," during which most software development organizations had not clearly differentiated between testing and debugging. Testing was an ad hoc activity associated with debugging to remove bugs from programs. Testing has since progressed to a "prevention-oriented" period, which describes best current testing practices and reflects the optimizing level 5 of both the SW-CMM and the TMM.

3. **Current industrial testing practices.** A survey of industrial practices also provided important input to TMM level definition (Durant 1993). It illustrated the best and worst testing environments in the software industry at that time, and has allowed the authors to extract realistic benchmarks by which to evaluate and improve testing practices.

4. **Beizer's Progressive Phases of Tester's Mental Model.** The authors have also incorporated concepts associated with Beizer's evolutionary model of the individual testers' thinking process (1990). Its influence on TMM development is based on the premise that a mature testing organization is built on the skills, abilities, and attitudes of the individuals who work within it.

At the time the TMM was being developed, two other models that support testing process assessment and improvement were reported. Gelperin and Hayashi's model (1996), the Testability Maturity Model, uses a staged architecture for its framework. Three maturity levels are described, along with six key support areas that are reported to be analogous to key process areas in the SW-CMM. The three levels are loosely defined as weak, basic, and strong. The internal level structure is not described in detail in the report, nor is it clear where the six key support areas fit into the three-level hierarchy. A simple score card that covers 20 test-process-related issues is provided to help an organization determine its Testability Maturity Model level (Gelperin 1996). No formal assessment process is reported.

Koomen and Pol (1998) describe what they call a Test Process Improvement Model (TPI), which does not follow a staged architecture. Their model contains 20 key areas, each with different maturity levels. Each level contains several checkpoints that are helpful for determining maturity. In addition, improvement suggestions for reaching a target level are provided with the model, which are helpful for generating action plans.

In contrast to these researchers, the authors have used a systematic approach to developing their TMM based on the four sources described, allowing them to satisfy the requirements for TMM development. The authors believe that their developmental approach has resulted in a TMM that is:

- More comprehensive and fine-grained in its level structure
- Supported by a well-defined assessment model
- Well defined and easier to understand and use
- Able to provide greater coverage of test-related issues
- Better suited to support incremental test process maturity growth

The TMM as described in this article is also more compatible and conceptually similar to the SW-CMM. This is beneficial to organizations involved in SW-CMM assessment and improvement drives.

THE MODEL STRUCTURE: A FRAMEWORK FOR THE LEVELS

The TMM is characterized by five testing maturity levels within a framework of goals, subgoals, activities, tasks, and responsibilities. The model framework is shown in Figure 1 (Burnstein, Suwanassart, and Carlson 1996a,1996b, 1996c). Each level implies a specific testing maturity. With the exception of level 1, several maturity goals, which identify key process areas, are indicated at each level. The maturity goals identify testing improvement goals that must be addressed to achieve maturity at that level. To be placed at a level, an organization must satisfy that level's maturity goals.

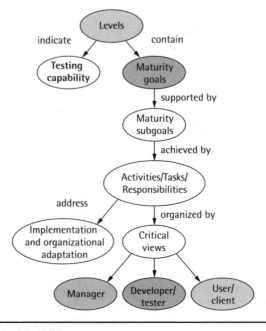

Figure 1   The framework of the TMM.

Each maturity goal is supported by one or more maturity subgoals, which specify less-abstract objectives and define the scope, boundaries, and needed accomplishments for a particular level. The maturity subgoals are achieved through a set of ATRs. The ATRs address implementation and organizational adaptation issues at a specific level. Activities and tasks are defined in terms of actions that must be performed at a given level to improve testing capability; they are linked to organizational commitments. Responsibility for these ATRs is assigned to the three groups that the authors believe are the key participants in the testing process: managers, developers/testers, and users/clients. In the model they are referred to as "the three critical views." The manager's view involves commitment and the ability to perform activities and tasks related to improving testing process maturity. The developer/tester's view encompasses the technical activities and tasks that when applied, constitute mature testing practices. The user/client's view is defined as a cooperating, or supporting, view. The developers/testers work with user/client groups on quality-related activities and tasks that concern user-oriented needs. The focus is on soliciting user/client support, consensus, and participation in activities such as requirements analysis, usability testing, and acceptance test planning.

MATURITY GOALS AT THE TMM LEVELS

The operational framework of the TMM provides a sequence of hierarchical levels that contain the maturity goals, subgoals, and ATRs that define the state of testing maturity of an organization at a particular level, and identify areas that an organization must focus on to improve its testing process. The hierarchy of testing maturity goals is shown in Figure 2 (Burnstein, Suwanassart, and Carlson 1996a, 1996b, 1996c). Following is a brief description of the maturity goals for all levels (except level 1, which has no maturity goals).

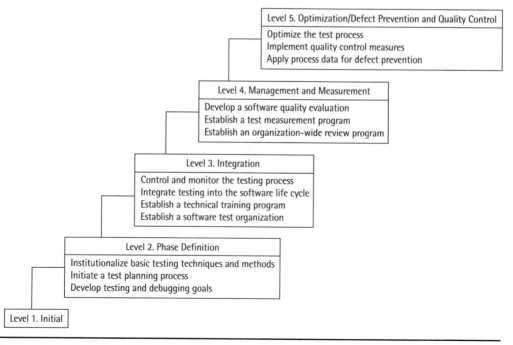

Figure 2 TMM maturity goals by level.

Level 2: Phase Definition

At TMM level 2 an organization begins to address both the technical and managerial aspects of testing in order to mature. A testing phase is defined in the software lifecycle. Testing is planned, is supported by basic testing techniques and tools, and is repeatable over all software projects. It is separated from debugging, the latter of which is difficult to plan. Following are the level-2 maturity goals:

1. **Develop testing and debugging goals.** This calls for a clear distinction between testing and debugging. The goals, tasks, activities, and tools for each must be identified and responsibilities must be assigned. Management must accommodate and institutionalize both processes. Separating these two processes is essential for testing maturity growth since they are different in goals, methods, and psychology. Testing at TMM level 2 is now a planned activity and therefore can be managed. Managing debugging, however, is more complex, because it is difficult to predict the nature of the defects that will occur and how long it will take to repair them. To reduce the process unpredictability often caused by large-scale debugging-related activities, the project manager must allocate time and resources for defect localization, repair, and retest. At higher levels of the TMM this will be facilitated by the availability of detailed defect and repair data from past projects.

2. **Initiate a test planning process.** Planning is essential for a process that is to be repeated, defined, and managed. Test planning requires stating objectives, analyzing risks, outlining strategies, and developing test design specifications and test cases. Test planning also involves documenting test-completion criteria to determine when the testing is complete. In addition, the test plan must address the allocation of resources, the scheduling of test activities, and the responsibilities for testing on the unit, integration, system, and acceptance levels.

3. **Institutionalize basic testing techniques and methods.** To improve testing process maturity, basic testing techniques and methods must be applied across the organization. How and when these techniques and methods are to be applied and any basic tool support for them should be clearly specified. Examples of basic techniques and methods include black-box and white-box (glass-box) testing strategies; use of a requirements validation matrix; and the division of execution-based testing into subphases such as unit, integration, system, and acceptance testing.

Level 3: Integration

Testing at TMM level 3 is expanded into a set of well-defined activities that are integrated into all phases of the software lifecycle. At this level management also supports the formation and training of a software test group. These are specialists who are responsible for all levels of testing, and along with software quality assurance professionals, serve as liaisons with the users/clients to ensure their participation in the testing process. Following are the level-3 maturity goals:

1. **Establish a software test organization.** Since testing in its fullest sense has a great influence on product quality and consists of complex activities that are usually done under tight schedules and high pressure, it is necessary to have a well-trained and dedicated group in charge of this process. The test group formed at TMM level 3 oversees test planning, test execution and recording, defect tracking, test metrics, the test database, test reuse, test tracking, and evaluation.

2. **Establish a technical training program.** A technical training program ensures that a skilled staff is available to the testing group. At level 3, the staff is trained in test planning, testing methods, standards, techniques, and tools. The training program also prepares the staff for the review process and for supporting user participation in testing and review activities.

3. **Integrate testing into the software lifecycle.** Management and technical staff now realize that carrying out testing activities in parallel with all lifecycle phases is critical for test process maturity and software product quality. Support for this integration may come from application of a development model that supports integration of test-related activities into the lifecycle. As a result of the integration efforts, test planning is now initiated early in the lifecycle. User input to the testing process is solicited through established channels during several of the lifecycle phases.

4. **Control and monitor the testing process.** Monitoring and controlling the testing process provides visibility to its associated activities and ensures that the testing process proceeds according to plan. Test progress is determined by comparing the actual test work products, test effort, costs, and schedule to the test plan. Support for controlling and monitoring comes from: standards for test products, test milestones, test logs, test-related contingency plans, and test metrics that can be used to evaluate test progress and test effectiveness. Configuration management for test-related items also provides essential support for this maturity goal.

Level 4: Management and Measurement

At TMM level 4 the testing process becomes fully managed; that is, it is now planned, directed, staffed, organized, and controlled (Thayer 1998). Test-related measurements are defined, collected, analyzed, and used by managers, software quality assurance staff members, and testers. The definition of a testing activity is expanded to formally include inspections at all phases of the lifecycle. Peer reviews and inspections serve as complements to execution-based testing. They are viewed as quality control procedures that can be applied to remove defects from software artifacts. Following are the level-4 maturity goals:

1. **Establish an organizationwide review program.** At TMM level 3 an organization integrates testing activities into the software lifecycle. The emphasis is on developing test plans early in the development process. At level 4 this integration is augmented by the establishment of a formal review program. Peer reviews, in the form of inspections and walk throughs, are considered testing activities and are conducted at all phases of the lifecycle to identify, catalog, and remove defects from software work products and test work products early and effectively. An extended version of the V-model as shown in Suwanassart (1996) can be used to support the integration of peer-review activities into the software lifecycle. Other means for integration of review/test activities can also be used.

2. **Establish a test measurement program.** A test measurement program is essential for evaluating the quality and effectiveness of the testing process, assessing the productivity of the testing personnel, and monitoring test process improvement. A test measurement program must be carefully planned and managed. Test data to be collected must be identified and decisions made on how they are to be used and by whom.

3. **Software quality evaluation.** One purpose of software quality evaluation at this level of the TMM is to relate software quality issues to the adequacy of the testing process. Software quality evaluation requires that an organization define measurable quality attributes and quality goals for evaluating each type of software work product. Quality goals are tied to testing process adequacy since a mature testing process should lead to software that is reliable, usable, maintainable, portable, and secure.

Level 5: Optimization/Defect Prevention and Quality Control

There are several test-related objectives at the highest level of the TMM. At this level one tests to ensure the software satisfies its specification, that it is reliable, and that one can establish a certain level of confidence in its reliability. Testing is also done to detect and prevent defects. The latter is achieved by collecting and analyzing defect data.

Since the testing process is now repeatable, defined, managed, and measured, it can be fine-tuned and continuously improved. Management provides leadership and motivation and supports the infrastructure necessary for continuously improving product and process quality. Following are the level-5 maturity goals:

1. **Application of process data for defect prevention.** Mature organizations are able to learn from their past. Following this philosophy, organizations at the highest level of the TMM record defects, analyze defect patterns, and identify root causes of errors. Action plans are developed, and actions are taken to prevent defect recurrence. There is a defect-prevention team that is responsible for defect-prevention activities. Team members interact with developers to apply defect-prevention activities throughout the lifecycle.

2. **Quality control.** At level 4 of the TMM organizations focus on testing for a group of quality-related attributes, such as correctness, security, portability, interoperability, usability, and maintainability. At level 5 organizations use statistical sampling, measurements of confidence levels, trustworthiness, and reliability goals to drive the testing process. The testing group and the software quality assurance group are quality leaders; they work with software designers and implementers to incorporate techniques and tools to reduce defects and improve software quality. Automated tools support the running and rerunning of test cases and defect collection and analysis. Usage modeling, based on a characterization of the population of intended uses of the software in its intended operational environment, is used to perform statistical testing (Walton, Poore, and Trammell 1995).

3. **Test process optimization.** At the highest level of the TMM the testing process is subject to continuous improvement across projects and across the organization. The test process is quantified and can be fine-tuned so that maturity growth is an ongoing process. An organizational infrastructure consisting of policies, standards, training, facilities, tools, and organizational structures that has been put in place by progressing up the TMM hierarchy supports this continuous maturity growth.

Optimizing the testing process involves: 1) identifying testing practices that need to be improved; 2) implementing the improvements; 3) tracking progress; 4) evaluating new test-related tools and technologies for adaptation; and 5) supporting technology transfer.

THE TMM ASSESSMENT MODEL: AN APPROACH TO DEVELOPMENT

The TMM Assessment Model (TMM-AM) is necessary to support self-assessment of the testing process. It uses the TMM as its reference model. The authors' research objectives for the TMM-AM were to: 1) provide a framework based on a set of principles in which software engineering practitioners could assess and evaluate their software testing processes; 2) provide a foundation for test process improvement through data analysis and action planning; and 3) contribute to the growing body of knowledge in software process engineering. The TMM-AM is not intended to be used for certification of the testing process by an external body.

The SW-CMM and SPICE assessment models were used to guide development of the TMM-AM (Paulk et al. 1995,1993a,1993b; ISO 1995; Zubrow et al. 1994). The goals were for the resulting TMM-AM to be compliant with the CMM Appraisal Framework so that in the future, organizations would be able to perform parallel assessments in multiple process areas (Masters and Bothwell 1995). A set of 16 principles has been developed to support TMM-AM design (Homyen 1998). Based on the 16 principles, the SW-CMM Assessment Model, SPICE, and the CMM Appraisal Framework, the authors have developed a set of components for the TMM-AM.

THE TMM-AM COMPONENTS

The TMM-AM has three major components: the assessment procedure, the assessment instrument (a questionnaire), and team training and selection criteria. A set of inputs and outputs is also prescribed for the TMM-AM (Homyen 1998). The relationship among these items is shown in Figure 3.

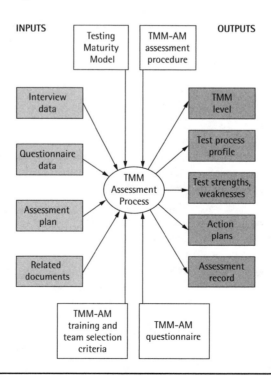

Figure 3   The TMM assessment process: components and inputs/outputs.

The Assessment Procedure

The TMM-AM assessment procedure consists of a series of steps that guide an assessment team in carrying out testing process self-assessment. The principal goals for the TMM assessment procedure are: 1) to support the development of a test process profile and the determination of a TMM level; 2) to guide the organization in developing action plans for test process improvement; 3) to ensure the assessment is executed with efficient use of the organizations' resources; and 4) to guide the assessment team in collecting, organizing, and analyzing the assessment data. A brief summary of the steps in the assessment procedure follows.

1. **Preparation.** This step includes selecting and training the assessment team, choosing the team leader(s), developing the assessment plan, selecting the projects, and preparing the organizational units participating in the assessment.

2. **Conducting the assessment.** In this step the team collects and records assessment information from interviews, presentations, questionnaires, and relevant documents. A test management support system as described by Hearns and Garcia (1998) is very helpful for automatically collecting and organizing test process related data and for use in cross-checking data from multiple sources. The TMM traceability matrix, as described later, can also be used to check data accuracy, consistency, and objectivity. This helps ensure that assessment results will be reliable and reproducible.

   An organization's TMM level, which is a measure of its current testing maturity level, is determined by analyzing the collected data and using a ranking algorithm. The ranking algorithm developed for the TMM-AM is similar to the algorithm described by Masters and Bothwell (1995) in their work on the CMM Appraisal Framework. The TMM ranking algorithm requires first a rating of the maturity subgoals, then the maturity goals, and finally the maturity level (Homyen 1998).

3. **Reporting the assessment outputs.** The TMM-AM outputs include a process profile, a TMM level, and the assessment record. The assessment team prepares the process profile, which gives a summary of the state of the organizations' testing process. The profile also includes a summary of test process strengths and weaknesses, as well as recommendations for improvements.

   The TMM level is a value from 1 to 5 that indicates the current testing process maturity level of the organization. Level values correspond to the testing maturity hierarchy shown in Figure 2.

   The assessment record is also completed in this step. It is a written account of the actual assessment that includes: names of assessment team members, assessment inputs and outputs, actual schedules and costs, tasks performed, task duration, persons responsible, data collected, and problems that occurred.

4. **Analyzing the assessment outputs.** The assessment team, along with management and software quality engineers, now use the assessment outputs to identify and prioritize improvement goals. An approach to prioritization is described in Homyen (1998). Quantitative test process improvement targets need to be established in this phase. The targets will support the action plans developed in the next step.

5. **Action planning.** An action-planning team develops plans that focus on high-priority improvements identified in the previous step. This team can include assessors, software engineering process group members, software quality assurance staff, and/or opinion leaders chosen from the assessment participants (Puffer and Litter 1997). The action plan describes specific activities, resources, and schedules needed to improve existing practices and add missing practices so the organization can move up to the next TMM level.

6. **Implementing improvement.** After the action plans have been developed and approved they are applied to selected pilot projects. The pilot projects need to be monitored and tracked to ensure task progress and goal achievement. Favorable results with the pilot projects set the stage for organizational adaptation of the new process.

The TMM Assessment Questionnaire

Assessment instruments, such as the questionnaire used by the authors, are needed to support the collection and analysis of information from an assessment, maintain a record of results, and provide information for assessment post mortem analysis. Use of a questionnaire supports CMM Appraisal Framework compliance (Masters and Bothwell 1995), facilitates integration with other process assessment instruments (Zubrow et al. 1994), ensures assessment coverage of all ATRs identified in each maturity goal for each level of the TMM, provides a framework in which to collect and store assessment data, and provides guidelines for the assessors as to which areas should be the focus of an interview.

It should be noted that the TMM questionnaire is not the sole source of input for determining TMM rank and generating testing assessment results. The data from completed questionnaires must be augmented and confirmed using information collected from interviews and presentations, as well as by inspection of relevant documents.

The TMM questionnaire consists of eight parts: 1) instructions for use; 2) respondent background; 3) organizational background; 4) maturity goal and subgoal questions; 5) testing tool use questions; 6) testing trends questions; 7) recommendations for questionnaire improvement; and 8) a glossary of testing terms (Homyen 1998; Grom 1998).

Parts 2 and 3 of the questionnaire are used to gather information about the respondent, the organization, and the units that will be involved in the TMM assessment. The maturity goal and subgoal questions in part 3 are organized by TMM version 1.0 levels and include a developer/tester, manager, and user/client view. The questions are designed to determine the extent to which the organization has mechanisms in place to achieve the maturity goals and resolve maturity issues at each TMM level. The testing tool component records the type and frequency of test-tool use, which can help the team make recommendations for the future. The authors added the testing-trends section to provide a perspective on how the testing process in the organization has been evolving over the last several years. This information is useful for preparing the assessment profile and the assessment record. The recommendations component allows respondents to give TMM-AM developers feedback on the clarity, completeness, and usability of the questionnaire.

Assessment Training and Team Selection Criteria

The authors have designed the TMM-AM to help an organization assess its testing process (the assessment is internal to the organization—it has initiated the drive toward test process improvement, and it will be the sole possessor of the assessment data and results). Upper management must support the self-assessment and improvement efforts, ensure that proper resources will be available for conducting the assessment, and ensure that recommendations for improvements will be implemented.

A trained assessment team made up of members from within the organization is needed. Assessment team members should understand assessment goals, have the proper knowledge experience and skills, have strong communication skills, and be committed to test process improvement. Assessment team size should be appropriate for the purpose and scope of the assessment (Homyen 1998).

The authors have adapted SPICE guidelines for selecting and preparing an effective assessment team (ISO 1995). Preparation, which is conducted by the assessment team leader, includes topics such as an overview of the TMM, interviewing techniques, and data analysis. Training activities include team-building exercises, a walk through the assessment process, filling out a sample questionnaire and other assessment-related forms, and learning to prepare final reports.

Forms and Tools for Assessment Support

To support an assessment team, the authors have developed several forms and a tool that implements a Web-based version of the TMM questionnaire (Grom 1998). These forms and tools are important to ensure that the assessments are performed in a consistent, repeatable manner to reduce assessor subjectivity and to ensure the validity, usability, and comparability of the assessment results. The tools and forms include the process profile and assessment record forms, whose roles have been described previously, as well as the following:

- **Team training data recording template.** This template allows the team leader to record and validate team training data. Completed instances of the template can be used in future assessments to make necessary improvements to the assessment training process.

- **Traceability matrix.** The traceability matrix, in conjunction with the assessment team training procedure, the team data recording template, and the traceability matrix review is introduced to address the issue of interrater agreement and general assessment reliability (El Emam et al. 1996). The matrix, which is completed as data are collected, allows the assessors to identify sources of data, cross-check the consistency and correctness of the data, and resolve any data-related issues. Review of the matrix data by the assessment team helps eliminate biases and inaccuracies. The matrix and the matrix review process help ensure data integrity and reproducibility of results.

- **Web-based questionnaire.** A complete version of the TMM-AM questionnaire (version 1.1) appears at www.cs.iit.edu/~tmm . The Web-based questionnaire was designed so assessment data could easily be collected from distributed sites and organized and stored in a central data repository that could be parsed for later analysis. Tool design also allows it to run on multiple operating systems and collect data from assessment teams around the world, thus providing support for test process assessment to local and global organizations. A detailed description of tool development is given in Grom (1998).

PRELIMINARY DATA FROM TRIAL QUESTIONNAIRE USAGE

Software engineers from two software development organizations evaluated the TMM questionnaire (Homyen 1998). The questionnaire evaluation for this study focused on: 1) clarity; 2) organization; 3) ease of use; and 4) coverage of TMM maturity goals and subgoals. Feedback from the evaluation made it possible to revise and reorganize the TMM questions for better understandability and sequencing. The glossary of terms was also upgraded. These revisions resulted in version 1.1 of the TMM questionnaire, which is displayed on the web site described earlier.

Trial usage of the TMM questionnaire focused on applying the questionnaire to software development and maintenance groups in actual industrial settings. The purpose of the trial usage was to further evaluate the usability of the questionnaire, experiment with the ranking algorithm using actual industrial data, generate sample action plans, and study problems of testing process improvement in real-world environments. One interesting result of the experiment was that although both organizations were evaluated at TMM level 1, the strengths and weaknesses of each were quite different. One of the organizations did satisfy several of the maturity goals at the higher levels of the TMM. Given the state of the existing test process for the latter, it should be able to reach TMM level 2 in a relatively short time period. More details concerning these experiments can be found in Homyen (1998).

It must be emphasized that a complete TMM assessment was not done in these experiments; a TMM level was determined only with the questionnaire data. In a formal TMM assessment, documents, interviews, and measurement data would also help determine TMM level. In addition, data integrity would be confirmed using the traceability matrix, and a more comprehensive view of strengths and weaknesses would be obtained for the final test process profile. While these small-scale experiments are promising with respect to the usability of the TMM questionnaire and the ranking algorithm, more industry-based experiments are needed to further evaluate the TMM with respect to the organization of the levels, the distribution of the maturity goals over the levels, and the appropriateness of the ATRs. The usefulness and effectiveness of the TMM for large-scale test process assessment and improvement must also be evaluated. The authors are now engaged in planning for these experiments and identifying organizations that are willing to participate in case studies.

TMM EVALUATION AND FEEDBACK

Throughout the development of the TMM the authors received feedback from software engineers, software testers, managers, and software quality professionals from more than 35 organizations around the world. Comments confirmed the need for a TMM since most correspondents believe that existing process improvement models do not adequately support the concept of testing process maturity and do not sufficiently address the special issues relevant to testing process assessment and improvement. An important issue for many practitioners was integration of maturity models and process assessments that would result in: 1) a common architecture and vocabulary; 2) common training requirements; and 3) support for performance of parallel assessments in multiple process areas. Fulfilling these requirements would ensure effective use of organizational resources, both for the assessment and the process improvement efforts.

Initially the authors viewed the TMM as a complement to the SW-CMM. They believed it would simplify parallel process improvement drives in industry if both the SW-CMM and TMM had corresponding levels and goals. In addition, they believed (and still believe) that test process maturity is supported by, and benefits from, general process maturity. Therefore, as part of the initial TMM development effort they identified relationships between TMM/SW-CMM levels and supporting key process areas. A matrix showing these relationships is shown in Figure 4 (Burnstein, Suwanassart, and Carlson 1996b).

In the course of their research, however, the authors realized that maturity model integration issues and intermodel support relationships are more complex than simple-level correspondences. Meeting industry requirements for maturity model integration required focusing research efforts in a new direction. These efforts have resulted in the development of a framework for building and integrating process maturity models for software development subdomains such as design and testing. The framework includes procedures, templates, and checklists to support maturity model development and integration in a systematic way (Saxena 1999). A publication on the work accomplished in this project is currently being prepared.

TMM Level	SW-CMM Level	Supporting Key Process Areas
2	2	Requirements management, project planning, software configuration management
3	2	Project tracking and oversight, SQA goals
3	3	Organization process focus, organization process definition, training programs
4	3	Peer reviews
4	4	Software quality management, quantitative process management
5	5	Process change management, technology change management, defect prevention

Figure 4   Examples of support for TMM maturity levels from SW-CMM key process areas.

SUMMARY

The authors have been developing a TMM to help organizations assess and improve their software testing processes. Feedback from industry concerning the TMM shows a need for a specific focus on testing process maturity and a need for a specialized test process assessment and improvement model.

Now that the complete model has been developed and trial tested, there must be wider industrial application of the TMM-AM. This will provide the additional data necessary to further evaluate and adapt the TMM so that it becomes an accepted and effective tool for test process improvement. Plans for these case studies are now being developed.

The authors' future plans also include the development of a tester's workbench that will recommend testing tools to support achievement of the maturity goals at each TMM level, as well as refinement of the TMM to include additional testing process concepts, such as certification of components. Research on integration mapping of the TMM with other maturity models also continues. The latter is especially important since success in this area will allow organizations to carry out parallel assessment and improvement efforts in multiple process domains, thus making optimal use of organizational resources.

REFERENCES

Beizer, B. 1990. *Software system testing techniques.* 2nd ed. New York: Van Nostrand Reinhold.

Bicego, A., and D. Kuvaja. 1993. Bootstrap, Europe's assessment method. *IEEE Software* 10, no. 3: 93–95.

Burnstein, I, T. Suwanassart, and C. Carlson. 1996a. The development of a testing maturity model. In *Proceedings of the ninth international quality week conference.* San Francisco: The Software Research Institute.

———. 1996b. Developing a testing maturity model: Part 1. *CrossTalk, Journal of Defense Software Engineering* 9, no. 8: 21–24.

———. 1996c. Developing a testing maturity model: Part 2. *CrossTalk, Journal of Defense Software Engineering* 9, no. 9: 19–26.

Coallier, F. 1994. How ISO 9001 fits into the software world. *IEEE Software* 11, no. 1: 98–100.

Durant, J. 1993. Software testing practices survey report (TR5-93). Software Practices Research Center.

El Emam, K., D. Goldenson, L. Briand, and P. Marshall. 1996. Interrater agreement in SPICE-based assessments: Some preliminary reports. In *Proceedings of the fourth international conference on the software process.* Los Alamitos, CA: IEEE Computer Society Press.

Gelperin, D., and B. Hetzel. 1988. The growth of software testing. *Communications of the Association of Computing Machinery* 31, no. 6: 687–695.

Gelperin, D., and A. Hayashi. 1996. How to support better software testing. *Application Trends* (May): 42–48.

Gelperin, D. 1996. What's your testability maturity? *Application Trends* (May): 50–53.

Grom, R. 1998. *Report on a TMM assessment support tool.* Chicago: Illinois Institute of Technology.

Hearns, J., and S. Garcia. 1998. Automated test team management—it works! In *Proceedings of the 10th software engineering process group conference.* Pittsburgh: Software Engineering Institute.

Homyen, A. 1998. An assessment model to determine test process maturity. PhD thesis, Illinois Institute of Technology.

International Organization for Standardization. 1995. ISO/IEC Software process assessment working draft—Part 3: Rating processes, version 1.0, Part 5: Construction, selection and use of assessment instruments and tools, version 1.0, Part 7: Guide for use in process improvement, version 1.0. Geneva, Switzerland: International Organization for Standardization.

Koomen, T., and M. Pol. 1998. Improvement of the test process using TPI. Available at www.iquip.nl .

Masters, S., and C. Bothwell. 1995. *A CMM appraisal framework, version 1.0* (CMU/SEI-95-TR-001). Pittsburgh: Software Engineering Institute, Carnegie Mellon University.

Paulk, M., C. Weber, B. Curtis, and M. Chrissis. 1995 *The capability maturity model guideline for improving the software process.* Reading, MA: Addison-Wesley.

Paulk, M., and M. Konrad. 1994. An overview of ISO's SPICE project. *American Programmer* 7, no. 2: 16–20.

Paulk, M., B. Curtis, M. Chrissis, and C. Weber. 1993a. Capability maturity model, version 1.1. *IEEE Software* 10, no. 4: 18–27.

Paulk, M., C. Weber, S. Garcia, M. Chrissis, and M. Bush. 1993b. *Key practices of the capability maturity model, version 1.1* (CMU/SEI-93-TR-25). Pittsburgh: Software Engineering Institute, Carnegie Mellon University.

Puffer, J., and A. Litter. 1997. Action planning. *IEEE Software Engineering Technical Council Newsletter* 15, no. 2: 7–10.

Saxena, G. 1999. A framework for building and evaluating software process maturity models. PhD thesis, Illinois Institute of Technology.

Suwanassart, T. 1996. Towards the development of a testing maturity model. PhD thesis, Illinois Institute of Technology.

Thayer, R., ed. 1998. *Software engineering project management.* 2nd ed. Los Alamitos, CA: IEEE Computer Society Press.

Walton, G., J. Poore, and C. Trammel. 1995. Statistical testing of software based on a usage model. *Software—Practice and Experience* 25, no. 1: 97–108.

Zubrow, D., W. Hayes, J. Siegel, and D. Goldenson. 1994. *Maturity questionnaire* (CMU/SEI-94-SR-7). Pittsburgh: Software Engineering Institute, Carnegie Mellon University.

BIOGRAPHIES

Ilene Burnstein is an associate professor of computer science at the Illinois Institute of Technology. She teaches both undergraduate and graduate courses in software engineering. Her research interests include: software process engineering, software testing techniques and methods, automated program recognition and debugging, and software engineering education. Burnstein has a doctorate from the Illinois Institute of Technology. She can be reached at Illinois Institute of Technology, Computer Science Department, 10 West 31st St., Chicago, IL 60616 or e-mail at csburnstein@minna.iit.edu .

Ariya Homyen holds a research position at the Ministry of Science, Technology, and Energy in Thailand. She has a doctorate in computer science from the Illinois Institute of Technology. Her research interests include test process improvement, test management, and process reuse.

Taratip Suwanassart is a faculty member at Chulalongkom University in Thailand. She has a doctorate in computer science from the Illinois Institute of Technology. Her research interests include test management, test process improvement, software metrics, and data modeling.

Gary Saxena is a member of the technical staff in the Telematics Communications Group at Motorola. He has a doctorate in computer science from the Illinois Institute of Technology. His research interests include software architecture, software development and system development processes, and software process maturity modeling.

Robert Grom is manager of data collection for SAFCO Technologies. He has worked as a hardware engineer and now designs software. He has a master's degree from the Illinois Institute of Technology. Grom's research interests include software testing and test process improvement.

Choosing a Tool to Automate Software Testing

Mark Fewster and Dorothy Graham, Grove Consultants

*C*hoosing which tool to buy is a project in its own right. Start by identifying the current problems in testing, and then evaluate different solutions, including the purchase of test automation tools. The cost justification for the tool should be written up as a business case. Organizational constraints on tool purchase must also be identified. The decision to purchase should be based on a business case for a realistic anticipated cost-benefit ratio. This article is based on Chapter 10 of the book Software Test Automation *(Addison Wesley 1999).*

Key words: business case, buy versus build, testing tools, tool selection, tool vendors

INTRODUCTION: TOOL SELECTION AND IMPLEMENTATION

The tool selection process evaluates the many test automation tools available and selects one that is appropriate for the organization. The tool implementation process then ensures that the selected tool is used effectively throughout the organization. The tool selection and implementation process is shown in Figure 1. This article covers the left-hand side of the diagram only.

The person in charge of selecting a tool to be used by many people within an organization must approach the selection process in a formal and detailed way. If a tool will be used on an experimental basis with only a few people, then the tool selection process will be on a smaller scale, less detailed, and less formal. If a tool will be used by many people in the organization, then the tool selection process will be more rigorous. In both cases, the process will be the same. If conducting a formal evaluation, all of the ideas in this article will probably be used; if conducting an informal evaluation, a few useful tips may be picked up from this article.

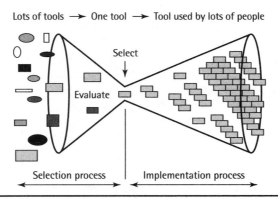

Figure 1 The tool selection and implementation processes.

This material is addressed because many of the people charged with selecting testing tools have never done a formal selection. There are books and courses that cover the topic of general tool selection and implementation processes in greater depth, including IEEE standards 1209 (IEEE 1992) and 1348 (IEEE 1995).

THE TOOL SELECTION PROCESS

In order to automate testing, if a testing tool has not yet been acquired, it is tempting to start by investigating what commercial tools may be suitable. Looking at the tool market, however, is not the place to start. It is important to start by evaluating the organization's requirements. This will ensure that the best decision is made within an appropriate time frame.

The ultimate goal of the tool selection process is to identify a tool for automating testing in the organization. How the tool is selected is important in achieving this goal. Choosing the wrong tool may at best set back the test automation efforts and sabotage them for some time. On the other hand, the right tool may be chosen in the wrong way. Even if the tool is suitable from a technical perspective, if the right people do not buy in to the selection process, they will be reluctant to use the tool once it has been acquired.

Choosing a test automation tool is a project in its own right and must be funded, resourced, and staffed adequately. The tool selection project must be made a priority, not only by the project's manager, but also by others involved. This will affect the scheduling and resourcing of "normal" projects. This is one reason why a tool solution should not be sought if there are serious time constraints for development or testing projects. Figure 2 provides an overview of the tool selection process. This is the left-hand side of the diagram in Figure 1.

THE TOOL SELECTION TEAM

A team of people should make the tool selection decision. The amount of time required from the team members need not be great, perhaps three to five days each, spread out over a month to six weeks. More time, however, would be needed from the team leader.

One person should be in charge of managing tool selection and evaluation. This should be someone with management skills or potential and the ability to build a team of people from different areas of the organization. This person should ideally be someone who has a broad view of the organization and is well respected.

The team should include representatives from each area of the organization that may want to automate its own testing. This may involve people from a number of projects, departments, or locations. As this is an important decision that may affect the efficiency

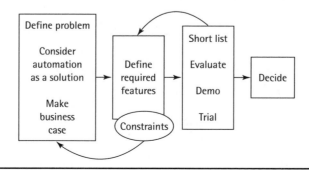

Figure 2   Overview of the tool selection process.

and productivity of the whole organization, team members should be knowledgeable about their own areas of the organization and capable of making an objective evaluation that can be justified to their colleagues.

The team should also include a variety of skills representing the different roles or jobs of the tool's target users. The tool selection team will become a network of communication with the rest of the organization to find out what is required in each area and help promote good test automation practice and "sell" the use of the tool once it has been acquired.

IDENTIFYING REQUIREMENTS

Some requirements for the tool will be related to the organization's current testing problems. Other requirements include the technical and nontechnical constraints on tool selection. These tool requirements must be identified first so there is something to evaluate the candidate tools against. Templates to help in the tool selection process are available from the authors' Web site at www.grove.co.uk .

What Are the Problems To Be Solved?

The starting point for tool selection is identifying what problems need to be solved where a tool might provide a solution. Specifying the problems ensures that everyone sees them the same way and they can be used as the basis for specifying test automation success criteria. Some examples of problems are:

- Manual testing problems (for example, too time consuming, boring, or error prone)
- No time for regression testing when small software changes are made
- Set-up of test data or test cases is error prone
- Inadequate test documentation
- Do not know how much of the software has been tested
- Testing is ineffective

Rank the problems by importance or current cost to the organization. The greatest benefit will come from addressing the organization's worst problems.

Look at each of the problems and consider a number of different solutions, not just tool-based solutions. It is important to consider nontool solutions to be able to assess whether the tools will actually give better value. There is often great enthusiasm for any automated solution (the "silver bullet" syndrome) without regard for alternative (and sometimes cheaper) solutions. This may lead to disillusionment when the tool does not solve all the problems completely.

In many cases a testing tool will help, but there may be other solutions that may be more effective in the situation. It is easy to leap to the conclusion that "a tool must be the answer," only to find that it is not.

Timing of Tool Selection

Having considered the current testing problems and concluded that a testing tool would be an appropriate solution (perhaps in addition to some others), the next step in tool selection is to consider whether it is the right time. There is a right and a wrong time to choose a testing tool. If the time is not right, even the best tool in the world is unlikely to succeed.

An automated solution often looks better and may be easier to authorize expenditure for than addressing the more fundamental problems of the testing process itself. It is important to realize that the tool will not correct a poor process without additional attention being paid to it. It is possible to improve testing practices while implementing the tool, but it requires a conscious effort. The right time is:

- When there are no major organizational upheavals or panics in progress
- When one person has responsibility for choosing and implementing the tool
- When people are dissatisfied with the current state of testing practice
- When there is commitment from top management to authorize and support the tooling-up effort

If one or more of these conditions do not apply, it does not mean the organization should not attempt to introduce test automation. It merely implies that doing so may be more difficult.

How Much Help Should the Tool Provide?

Once a problem is identified for which tool support is a viable solution, it is important to be able to tell whether a tool has actually helped. Depending on the circumstances, it helps to set measurable goals as the success criteria for the tool. For example, if the time taken to run tests manually is the problem, how long does it currently take to run a set of tests manually? What is a reasonable length of time to run them once the test automation regime has been set up?

A realistic measurable criterion for a test execution tool might be set out as follows: Manual execution of test cases currently takes four staff-weeks. After three months of using the tool, 50 to 60 percent of these test cases should be automated, reducing the execution time for all the tests down to two to two-and-one-half staff-weeks. After 12 months the aim is to have 80 percent of the test cases automated with the equivalent test suite being run in four staff-days.

When considering the measurable benefits it is best to be conservative. It always takes longer when a tool is being used for the first time, so the learning curve must be considered. It is important to set realistic goals and not expect miracles.

If people argue about the numbers that are used, ask them to supply more accurate figures to give a better evaluation. Do not spend a great deal of time "polishing" the estimates. The tool evaluation process should be only as long as is needed to come to a decision and no longer. The estimates should reflect this granularity.

How Much Is This Help Worth? Making the Business Case

Some organizations will require a business case to justify the purchase of a tool. If so, this section will help in preparing one. If a business case is not required, it can still be useful to think about the issues described here. Do not spend a great deal of time, however, preparing something that is not going to be used.

A business case quantifies what the help provided by a tool is worth to be able to tell if the tool is affordable and will provide any cost benefit to the organization. One of the simplest ways to quantify the benefits is to measure the time savings and multiply that by approximate staff costs.

For example, if regression tests that normally take four staff-weeks manually can be done in two staff-weeks; the organization will save two staff-weeks of effort whenever those tests are run. If they are run once a quarter, the organization will save eight staff-weeks a year. If they are run once a month, the organization will save 24 staff-weeks a year. If a staff-week is costed at say, $3000, the organization will save $24,000 if they are run once a quarter or $72,000 if they are run once a month.

There will also be other benefits, which may be difficult if not impossible to quantify but should also be mentioned. The risk of an embarrassing public release may be reduced, for example, but it may not be possible to put a monetary value on this. Morale among testers may improve, which is likely to result in increased productivity, but it may not be possible or desirable to separate this from the productivity increase from using the tool.

The business case could contain the following information:

- **Cost of current manual testing.** This could be done per test cycle or for the testing done in a fixed time period (say per quarter or per year). These numbers do not need to be very accurate; only approximate costs. Determine what the future costs of manual testing would be in say two or three years' time. This may include tests on more software or on more platforms, for example.

- **Coverage of current manual testing.** How much of the software is currently not tested, especially because of limitations that test automation could overcome?

- **Cost of defects not found by current testing in the past year.** This could be calculated by multiplying the number of defects found by users (missed by testing) by an average cost, for example, $1500 per defect. (In the authors' experience this is a very conservative figure and, therefore, a good one to use until a more accurate one can be determined.)

- **Cost of the first tool use.** This would include tool purchase or initial leasing cost, training in use of the tool, and additional hardware and software. It may be a good idea to include additional time for the learning curve; for example, analyzing test results will probably take longer the first few times. This cost would also include time needed to set up a workable automation regime. The cost of automating a test for the first time is normally at least four times longer than running the same test manually.

- **Cost of subsequent use of the tool.** This is where the benefits would be seen, such as where more tests could be run. There are also costs associated with continuing use, such as license fees, effort to maintain tests, and effort to improve the automation regime.

- **A calculation of the break-even point, taking the costs and benefits into account.**

The business case should also include the assumptions that were made in constructing it. This may include assumptions about testing in general, such as what test activities need to be done, the number of tests expected to fail, the number of test iterations (tests rerun after fixes), new functionality to be tested, and so on. There may also be assumptions about the test automation, such as time taken to add verification, time for test maintenance, and setting up standards for the testing regime. An example business case summary is shown in Figure 3.

Welcome any input regarding the figures. The more accurate they are, the more confidence there will be in the business case. Do not let anyone say they "don't like the figures" or they "don't think they are right" without supplying better figures. In any case, the figures do not have to be perfect, only good enough to justify a decision.

Ensure that the business case is conservative. Making extravagant claims for savings makes it difficult to achieve them. Instead, make realistic claims to set realistic expectations. This provides the possibility for exceeding the initial benefits, which will make the test automation effort look even better.

Business case for tool _____

Prepared by _____ Date: _____

Costs	Without tool		With tool	
	Test Cycle 1	Test Cycle 2	Test Cycle 1	Test Cycle 2
Test cycle	$16,000	$25,000	$29,000	$11,000
Tool			$33,000	
Evaluate			$13,000	
Implement			$22,000	
Other	none	none	none	license per cycle: $550
Totals	$16,000	$25,000	$97,000	$11,550
Break even			Cycle 8, 16 months	
	Savings: Year 1		($22,150)	
	Savings: Year 2		$45,950	
	Savings: Year 3		$114,050	

Assumptions:

1. One cycle every two months, six per year
2. License fee of 10 percent of purchase cost for second and subsequent years
3. All tests will be rerun after last fix for second and subsequent cycles
4. Failure estimates assume:
    i) One-third of new tests will fail each time they are run
    ii) Previously failed tests are rerun
    iii) Four test runs will be necessary
    iv) Ten percent of old tests will fail
5. Cycle 2 for both manual and tool-supported testing represents an estimated typical "snapshot" in one year's time. (Calculation based on Cycle 1 plus n*Cycle 2.)
6. Twenty-five percent increase in new functionality to test over the year (new tests to write)

Figure 3   Example of a one-page business case for implementing a test execution automation tool.

IDENTIFYING CONSTRAINTS

Having established the testing problems and that it is a good time to introduce a test automation tool, it is time to begin looking at the tool market. There will be many factors that will constrain the tool choice. Identifying them initially can save a lot of time and effort investigating tools that will be rejected anyway.

Environmental Constraints

Testing tools are software packages and therefore will be specific to particular hardware, software, or operating systems. There is no point spending time considering a tool that runs only on a Unix platform when there is only a Windows environment available and no possibility of acquiring or using anything else.

It may be desirable to acquire additional hardware or software along with the tool. This is sometimes more of a psychological barrier than a technical or economic one. In the tool selection process, especially if there are not many for the "home" environment, it is worth considering tools based on a separate environment, even though this will add to the purchase price.

It may be necessary to acquire extra hardware or software, however, even for a tool that runs on the current environment, such as extra disk space to store test scripts or a specialized comparator tool to help verify test outcomes.

Commercial Supplier Constraints

The company that supplies the tool may be an important factor in the future. To get the best from the tool, it is useful to take advantage of the tool vendor's expertise. A good relationship with the vendor can help the test automation progress in the desired direction.

Here are some factors that should be considered when evaluating the tool vendor's organization.

- Is the supplier a *bona fide* company? The commercial details of the supplier can be checked in various testing tool reports or the normal commercial channels for such information.

- How mature are the company and the product? If the company is well established this gives confidence, but if the product has not changed significantly in recent years, it may be out of date.

- Is there adequate technical support? What would their response be to major or minor problems? Does the vendor run a help desk? During what hours is help available (in your time zone)? What training courses are provided? How responsive are they to information requests?

- How many other organizations have purchased this tool? How many are using the tool well and achieving benefits? An organization may not want to be the first commercial user of a new tool. Is it possible to talk to other tool users? Is there a user group, when does it meet, and who controls it? Will the vendor provide reference sites?

- What is the tool's history? Was it developed to support good internal testing practices, to meet a specific client need, or as a speculative product? How many releases have there been to date, and how often is the tool updated? How many open faults have been reported in the tool itself?

The organization's relationship with the tool vendor starts during the selection and evaluation process. If there are problems with the vendor now, there are likely to be more serious problems later.

Cost Constraints

Cost is often the most stringent and visible constraint on tool selection, but the tool's purchase price may be only a fraction of the cost of fully implementing the tool. Of course there must be guidelines, but it is also important not to be too rigidly bound by what may be an arbitrary number. Cost factors include:

- Purchase or lease price (one time, annual, or other renewal period)
- Cost basis (per seat, per computer, and so on)
- Cost of training in the use of the tool (from the tool vendor)
- Any additional hardware needed (for example, PCs or additional disk space or memory)
- Any additional software needed (for example, updates to operating systems or netware)
- Support costs (maintenance agreements)
- Any additional start-up costs (for example, consultancy to ensure the tool is used in the best way)

- Internal costs (for tool maintenance, establishing the internal test automation regime, implementing the tool within the organization, and so on)
- Purchase of books or training in general test automation techniques (that is, not tool specific)

Note that the internal costs will be far more significant in the long term than the others.

Political Constraints

Political factors may override all the other constraints and requirements. For example, the organization may be required to buy the same tool its parent company uses. There may be a restriction against buying anything other than a tool supported in one's own country. Or an employee's boss may have a brother who works for a tool vendor. It is frustrating to tool selectors to discover these factors late in the selection process, so make inquiries now.

Do not underestimate the role of political factors. Although people like to think that tool purchase decisions are always based on rational technical factors, decisions are often based on emotional and irrational factors.

Quality Constraints

What are the required quality characteristics of the tool? This may include both functional aspects and nonfunctional aspects. Here are some suggestions to consider.

- How many people can use the tool at once? Can test scripts be shared?
- What skill level is required to use the tool effectively? How long does it take to become proficient? What programming skills are needed to write test scripts?
- What is the quality of the documentation supplied with the tool (paper or on line)? How thorough is it? How usable is it? Are there quick reference guides, for example?
- What about the help line, Web site, or other support for the tool itself from the vendor?
- What is the frequency of failures during realistic use?
- Can it corrupt any of the data?
- What overheads are caused by the tool (how much time or resource does the tool use)?
- Can the tool integrate with other tools already in use (for example, configuration management and project management tools)?

The authors have found it useful to apply a technique (known as the quality attribute technique) developed by Tom Gilb for specifying and testing nonfunctional qualities. An example of the use of Gilb's Quality Attribute Table for evaluating test execution tools is shown in Figure 4. Note that the numbers in the "must do" and "planned" levels reflect a set of requirements that may be different for other organizations. The table is intended to show the types of nonfunctional attributes that can be expressed in this way, based on a real example.

The "DM" mentioned in Figure 4 is an abbreviation for "defect measure." This is defined as defects multiplied by a weighting factor reflecting their severity, so a single defect would count as one, five, or nine units of defect measure. The "DM rate" is defect measure realized by one hour of test effort. Further details on using the quality attribute technique can be found in Gilb (1988).

Note that the "must do" level for reliability in Figure 4 does not mean that at least one defect must be found—it means that one defect is the maximum that is acceptable.

Attribute	Test		Scale	Must do	Plan	Comment
Ease of use	Average time for at least three different people to complete the following tasks.	Invoke tool, select and start a sample of 10 tests.	Minutes	3	1	Must be an assorted subset of tests.
		Record 5 minute test case with 3 dynamic comparisons.	Minutes	20	10	Use three different comparisons at different points within the test case.
		Obtain summary statistics from run of set of test cases.	Minutes	3	1	Should involve at least 100 test cases.
Documentation usefulness	Time to learn how to perform four basic tasks (add a new test, add dynamic verification, execute test, analyze results)		Minutes	40	20	Use at least three people and take the average time.
Reliability (of the tool)	Number of defects found weighted by severity.		Defect measure (DM rate)	1.0	0.1	Severe = 9, Moderate = 5, Minor = 1
	Number of critical defects found in evaluation.		Number	1	0	
Availability	Time tool is available for effective use during evaluation.		Percentage of total time in use.	90%	100%	Evaluation period not less than 20 work hours.
Support service	Assessment by evaluation team grading on a scale of 1 (unacceptable) to 5 (excellent). (Intermediate grades are: poor; fair; good).		Average grade.	3 (Fair)	4 (Good)	
Usefulness	Percentage of typical regression test cases that it is estimated can be automated within a reasonable time.		Percent of test cases.	3 months: 10% 12 months: 50%	3 months: 20% 12 months: 70%	Consensus of all people involved in evaluation.
Disk use	Count of working files created in using the tool.		Number of extra files for each test.	7	3	
	Largest amount of extra disk space used at any time during the execution of a set of tests.		Factor of disk space used by manual tests.	five times more	two times more	

Figure 4   Quantified evaluation criteria for a test execution tool.

Build or Buy?

After evaluating the commercial market, there may not be any tools that meet the organization's requirements. It is worth considering whether it might be better to build a tool (or wait for the market to catch up).

If building a tool:

- It will be most suitable for the organization's needs
- It may be possible to compensate in the tool for a lack of testability in the software under test
- The tool may be able to assume knowledge of the applications thereby reducing the work necessary to implement automated tests
- It will probably not be well supported in terms of documentation, help, and training

- It may suffer from "image" problems ("something developed by Joe in the next office cannot possibly be as good as the tool described on this glossy color brochure from a tool vendor")
- The user interface may leave something to be desired (a tool developed by technical people often considers ease of use to be unimportant)

If buying a commercially available tool:

- It will probably be considerably cheaper to achieve a given level of features and quality (such as usability and so on) than the cost of developing the tool oneself
- It should be well supported in terms of documentation, help, training, and so on
- It is often seen as "sexy"—something people want to be involved with
- Buying a tool does not entirely avoid building some tailored tool support; it will still be necessary to build utilities and so on for the internal test automation regime

If building a tool, do not attempt to produce a tool on the same scale as the commercial tools. Remember, most have been under development for many years, funded by numerous users in many organizations. Build the smallest and simplest tools that will provide immediate and real benefit. Perhaps start by building some filters to use with existing comparison tools. Start by collecting information about any existing tools or utilities that people or groups in the organization have already developed to meet some need within their own scope. These starting points can often be developed at minimal cost to give more general benefits to the organization.

IDENTIFYING WHAT IS AVAILABLE ON THE MARKET

Feature Evaluation

The next step is to become familiar with the capabilities of the commercial test automation tools available. Which features are the most important for meeting the needs and objectives of the current situation? For example, if it is necessary to synchronize with a database or a network, the tool should be able to detect the relevant signals so the tests will stay in step with the application being tested.

Make a list of the features, and classify them into categories, such as "mandatory," 'desirable,' and 'don't care.' Note that the feature list will change throughout the evaluation process, as new desirable features are discovered over time.

Some tool features are either present or absent. Evaluating this type of feature is straightforward. If the feature is mandatory, then any tool without it is eliminated from further consideration. Other features may be present to a degree, or the tool may offer support for a requirement but only partially. Some tools may be easier for nontechnical people to use but tedious for the technical test automator.

Evaluating this kind of feature is not as straightforward, as there may need to be a value judgment on some scale. The DESMET project (an ESPRIT method for rigorous method and tool selection) suggests a seven-point scale, provided here in a slightly modified form.

- 5: Has the greatest effect or fully supports the requirement
- 4: Very strong support but not fully complete
- 3: Strong support, probably adequate
- 2: Some support, but leaves much to be desired
- 1: Very little support, may be survivable

- 0: No support whatever for this feature
- -1: Actually makes it more difficult to meet a requirement or makes things worse. More information on the DESMET methodology can be found in Kitchenham et al. (1997) and Kitchenham (1996).

Producing the Long List

In a thorough tool selection process, all the commercially available tools should be investigated, but it can be difficult to know whether they have all been identified. There are many tools that provide support for testing, and the marketplace is constantly changing. By not casting one's net wide enough, it is possible to miss a tool that could be just the right thing. The place to start is with "information about the information" (that is, lists of current testing tools).

Some of these sources may just be contact details for vendors with no information about what the tools do. Others may have summaries about what each tool does, so tools that are not of interest can be eliminated. Still others may contain evaluations of the tools themselves, with comments on how well they work. The organization's long list will contain all potentially suitable tools.

Constructing the Short List

If there are more than three or four tools on the organization's long list, it should use the list of desirable features to eliminate some. If the long list contains only one tool, it may be best to go ahead and evaluate that one for suitability. After all, only one tool is needed in the end.

If the long list is empty, either relax the constraints or mandatory features list and try again, or consider building a tool or decide not to opt for tool support at this time.

To find out about what tools are available, here are some possible sources:

- Check internal "informal" tools or utilities
- Ask the vendors of other software or hardware products
- Ask the vendors of testing tools that are almost suitable (for example, if it does not yet run on the required platform, ask if there are plans to port it soon)
- Investigate whether the tool can be used in a different environment than it was purchased for
- Check the testing features of other software development tools, such as computer-laided software engineering (CASE) tools
- Attend a testing conference or event with a tools exhibition
- Look for tools sourced from another country
- Check tool evaluation reports from independent organizations such as Ovum

The result of this part of the evaluation process is to have a list of two or three tools that look suitable on paper. Having several tools means that there should be a choice. This should help to better meet the organization's needs, both for tool functions and features and for nonfunctional aspects of the tools.

EVALUATING THE SHORT-LISTED TOOLS

Feature Comparison

1. **Contact vendors of short-listed tools for information.** Study the information and compare features. Request further information from the vendors if the literature sent does not explain the tool function clearly enough. The function and feature list will be evolving at this point, depending on the information being gathered and the greater understanding of what the tools can do. This should help in making the choice between the tools. (A list of questions to ask the vendors is given in the on-line appendix to this article at www.sqp.asq.org .)

   This is the time to consult one or more of the publications that have evaluated testing tools. These reports are often perceived as being very expensive. The cost of the report, however, should be compared to the cost of someone's time in performing similar evaluations, and the cost of choosing the wrong tool because one did not know about something that was covered in published material. (Remember to allow time to read the report!)

2. **Ask the short-listed vendors to provide the names of a few of their existing customers as references.** If there are user groups for any of the tools, contact them and attend one of their meetings if possible. Contact the reference sites from short-listed vendors and ask them about the tool. An example list is shown in the on-line appendix to this article.

   Remember that the reference sites supplied by the vendor will be their best customers, and so they will likely be happy with the tool. The user group is a better source of reference sites as one will find a better cross-section of experience with the tool. But those who have had the least success with this tool may not attend the user group either. One may be able to find people with both positive and negative experience with the tool by attending a special interest group in testing or a testing conference.

   At any point in the selection and tool evaluation process it may become clear which tool will be the best choice. When this happens, any further activities may not influence the choice of tool but may still be useful in assessing how well the chosen tool will work in practice. It will either detect a catastrophic mismatch between the selected tool and the current environment or will give more confidence in the selection.

In-House Demonstrations

The advice in this section assumes that the short-listed tools are not of the shrink-wrapped, off-the-shelf, take-it-or-leave-it, cheap-and-cheerful variety. If going for this type of tool, the demonstration will be done by the tool selection team. The advice for what and how to demonstrate will still apply, but more work is required to be as thorough.

Before contacting the vendor to arrange a tool demonstration, some preparatory work will help make the assessment of the competing tools more efficient and unbiased. Prepare two test cases for tool demonstration: 1) One of a normal test case; and 2) One of a nightmare case (or something more complex than normal). Rehearse the tests manually to discover any defects in the test cases themselves. It is important that the tools be set up and used on the organization's own premises, using the current internal environment and configuration.

1. **Invite the vendors of all short-listed tools to give demonstrations within a short time frame, such as during the same week.** This will ensure that the memory of one tool is still fresh when seeing different tools.

2. **Give vendors both of the test cases in advance to be used in their demo.** If they cannot cope with these two cases in their demo, there probably is not much hope of their tool being suitable. Be prepared, however, to be flexible about the pre-pared test cases. The tool may be able to solve the underlying problem differ-ently than had been initially envisioned. Test cases that are too rigid may cause a tool to be eliminated that would actually be suitable.

3. **Find out what facilities the vendors require and make sure they are available.** Prepare a list of questions (technical and commercial) to ask on the demo day. Allow time to write up reactions to the tools immediately after each demonstration.

   Prepare evaluation forms or checklists for:

   • General vendor relationship (responsiveness, flexibility, technical knowledge)

   • Tool performance on the organization's test cases. Set measurable objectives, such as time to run a test case for the first time, time to run a reasonable set of test cases, or time to find an answer to a question in the documentation.

   • Typical test cases that one might wish to automate

4. **Prepare one additional test case that is not supplied to the vendor in advance.** After they have shown what the tool can do with the other two test cases, see how easy it is to put this new one into the tool from "cold." This test case should not be too easy nor too complex. This is illustrated in Figure 5.

5. **Provide facilities for the vendor's presentation and demonstration.** Listen to their presentation and ask questions.

6. **Observe what happens when they set up the tool in one's own environment.**

7. **Ask (and note) any more questions that may come up.** Note any additional features or functions of the tool. Note any features or functions that the tool does not provide but may be needed.

8. **Try to keep all demonstrations the same.** It is easy for the last one to incorporate improvements learned during previous demonstrations, but this is not fair to the first one.

9. **Thank and dismiss the vendor and then write up observations and reactions to its tool.**

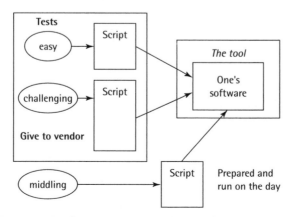

Figure 5   Overview of the test-tool demonstration process.

10. **After the demonstration, ask the vendors that presented earlier any questions that came up when watching a later vendor's presentation or demonstration.** This will give the fairest comparison between tools.

11. **Assess tool performance against measurable criteria defined earlier, taking any special circumstances into account.** Compare features and functions offered by competing tools. Compare nonfunctional attributes, such as usability. Compare the commercial attributes of vendor companies. It might also be helpful to test the technical support by ringing their help line and asking a technical question or two.

Test of Script Maintenance

Another important aspect to investigate is how easy it will be to maintain the test scripts. This is an important investigation both for vendor in-house demonstrations and for shrink-wrapped tools.

Prepare an altered version of the software being tested. Make changes to it in line with what typically happens from release to release of the organization's system. For example, if screen layouts usually change, then change the screen layout. If new fields are added, add a new field.

Now replay one of the test cases through the new version of the software to see how the tool copes. Next edit the scripts until they run successfully. Note how easy or difficult this is, how error-prone it is, how much editing is necessary, and so on. Remember that the approach to implementing automated test cases will ultimately be adjusted to minimize this type of effort. Some tools may be less susceptible to frequent types of software change than others, which will make the basic script editing easier. This is illustrated in Figure 6. What is easiest to do in a small-scale evaluation or trial (such as record tests) will not be the best long-term strategy.

If a clear winner is now obvious, select the winning tool. Otherwise select two tools for a final competitive trial. Inform the nonselected vendors of the decision and give the reason for their elimination.

Competitive Trial

An in-house competitive trial will provide a clearer idea of how the tool will work in the organization's situation. This involves additional effort and is probably more appropriate for larger organizations where the tool chosen will eventually be used by a large number of people.

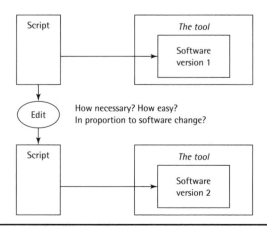

Figure 6   Investigating the script maintenance effort.

Many tool vendors will allow short-term use of the tool under an evaluation license, particularly for complex tools that represent a major investment. Such licenses will be for a limited time period, and the evaluation team must plan and prepare for that evaluation accordingly.

The preparation for the trial period includes selecting or designing a set of test cases to be used by the tools in the trial. Measurable success criteria for the evaluated tools should be planned in advance, such as length of time to record or construct a test case (perhaps expressed as a multiple of the time taken to run the test case manually), and the number of discrepancies found in comparison (real, extraneous, and any missed). Attending a training course for each tool will help to ensure that the tools will be used correctly during the evaluation period.

When performing the competitive trial evaluation, install each tool and run the chosen test cases. Ensure that all mandatory requirements are met. Use the discriminatory factors and the ranked list of features and functions to give an objective score to each tool. Measure the success criteria and estimate the potential savings.

Finally, analyze the results of the trial. Compare the features and functions offered by the tools. Compare the nonfunctional attributes, especially usability and general gut feel. Compare the commercial attributes of vendor companies and experience in tool installation and support during the trial. Compare other users' experiences in using the tool, from reference sites. A tool that looks impressive at a one-day demonstration may not be the best tool at the end of the trial.

Assess any features that were not evaluated in this trial but are likely to be required later. This may influence the choice of tool, especially if there is more than one suitable tool in all other respects.

MAKING THE DECISION
Assess against the Business Case

Having spent considerable effort assessing the tools, the evaluation report would normally recommend purchasing the tool that would best meet the organization's requirements and constraints.

Before making this recommendation, assess the business case: Will the potential savings from this tool give a good return on investment, including purchase/lease price, training costs, and ongoing internal tool costs? The likely benefits need to be clearly communicated so expectations are realistic. Deciding not to purchase any of the tools investigated could be the best economic decision at the time; do not be afraid to make it if a tool is not justified.

When to Stop Evaluating

If there is only one clear candidate tool, the evaluation process could stop as soon as this became obvious. It may be better, however, to continue with the evaluation process until everyone involved is happy with the final decision. Otherwise, there may be future problems if some people believe the evaluation was not thorough enough (see Figure 7).

If a clear-cut winner is still not obvious, then any of the short-listed tools are likely to be equally successful. Commercial factors such as the status of the tool supplier, the flexibility of licensing arrangements, or the company most willing to be flexible on some other aspect of the purchase may now become the deciding factor. If the commercial factors have not swayed the decision to a particular vendor, then further agonizing over the choice will not be profitable. If technical and other issues cannot make the decision, then trust intuitive feelings about the people involved. (Or just flip a coin!)

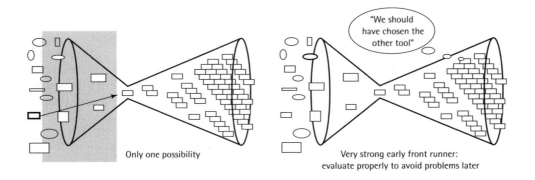

Only one possibility

"We should have chosen the other tool"

Very strong early front runner: evaluate properly to avoid problems later

Figure 7   When to stop evaluating.

Completing the Evaluation and Selection Process

Let the winning vendor know what the organization's purchasing procedure is. For example, if a management meeting has to approve the expenditure and purchase orders have to be raised, it may be several weeks or months before the organization can begin using the tool. It is also an important courtesy to inform those not chosen and to let them know the reasons for the decision.

Prepare a short written report on the evaluation, including the organization's selection criteria and the scores of each of the evaluated tools. Be as brief as possible, but do include enough information so anyone not involved in the selection process can see what happened.

The selection and evaluation process should be limited in time; once the winning tool has been identified, the more significant process of implementing the tool within the organization can start.

SUMMARY

Choosing which tool to buy is a project in its own right. It requires a team of people and a team leader to guide the selection process. The place to start is to identify the current problems in testing and to evaluate different solutions, including the purchase of test automation tools. The cost justification for the tool should be written up as a business case. Organizational constraints on tool purchase must also be identified, such as environment, cost, quality, commercial, and political factors. Any tools that meet the requirements will go into the initial long list for consideration.

A list of features that are mandatory, desirable, or optional is prepared, and available tools are compared to this list. The feature analysis will help to eliminate the less suitable tools to form a short list of perhaps three candidate tools.

The short-listed tools are compared with each other in more detail. Evaluation reports and reference sites give an idea of other people's experiences using the tools. If appropriate, in-house demonstrations are organized with each vendor. The tools should be tested with realistic test cases, and the maintenance of the test cases when the software changes should also be investigated. If needed, a competitive trial of the top two tools is then carried out. The decision of whether to purchase should be based on a business case for a realistic anticipated cost-benefit ratio.

REFERENCES

Fewster, M., and D. Graham. 1999. *Software test automation.* Harlow, England: Addison Wesley.

IEEE Standard 1209: *Recommended practice for the evaluation and selection of CASE tools.* 1992. New York: Institute of Electrical and Electronics Engineers, Inc.

IEEE Standard 1348: *Recommended practice for the adoption of computer-aided software engineering (CASE) tools.* 1995. New York: Institute of Electrical and Electronics Engineers, Inc.

Gilb, T. 1998. *Principles of software engineering management.* Harlow, England: Addison Wesley.

Gilb, T., and D. Graham. 1993. *Software inspection.* Harlow, England: Addison Wesley.

Kitchenham, B. 1996. DESMET: A methodology for evaluating software engineering methods and tools. Keele University Technical Report (TR96-09).

Kitchenham, B. A., S. G. Linkman, and D. Law. 1997. DESMET: A methodology for evaluating software engineering methods and tools. *IEEE Computing and Control Journal.* (June): 120–126.

BIOGRAPHIES

Dorothy Graham is founder of Grove Consultants, which provides advice, training, and inspiration in software testing, testing tools, and inspection. Graham is originator and coauthor with Paul Herzlich of the CAST Report on computer-aided software testing tools, published by Cambridge Market Intelligence, and is coauthor with Tom Gilb of the book, *Software Inspection* (Addison Wesley 1993). She has written articles for Ovum and a number of technical journals, and is a frequent and popular keynote and tutorial speaker at conferences and seminars.

Graham was program chair for the first EuroSTAR conference in 1993. She is on the editorial board of the *Journal for Software Testing, Verification, and Reliability,* a member of the program committee for the Object Technology conferences, and for the U.S. Professional Development Institute's series of annual software testing conferences in Washington, D.C.

Graham has served on the BCS SIGIST committee and the BCS Software Component Test Standard Committee, and is a member of the Information Systems Examination Board (ISEB) working on a training and qualification scheme for testing professionals. She can be reached at Grove Consultants, Grove House, 40 Ryles Park Rd., Macclesfield, U.K. SK11 8AH, or by e-mail at Dorothy@grove.co.uk .

Mark Fewster has more than 18 years of experience in the software industry, with more than 10 years in automating software testing. He has been a software developer and manager for a multiplatform graphical application vendor, where he implemented a testing improvement program and successfully developed and implemented a testing tool that has led to dramatic and lasting savings for the company.

Fewster spent two years as a consultant for a commercial software testing tool vendor, providing training and consultancy in both test automation and testing techniques.

Since joining Grove Consultants in 1993, Fewster has provided consultancy and training in software testing, particularly in the application of testing techniques and all aspects of test automation. He is a popular speaker at national and international conferences and seminars. Fewster has served on the BCS SIGIST committee and the BCS Software Component Test Standard committee, and is a member of the Information Systems Examination Board working on a training and qualification scheme for testing professionals. He can be reached by e-mail at mark@grove.co.uk .

PART SEVEN

Audits

The fundamentals of the audit process—the planning, conduct, reporting, and follow-up—are universally applicable and well treated in other ASQ Quality Press volumes such as *The Quality Audit Handbook* and *Quality Audits for Improved Performance.* What is unique about auditing in a software development environment is the nature of the various intermediate and final products as well as the process standards by which development proceeds.

The two articles in this section address these unique aspects of software auditing. Functionality has traditionally been, if not the only, at least the greatest software quality factor to be evaluated. But with humans in the interactive loop, a system also has to be evaluated for usability in all its manifestations. And as computers emerged from isolation, and especially as they began to be connected with one another, security in its many different dimensions has arisen as another major issue.

Jørgen Bøegh (**"Quality Evaluation of Software Products"**) provides a worldwide survey of product evaluation and certification arrangements. Beginning with an overview of international standards efforts, he reports on recognition processes currently in use throughout Europe and ranging as far as Brazil and Korea. His own specific experiences are from a successful commercial assessment service focusing on usability, maintainability, and functionality.

Early defect removal is especially critical for embedded software in consumer electronics products, where the cost of repair after shipment is all the greater because it usually means physical replacement of thousands upon thousands of units. Inspections and structured testing are the primary techniques described by Erik van Veenendaal in **"Practical Quality Assurance for Embedded Software."** In this article, the author provides data that demonstrate a positive payback and discusses the success factors that contributed to reduced project risk, improved quality awareness, and on-time delivery.

CHAPTER 7.1

Quality Evaluation of Software Products

Jørgen Bøegh, DELTA Software Engineering

S *oftware quality evaluation is the systematic examination of the software's capability to fulfill specified quality requirements. This article discusses the needs for and advantages of software product evaluation. It reviews the relevant international standards, both published and forthcoming.*

Practical software evaluation schemes have been introduced in recent years. Some of these schemes are described and their market acceptance is reviewed. Finally, the experiences gained with the MicroScope evaluation scheme based on almost 80 commercial evaluations are presented.

Key words: accreditation, certification, quality characteristics, requirements, standards, testing laboratories

INTRODUCTION

Software use is growing dramatically and so are the number of critical computer systems. Faults in critical systems can lead to serious consequences. Therefore, the quality of these systems' software is important for individuals, companies, and society in general, which leads to a growing demand for quality evaluation of software products.

CRITICAL APPLICATION

Most software quality evaluations are conducted for critical applications. This includes national critical applications such as defense systems, where large software developments are carried out. Here the evaluation effort is often of the same magnitude as the development effort.

Until now, life-critical systems have been the main target for independent third-party quality evaluations. Such systems include traffic-control systems, medical systems, process-control systems, robots, and so on. The evaluation effort for this type of application can be large; public authorities often require independent evaluations of these systems.

Other systems are equally critical. Modern society depends on such software systems as electronic payment systems, public-administration systems, and telephone systems. These have equally high quality requirements and extensive quality evaluations.

Similarly, corporate-critical systems such as production systems, financial systems, and consumer products (including software and customer databases) should be considered systems with high-quality requirements. This type of software, however, is often neglected with respect to quality evaluation. As companies realize the advantages of ensuring the quality of their software, the market for software evaluations should increase substantially.

Market Advantages

Currently most independent quality evaluations are done because they are required by law or public authorities. There are, however, other reasons for demanding software evaluations. In some cases a software company may be asked by an acquirer to accept an independent quality evaluation as part of the development contract. This can actually be an advantage for both parties since disputes about the delivered software can be referred to the evaluation, and therefore, legal actions can be avoided.

Some evaluation schemes are devoted to issuing quality marks or seals. The aim is to give a marketing advantage to good quality software products. A few quality marks have been introduced, but until now, they have not been generally accepted in the market.

Yet another group of evaluation schemes is used for comparing similar software products. Many software magazines apply this approach for benchmarking software packages, but it is also relevant in other circumstances, such as when choosing a software supplier. In any case, a quality seal should have a positive influence on a buying decision.

INTERNATIONAL STANDARDIZATION

It is generally accepted that a professional development process is a prerequisite to achieving quality products. This is the background for process-related standards such as ISO 9000 and ISO/IEC 12207: Software Lifecycle Processes (ISO/IEC 12207 1995). A good development process alone, however, cannot guarantee a high-quality product. When product quality is important it is also necessary to consider the product itself. The process view and product view should therefore complement each other. This article is mainly concerned with the product view of software quality.

The need for product quality evaluations is reflected in standardization activities. Currently several international standards are either being finalized or revised to fit the present state of the art. The requirements of the standardization work and the most important standards are presented here.

Evaluation Requirements

By definition, quality evaluation is the systematic examination of the extent to which an entity is capable of fulfilling specified requirements. Hence, software product evaluation must follow some strict rules and satisfy some basic requirements, or evaluation results will not be valid. This is especially true for independent third-party evaluation. Requirements for testing laboratories can be found in ISO Guide 25: General Requirements for the Technical Competence of Testing Laboratories (ISO Guide 25 1990). It emphasizes the following requirements for evaluation:

- **Repeatability.** Repeated evaluation of the same product to the same evaluation specification by the same evaluator will give the same result.
- **Reproducibility.** Repeated evaluation of the same product to the same evaluation specification by different evaluators will give the same result.
- **Impartiality.** Evaluation will be free from unfair bias toward achieving any particular result.
- **Objectivity.** The evaluation will be obtained with the minimum of subjective judgment.

These requirements must be fulfilled by any reliable evaluation scheme. In addition, there may be other considerations, such as cost effectiveness of the evaluation, inclusiveness (the evaluation covers all quality characteristics), and indicativeness (when some discrepancies or other problems are found by the evaluation, their causes and required actions are indicated).

ISO/IEC 9126: Quality Characteristics

ISO/IEC 9126 (ISO/IEC 9126 1991) is the relevant standard for defining software quality and is recommended for quality evaluations in most situations. In ISO quality is defined as "the totality of characteristics of an entity that bear on its ability to satisfy stated and implied needs." ISO/IEC 9126 suggests a hierarchical quality model with six quality characteristics and attached subcharacteristics:

- **Functionality.** A set of attributes that bear on the existence of a set of functions and their specified properties. The functions are those that satisfy stated or implied needs. Subcharacteristics are suitability, accuracy, interoperability, compliance, and security.

- **Reliability.** A set of attributes that bear on the capability of software to maintain its level of performance under stated conditions for a specified time period. Subcharacteristics are maturity, fault tolerance, and recoverability.

- **Usability.** A set of attributes that bear on the effort needed for use and on the individual assessment of such use by a stated or implied set of users. Subcharacteristics are understandability, learnability, and operability.

- **Efficiency.** A set of attributes that bear on the relationship between the software's performance level and the resources used under stated conditions. Subcharacteristics are time behavior and resource behavior.

- **Maintainability.** A set of attributes that bear on the effort needed to make specified modifications. Subcharacteristics are analyzability, changeability, stability, and testability.

- **Portability.** A set of attributes that bear on the ability of software to be transferred from one environment to another. Subcharacteristics are adaptability, installability, conformance, and replaceability.

ISO/IEC 9126 is applicable to most types of software. In some situations, however, it may be better to use another quality model (such as for security evaluations).

ISO/IEC 12119: Quality Requirements and Testing

This standard (ISO/IEC 12119 1994) is based on the German standard DIN 66285 and is applicable to software packages. It establishes a set of quality requirements and provides instructions on how to test software against these requirements. In contrast with ISO/IEC 14598 (ISO/IEC 14598 1998), it only deals with software as offered and delivered; it does not deal with the production process, including development activities and intermediate products such as specifications and source code. ISO/IEC 12119 uses ISO/IEC 9126 as the underlying standard for defining software quality.

ISO/IEC 14598: Software Product Evaluation

ISO is currently preparing a new standard for software product evaluation. It is also intended to be used in conjunction with ISO/IEC 9126. The new standard consists of the following parts:

Part 1: General overview. This part provides an overview of the other parts and explains the relationship between ISO/IEC 14598 and the quality model in ISO/IEC 9126. It defines the technical terms used in the standard, contains general requirements for specification and evaluation of software quality, and clarifies the concepts. Additionally, it provides a framework for evaluating the quality of all types of software products and states the requirements for methods of software product measurement and evaluation.

Part 2: Planning and management. Part 2 provides requirements and guidelines for a support function responsible for the management of software product evaluation and technologies necessary for software product evaluation. The responsibilities of this support function include people motivation and education relevant to the evaluation activities, preparation of suitable evaluation documents, standards, and response to queries on evaluation technologies. The main targets for evaluation support are the software development and system integration projects, which include software acquisition, both at a project and organizational level.

Part 3: Process for developers. This part provides requirements and recommendations for the practical implementation of software product evaluation when the evaluation is conducted in parallel with development and carried out by the developer. The evaluation process described defines the activities needed to analyze evaluation requirements; specify, design, and perform evaluation actions; and conclude the evaluation of any software product. The evaluation process is designed to be used concurrently with the development. It must be synchronized with the software development process and the entities evaluated as they are delivered.

Part 4: Process for acquirers. Part 4 contains requirements, recommendations, and guidelines for the systematic measurement, assessment, and evaluation of software product quality during acquisition of off-the-shelf software products, custom software products, or modifications to existing software products. The evaluation process helps meet the objectives of deciding on the acceptance of a single product or selecting a product. The evaluation process may be tailored to the nature and integrity level of the application. It is also flexible enough to cost-effectively accommodate the wide range of forms and uses of software.

Part 5: Process for evaluators. This part provides requirements and recommendations for the practical implementation of software product evaluation when several parties need to understand, accept, and trust evaluation results. The process defines the activities needed to analyze evaluation requirements; specify, design, and perform evaluation actions; and conclude the evaluation of any kind of software product. The evaluation process may be used to evaluate already existing products, provided that the needed product components are available, or to evaluate products in development. This part may be used by testing laboratories when providing software product evaluation services.

Part 6: Documentation of evaluation modules. This part describes the structure and content of an evaluation module. An evaluation module is a package of evaluation technology for a specific software quality characteristic or subcharacteristic. The package includes descriptions of evaluation methods and techniques, inputs to be evaluated, data to be measured and collected, and supporting procedures and tools. This part should be used by testing laboratories and research institutes when developing evaluation modules.

In 1997 "Part 5: Process for Evaluators" was approved as an international standard (ISO/IEC 14598-5 1997) and "Part 1: General Overview" is currently in the final-ballot stage. The other parts are expected to become international standards sometime this year.

PRACTICAL EVALUATION SCHEMES

There are a number of practical software quality evaluation schemes, some of which are outlined here. The selection is not exhaustive, but it gives an impression of the trends in the area. Most activities are currently taking place in Europe, but South America and Asia are beginning to appear on the scene. Figure 1 provides an overview of the evaluation schemes and relevant standards discussed.

Evaluation scheme	Area	ISO/IEC 9126	ISO/IEC 14598	ISO/IEC 12119	ISO/IEC 12207
GGS	Germany	X		X	
SCOPE	Europe	X	X		
Microscope	Denmark, Greece, Hungary	X	X		
TÜV Nord	Germany	X		X	
Assespro	Brazil	X	X	X	
Squid	Denmark, Germany, Italy, United Kingdom	X	X		
NF-Logiciel	France	X		X	
Medical software	Ireland	X	X		
Q-Seal	Italy	X			
Product and process	Korea	X	X		X
Product evaluation	The Netherlands	X	X		
Product evaluation	Sweden	X	X		

Figure 1   Examples of product evaluation schemes and related standards.

The Gütegemeinschaft Software Seal

One of the first initiatives to develop a quality seal for software products was the German GGS controlled by the Gütegemeinschaft Software Association (Knorr 1990). The GGS association was founded in the mid-1980s with the aim of defining quality criteria for software products and organizing a software quality certification scheme. This resulted in the publication of the German standard DIN 66285 in 1990, which defines the quality requirements for a software package and specifies the testing procedure that could lead to a certificate. This standard was adapted for international standardization and published by ISO in 1994 as standard ISO/IEC 12119.

The GGS seal has never been very successful in Germany and has only been awarded to a few software products.

The SCOPE Experiment

The ESPRIT project SCOPE (Software Certification Program in Europe) was the first major international attempt to set up a certification scheme for software product evaluation (Robert and Roan 1990). SCOPE lasted from 1989 to 1993. The project involved 13 companies from eight countries with a total effort of 110 person-years.

The SCOPE project was successful, although it failed to set up a certification scheme. Its main achievement was the development of a framework for software quality evaluation that is now widely accepted and used as a basis for evaluations around the world.

The main results of SCOPE were an evaluation method, a collection of evaluation technologies, and extensive practical experience. Additionally, a thorough review of the legal aspects of evaluation and certification was carried out, including the legal view of software, rights exclusion clauses, criteria for successful claims, common legal defenses, and the implications of the European Communities Directives on product liability (Rae, Robert, and Hausen 1995).

The SCOPE project carried out 30 trial evaluations (Welzel, Hausen, and Bøegh 1993). These case studies were conducted in two phases. In the first phase six evaluations were carried out applying different evaluation procedures and techniques. The results were analyzed and used for planning the second phase. Here all evaluations followed the same procedure, and care was taken to select software products that covered a wide range of applications and software development approaches.

The SCOPE evaluation method was developed as a result of an analysis of the trial evaluations. It was documented in the "Evaluators Guide," which was submitted to ISO for consideration (Bøegh, Hausen, and Welzel 1992). This document has now been adapted and published as ISO/IEC 14598-5: Process for Evaluators.

The concept of evaluation modules was also an important outcome from SCOPE (Bøegh 1995). It was introduced to make it easy and flexible to manage the use of the different evaluation technologies.

MicroScope Evaluations

The MicroScope approach to software evaluation was introduced in Denmark by DELTA Software Engineering in 1991 (Kyster 1995). MicroScope is based on the results of the SCOPE project and follows standards ISO/IEC 9126 and ISO/IEC 14598-5.

The MicroScope evaluations are being used in many situations. The most common purposes are to state the conformance to a specified external standard or regulation and to validate that the level of documentation and safety for a software product is satisfactory.

The evaluations are based on an agreement between a client and DELTA on which quality characteristics of the software product should be considered and evaluation modules should be used. The MicroScope evaluation modules are checklist based. There are 12 modules covering all six characteristics of ISO/IEC 9126. The evaluations are performed at one of four possible levels for each relevant characteristic corresponding to the criticality of the product.

MicroScope emphasizes the evaluation of the workmanship of the software and related documentation (for example, that design descriptions, coding standards, test documentation, and so on comply with the best state of practice in the software industry). Experiences with the MicroScope approach will be discussed more in detail later.

TÜV Nord Evaluations

TÜV Nord in Germany has developed an evaluation method aimed at process control and real-time systems with safety relevance. The evaluation method is based on several standards, including IEC 880, draft IEC 1508/IEC 65A, DIN V VDE 801, and DIN 19250. TÜV Nord received an accreditation by DEKITZ as a software testing laboratory for evaluating software according to these standards. Off-the-shelf software is evaluated based on ISO/IEC 12119. TÜV Nord is accredited as a testing laboratory by the Gütegemeinschaft Software Association.

The mentioned standards are mainly concerned with functionality. TÜV Nord is also elaborating quality profiles based on ISO/IEC 9126 using the TASQUE approach (Anders and Flor 1994). They have been involved in national and European research projects, which have resulted in the adoption of new methods and tools such as CATS (Technischer Fachbericht 1993) and SQUID (Kitchenham et al. 1997a). These tools are used to enhance the evaluation capabilities.

The ASSESPRO Prize

In Brazil the Technological Center for Informatics Foundation (CTI) is in charge of a major effort to provide software product evaluation services to the Brazilian software industry (Tsukumo et al. 1995; Tsukumo et al. 1996; and Tsukumo et al. 1997). They have developed the method MEDE-PROS based on the international standards ISO/IEC 9126, ISO/IEC 12119, and ISO/IEC 14598 drafts.

The checklist-based method has similarities to the MicroScope approach. The checklists are continuously being improved and now include more than 100 questions. The method evaluates the product description, documentation, and programs and data according to ISO/IEC 12119. The main emphasis of MEDE-PROS evaluations are on functionality and usability for software packages.

The evaluation method is applied by the Brazilian Association of Software Houses (ASSESPRO) for awarding the best software product of the year in Brazil. The ASSESPRO prize only includes software packages and is given in six categories:

- Systems for documentation and planning support
- Systems software and systems of support to software development
- Tools for graphic design
- Information and services automation systems
- Engineering, scientific, and industrial automation systems
- Education and entertainment systems

Each year since 1993 between 20 and 50 software packages have been evaluated for the ASSESPRO prize, and considerable statistical material has been collected. Currently the MEDE-PROS evaluation method is also being applied to support a Brazilian software export initiative with the aim of increasing the Brazilian share of the world market.

The SQUID Approach

The SQUID approach to software quality evaluation is slightly different from the others. It is intended for use during software development as described in ISO/IEC 14598-3 (Bøegh and Panfilis 1996). The aim of the SQUID method is to provide support to a software developer. It is an approach to modeling, measuring, and evaluating software quality during the development process. SQUID is supported by a toolset currently under development.

The toolset assists in quality specification, planning, control, and evaluation. More specifically, for quality specification it provides the means to establish targets for the product quality requirements and evaluate their feasibility. Then, the toolset supports the identification of internal software product and process attributes that must be controlled during the development process to fulfill project quality requirements. This is called quality planning and control. Finally, the toolset helps assess the fulfillment of project quality requirements.

Ongoing evaluation of the SQUID approach and toolset is part of the work (Kitchenham et al. 1997b). One experiment is to apply SQUID as a supporting tool for third-party testing laboratories in connection with independent software product evaluations. This study is carried out by TÜV Nord in cooperation with DELTA Software Engineering.

Other Initiatives

Several other attempts to develop quality certification schemes and seals have taken place in different countries during recent years. In 1996 the French national standardization body initiated the development of a software product marking called NF Logiciel (Geyres 1997). This quality mark should be applicable to any type of software product. It is based on ISO/IEC 12119 and requires a product to be composed of product description, user documentation, and program and data. For a software product to obtain a NF Logiciel marking, the claims in user documentation must be able to be verified in the program and data by an independent evaluator. Several trial evaluations were started, but the quality mark has not yet been adopted in France.

In Ireland an evaluation scheme based on the SCOPE approach and standards ISO/IEC 9126 and ISO/IEC 14598 was established in 1994 (O'Duffy 1997). This scheme was extended to a certification scheme covering products for practice management for general practitioners in Ireland. In 1997 a total of nine software products had received certification.

In Italy an initiative to implement an evaluation scheme for software based on ISO/IEC 9126 called Q-Seal was initiated. It applies a predefined profile based on characteristics, subcharacteristics, and levels. Some case studies were conducted in 1995 and 1996.

In 1996, the National Computerization Agency in Korea started to set up a software product evaluation scheme. It decided from its organization's perspective to concentrate on custom-made software, and it is following an approach to integrate software product evaluation and software process evaluation into a common framework. The process evaluation is based on the software lifecycle processes defined in ISO/IEC 12207: Software Lifecycle Processes.

In the Netherlands KEMA has recently developed a technique for third-party evaluation of quality characteristic maintainability (Punter 1998). The technique combines the use of quality metrics (such as number of statements, comment frequency, and number of levels) with checklists. KEMA's evaluation procedure complies with ISO/IEC 14598-5.

Finally, the Swedish Association of Software Houses SPI (Föreningen Svensk Programvaruindustri) has prepared an annotated translation of ISO/IEC 14596-5 (Battison et al. 1996) and developed a series of small evaluation modules. A first experimental software product evaluation was successfully completed in 1997.

MicroScope Experiences

MicroScope is an example of a commercially successful software evaluation scheme. Many evaluations have been conducted since its introduction in 1991. The accreditation to the European standard EN 45001 obtained in 1996 confirmed the soundness of the scheme.

Evaluation Procedure

The MicroScope evaluation procedure consists of five activities that are conducted in cooperation with the client of the evaluation. The activities are performed on the basis of data and other information provided by the client or produced by other activities during the evaluation. Figure 2 shows the evaluation process.

Analysis of evaluation requirements. The purpose is to establish the objectives of the evaluation. Such objectives relate to the intended use of the software product and its associated risks. The client of the evaluation must provide an initial version of the evaluation requirements. The evaluator will then assist in analyzing these requirements.

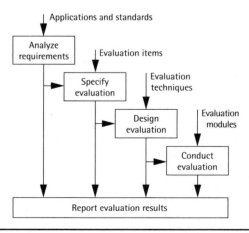

Figure 2   The evaluation process.

The application domain; critical issues such as safety, security, economic, or environment aspects; and regulations and laws are taken into account. How extensive the coverage of the evaluation should be must also be stated and agreed upon.

Specification of the evaluation. The purpose is to define the scope of the evaluation and the measurements to be performed. The level of detail should be such that the repeatability and reproducibility of the evaluation are ensured. The activity of specifying the evaluation includes three subactivities:

1. Analyzing the product description
2. Specifying the measurements to be performed on the product and its components
3. Verifying the specification produced with regard to the evaluation requirements

This activity may be supported by predefined evaluation specifications. These specifications should be in the form of evaluation module specifications as recommended in ISO/IEC 14598-6.

Design of the evaluation. The evaluator must produce a plan that describes the resources needed to perform the specified evaluation. This activity is composed of three subactivities:

1. Documenting evaluation methods and producing a draft plan. In most cases this means selecting appropriate evaluation modules.
2. Optimizing the evaluation plan.
3. Scheduling evaluation actions with regard to available resources.

The goal of this activity is to combine the specified measurements with various product components. The measurements must be selected to ensure an objective and impartial evaluation.

Execution of the evaluation plan. This consists of inspecting, modeling, measuring, and testing elements of the product according to the evaluation plan. The actions performed by the evaluator are recorded, and the results are put in a draft-evaluation report. To execute the evaluation plan the evaluator shall:

1. Manage the product components provided by the client
2. Manage the data produced by the evaluation actions
3. Manage the tools used to perform the evaluation actions

Conclusion of the evaluation. This consists of finalizing and approving the evaluation report and disposing of the product components evaluated.

The MicroScope evaluation procedure complies with the international standard ISO/IEC 14598-5: Process for Evaluators.

Commercial Evaluations

DELTA Software Engineering has obtained considerable experience by offering the MicroScope evaluation service on commercial conditions. MicroScope was launched in 1991, and about 80 software evaluations have already been conducted.

The evaluations cover many application areas, including fire alarms, burglar alarms, offshore systems, gas burners, railway signals, process-control systems, medico systems, automatic weighting systems, and windmills. Most evaluations have been in safety-critical areas. To identify the main areas of commercial interest in the MicroScope evaluation service, Figure 3 shows the evaluation effort used on different application categories.

Application category	Effort
Offshore	48%
Fire alarms	23%
Railway	12%
Other	17%

Figure 3   Effort used on different application categories.

The offshore evaluations weigh heavily in this summary because of the size of the evaluations. In numbers, however, they account for less than 10 percent of the evaluations. Software developers learn from their evaluation experiences: The second time a company applies for an evaluation the quality of its software is higher than the first time.

In particular the quality of the development documentation has increased. A few years ago companies seemed to produce limited documentation, whereas now it is common to see extensive and good quality documentation, such as design documents and well-documented source code.

Evaluation Modules

An evaluation module is defined as a package of evaluation technology for a specific software quality characteristic or subcharacteristic. The package includes descriptions of evaluation methods and techniques, inputs to be evaluated, data to be measured and collected, and supporting procedures and tools.

MicroScope includes a set of 12 evaluation modules. They are checklist based and contain more than 1800 questions. A disadvantage of the checklist approach is that answers to the questions often rely on the evaluator's judgment. This loss of objectivity can be minimized by carefully formulating the questions so they can be answered unambiguously and by avoiding very short checklists. Some experiences with checklist-based evaluations are reported in *Software Metrics for Product Assessment* (Andersen and Kyster 1994).

The possible answers to the checklists are such that zero, one, and two points are given, or it is decided that the answer is not applicable (N/A). Two points indicates that the feature is present and the formulation is such that this is positive for the product. Zero points implies an absence of a desired feature.

A score is calculated for each checklist by counting the number of points given and the number of points the product could have received when excluding the N/A questions. The ratio between these two numbers is multiplied by 10 to arrive at a final score for a checklist between zero and 10, independent of the number of questions on the checklist. The evaluation modules cover all quality characteristics identified in ISO/IEC 9126. Figure 4 categorizes the evaluation modules accordingly.

In practice, the application of some evaluation modules may be irrelevant for an evaluation, and in other cases, it may be convenient to restrict the scope of application of some of the chosen evaluation modules to samples from the documentation received for evaluation. In any case, to keep the evaluation within reasonable time and cost limits, an agreement must be reached concerning the choice of evaluation modules and the depth to which they are used.

Before starting an evaluation, the evaluator must ensure that the needed product information is made available by the client. The specific product information requirements are stated in the evaluation modules.

Quality characteristic	Evaluation module	Description
Functionality	Requirements specification	Checklist for assessing the quality of the requirement-specification document
	Safety	Checklist that takes all product parts and guides the evaluator through a cross examination of the product
	Test documentation	Checklist concerning the test documentation and the test planned and executed
	Fire-alarm regulations	Checklist covering the requirements relating to software of the standard prEN 54-2: Control and Indicating Equipment
	Nonautomatic weighing instrument	Checklist based on the WELMEC guide for examining software of nonautomatic weighing instruments
Reliability	Reliability	Checklist taking as input the design documentation and source code. The assessment is restricted to qualitative aspects of reliability
Usability	User manual	Checklist concerning the user manual, not the usability of the system under evaluation
	ISO/IEC 9241	Checklist guiding the assessment of the user interface according to the software-related parts 12 to 17 of ISO 9241
Efficiency	Source code	Checklist guiding the assessment of the source code assessed through the analysis of the software aspects: Time behavior and resource behavior
Maintainability	Design documentation	Checklist concerning the quality of the design documentation for the software product
	Source code	Checklist concerning the quality of the source code as written in any traditional programming language or as logic or ladder diagrams for PLC program
Portability	Source code	Checklist concerning the independence of the source code from any particular hardware and/or operating system platform

Figure 4   The MicroScope evaluation modules.

An Evaluation Example

A MicroScope evaluation of the software part of a fire alarm, which is a typical example of a small evaluation, requires one to two weeks' effort. A full evaluation of a fire alarm also requires a thorough hardware and system evaluation, including both design and implementation aspects and practical fire tests of the alarm. It is the combined results of these evaluations that form the basis for the approval decision by the authorities (in this case the Danish Institute of Fire Technology).

Before an evaluation starts the manufacturer must provide the necessary input for the evaluation. This includes product identification information (name, version, date, type, hardware and software platform, programming language, compiler name and version, and so on) design documentation, program description, source code, and user manual. Furthermore, requirements specification, test documentation, executable code, maintenance manual, quality assurance plans, and project plans are also requested.

This type of MicroScope evaluation usually requires the application of four evaluation modules:

- **Usability: User manual.** A Checklist with 97 questions concerning the user's manual as such for the software (or the system as a whole).

- **Maintainability: Design documentation.** A Checklist with 110 questions concerning the quality of the design documentation for the software product.

- **Functionality: Safety.** A Checklist with 195 questions concerning the safety and security of the software product as a whole.

- **Functionality: Fire-alarm regulations.** The purpose of applying this evaluation module is to demonstrate compliance to European fire-alarm regulations.

The criteria for selecting these four evaluation modules are the requirements from public authorities and the cost of the evaluation. In other words, to answer the questions of evaluation module "Functionality: Fire-alarm regulations" the evaluator must have a thorough understanding of the system. This is obtained by answering the questions of the three other evaluation modules. Since these types of evaluations are cost sensitive (due to competition) the selected evaluation modules constitute a minimal set necessary to carry out the evaluation.

In a real MicroScope evaluation conducted at DELTA Software Engineering the following scores were achieved and observations made:

- **Usability: User Manual: Score 8.6.** The user manual is well structured, with the appropriate level of details for users who have been trained in the operation of the system. On the other hand there lacks an upper-level description of the system including examples of typical systems. There is no identification of the software version for which it is relevant. Of the questions on the checklist, 25 percent were N/A because the system is embedded and the user manual does not need to cover explanations of platform, operating system, software environment, back up, and so on.

- **Maintainability: Design documentation: Score 7.5.** The modularity and breakdown of the system are very good, and it is a convincing reflection of the implementation. The completeness and consistency of the design documentation is also good. On the other hand, a simple introduction to the system and its design is lacking, together with descriptions of data structures and explanations of variables and constants. The self-descriptiveness of the design documentation is weak, as illustrated through lack of consistent document identification, tables of contents, glossaries, and introductions.

- **Functionality: Safety: Score 7.3.** The self-test facilities and the supervision of the hardware are good from a safety point of view, as well as the user interface. The programming style is well structured. On the other hand, the documentation of fault handling is weak and is mainly restricted to information contained in module headers. Thus, there is no central place to identify what may happen and what the systems' reactions are. Use of interrupts complicates the safety analysis, as does use of the language C. Of the questions on the checklist, 25 percent were N/A because they were related to fail-safe features. No true fail-safe features are present in the software, but because of the application, they are not needed.

- **Functionality: Fire-alarm regulations.** Here "passed" or "failed" is given for each of the requirements from the standard. In this case, 15 out of 16 requirements from fire-alarm regulations were passed.

- **Conclusion of the evaluation.** The software and the corresponding documentation for the fire-alarm unit have been assessed regarding its conformity with the relevant requirements of the fire-alarm regulations. This was done by conducting a MicroScope evaluation to assess the design documentation, the user manual, the safety features of the software system, as well as the conformity with the fire-alarm regulations.

The conclusion is that the software sufficiently conforms with the standard for use in a fire-alarm unit. With regard to the nonconformity found with one of the requirements of the fire-alarm regulations, it should be noted that the judgment is based on the fact that no documentation was found for the requested feature. If the software is in conformance, this may be documented. If the nonconformity is real and the matter is deemed to be sufficiently important, restrictions may be introduced so that the system can only handle 512 fire detectors or manual call points.

ISO Guide 2:	General terms and their definitions concerning standardization and related activities
ISO Guide 25:	General requirements for the technical competence of testing laboratories
ISO Guide 38:	General requirements for the acceptance of testing laboratories
ISO Guide 43:	Development and operation of laboratory proficiency testing
ISO Guide 45:	Guidelines for the presentation of test results
ISO Guide 49:	Guidelines for development of a quality manual for testing laboratories

Figure 5   The ISO guides related to EN 45001.

Accreditation

At the beginning of 1996 DELTA Software Engineering received an official accreditation of MicroScope according to the European standard EN 45001: General Criteria for the Operation of Testing Laboratories. Accreditation means formal recognition by an authoritative body that an organization is competent. The MicroScope accreditation, which is issued by the Danish Accreditation Service (DANAK), confirms the compliance of MicroScope with ISO/IEC 9126 and ISO/IEC 14598-5. The accreditation gives the right to issue MicroScope evaluation reports using the DANAK logo.

DANAK is a member of the European Cooperation for Accreditation of Laboratories, an organization of the national bodies of all EU/EFTA member countries that accredit testing laboratories. The national accreditation bodies evaluate each other frequently to ensure that each is operating in accordance with international standards. A multilateral agreement exists between national accreditation bodies ensuring that reports issued by accredited testing laboratories have the same degree of credibility in all member countries. The purpose of this European acceptance of reports is to help international business by removing barriers to trade.

To achieve the accreditation, a quality documentation consisting of 39 documents, totaling 2100 pages, was produced. The documentation includes a quality system, relevant standards, operating procedures, and test instructions. The experiences with the accreditation process were positive. The accreditation body handled the process fast and efficiently. It took six months from when the application was forwarded until the accreditation was issued. To keep validity, the MicroScope accreditation must be renewed every year.

It should be noted that European standard EN 45001 is based on the ISO guides listed in Figure 5. In some instances the text from these guides has been modified or clarified for European purposes; however, such changes are the exception rather than the rule.

Licenses

The MicroScope evaluation method and evaluation modules have been licensed to companies in Greece and Hungary, and other companies have expressed interest. Such arrangements provide an efficient start-up of software evaluation services for testing laboratories, which are new in this field.

CONCLUSION

As the number of critical software applications grows, the need and demand for software quality evaluation increases. International standards are being prepared to support evaluation, and practical software product evaluation schemes are available to the market. But the field is not mature yet, and there is still a need to experiment, collect experiences, and improve the evaluation methods and technologies.

References

Anders, U., and R. Flor. 1994. TASQUE-TÜV. In *Software metrics for product assessment*, R. Bache and G. Bazzana, eds. London: McGraw-Hill.

Andersen, O., and H. Kyster. 1994. Reproducibility of checklists. In *Software metrics for product assessment*, R. Bache and G. Bazzana, eds. London: McGraw-Hill.

Battison, R., J. Bengtsson, R. Källgren, L. Piper, M. Ran, H. Samuelsson, and J. Stiernborg. 1996. *Manual för utvärdering av programprodukter enligt ISO 14598-5 och ISO 9126*. Stockholm: Föreningen Svensk Programvaruindustri.

Bøegh, J., H. L. Hausen, and D. Welzel. 1992. Guide to software product evaluation: The evaluator's guide. *SCOPE Technical Report* SC.92/099/ECT.jb. GMD.hlh.dw/T2.1.2/DR/04.

Bøegh, J. 1995. Evaluation modules: The link between theory and practice. In *Proceedings of the second IEEE international software engineering standards symposium*. Los Alamitos, CA: IEEE Computer Society Press.

Bøegh, J., and S. de Panfilis. 1996. SQUID: A method for managing software quality during the development. In *Proceedings of the European Space Agency product assurance symposium and software product assurance workshop*. Noordwijk, The Netherlands: ESA Publication Division.

EN 45001: *General criteria for the operation of testing laboratories*. 1991. CEN/CENELEC.

Geyres, S. 1997. NF Logiciel: Affordable certification for all software products. In *Achieving software product quality*, edited by E. van Veenendaal and J. McMullan (September): 125–135.

ISO Guide 25: *General requirements for the technical competence of testing laboratories*. 1990. Geneva, Switzerland: International Organization for Standardization.

ISO/IEC 9126: *Information technology–Software product evaluation–Quality characteristics and guidelines for their use*. 1991. Geneva, Switzerland: International Organization for Standardization.

ISO/IEC 9241: *Ergonomic requirements for office work with visual display terminals*. 1994. Geneva, Switzerland: International Organization for Standardization.

ISO/IEC 12119: *Information technology–Software packages–Quality requirements and testing*. 1994. Geneva, Switzerland: International Organization for Standardization.

ISO/IEC 12207: *Information technology–Software lifecycle processes*. 1995. Geneva, Switzerland: International Organization for Standardization.

ISO/IEC 14598: *Information technology–Software product evaluation* (draft multipart standard). 1998. Geneva, Switzerland: International Organization for Standardization.

ISO/IEC 14598-5: *Information technology–Software product evaluation–Process for evaluators*. 1997. Geneva, Switzerland: International Organization for Standardization.

Kitchenham, B., A. Pasquini, U. Anders, J. Bøegh, S. de Panfilis, and S. Linkman. 1997. Automating software quality modeling, measurement and assessment. In *Reliability, quality and safety of software-intensive systems*, edited by D. Gritzalis. London: Chapman & Hall.

Kitchenham, B., S. Linkman, A. Pasquini, V. Nanni. 1997. The SQUID approach to defining a quality model. *Software Quality Journal* 6: 211–213.

Knorr, G. 1990. The Gütegemeinschaft software: A major concept in the certification of software quality. In *Approving software products*, edited by W. Ehrenberger (September): 135–138.

Kyster, H. 1995. MicroScope: *The evaluation of software product quality* DQD-5012200. Horsholm, Denmark: DELTA Danish Electronics.

O'Duffy, M. 1997. Certification of software for medical practitioners. In *Achieving software product quality*, E. van Veenendaal and J. McMullan, eds. (September): 137–143.

Punter, T. 1998. Developing an evaluation module to assess software maintainability. In *Proceedings of empirical assessment in software engineering conference*. Staffordshire, England: University of Keele.

Rae, A., P. Robert, H. L. Hausen. 1995. *Software evaluation for certification.* London: McGraw-Hill.

Robert, P., and A. Roan. 1990. The SCOPE project: An overview. In *Approving software products,* edited by W. Ehrenberger (September): 9–22.

Tectnicher Fachbericht. 1993. Werkzeuge für den standardisierten software-sicherheitsnachweis (SOSAT-3), supported by Bundesministerium für Bildung und Forschung. Hamburg, Germany: Tectnicher Fachbericht. (March).

Tsukumo, A. N., C. R. Capovilla, C. M. Rêgo, M. Jino, and J. C. Maldonado. 1995. ISO/IEC 9126: An experiment of application on Brazilian software products. In *Proceedings of the second IEEE international software engineering standards symposium.* Montréal. Los Alamitos, CA: IEEE Computer Society Press.

Tsukumo, A. N., A. Oliveira, C. M. Rêgo, G. F. Azevedo, J. C. Maldonado, M. T. Aguayo, M. Jino, and R. Tutumi. 1996. The second experiment of application of ISO/IEC 9126 standards on quality evaluation of Brazilian software products. In *Proceedings of the 6th international conference on software quality.* Ottawa, Ontario.

Tsukumo, A. N., A. Oliveira, C. M. Rêgo, C. S. Salviano, G. F. Azevedo, M. C. Costa, R. M. T. Colombo, and M. Jino. 1997. A framework for incremental evaluation of software product quality based on ISO/IEC 9126. In *Proceedings of the 6th software quality management conference.* Bath, England.

Welzel, D., H. L. Hausen, and J. Bøegh. 1993. A metric-based software evaluation method. In *Software testing, verification, and reliability.* New York: John Wiley & Sons.

Biography

Jørgen Bøegh has a degree in mathematics and computer science from Aarhus University in Denmark. He is currently a project manager for DELTA Danish Electronics, Light and Acoustics Division.

Bøegh has been involved in research in communication security and personal safety of software-based systems. He was involved in the ESPRIT 1 project REQUEST (Reliability and Quality in European Software Technology) from 1985 to 1987. From 1986 to 1989 he was responsible for DELTA's participation in the MAP projects "Network Security" and "Software Integrity." In 1988 and 1989 he managed an industrial collaborate project on integration of computer-aided engineering tools within the Danish electronics industry.

From 1989 to 1993 he was involved in the ESPRIT II project SCOPE (Software certification program in Europe) and from 1994 to 1996 he was responsible for DELTA's participation in the ESPRIT III project PET (Prevention of errors through test). Since 1995 he has been responsible for DELTA's participation in the ACTS project Prospect, and from 1997 also for the project VALSE (validating SQUID in real environments) and the ESSI project EPIC (exchanging process improvement experiences across SMEs by conferencing on the Internet).

Bøegh is head of the Danish delegation to the international standardization group ISO/IEC JTC1 SC7 and was appointed editor of ISO/IEC 14598 parts 3 and 6. He is the author of several scientific papers and a book on object-oriented software development. His research interests include software quality specification and evaluation, software measurement and testing, and software best practices. Bøegh can be reached by e-mail at jb@delta.dk .

CHAPTER 7.2

Practical Quality Assurance for Embedded Software

Erik P. W. M. van Veenendaal

*I*nspections are generally accepted as a means for effectively and efficiently improving the quality of software products. Yet inspections are not a standard practice in many software projects and organizations. Introducing and implementing inspections is often tedious and difficult because software engineers must be personally convinced of the effectiveness of new methods before they will consistently use them.

This article describes the applications of inspections and structured testing as measures for quality assurance in a television set software project at Philips Semiconductors. Inspections were used to reduce project risks and assure product quality. Implementation of inspection and structured testing is described, as are the results achieved and some critical success factors.

Key words: defect detection, inspection, software quality management, success factors, testing, walkthroughs

INTRODUCTION

In every phase of software development defects are introduced, defects are found, and rework is done. Most defects, however, are found when the software product is almost finished (such as during the system and acceptance testing phase or even during operation). The rework for defects found during the testing phase on almost-finished software products is time consuming. Finding these defects earlier in the process would save the development organization a lot of time.

Inspections are an effective and efficient technique for improving the quality of software products early on. They can also be used to prevent defects. By analyzing the defects that are found, the software development processes can be adapted and optimized to prevent these defects from occurring in the future.

Inspections can be defined as structured reviews of an engineer's software work product carried out by colleagues to find defects and to enable the engineers to improve the product's quality (Fagan 1986). The reason for having inspections can be explained by using Gerald M. Weinberg's concept of egoless engineering (1971). Weinberg refers to cognitive dissonance as the human tendency to self-justify actions. Since people tend not to see evidence that conflicts with their strong beliefs, their ability to find errors in their own work is impaired. Because of this tendency many engineering organizations have established independent test groups that specialize in finding defects. Similar principles have led to the introduction of software inspections.

CONSUMER ELECTRONICS

In the world of consumer electronics the amount of embedded software is growing rapidly. The amount of software in high-end television (TV) sets has increased approximately eight times over the last six years (Rooijmans, Aerts, and van Genuchten 1996). The increasing complexity of software in consumer electronics calls for a high level of quality assurance activities. The challenge is even greater if one considers that in principle no field defects can be allowed; it is almost impossible to recall consumer products from the market since the location of these products is generally unknown. Implementing software product quality is no longer an option, it is mandatory.

Along with the need for a high-quality product, which requires time and effort to develop, are the demands that come from a highly competitive market. The time to market for consumer electronics is decreasing rapidly, putting more pressure on software development groups to deliver on time. Being one month late on market introduction will result in a substantial loss of profits. In addition, the consumer electronics market has been faced with a 5 percent to 10 percent price erosion per year (Rooijmans, Aerts, and van Genuchten 1996). The price of a product is, among other things, determined by the microcontroller used. Therefore, the use of computing resources remains under high pressure in consumer electronic products, leading to severe restrictions on code size. Time to market and price are thus putting extra tension on the objective of developing high-quality software products.

This article describes a project within consumer electronics that had the objective of developing the leading versions for a low-end TV software product. It focuses on the way software quality activities testing and inspections were planned and performed. The TV software development project was conducted by a software group within Philips Semiconductors. Philips Semiconductors is one of many companies in the electronics industry that is in transition from the hardware stage to the embedded software stage. Companies in this position are starting to add software to their hardware products to add value and achieve a higher level of flexibility within their products. Development, however, is still dominated by hardware (Gal and van Genuchten 1996).

The low-end TV software project was carried out at locations throughout the world. Eindhoven in The Netherlands and Singapore were the main development sites. Two other sites were used for reasons of specific knowledge and skills on teletext and closed captioning. Initially, the project was faced with tight deadlines and difficulties obtaining adequate staffing. The final staff consisted of engineers experienced both in software development and in the application domain, experienced engineers with no practical knowledge of the application domain, and less-experienced engineers who had just completed their education. During the development a quality system certified to ISO 9001 was used, and within the software organization, the Capability Maturity Model (Humphrey 1989) was used for continuous software process improvement.

Trying to meet the objectives of developing a high-quality product (zero field defects) on time according to the agreed functional requirements presented a few challenges:

- **Less-experienced staffing.** As stated earlier only some of the staff were experienced. Little time was available for training, so most of it had to be done on the job. Additional attention was needed for ensuring the quality of the various software work products.

- **More than one location.** The project was carried out at various locations, mainly Eindhoven and Singapore. Again this provided a number of challenges considering methods and standards used, interfaces between components, planning and tracking, and quality in general. These challenges were exaggerated by the cultural differences between Europe and Asia.

- **Project size.** Although the software organization had experience in developing TV software, the size of the project introduced a new dimension. Project planning, tracking, and oversight principles had to be expanded for this project toward a new environment. A number of project management activities were to be carried out for the first time at this level.

In response to these factors, project management and the project sponsor decided that quality needed explicit attention. A separate software quality plan was written in which the quality strategy was one of the most important issues, and quality engineering was defined as a dedicated role within the project.

THE QUALITY STRATEGY USED

One of the most important elements in the software development process is the definition of the quality strategy. The quality strategy defines what quality activities (for example, testing and inspections) will be carried out on which software work products and how thorough the activities will be. Choices must be made because it is impossible to evaluate a software product completely. One hundred percent coverage on all components and quality characteristics is perhaps possible in theory, but no organization has the time nor the money to achieve this.

The quality strategy of the TV software project was determined via a communication process within the software development team, trying to identify the product's most important components and quality characteristics and making use of past experiences with TV software projects. The aim was to focus on the most important and complex components and quality characteristics of the software.

The V-model (see Figure 1) was adapted as a starting point for evaluating the software product. This means that in parallel to phased software development, starting with the customer requirements specification (CRS), a sort of phased model is used for software quality activities testing and inspections. The arrows in the V-model show which documentation was used as a reference for each type of testing. To improve the quality of the starting documentation, providing a solid basis for testing and trying to detect defects as early as possible in the development process, the V-model was supplemented with various inspection activities.

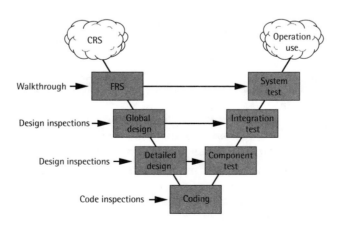

Figure 1 The V-Model.

Requirements Walkthrough

At the time the quality strategy was defined and inspections were introduced, the functional requirements specification (FRS) document was almost finished. The tight deadline put on the delivery date of the FRS left little time for internal reviews or inspections by the software development team. The FRS was reviewed, however, by means of a walkthrough with representatives of the customer and product management. Walkthroughs can cover more material than inspections and reviews because the presenter is the author, and the other participants do not have a heavy participating workload. Therefore, they provide an opportunity for many people to become familiar with the material.

Walkthroughs are used more for communication than for discovering defects. For instance, software may be inherited; exactly what is there is not known, so a walkthrough is organized to go through it, page by page, with the key people in the room. It is fine if defects are found; the main objective is to become familiar with the product. In the TV software project the walkthrough served as a means to reach formal agreement with the customer on the documented functional requirements.

Important Quality Characteristics

In addition to the quality strategy based on the V-model, a number of quality characteristics according to ISO 9126 (ISO/IEC 9126 1991) were identified that needed special attention during software development:

- **Efficiency.** As previously stated, price, and therefore code size, are important issues within consumer electronics software products. During software inspections special attention was given to the efficiency of the software code. In the final stages of the project a tool was used to track the code size after compilation for the various leading versions.

- **Maintainability.** Because of business requirements such as time to market and reduction of production cost, the importance of reusable and easy-to-maintain software is high. Within the project a static-analyzer tool was used to evaluate the number of code lines, number of function calls, cyclomatic complexity, maximum number of control structures, and comment density of the developed software components and functions. Acceptance criteria per metric were defined in a discussion meeting with the software engineers. This was done to ensure feasibility and commitment on the criteria by the engineers. As a result, 92 percent of the software code complied to all criteria and was classified as being excellent.

- **Portability.** Three variations of a certain microcontroller were used for the various leading versions (nonteletext, teletext, and closed captioning). This meant that the interface functions for hardware pinning had to be developed separately from the standard components. Fulfilling the customer requirement of one standard user interface regardless of the microcontroller used meant that the basic functionality for user interface was limited to the possibilities of the nonteletext microcontroller. This customer requirement was thus putting constraints on the specifications and design to achieve the required portability.

- **Usability.** Usability is an important quality characteristic within consumer electronics; however, it was not always dealt with by the software development team. A specialized corporate design unit designed and specified the user interface and human interactions as part of the FRS. The same unit also performed usability testing based on a prototype user interface to improve the usability of the final software product.

SOFTWARE TESTING

Component Testing

Initially it was decided that all newly developed software components would be subject to component testing by a software engineer (preferably not the same one who wrote the software code). No formal testing techniques would be mandated, so the software engineers themselves were to decide how component testing was to be carried out against the global and detailed designs. Component test cases that were identified, however, would be embedded in the source code to enable reuse and reproducibility of the tests performed. A test case can be defined as a set of test inputs, execution conditions, and expected results developed for a particular objective.

To assist the software engineer in doing a thorough component test, a test-coverage tool was made available. A test-coverage tool can provide information on the level of statement coverage that is reached during testing, which gives the software engineer an understanding of the thoroughness of the testing.

The project team decided that a statement coverage of 75 percent was required for component testing. If a large number of defects were found, however, the requirement statement coverage was raised to 85 percent. Statistics show that the number of defects found on 75 percent coverage will double when the coverage is increased to 85 percent (Kit 1995).

The main problem for component testing is an adequate testing environment. For embedded software this means having dummy components for both hardware and software interface. Developing these dummy components is often time consuming. In practice, because of time constraints and the problem related to dummy components, component testing was limited to a small number of critical and complex components. To reduce the risk associated with not performing component testing according to the defined quality strategy, project management decided to place more effort on code inspections and enlarge the number of test cases for integration and system testing. Defining these actions brought the risk under control, enabling the software development team to deliver a quality product on time. The test-coverage tool was deferred until integration and system testing.

Integration Testing

The integration test aims at testing the interfaces between the components in an integrated hardware/software environment. For the integration tests, a more formal approach was used. The integration test was prepared by the software engineers together with independent test engineers, defining test cases for each interface specified in the global design document and the hardware-software interface document. The data flow testing technique was used for specifying the test cases (Pol, Teunissen, and van Veenendaal 1995; Pol and van Veenendaal 1999).

The starting point for the data flow test is the data (triggers) that flow from one component to another by means of a function call. The technique focuses on the possible values of the parameters in the function call. A test case consisted of identifying the interfaces being tested, the input, and the expected results (on a logical level). Relevant environmental needs and preconditions were also specified. Test execution was done by the software engineers using the prepared (and inspected) test cases, and the results were logged on a test report form.

System Testing

The objective of the system test was to test the entire software product against the functional requirements, treating the software product as a black-box. The system test was prepared by the software engineers and the independent test engineers, defining test cases for each functional requirement defined in the FRS document. The decision-table testing technique was used for specifying the test cases (Pol, Teunissen, and van Veenendaal 1995; Pol and van Veenendaal 1999).

The decision-table technique is a formal technique, which means that the test cases are derived from the FRS documentation in a deterministic way according to a fixed set of rules. It focuses on the completeness and accuracy of the processing. It was originally developed for glass-box testing, but has been applied successfully during black-box testing (system and acceptance testing), especially in embedded software environments. The test cases based on this technique were enriched with error-anticipating test cases focusing on invalid and unexpected conditions. To improve the quality of testing, test cases were subject to inspections. Again, test execution was mainly done by software engineers, using the test report form as a logging mechanism. All test cases were put under configuration management to assure reuse of the test cases in regression testing and future projects.

INSPECTIONS

Implementation

While the importance and benefits of software project inspections are understood within the industry, few engineers apply this technique to their own work. Even when statistical evidence exists, the adoption of improved software methods is often slow because software engineers must be personally convinced of the effectiveness of new methods before they will consistently use them. This is particularly true in software development because of several factors (Humphrey 1995):

- Software engineers' methods are largely private and not obvious from the products they produce. Thus, if they do not use proper methods, it is unlikely that anyone else will know.

- Software engineers are generally not trained to follow the planning and measurement disciplines needed to rigorously evaluate the methods they use.

- Even when software groups have a common set of defined practices, these practices are not consistently followed.

- Current industrial environments do not require the use of the best-known software engineering methods.

A principal issue, therefore, is how to motivate and implement inspections within a software organization. Some software engineers working on the TV software project initially showed a negative attitude toward inspections. In previous projects they had experienced a somewhat theoretical introduction of inspections, resulting in the discovery of a large number of minor textual defects.

As a result two types of inspections were introduced: team review and formal inspections. Both types were carried out using initiation, preparation, meetings, rework, and follow-up as the main phases (a description of the inspection procedures is provided in the next section). For the formal inspection a moderator was appointed, roles were assigned, and separate logging and causal analysis meetings were held. These issues and aspects were not part of the inspection process when a team review was conducted. For both types of inspections a procedure was developed and maintained throughout the project by the quality coordinator.

In principle, the author of the design document or software code to be inspected had to decide which inspection method to use. An exception to this rule was made when the object to be inspected was larger than 15 pages or when the quality strategy identified the component as highly important and complex. In these cases the formal inspection method was used.

The implementation of inspections within the Singapore team was another matter. The Singapore team members were not used to commenting on software products made by other team members. Comments can be taken personally, particularly during inspection meetings where many people are present. Because of this it was decided that all inspections would be performed at Eindhoven. A co-author from the Eindhoven team was assigned to each software work product developed at Singapore. The co-author coordinated the inspection and provided written feedback on the results to the original author. This way of working proved to be beneficial throughout the project.

Inspections Conducted

All project design documents, both global and detailed, were inspected. Because of the number of detailed design documents, extra attention was given to the authors' objective (for example, the specific questions that had to be answered). Emphasis was put on best practices, and discussions on functionality or architecture were not allowed since this was not cost effective. All software code was also inspected, giving special attention to the issue of code size (performance). When performing code inspections, optimization of code size is the main objective next to conformance to standards. The team-review method was selected for use in code inspections.

A total of 123 inspections were carried out throughout the project's lifecycle. The total effort spent was approximately nine person weeks for finding the defects and another nine person weeks for rework and follow up. No fewer than 1465 defects were found during inspections. The defects within the project were classified into three groups:

- **Critical.** A defect that would get through to testing or operational stages if not found during inspection and has a scope beyond the component being inspected.

- **Major.** A defect that would get through to testing or operational stages if not found during inspection but only has an impact on the component being inspected.

- **Minor.** A defect that only impacts the document under inspection. If this defect is not found during inspection it will not result in a testing or operational defect.

Note that instead of the common categorization for defects relating to risk or the amount of rework, the focus is on preventing test failures (Rooijmans, Aerts, and van Genuchten 1996), and thus, saving effort. The category distribution of defects is shown in Figure 2.

Defect category	Total number of defects	Percentage
Critical defects	50	4%
Major defects	691	47%
Minor defects	724	49%
Total	1465	100%

Figure 2 Defect distribution.

It can be calculated from the data presented that on average one critical or major defect was found per hour spent (including rework). Looking at the differences between team review and formal inspection, the average number of defects found per hour for formal inspections was 1.5. This means that although there was some initial opposition to formal inspections, they were more efficient during the project. Data resulting from the engineers' own organization or project will convince them more readily of process changes needed (for example, more formal inspections instead of team reviews). It was also calculated that an average of 0.9 defects were found per page, and 27 defects were found per thousand lines of code, only taking the critical and major defects into account.

THE INSPECTION PROCEDURE

The inspection procedures are based on the generic inspection procedure described in the organization's quality system. Adaptations were based on the specific project environment. The procedure for formal inspection consisted of eight steps, and the team-review procedure consisted of five steps. Hereafter, the formal-inspection procedure that was developed is described, identifying the differences with the team-review procedure. When the term "document under inspection" is used it also refers to "software code under inspection."

1. **Request:** Initiating the inspection process. The inspection process begins with a request for inspection by the author of the software to the quality coordinator. The quality coordinator assigns a moderator to the inspection, who performs an initial entry check. The purpose of the entry check is to reduce the probability that the team will waste scarce resources, only to discover items that could easily have been corrected by the author before the inspection began. In the case of a team review, no moderator is assigned to the inspection; the author and the quality coordinator take care of moderator's activities.

2. **Planning the inspection.** When the design document or software code has passed the entry check the quality coordinator gives the moderator (or the author in the case of a team review) an inspection-process form. During the planning phase the dates, times, and place are set. Participants are selected and informed on these issues and are assigned to one or more so-called roles. Roles are used to ensure that each participant has a unique viewpoint and discovers unique defects, making the inspection process more effective. An inspection team typically consisted of two or three software engineers, both experienced and less experienced. The following roles can be distinguished according to the "1 to 4" model (see Figure 3) for inspections:

   • Focus on related documents on the same level (for example, interfaces between software functions).

   • Focus on standards (for example, best practice, internal consistency, clarity, and naming conventions).

   • Focus on higher-level documents (for example, does the design comply to the FRS?)

   • Focus in use (for example, for design testability, programmability, and maintainability).

   The author can raise specific issues (roles) that must be addressed during the inspection process. During a team review, however, the concept of roles is not mandatory. It is up to the author to raise specific questions and issues during the planning phase. Because no separate kickoff is held during a team review, the author distributes the document to be inspected and other relevant information at the end of the planning phase and provides participants with the necessary explanation.

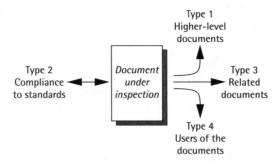

Figure 3 The "1 to 4" model.

3. **Kickoff.** The moderator distributes the document to be inspected and other relevant documents. The participants receive a short introduction on the objectives of the inspection and the documents. Role assignments and other questions are also discussed. The kickoff meeting may also include feedback on inspection process changes and training on inspection procedure. As stated before, a kick-off meeting is not held during a team review.

4. **Preparation.** Participants work separately on the document under inspection using the documents, procedures, and checklists provided. The defects are identified according to the understanding of the individual participant and are recorded on the document under inspection. If necessary, these copies of the document will be given to the author at the end of the logging meeting. This step is identical during a team review.

5. **Logging meeting.** During the meeting the defects that have already been identified during the individual preparation are logged on the logging form by the author. To assure progress and efficiency no discussions are allowed during the logging meeting. Items that need to be discussed and questions that are raised are logged in and addressed later during the discussion meeting. In a team review, however, discussions are allowed during this meeting. At the end of the logging meeting the author asks for suggestions for improvements, possibly leading to change requests on related documents, standards, and the review process. How the follow-up should take place is also discussed and agreed upon at the end of the logging meeting during a team review.

6. **Discussion meeting.** The discussion meeting normally takes place immediately after the logging meeting, and items identified during the logging meeting are addressed. This meeting may include issues on how to solve the detected defects. At the end of the meeting the moderator asks for remarks on improvements, possibly leading to change requests on related documents, standards, and the inspection process. The way the follow-up should take place is also discussed and agreed upon, if possible including throughput time. There are five options to choose from:

   - The follow-up is done by the moderator
   - The follow-up is done by the moderator in cooperation with the participants
   - A new team review is required for the document
   - A new formal inspection must take place on the same document
   - A separate discussion meeting is not conducted during a team review

7. **Rework.** Based on the defect logging the author will improve the product. The author may also make improvements or corrections to the document not based on the defect logging. This step also applies to the team review.

8. **Follow-up and exit.** The moderator (or the quality coordinator in case of a team review) checks whether satisfactory actions have been taken on logged defects, improvement suggestions, and change requests. Although the moderator checks to make sure that the author has taken action on all known defects, he or she does not have to check the corrections themselves. If decided at the end of the discussion meeting, the design document is once again distributed among the participants to check whether the defects are corrected.

Finally, the document leaves the inspection process and is put under formal configuration management. The moderator completes the inspection-process form and presents it to the quality coordinator, who will use these forms as a basis for reporting and gathering metrics.

RESULTS

Of course, inspections and testing are only a means to achieving project objectives. Therefore, the most important questions have yet to be answered:

- Did the project meet its objectives?
- How did the defined and implemented quality strategy contribute to these objectives?
- What other results were achieved by carrying out inspections and structured testing?

A Quality Product on Time

The primary project objective—a quality product delivered on time—was met by the software development team. Inspections and testing improved the quality of the product without delaying the project. This is especially true since inspections were used at various development stages, such as global design, detailed design, and coding. Using inspections during the various stages helped catch defects that had slipped through inspections at earlier stages. Structured testing, by means of well-prepared test cases, proved to be successful in finding the remaining defects and showed an extremely high level of coverage.

Since the test cases were prepared during an earlier phase, making the test-execution phase an efficient one, the overall throughput time of testing did not exceed its initial plan. Statistics also showed that the project did not lose any time on inspections but in fact gained some time (see Figure 4). Delivering a quality product on time ultimately means customer satisfaction, which is likely to result in an assignment for software development of another TV range.

Total number of critical or major defects found by inspections	741
Average time to solve a defect in testing	70 minutes
Potential effort needed to solve defects in testing	864 hours
Total effort spent on inspections	720 hours
Effort saved by carrying out inspections	144 hours

Figure 4   Net time saved by inspections.

Reduction of the Project Risks

One of the main reasons for having a thorough quality strategy and using inspections was to control the identified project risks. In practice, inspections proved to be a powerful means for controlling these risks. The risks that were identified earlier are again briefly addressed:

- **Staffing.** Having both experienced and less-experienced engineers on each inspection team allowed a lot of knowledge to be transferred during inspection meetings. Inspections were thus used as an on-the-job training mechanism.

- **More than one location.** Since all software work products developed in Singapore were inspected by the Eindhoven team, product quality information was provided at a detailed level to project management. This information enabled project management to track product quality and take appropriate action when necessary. Although not initially intended this way, carrying out all inspections at Eindhoven turned a problem into an opportunity and became beneficial to the project.

- **Project size.** The inspection phases "initiation" and "follow-up and exit" were used as checkpoints for project tracking and oversight at a detailed level. In the beginning of the project there was much discussion about tasks that were "almost done" or "90 percent done" according to software engineers. Using the inspection checkpoints as a basis for project tracking made tracking more objective and tangible since the results of a certain task—for example, a design document or software code—had to be available at the beginning of an inspection. Inspection thus provided an effective way to track the project's progress.

Earlier and Cheaper Defects

Another reason for conducting inspections is to improve productivity. The longer a defect remains in a product, the more costly it is to remove. The only other widely applicable technique for detecting and eliminating defects is testing, and since inspections can eliminate defects more cheaply than testing, they can also be used to improve productivity. During the TV software project data were collected on the rework effort for critical and major defects during the various development phases. As shown in Figure 5, the average rework effort (shown in minutes) on testing defects is significantly higher than during earlier phases.

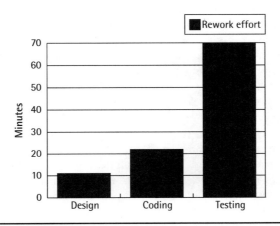

Figure 5 Rework effort on defects.

It is even possible to calculate the time saved by using inspections, giving an indication of the improved productivity. Although inspections were used for a number of reasons, including improved product quality and risk reduction, the project ultimately did not lose time on inspections. The calculation of the net time saved is shown in Figure 4.

A Structured Testing Process

In addition to improved product quality and higher productivity, inspections provide for a more structured testing process. Since many defects have already been detected during earlier phases, the initial input quality of the software product to be tested is higher. Inspections reduce the chaos that usually exists at the start of testing. Chaos is most prominent when the big-bang approach is used: nonreproducible defects, tests scripts that cannot be completed, unexplainable system failures, test cases that cannot be executed, and test cases that are inconsistent with specifications and design. Using inspections within the TV software project meant that most test scripts were fully executed during the first test run.

Testing with the prepared test cases led to reproducible testing defects, making it easier for software engineers to solve the problem. All versions of the TV software product were subject to a thorough evaluation cycle, which included at least three full integration and system tests. This meant the test scripts and test cases were reused, giving a satisfactory return on the initial effort invested in the identification and specification of the test cases.

While performing an integration and system test for a specific software version, the code-coverage tool was used to measure the statement coverage and the effectiveness of testing using structured testing techniques. All tests (full integration and system test) showed a statement coverage of at least 95 percent, which is high compared to the average of 40 percent for commercially released software (Fenton 1991). Note that statement coverage requires every statement in a program to be executed at least once; it is a necessary but in no way sufficient criterion for a quality test. Stronger criteria include decision coverage or branch coverage.

Improved Quality Awareness

The project created additional awareness on software product quality issues both on a managerial and operational level. On the operational level, two engineering groups can be distinguished: the engineers involved in the project and the other engineers. The project engineers experienced the benefits of using inspections and performing structured testing. For them it has become a way of working that goes without saying. Other software engineers within the organization have since become interested. They want to know more about the way the quality activities were carried out and how to use them in their own projects. A separate presentation was made to them, explaining and discussing in detail the way of working, results, pitfalls, and so forth.

Since the project was of strategic importance to the organization, management watched it closely. Since the project was a success—a quality product delivered on time and a satisfied customer—a presentation was made to senior and middle management on software product and project quality. At the end of the presentation it was decided that some additional software process improvements (SPI) would be defined and carried out for which budget would be made available. One of the three SPIs that has been defined, proposed, and accepted is the implementation of inspections and reviews throughout the entire software organization.

Metrics and Data

Although often underestimated, an important aspect of each SPI program should be measurement. SPI programs often require substantial investments. In the beginning these investments can be justified by the successes of other organizations. After a certain period, however, an organization should be able to justify its investments by showing that the SPI program has been effective (for instance, the targets set for the SPI objectives have been met). This can be achieved by defining and implementing corresponding metrics. The TV software project delivered metrics that will be used as a baseline, describing the current situation of software development within the organization. Two types of metrics have been delivered:

- **Quality metrics.** Metrics related to testing, inspections, and the number of defects found per development phase.

- **Predictability metrics.** Metrics relating to slip on lead time, effort, and code size.

Defect data that have been gathered throughout the project, as a result of both inspections and testing, can also be used for SPI. An analysis of the defect data by type and cause will result in more knowledge on the development process. It will identify problem areas, enabling the organization to improve the process in a more focused manner.

CRITICAL SUCCESS FACTORS

It should be clear from the previous discussion that the use of inspection and structured testing has been a success within the project. It is, of course, interesting to learn the reasons for success, especially how the implementation and introduction of new methods and techniques were accepted by the software development team. These issues were discussed with team members, and five critical success factors were identified.

- **A separate quality engineer and quality consultant.** It is clear that quality is important. Nevertheless, the required quality is often not achieved. This is because quality is everyone's second-highest priority. Unfortunately, people have to work overtime just to fulfill their first priority, leaving no time left for their second. Hence, this is the main motivation for having someone on a project team who can focus on quality as his or her first priority. Of course, quality is still everyone's responsibility, but it is the role of the quality engineer to assist the other engineers in fulfilling that responsibility. As with any other role, quality engineering requires skill, knowledge, and experience. Since the project quality engineer did not have all of these, an external consultant was asked to support the project. Project management thus showed it was taking product quality seriously and looking upon quality engineering as a true profession.

- **Supporting procedures, forms, and tools.** Today, many software organizations have a quality system in place, sometimes certified to ISO 9001. Each project, however, has different characteristics demanding a tailored version of the organization's standard software process to address these characteristics. In close cooperation with the development team, the quality engineer developed and maintained specific project procedures and supporting forms. This enabled the engineers to perform their tasks more efficiently and effectively. Support tools were implemented and used, particularly for engineering, testing, and configuration management activities.

- **Realistic implementation.** As stated previously, every project has its own characteristics, meaning that the standard procedures are not always fully applicable. Each situation must be evaluated to determine which parts of the procedures are meaningful and add value. Bureaucratic application of procedures only results in opposition. A procedure is only a means, not an objective. If the way of working differs from the standard procedures, however, this must be documented, including the reasons for doing so.

- **Management commitment.** No matter how hard one tries, the implementation of inspections and structured testing will not be successful if there is no management commitment. Commitments are not met by inspections, procedures, or tools, they are met by committed people. Both the project manager and the project sponsor showed great commitment toward achieving product quality. Commitment is not something to be taken lightly; it means one has to get involved. Within the TV software project, management demanded inspections and testing on every software product even when time was running out, participated in reviews, attended software quality meetings, and arranged additional budget for quality support.

- **The right people.** Perhaps the most critical success factor is the people working on a project. A quality product is always realized by people working together as a team. The TV software project consisted of engineers who, throughout the project's lifecycle, became a strong and solid team. Having the right mix of engineers helps the team-building process when one also wants to make changes to the way of working. The combination of experienced engineers (not always willing to make changes but highly skilled) and less-experienced engineers (enthusiastic and willing to try and learn new things) supported by open-minded project management and experienced quality engineering proved to be successful.

The previously mentioned factors all relate to the implementation and support delivered to the engineers. Undoubtedly, inspections and structured testing were successful in every way in the project. Making it work in the end, however, comes down to how to motivate and implement the methods and techniques in an organization with management support. Remember, "Willing people make failing systems work, unwilling people make working systems fail."

REFERENCES

Fagan, M. E. 1986. Advances in software inspections. *IEEE Transactions on Software Engineering* 12 (July)

Fenton, N. E. 1991. *Software metrics: A rigorous approach.* London: Chapman & Hall.

Gal, R., and M. van Genuchten. 1996. Release the embedded software: The electronics industry in transition. *International Journal of Technology Management* (June).

Humphrey, W. S. 1989. *Managing the software process.* Reading, MA: Addison-Wesley.

———. 1995. *A discipline for software engineering.* Reading, MA: Addison-Wesley.

ISO/IEC 9126: *Information Technology—Software product evaluation: Quality characteristics and guidelines for their use.* 1991. Geneva, Switzerland: International Organization for Standardization.

Kit, E. 1995. *Software testing in the real world.* Reading, MA: Addison-Wesley.

Pol, M., R. A. P. Teunissen, and E. P. W. M. van Veenendaal. 1995. *Testing according to TMap.* Hertogenbosch, The Netherlands: UTN Publishing.

Pol, M., and E. P. W. M. van Veenendaal. 1999. *Structured testing of information systems: An introduction to TMap.* Deventer, The Netherlands: Kluwer Publishing.

Rooijmans, J., H. Aerts, and M. van Genuchten. 1996. Software quality in consumer electronic products. *IEEE Software* (January): 55–64.

Weinberg, G. M. 1971. *The psychology of computer programming.* New York: Van Nostrand Reinhold.

Biography

Dr. Erik P. W. M. van Veenendaal is a certified information system auditor who has been working as a practitioner and manager within software quality for a number of years, carrying out assignments in the field of quality management, project control, electronic data processing auditing, and software testing. Within this area he specializes in software testing and is the author of a number of papers and books, including *Testing According to TMap and Software Quality From a Business Perspective.*

As a consultant to Philips, van Veenendaal has been involved in the mentioned TV software project, being responsible for the implementation and coordination of the quality activities. He is a regular speaker at conferences and a leading international trainer in the field of software quality and testing. Veenendaal is the founder and managing director of Improve Quality Services, a company that provides services in the area of quality management, usability, and testing. He is involved in lecturing and research activities as part of the Eindhoven University of Technology, Faculty of Technology Management, and he is on the Dutch Standards Institute committee for software quality.

Van Veenendaal can be reached at P. van Vroonhovenstraat 2A, 5554 HJ Valkenswaard, The Netherlands, or reached by e-mail at e_van_veenendaal@hotmail.com .

PART EIGHT

Configuration Management

Identification, change control, and status accounting—these are the classic components of configuration management. Given the immaterial nature of software, its ease of modification, the complexity of modern software-based systems, and the potential for unintended consequence of changes, software configuration management is often a daunting challenge.

The ecologists have a saying that "You can't do only one thing." In other words, there are side-effects in any interdependent system, often unanticipated and far more profound than one might expect from a supposedly "simple" intervention. Impact analysis—projecting the consequences of a proposed change—thus becomes a key task for practitioners of software configuration management.

Someone has also humorously declared, "Software isn't released; it escapes." The pressures of fixed schedules, budgets, and market-driven expectations can have a troublesome impact on the decision of when to release a software product into production. Careful analysis of this process, and its past results, may equip an organization to better manage this key step.

"Software Configuration Management for Project Leaders," offers the experiences of Tim Kasse and Patricia McQuaid. Configuration management is not only one of the most essential functions in software development, but also one of the least appreciated. The authors discuss the purposes, components, and applications of processes for managing the inevitable changes in any project. They present practical suggestions on which techniques promise the project leader the visibility and control necessary for success.

"Applying Quantitative Methods to Software Maintenance" is Ed Weller's report on analysis of data from three years of software maintenance activities that led to meaningful indicators of quality, productivity, and predictability. His account is of measuring post-release support of an operating system to evaluate the impact of process changes as well as the performance of the team against perceptions of their performance. Weller introduces the term "recidivism ratio" to describe incorrect fixes or fixes that resulted in new defects. He sees ample evidence that the "pay me now or pay me later" rule holds for software, and he concludes with lessons that should be applicable to others' efforts, too.

Software Configuration Management for Project Leaders

Tim Kasse and Patricia A. McQuaid, Kasse Initatives, LLC,
and California Polytechnic State University

*A*s the systems being built today increase in software content, the need for software configuration management continues to rise. Prime contractors are integrating millions of lines of code from multiple subcontractors. Companies are required to produce and maintain variants of their main product to reach out to a diversified market. Project leaders are aware of the need to better manage and control their projects.

Change is a fact of life in software development: Customers want to modify requirements, developers want to modify the technical approach, and management wants to modify the project approach. Modification is necessary, because, as time passes, all parties know more about what they need, which approach would be best, and how to get it done and still make money. The additional knowledge becomes the driving force behind most changes. But, these changes must be carefully controlled.

This article brings together most of the software configuration management concepts to be analyzed from the project leader point of view. Configuration management will be shown as a project management support function that indeed helps project leaders manage and control their projects better.

Key words: baselines, Capability Maturity Model, change control, CMM, configuration control, process improvement, project leader, software configuration audits, software quality assurance

PURPOSE OF SOFTWARE CONFIGURATION MANAGEMENT

According to the Software Engineering Institute's (SEI's) Key Process Areas definition of software configuration management (SCM) (Paulk et al. 1993a; Paulk et al. 1993b), the purpose of SCM is to establish and maintain the integrity of the products produced throughout the project's software lifecycle. Knowing the state of the product that a project is developing and knowing that it satisfies the customer's requirements are of utmost importance for any project leader. SCM then can be viewed as a support function that helps a project leader better manage and control the project (IEEE 1997).

The Need for SCM

In many software companies, software support functions such as software quality assurance and SCM are not perceived as value-added by project leaders and software developers alike. SCM is frequently viewed by developers as a hindrance to product improvements because of the overhead associated with the change control function of SCM. But on closer examination, one can see that the most frustrating software problems are often caused by poor configuration management. Some examples of poor practices are (Babich 1986):

- The latest version of source code cannot be found
- A difficult defect that was fixed at great expense suddenly reappears
- A developed and tested feature is mysteriously missing
- A fully tested program suddenly does not work
- The wrong version of the code was tested
- There is no traceability between the software requirements, documentation, and code
- Programmers are working on the wrong version of the code
- The wrong versions of the configuration items are being baselined
- No one knows which modules comprise the software system delivered to the customer

Most of these problems were revealed during software process assessments conducted by the authors (Kasse 1995). Projects, under great pressure to meet difficult deadlines, found their scarce time resource constantly under attack because of the rework caused by these reasons. One developer stated that he had "fixed" a problem three times, and three months after each delivery the problem recurred. Project leaders cannot afford to have their software developers redoing what was already done.

The cost of rework adds greatly to the cost of developing software and can be reduced by implementing an effective SCM program. The principles behind the modern cost-of-quality concept were derived for manufacturing applications and can be found in the works of J. M. Juran (Juran and Gryna 1988). In 1988 Raytheon Electronic Systems began using a cost of software quality model derived from Philip Crosby (1984) and process improvement methods to increase efficiency. According to Herb Krasner (1997), one of the leading researchers in the field of the cost of quality, by 1991, Raytheon moved from capability maturity model (CMM) level 1 to level 3; by 1994 it decreased rework costs from 41 percent to 20 percent of project costs. In 1995 it reached level 4. Between 1988 and 1994, Raytheon's cost of rework from both internal and external nonconformances was reduced to less than 10 percent of development cost, and the productivity of the development staff increased by a factor of 170 percent. Additional material on this topic can be found in Krasner (1998), Dion (1993), and Haley (1996).

Another example of how a strong SCM program can reduce the cost of rework is that of Gunter Air Force Base in Montgomery, Ala. Gunter's first assessment was conducted in 1987 by Watts Humphrey. The base was supplying MIS software support for the entire Air Force. They had about 500 outstanding Trouble Reports and so much pressure to get the defects fixed that they were sending out a release per month and patches in between. Based on the statistic that for every four defects one detects and "fixes" a new defect is introduced, one can imagine the chaos. While they did not keep statistics, they were probably introducing two to three errors for every four that they fixed. After the assessment, they focused on configuration management. When one of the authors conducted the follow-up assessment in 1989 while working at the SEI, the Air Force base was still not at CMM level 2, but they had made such a distinct business difference in configuration management they told the whole world how well they had done. It was not surprising that the number of trouble reports went from 500 to 50 and product releases went from once per month to once every six months. The results were impressive for any organization.

A key role of SCM is to control changes actively in order to answer the following questions (Babich 1986): What is the current software configuration? What is the status of the modules? What changes have been made to the software? Do anyone else's changes affect the software? SCM provides visibility into the status of the evolving software product. SCM answers who, what, when, and why. Who made the changes? What changes were made to the software? When were the changes made? Why were the changes made? Project leaders must be able to obtain answers to these questions in order to manage the project's technical activities and determine actual product evolution.

SCM VERSUS CHANGE CONTROL

SCM is often equated to change control. Indeed change control is a critical component of SCM, but it is only one of many. Following is a brief look at the components of SCM and how they connect to supporting a project leader's ability to manage and control the project.

Configuration Identification

Configuration identification supports the identifying of the structure of the software system and identifying the related lifecycle work products. It provides a unique identifier for each work product, and it supports traceability between the requirements and all other related software products.

Two structures that SCM is concerned with directly affect a project:

- **Problem-solving structure.** The system concept evolves through the lifecycle by successive refinement and elaboration of the resulting work products.

- **Product system structure.** The system is composed of subsystem components, which are themselves composed of subsystem components.

Figure 1 shows a V-Software lifecycle (McDermid 1994) out of which comes a number of predefined work products. Examples of work products that should be considered for placement under configuration control include:

Source code modules	Quality plans
System data files	Configuration management plans
System build files/scripts	Compilers
Requirements specification	Linkers/loaders
Interface specifications	Debuggers
Design specifications	Operating systems
Software architecture specification	Shell scripts
Test plans	Third-party tools (STSC 1994)
Test procedures	Other related support tools
User documentation	Procedure language descriptions
Software development plan	Development procedures & standards

Figure 2 is a simple example of a software product system composed of subsystems and modules (Walker 1996). Each system or subsystem component may have associated with it an "include" file for code or data and a "make" file for creating compiled and linked systems or subsystems. A discussion between the project and the SCM representative can help the project leader look critically at the software architecture and plan for evolutionary builds that can be controlled and tested at the developmental and system level.

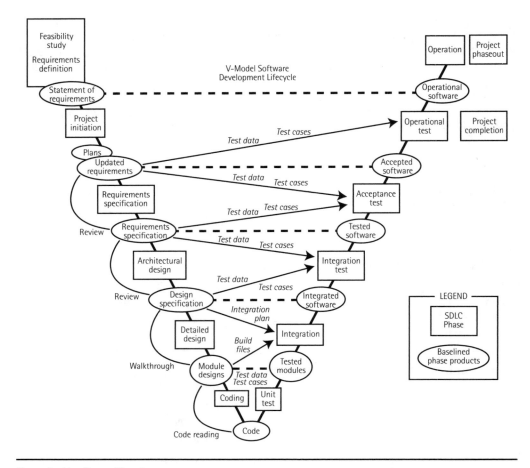

Figure 1   V-software lifecycle.

A software product system is composed of subsystems, which are in turn composed of subsystems, which are composed of modules, which are composed of lines of code.

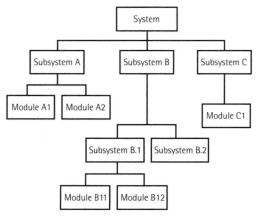

Figure 2   Product structure.

Baselining

Change is a fact of life in software development: Customers want to modify requirements, developers want to modify the technical approach, and management wants to modify the project approach. Modification is necessary, because, as time passes, all parties know more about what they need, which approach would be best, and how to get it done and still make money. The additional knowledge becomes the driving force behind most changes.

The fundamental success of any development effort depends on well-defined reference points against which to specify requirements, formulate a design, and specify changes to these requirements and the resultant designs. The term *baseline* is normally used to denote such a reference point. A baseline is an approved snapshot of the system at appropriate points in the development lifecycle. A baseline establishes a formal base for defining subsequent change. Without this line or reference point, the notion of change is meaningless. A baseline could be:

- A specification (for example, requirements specification, design specification)
- A product that has been formally reviewed and agreed upon
- A partial system

A baseline is a record of a contract and serves as the basis for further development. It should be changed only through an agreed-upon change procedure. A baseline helps a project to control change without seriously impeding justifiable change. It will help a project to control the identified configuration items but not constrain early development excessively from the aspects of time, money, or resources. Before a baseline is established, change may be made quickly and informally. Once a baseline is established, change can be made but a specific, formal procedure must be applied to evaluate and verify each change. The items in the baseline are the basis for the work in the next phase of the software development cycle. The items of the next baseline are measured and verified against previous baselines before they become baselines themselves.

Figure 3 illustrates both the types of baselines that are typical and the quality functions that may be used to ensure that the work products are of the highest quality before they are baselined (Bersoff, Henderson, and Siegel 1980; Bryan and Siegel 1988; Humphrey 1990). The functional baseline, allocated baseline, and product baseline are most often thought of as organizational or system baselines. The requirements baseline, design

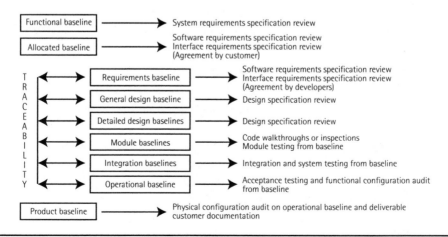

Figure 3   Mapping of system and developmental baselines.

baselines, module baselines, integration baseline (component and system), and operational baseline are often thought of as project or developmental baselines. System baselines are the records of contract made with the external customer. Developmental baselines are agreements to assure the project leader that the product integrity remains as it moves from phase to phase.

Configuration Control

In the ideal world, once a configuration item is fully approved there would be no need to change. In the real world, new versions of a configuration item are needed for a variety of reasons:

- The requirements for the system change
- The boundaries between items in the design hierarchy change
- The specification of an item is incomplete or wrongly interpreted
- An error is found that was not detected during the configuration items review
- The software environment changes in a way that necessitates change

In each case, a new version of a configuration item is needed that supersedes the earlier version. Without change control, a software engineer could make an important change to a configuration item or its interfaces without a lot of extra work and red tape. *No record would be kept of what the change was, however, why the change was requested, who approved the change, who made the change, and who verified the change would be* (IEEE 1997; Whitgift 1991). In addition, it would be hard to find answers to the following questions:

- "Why doesn't my software link this morning? It linked last night!"
- "Why does this regression test fail now? It worked yesterday!"
- "Why does the product behave this way now? It didn't before!"
- "Why are we running out of memory now? We did not have that problem yesterday!"

All changes made to the configuration management baselines or baselined software configuration items should be done according to a documented change control process. The change control process should specify:

- Who can initiate the change requests
- The individuals, group, or groups who are responsible for evaluating, accepting, and tracking the change proposals for the various baselined products
- What the criteria are for placing the software components under formal change control
- The "change impact" analysis expected for each requested change
- How revision history should be kept
- The check-in/check-out procedures
- The process the software configuration control board (SCCB) follows to approve changes
- How change requests will be linked to the trouble-reporting system
- How change requests are tracked and resolved
- The reviews and/or regression tests that must be performed to ensure that changes have not caused unintended effects on the baseline
- The procedure that will be followed to update all affected software lifecycle components to reflect the approved changes

To control the organizational or system baselines or contracts with the external customers, many organizations establish one or more SCCBs. The purpose of the SCCB is to ensure that every change is properly considered and coordinated. This SCCB may include members from program management, systems engineering, software engineering, software quality assurance, SCM, independent test, documentation, hardware engineering, and may even include a customer representative. The SCCB is responsible for receiving and initially evaluating the change requests that come from all sources (that is, customer, engineering, marketing, trouble reports, program management) and performing triage to get the most critical or significant change requests to the right people for impact analysis. Following the impact analysis, the SCCB ensures that all affected groups are able to recommit to the new requirements. The SCCB can make the decision to implement the change request, defer it to the next release, or discard it altogether. It is also possible that the SCCB will have to seek additional information before a decision can be made.

Project Leader Approval of Baseline Changes

Once the allocated baseline is created and the customer has accepted the software requirements specification and interface specification, the control of the work products and system components comes under developmental configuration control. Normally this means that decisions to make changes are decided by the project leader. If a change to a software module results in a required change to an interface module to a hardware device, the project leader may share the approval responsibility with the appropriate hardware manager. When the software passes to the integration and test stage, the project leader may share approval authority to make changes with the integration and test manager. When the product is ready to be shipped to the customer and a product baseline is established, the SCCB again becomes the approval authority. What baselines, when they are created during the software lifecycle, and who the approval authorities are become part of each project's SCM plan.

Configuration Management Status Accounting

Configuration management status accounting involves maintaining a continuous record of the status and history of all baselined items and proposed changes to them. It includes reports of the traceability of all changes to the baseline throughout the software lifecycle, and it should identify what changes have been made to the system and what changes remain to be implemented.

Configuration management status accounting provides visibility into the system evolution by recording and reporting the status of all items and the status of all requests for change. Questions that configuration management status accounting should be able to answer include (IEEE 1997; Whitgift 1991):

- **What is the status of an item?** A programmer may want to know whether a specification has been fully approved. He or she may want to know whether a subsystem has been tested so the programmer can test his or her modules that interface with that subsystem. A project leader will wish to track the progress of a project as items are developed, reviewed, tested, and integrated.

- **Has a change request been approved or rejected by the SCCB?**

- **Which version of an item implements an approved change request?** Once a requested enhancement of a library routine is implemented, the originator and other developers will want to know which version of the routine contains the enhancement. Without this timely information, the project leader has inadequate control as to how to direct his or her project's technical activities.

- **What is different about a new version of a system?** A new version of a software system should be accompanied by a list of changes from the previous version. The change list should include both enhancements and fixes to faults. Any faults that have not been fixed should also be identified. This, of course, provides project progress information to the project leader.

- **How many faults are detected each month and how many are fixed?** Faults are continuously detected during the operational use of the system. Comparing the number of detected and fixed faults helps the project leader, SCM, SQE, test, and other project support teams to assess the stability of the system's latest release. Tracking the number of faults also helps the program manager decide when to make a new release of the system.

- **What is the cause of the trouble report?** Trouble reports can be categorized by their causes: violation of programming standards, inadequate user interface, or customer requirements that have been left out. Sometimes when it is discovered that many faults have a similar cause, action can be taken to improve the process and stop such faults from recurring. This information can help the project leader make any necessary process improvements (Kasse and McQuaid 1998) at the project level, and provide the organization's process improvement group with information to make necessary changes to the organization's standard software processes.

Configuration management status accounting is the means by which key project or system information can be communicated to everyone. Project members can easily determine which configuration item should be used, whether it is subject to a change request, and what a build consists of. Project leaders can easily determine what configuration items passed review, which changes have been completed, which changes are still in progress, how many changes have been accepted, which modules are the most volatile, what a build consists of, and what has been delayed to the next release.

Configuration Management and the Use of Peer Reviews

Configuration management status accounting can help the project leader make decisions on what degree of formality peer reviews should follow. For example: The product the project is building consists of 50 modules or units. Status accounting information reveals that 45 of the modules have changed once in six months, but five of the modules have changed 10 times per month for the past two months. With this configuration status information, the project leader can choose to conduct formal software inspections on the five modules that are experiencing rapid change and use less formal walkthroughs to ensure the integrity of the 45 modules that change infrequently.

Interface Control

The definition of interfaces is one of the most important SCM planning and tracking activities (IEEE 1997). There must be agreement of each group or organization's responsibility. Any proposed changes to the product or baselined configuration items can be considered and evaluated by all affected groups.

There are two basic types of interfaces that must be considered: organizational interfaces and technical interfaces. Organizational interfaces are those in which configuration management controls the transfer of configuration items from vendor to customer, project to project, and co-developer to co-developer. SCM ensures that the correct configuration items are sent to the correct people. Organizational interfaces also include lifecycle phase interfaces. Phase interfaces become critical when control of the product is being transitioned between different groups (for example, software development group to independent test group for formal testing). Technical interfaces are descriptions that should be placed under configuration management control like any other configuration item. Technical interfaces include system, user, software, hardware, and communication interfaces.

Subcontractor Control

If a portion of a software development project is to be subcontracted to another organization, the responsibility for the SCM generally belongs to the contracting organization and specifically the project leader of the project that requires this outside support. The subcontractor is normally only responsible for the portion of the work that his or her organization is tasked to perform. The integration of the subcontracted work is normally the responsibility of the organization that subcontracted portions of the work.

> *The cost of rework adds greatly to the cost of developing software*
> *and can be reduced by implementing an effective SCM program.*
> *The principles behind the modern cost-of-quality concept were derived for*
> *manufacturing applications and can be found in the works of J. M. Juran.*

An effective SCM system greatly increases the opportunity to have portions of the product subcontracted out and then integrated back into a whole that satisfies the customer's technical and quality requirements. SCM must be applied to a subcontractor to ensure that the subcontractor is able to maintain the integrity of the subsystem for which it has contracted (Paulk et al. 1993a; Paulk et al. 1993b). This includes placing necessary lifecycle products under configuration control to ensure consistency with the main development effort and maintaining a subcontractor's software library that will release the agreed-upon configuration items or subsystems to the contracting organization.

Software Configuration Audits

Configuration auditing verifies that the software product is built according to the requirements, standards, or contractual agreement. Auditing also verifies that all software products have been produced, correctly identified and described, and that all change requests have been resolved (IEEE 1997; Kasse 1995).

A software configuration audit should be performed periodically to ensure that the SCM practices and procedures are rigorously followed. The integrity of the software baselines must be assessed and the completeness and correctness of the software baseline library contents must be verified. The accuracy of the implementation of the changes to the baselines must be verified to ensure that the changes were implemented as intended. It is recommended that a software configuration audit be performed before every major baseline change.

Software configuration auditing should be continuous, with increased frequency and depth throughout the lifecycle. Types of configuration audits include functional configuration audits, physical configuration audits, in-process audits, and traceability audits (see Figure 4).

Functional configuration audits. The objective of the functional configuration audit (FCA) is to provide an independent evaluation of the software products, verifying that each configuration item's actual functionality and performance is consistent with the

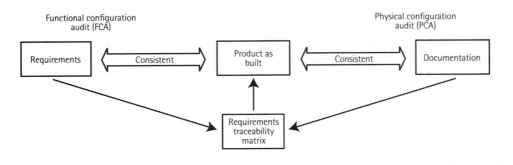

Figure 4   Functional and physical configuration audits.

software requirements specification. An FCA audit must be concerned not only with functionality but also with performance. An FCA includes:

- An audit of the formal test documentation against test data
- An audit of the verification and validation reports to ensure their accuracy
- A review of all approved changes (problem reporting and corrective actions) to ensure they have been correctly technically incorporated and verified
- A review of the updates to previously delivered documents to ensure their accuracy and consistency
- A sampling of the design review outputs to ensure that all findings were completed and incorporated
- A comparison of the code with the documented software requirements to ensure that the code addresses all and only the documented requirements
- A review to ensure that all testing was accomplished with appropriate test documentation and approved test data to ensure that all configuration items meet the established performance criteria

Physical configuration audits. The objective of the physical configuration audit (PCA) is to provide an independent evaluation of the system configuration items to confirm that each item that makes up the "as built" system maps to its specifications. The audit is held to verify that the software and its documentation are internally consistent and ready for delivery to the customer or end user. Appropriate customer deliverable documentation includes installation manuals, operating manuals, maintenance manuals, and release notes or version description documents. A PCA includes:

- An audit of the system specification for completeness
- An audit of the FCA report for discrepancies and actions taken
- A comparison of the architectural design with the detailed design components for consistency
- A review of the module listing for compliance with approved coding standards
- An audit of the manuals for format completeness and conformance to systems and functional descriptions; such manuals include user's manuals, programmer's manuals, and operator's manuals

In-process audits. In-process audits are held during the design and development phases prior to the FCA and PCA to verify the consistency of the design as it evolves through the development process. In-process audits are performed to determine:

- Are the hardware and software interfaces consistent with the design requirements?
- Is the code fully tested to ensure that the functional requirements are satisfied?
- Is the design of the product, as it is evolving, satisfying the functional requirements?
- Is the code consistent with the detailed design?

Traceability audits. Traceability auditing is necessary to be able to verify throughout the software development process:

- Can the software requirements be traced back to the system requirements allocated to software?
- Can the architectural design be traced back to the software requirements?
- Can the detailed design(s) be traced back to the architectural requirements?
- Can the code modules be traced back to detailed design modules?
- Can the module tests, integration tests, and system tests be traced back to the software requirements?

Traceability audits are also necessary to be able to answer the following questions:

- Can it be proven that what one is doing is required?
- How does one know that what he or she is delivering is what the customer asked for?
- Are the software lifecycle work products consistent as the system evolves and change requests are processed?

Software configuration audits check that the configuration management system and practices are effective and efficient for the project and the organization.

Software Library

The software library should contain the items that are important to a software project, including source code, user documentation, system documentation, test data, support software, specifications, and project plans. The SCM library typically stores the configuration items and prevents unauthorized changes to the baselined items. The library system (Whitgift 1991):

- Supports multiple control levels of SCM
- Provides for the storage and retrieval of configuration items
- Provides for the sharing and transfer of configuration items among affected groups and among control levels within the library
- Provides for the storage and recovery of archive versions of configuration items
- Provides service functions, such as checking status, verifying the presence of all built items, and integrating changes into a new baseline
- Ensures the correct creation of products from the software baseline library
- Provides for the storage, update, and retrieval of SCM records
- Supports the production of SCM reports
- Supports the tracing of requirements, forward and backward, throughout the lifecycle

A software library provides safe and secure storage for configuration items (key project components) so they cannot be changed without authorization. Acceptance of items (new or revised) into the library is strictly controlled to ensure that everyone accessing items in the library can have complete confidence in their integrity. A number of different libraries may be established to hold different types of items or provide different levels of control.

SCM Plan

The SCM plan is the document that describes how a project will manage configurations (Paulk et al. 1993b; Whitgift 1991). The SCM plan should cover:

- The scope of the plan, including the project, the software to be developed, and the lifecycle phases
- The relationship between the SCM plan and the other standards or plans that describe how the project will be managed (for example, software development, SQA plan)
- SCM roles and responsibilities
- Configuration identification
- Baselining
- Configuration control
- Configuration management status accounting
- Interface control
- Subcontractor control
- Software configuration audits
- Software library

SUMMARY

SCM is one of the most important process improvement tools that project leaders can use to evolve and deliver their product in a controlled manner. Knowing the state of the product that a project is developing and knowing that it satisfies the customer's requirements is of utmost importance for any project leader. Since many of the most frustrating software problems are often caused by poor configuration management, proper configuration management is critical.

System baselines are the records of contract made with the external customer. Developmental baselines are agreements to assure the project leader that the product integrity remains as it moves from phase to phase.

Even if an organization has little or no configuration management in place and is just getting started with a configuration management program, five simple steps will add a great deal of control and project tracking information: 1) Formalize the use of reviews before a configuration item is baselined; 2) Uniquely identify system components; 3) Establish simple change control; 4) Build up a repository of configuration items, change requests, and problem reports; and 5) Restrict access to the project library.

A good place to start is with simple status reports, which may include only the versions one has. When developing a change history, one can expand to a status accounting system, which includes who changed it, when, why, how, and what was affected, as described earlier in the article. Then, a configuration audit can be performed to make sure the approved change requests have been implemented completely and correctly. Once established, FCAs would be the next step to ensure that the system matches what was approved, and nothing more. Then, a physical audit can be added to ensure that the documentation matches the changes.

It is important to implement requirements traceability from the beginning through systems testing, implementing lifecycle work-product consistency checks. This means that if a requirements change request has been accepted, one must go through lifecycle phases to determine if it is necessary to make a corresponding change. Without the ability to trace through the lifecycle process, it cannot be done. Once one has the design document, he or she needs the ability to go backward and forward to look at the other lifecycle work products.

After expanding to multisite, multicountry, and multicultural projects, one may be looking at implementing at multiple levels of control boards and need to ensure that all parts are being managed and controlled with consistency and integrity. Otherwise, it cannot all be brought together and integrated into a working and maintainable system. Ultimately, some project leader is responsible for the entire integrated product!

REFERENCES

Babich, W. 1986. *Software configuration management.* Reading, MA: Addison-Wesley.

Bersoff, E. H., V. D. Henderson, and S. G. Siegel. 1980. *Software configuration management.* Upper Saddle River, N. J.: Prentice-Hall.

Bryan, W. L., and S. G. Siegel. 1988. *Software product assurance.* New York: Elsevier Science Publishing Co.

Buckley, F. J. 1996. *Implementing configuration management.* Computer Society Press.

Crosby, P. 1984. *Quality without tears.* New York: McGraw-Hill.

Dion, R. 1993. Process improvement and the corporate balance sheet. *IEEE Software* (July): 28–35.

Haley, T. J. 1996. Software process improvement at Raytheon. *IEEE Software* (November): 33–41.

Humphrey, W. 1990. *Managing the software process.* Reading, MA: Addison-Wesley.

IEEE. 1997. *IEEE Software engineering standards collection.* Washington, DC: IEEE Press.

International Organization for Standardization (ISO). 1994. ISO 9000 Quality Management, ISO Standards Compendium. Geneva, Switzerland: International Organization for Standardization.

Juran, J. M., and F. M. Gryna. 1988. *Juran's quality control handbook.* 4th ed. New York: McGraw-Hill.

Kasse, T. 1995. Project leader exploratory question database. Antwerp, Belgium: Institute for Software Process Improvement, internal document.

Kasse, T., and P. McQuaid. 1998. Entry strategies into the process improvement initiative. *Software Process Improvement and Practice Journal* 4, no. 2: 73–88.

Krasner, H. 1997. Accumulating the body of evidence for the payoff of software process improvement. URL document www.utexas.edu/coe/sqi/archive .

———. 1998. Using the cost of quality approach for software. *Crosstalk, The Journal of Defense Software Engineering* (November) (or see URL www.stsc.hill.af.mil/crosstalk/1998/nov/krasner.asp).

McDermid, J. 1994. *Software engineer's reference book.* Florida: CRC Press.

Paulk, M. C., B. Curtis, M. B. Chrissis, and C. V. Weber. 1993. *Capability maturity model for software, version 1.1.* (CMU/SEI-93-TR-24). Pittsburgh: Software Engineering Institute, Carnegie Mellon University.

Paulk, M. C., C. V. Weber, S. M. Garcia, M. B. Chrissis, and M. Bush. 1993. *Key practices of the capability maturity model, version 1.1.* (CMU/SEI-93-TR-25). Pittsburgh: Software Engineering Institute, Carnegie Mellon University.

Pressman, R. S. 1987. *Software engineering.* New York: McGraw Hill.

Schulmeyer, G. G., and J. I. McManus, eds. 1987. *Handbook of software quality assurance.* New York: Van Nostrand Reinhold.

STSC. 1994. Software configuration management technology report, Software Technology Support Center. (This document provided by the STSC is a checklist of criteria to help organizations develop their requirements for selecting configuration management tools.)

Walker, G. 1996. What is configuration management? Alcatel Alsthom internal presentation. Paris, France.

Whitgift, D. 1991. *Methods and tools for software configuration management.* New York: John Wiley & Sons.

BIOGRAPHIES

Tim Kasse is manager and principal consultant of Kasse Initiatives LLC, founded in 1999. Previously he served as the chief executive officer and principal consultant for the Institute for Software Process Improvement (ISPI), which he co-founded with Jeff Perdue in 1991. His focus is on innovative solutions for process improvement of business, systems, software, people, and lifestyles. He is the architect of the Action Focused Assessment, which has been applied in major organizations throughout Europe and has been commercialized in the Netherlands.

Kasse is the primary or co-developer of many of Kasse Initiatives' workshops. He is a recognized speaker at major conferences around the world, including the SEI's SEPG conference, the European SEPG conference, the European Software Process Improvement Conference, the Software Technology Conference, and the World Congress of Software Quality.

Prior to starting ISPI, Kasse spent four years at the Software Engineering Institute. He was a major contributor to the development of the Capability Maturity Model, which provides the framework for the SEI's assessments and evaluations. Kasse has a master's degree from Southern Methodist University and a bachelor's degree in systems engineering from the University of Arizona. He is a member of IEEE and has participated in the development of the IEEE standard on reviews and audits. Kasse can be reached at Kasse Initiatives, LLC., 30 W. Sheffield Ave., Gilbert, AZ 85233, or by e-mail at kassetc@aol.com .

Patricia McQuaid is an associate professor of management information systems at California Polytechnic State University. She has taught a wide range of courses in both the college of business and college of engineering. She has industry experience in information systems auditing in both the banking and manufacturing industries, and is a certified information systems auditor (CISA). Her research interests include software quality, in particular, the areas of software process improvement, software testing, and complexity metrics. McQuaid is serving as the chair for the Americas for the Second World Congress for Software Quality, to be held in Japan in September 2000.

McQuaid has a doctorate and a master's degree in computer science and engineering from Auburn University, an MBA from Eastern Michigan University, and an undergraduate degree in accounting from Case-Western Reserve University. She is a Senior member of ASQ, and a member of the Association for Computing Machinery, IEEE, IEEE Computer Society, the International Function Point Users Group, the Information Systems Audit and Control Association, and the Decision Sciences Institute. She can be reached at California Polytechnic State University-MIS, College of Business, San Luis Obispo, CA 93407, or by e-mail at pmcquaid@calpoly.edu .

CHAPTER 8.2

Applying Quantitative Methods to Software Maintenance

Ed Weller, Bull HN Information Systems, Inc.

*S*oftware maintenance processes can generate large amounts of data that are useful in *evaluating a maintenance operation. The challenge is often finding ways to make sense of the data, breaking it down into meaningful indicators of quality, productivity, and predictability. Data from three years of software maintenance activities were used in the analysis. Detailed results for the first year are presented in this article with references to following years' analysis. The questions that prompted the analysis and the answers to the questions, as well as the follow-up results of a major process change, are included.*

Key words: corrective maintenance, defective fixes, quantitative analysis, software process, stable process

INTRODUCTION

A major release to Bull Information Systems' GCOS 8 Operating System created the need to understand in detail the operation of its software maintenance team (SMT), the group responsible for software maintenance (maintenance in this discussion refers to corrective maintenance, that is, fixing defects reported by customers). By looking at the SMT process data, the company wanted to find what was working well and duplicate those processes, as well as identify less effective processes and eliminate them. It also wanted to measure the typical process metrics to allow year-to-year comparisons to evaluate the impact of process changes, as well as to evaluate the performance of the team against perceptions of its performance. This article concentrates on the metrics used by the SMT and shows how quantitative methods can be used to evaluate maintenance work. The evaluations cover three years of data. Several of the process changes introduced as a result of the studies are also covered.

DATA CHARACTERISTICS

The GCOS 8 Operating System (exclusive of third-party products) includes about 7 million lines of source code split across about 320 product IDs (PIDs). A major release in 1995 resulted in an expected flow of customer reported defects. As these defects were repaired, the company monitored a number of the process metrics to evaluate the effectiveness of the repair process. The GCOS 8 Operating System is divided into logical groupings, or PIDs, that might be as large as 400,000 lines of source code and contain up to 300 modules. In some cases, several PIDs combine to provide the larger product areas within the operating system, such as the memory manager, COBOL Compiler, or I/O Supervisor.

In 1995, 82 percent of the fixes were isolated to 5 percent of the (320) PIDs, and in 1996, 84 percent of the fixes were isolated to 5 percent of the PIDs. By concentrating on the 15 PIDs with the highest change volume, the data analysis effort was manageable. In three cases, PIDs that covered the same product area were combined, so most of the charts show only 12 data points. The 1996 data were extended to include a 13th PID.

Grouping by PIDs appears to be a logical approach, in that PIDs have a common technical domain or product area, and for the most part, the people working on problems in each PID are the same. Problem analysis, resolution, and verification methods within each group tend to be consistent, so differences in the metrics from the different PIDs might indicate processes that should be transferred from one group to another. Since this grouping may also be sensitive to the relative complexity of the different product areas, as well as the familiarity of the maintenance staff with the product areas, some judgment was required when evaluating these differences.

SMT PROCESS

The SMT was set up as a separate organization to allow a dedicated team of maintenance specialists to focus on customer reported problems. Key elements of the process include daily reviews of open problems, pairing specialists on problems that have not been resolved within goals (or at the request of the person working the problem), and critical problem reviews (CPR) for especially difficult or longstanding problems. Over several years, the productivity of the SMT, measured by the effort per system technical action request (STAR), more than doubled. Metrics are collected using an internally developed problem tracking system called problem analysis and solution system (PASS). This system recorded the usual data elements seen in today's problem tracking systems. Some of the 58 fields include date opened/closed, customer, priority, assigned to, closure code, and PID. This system also provides links into the company's configuration management system to allow the specific code transmittals issued to correct a problem to be tracked against that problem.

Additional data include a separate database for all fixes shipped as site-specific corrections (SSCs) and emergency patches (EPs). In particular, this database is used to track replacements to EPs and the reason for the replacement (such as bad fix, regression, fix overlap—current fix overlays a previous one). Also, all fixes are inspected, and the inspection results are captured in a site database that has inspection results starting in 1990. The primary linkages between these databases are the STAR number and PID.

Although the SMT uses a large number of metrics, the following are of the most interest to Bull's customers and its management as indicators of quality and predictability.

- Response time by problem priority level—as measured by entry to and exit from the software maintenance team (open/closed date in PASS).

- Inspection "hit ratio," or the percentage of inspection meetings of fixes that yield a major defect (a major defect is one that is visible to the end user). This is more useful than the usual "defects per thousand lines of code" used to measure inspection effectiveness.

- Defective fix ratio or "recidivism ratio." This is a measure of defective fixes shipped to customers, and does not include defects found via inspection or test, although the company does have these numbers and uses them to identify above/below effectiveness in inspection and test as a means of identifying process improvements.

"Quality" of the corrective maintenance process in the eyes of Bull's customers means the defect is fixed on the first attempt. Response time as measured in the company's problem tracking system is the end-to-end time in the SMT for the final fix transmitted to the source control system. Typically, a work-around, avoidance, or temporary fix is provided on a site-specific basis as soon as possible. The permanent fix that is made available across the customer base goes through a longer development and test cycle, which is the "response time" used in this article.

WHAT DID THE COMPANY WANT TO DISCOVER?

Once these metrics are selected as the quality measure of the work, as seen by Bull's customers, what questions might one ask about them that will reveal something (useful) about the SMT process? This article looks at the following:

- Is there a relationship between the volume of STARs and response time?
- Is there a relationship between the PID in which the defect is repaired and response time?
- Is there a relationship between the volume of STARs or PID and quality?
- Does inspection effectiveness affect quality?
- Does response time affect quality?

Answers to these questions should enable the company to answer a number of process related questions:

- Is the company applying its resources optimally?
- Would a detailed look at the data show obvious areas for process improvement?
- Does the volume of change or length of response time affect quality in any way? (There was a perception in some areas that faster response time was accomplished by "rushing the fixes" and tacitly accepting lower quality.)

Introducing inspections in 1990 to 1993 had reduced the recidivism ratio to one-third of the preinspection values (Weller 1993). Over the four years the company gained another 33 percent improvement but had stabilized at a 4 percent ratio. Bull was looking to better understand the underlying processes to see what could be changed to improve further.

ANALYSIS TECHNIQUES

The data available for analysis were limited by what was collected in the problem reporting system, the site inspection database, and the EP database ("emergency patch," while historically a meaningful definition, now means an object code fix shipped between releases) kept by the change control board that manages EPs. The company did not have the luxury of adding additional data to the problem reporting system necessary to conduct rigorous experiments. The analysis was a "do what you can do with the available data" project.

Scatter plots, correlation analysis, and detailed comparisons of metrics across PIDs were used to indicate trends, relationships, and best-case/worst-case process differences between the extreme performance groups. The drawing in Figure 1 illustrates this process. A large amount of data are available for analysis, but the best way to look at the data is not obvious.

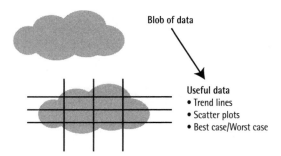

Blob of data

Useful data
• Trend lines
• Scatter plots
• Best case/Worst case

Figure 1   Larger amounts of unorganized data.

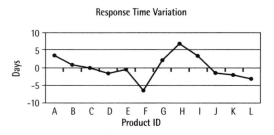

Figure 2   A STAR response time.

DATA RESULTS AND INTERPRETATION

In the following figures, a STAR is a system technical action request (problem report) that may be caused by a product defect, user misunderstanding of product documentation, duplicate error report, and so on.

In the following charts, "response time" is the end-to-end time spent in the SMT for analysis, problem correction, inspection, verification, and release into the source code control system. "Recidivism" is the defective fix ratio for the problem report. "inspection hit ratio" is the percentage of inspections of fixes that find major defects.

Figure 2 shows the response time for priority A (highest) STARs across a group of 12 PIDs. In Figure 2, PIDs A, H, and I have the largest positive (longer response time) variation. Products A and H were developed in the same project, and are consistently on the outer limits in all of the charts in this article. This project was "grandfathered" into the release without being inspected, which caused poor quality product turnover to the maintenance group. Product I will be discussed in the next section.

Lessons Learned

- Inspections work (this is a no-brainer, but at the time of the grandfathering a decision not to inspect completed work was clearly wrong. There is always time to do it right.)
- The company needed to define exit criteria for turnover from development to maintenance.

DEVELOPMENT IMPACT ON MAINTENANCE

Figure 3 shows a plot of the recidivism ratio by PID. Again, PID A is clearly out of the box, with a high response time and lower quality. The analysis of the problems with this PID indicate the design was not documented and that it was not inspected. Without design documentation, the only way the team could decipher the design was by reverse engineering the code. The high defect ratio that was visible meant the rest of the code could not be trusted to reflect the required design, and the original designer was not available to question. This is probably the worst-case scenario for software maintenance.

Two PIDs (I and L) have a zero defect ratio. Two items were noted as possible causes: long familiarity with the product by the maintainers, and recent "source rolls" that "cleaned up" one of the PIDs. Also, PID I had a longer response time (see Figure 2), which might indicate a relationship between response time and quality, which will be investigated later. Source rolls are a method of integrating a series of overlapping changes into "clean" source code. One of the characteristics of the legacy, proprietary language used in parts of the operating system is that there is a tradeoff between frequent source rolls and the cost of the activity.

Lessons Learned

- Evaluate "source roll" (source-code cleanup) frequency to ensure the proper balance between the cost of the source roll and increased maintenance effort.
- Improve product familiarity (another no-brainer; however, if the work force is optimally allocated, moving people around will not work, so product training may be the only way to achieve this end. Ultimately, this may mean on-the-job training or experience.)

RESPONSE TIME VERSUS RECIDIVISM RATIO

The discussion of the data in Figure 3 suggests response time might have an impact on quality. This relationship is shown in Figure 4. There does not appear to be sufficient correlation to draw any conclusions. The correlation is low, and the point above 10 percent is the now infamous PID A.

Lessons Learned

- Response time did not appear to impact the quality of the work, which was contrary to a view that the faster response time had been accomplished by "rushing" the fixes and accepting lower quality.

Figure 5 plots the inspection hit ratio (percentage of inspections of fixes that find defects) to volume of fixes to see if higher change rate affected the inspection results. Although this set of data has one of the higher correlation values in this analysis ($R = .63$), there is an indication that as the volume of inspections in a product area increases, the team finds more defects in the rework. The reasons could include:

- More defects caused by a higher volume of work, providing more opportunities for the inspection teams
- More inspections allow the team to become more proficient in finding defects

As a test for the first hypothesis, the company looked at the relationship of inspection hit ratio to recidivism, shown in Figure 6.

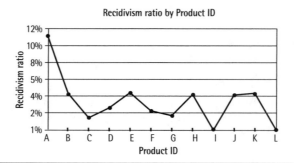

Figure 3　Development impact.

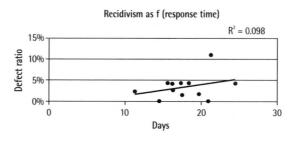

Figure 4　Recidivism as a function of response time.

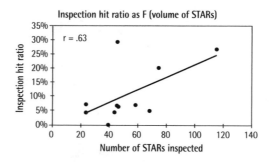

Figure 5　Inspection hit ratio as a function of volume of STARs.

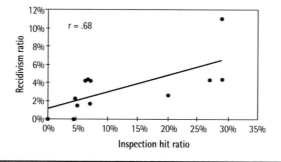

Figure 6　Recidivism ratio versus inspection hit ratio.

Readers may have heard that "defective products stay defective through the entire debug cycle." Figure 6 is an attempt to see if this holds true for fixes. It has the highest correlation (R = .68) seen so far, but it is still questionable that product quality can be predicted by inspection hit ratio. If PID A in the upper right corner is removed, the relationship (R = .56) is less conclusive.

A Different View

When these data were first presented at the 1996 Applications of Software Measurement Conference, Shari Lawrence-Pfleeger asked the author of this article if he had looked at the data individually, rather than the groupings by PID. He had not, primarily because the organization of the data and extraction tools made it relatively easy to view the data by PID, and extremely time consuming to look at each fix. A recent review of the data on a fix-by-fix basis revealed a slight trend indicating the longer it took to fix a problem, the higher the recidivism ratio.

SUMMARY: YEAR 1

It seems as if nothing is easy in software engineering. It would have been much easier if one or more of the analyses had shown a strong correlation, or if there had been a series of obvious outliers that would have guided corrective action. One might ask, "What did Bull gain by this effort?" The company learned that:

1. Quality is maintained in spite of pressures to respond quickly.
2. There is reinforcement that poor process leads to poor results.
3. Further improvements will need to be broad-based process improvements, rather than fixing exception conditions. The company did find several indications that suggested a process changed (source roll frequency).
4. This analysis sets a baseline for future comparisons.
5. Response time seems to be under control across 12 PIDs, suggesting that resource allocation is managed fairly well.

THE NEXT YEARS

The analysis was repeated the next two years. Several of the more interesting observations are shown in Figure 7. One can see the recidivism ratios for the same set of PIDs as in the first year with the addition of PID M.

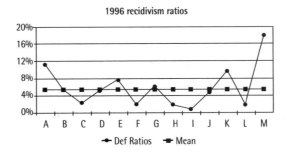

Figure 7   Recidivism year 2.

Product A was still a problem, however, it was replaced by a new PID (M) as the "worst behaved." PID M was the result of a project with poor documentation and no inspections, creating a repeat nightmare. Unfortunately, the root causes for PID M problems were well established before the lessons of the previous year were available. The average recidivism ratio was up considerably, from 4.1 percent to 5.4 percent, a 31.7 percent increase. Since the STAR volume for the year was nearly double (reflecting the increased number of installations of the new release), this suggests the STAR volume has an influence on recidivism ratio. If the two worst PIDs are removed (A and M), however, the difference is 3.9 percent to 4.4 percent on a year-to-year comparison (12.8 percent). This suggests that controlling the volume of changes might improve the recidivism ratio.

LESSONS LEARNED, ACTIONS TAKEN, AND RESULTS

The lessons learned from the second year of data reinforce the first year of data, that low quality products are difficult to maintain and will have a high(er) defect ratio in repair than well-designed products. This is not an earth-shattering revelation, but sometimes one must have these data to prove the "pay me now or pay me later" rule holds for software just as well as for oil filters and auto engines. There were several significant changes in the processes (or enforcement of processes) in the following years.

First, the company realized the existing maintenance processes were not capable of better performance and instituted a major change in the testing process. EPs that were distributed beyond the site-specific correction were subjected to longer testing. This delayed the availability of the correction, but is in agreement with the recognized defect to failure ratio relationship published by Adams (1984). Second, the company reduced the frequency of EPs. By taking a more conservative approach to distributing corrections (again consistent with the Adams' work, especially in the second or third year of corrective maintenance), it avoided taking site-specific corrections to a second site where they were not needed. This effectively reduced the recidivism ratio to zero. (Since the middle of 1997, eight or more months of the year see 0 percent recidivism ratio). The change was so significant that the company was not able to repeat the analysis in the third year. The number of defective fixes was so low that it was not possible (or necessary) to use the same analysis methods.

Second, the company strictly controlled the development processes on the next release. It introduced defect-depletion tracking across the full development lifecycle. It developed quality goals for the next release, and predicted and measured conformance to these goals (Weller 2000). The stated objective of development was "to put the SMT out of business" by reducing the STAR rates to the point where the volume would not sustain a separate maintenance organization.

THE PAYBACK

One measure of improvement from release to release is to measure the reported defects against the system-years of operation. This normalizes for different migration rates and number of systems. Figure 8 shows the comparison between the release that generated the data in this article with its follow-on release. The follow-on data were subdivided to show the contribution of the new products in the follow-on release. The follow-on release was as stable as its mature predecessor 12 months after initial exposure because the defect ratio of the new product was significantly better than its predecessor. The current ratio is about 40 times better, but actual exposure of the post-Y2K release is still limited. The company expects the final result to be in the 10-to-20-to-1 range. Note that

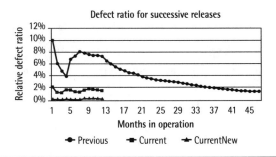

Figure 8   The payback.

all of these gains were not due to the results of this study, but several key changes, including the absolute need for design and inspection, were rigorously enforced on all products going into the follow-on release.

SUMMARY

What did Bull Information Systems learn? Obviously, the first lesson is "do it right the first time." Looking strictly at the analysis of the SMT process, the company concluded the existing defect removal processes were delivering the best the company could expect, and that any improvements would require major changes to the process.

Are these results transferable to another company? To investigate the approach used to do this analysis, readers can try the following with their own data:

- Find ways to divide data into repeating or related groups, whether time based, product identity, or other division
- Consider scatter plots and values by group (for example, see Figure 1)
- Look at the outliers (best case/worst case)

If there are outliers, see if one can reconstruct their history. Look at both the good and bad to propagate the good processes as well as avoiding the bad (or nonexistent) processes.

A few warnings might include:

- Do not be fooled by coincidental correlations. Just because the data look the way one expects or wants them to, do not accept it.
- If a company has to maintain its products, be sure to document the designs, and inspect the designs and code. If responsible for product maintenance, refuse to accept a product that fails to meet these criteria, or allow sufficient budget to handle a high rate of problems (and repeat problems).
- Look for distortions caused by a large subset of data from one project.
- Do not ignore outliers, but do look at the data with outliers removed.
- Ensure data sets have a large enough population.
- Consider product age—are older products better or worse than newer products?
- Consider the people who are doing the work—training, familiarity with product, and so on, but never blame the people for the problems.
- Apply common sense!

ACKNOWLEDGMENTS

Without the detailed EP data collected by Jim Hensley, this study would not have been possible. I would also like to thank the many valuable comments from the reviewers.

Much of this work was presented in 1996 and 1997 at the Application of Software Measurement Conferences. The material was presented here with the benefit of four to five years of hindsight, and the results of some of the improvements made since then.

REFERENCES

Adams, E. 1984. Optimizing preventive service of software products. *IBM Journal of Research and Development* 28, no. 1.

Bencher, D. L. 1994. Programming quality improvement in IBM. *IBM Systems Journal* 33, no. 1: 218–219.

Jones, C. 1991. *Applied software measurement.* New York: McGraw-Hill.

Weinberg, G. 1986. Kill that code. *IEEE Tutorial on Software Restructuring.* Washington, DC: IEEE Computer Society Press.

Weller, E. F. 1993. Lessons from three years of inspection data. *IEEE Software* (September): 38–45.

———. 1995. Applying statistical process control to software maintenance. In *Proceedings of the applications of software measurement conference.* Orange Park, FL: Software Quality Engineering.

———. 1996. Managing software maintenance with metrics. In *Proceedings of the applications of software measurement conference.* Orange Park, FL: Software Quality Engineering.

———. 2000. Practical applications of statistical process control. *IEEE Software* (May/June): 48–55.

BIOGRAPHY

Ed Weller is a Fellow at Bull HN Information Systems in Phoenix, Ariz., where he is responsible for the software processes used for their mainframe operating systems group. Prior to joining Bull HN, he was a technical staff engineer and manager of the Systems and Software Engineering Process Group at Motorola's Satellite Communications Division. He is an authorized lead assessor in the Software Engineering Institute's Appraiser Program for CMM-based Appraisals for Internal Process Improvement.

Weller received the IEEE Software "Best Article of the Year" award for his September 1993 article, "Lessons from Three Years of Inspection Data," and was awarded Best Track Presentation at the 1994 Applications of Software Measurement Conference for "Using Metrics to Manage Software Projects." Weller has more than 30 years of experience in hardware, test, software, and systems engineering of large-scale hardware and software projects and is a Senior member of IEEE. He has a bachelor's degree in electrical engineering from the University of Michigan and a master's degree from the Florida Institute of Technology. Weller can be reached at Bull Information Systems, Inc., 13430 N. Black Canyon, MS Z-68, Phoenix, AZ 85029 or by e-mail at Ed.Weller@Bull.com .

Closing Thoughts

We need to do more to praise software, not to blame it.

Despite all the horror stories, computers and computerized systems have had an influence on our lives that is far more positive than negative. And because it is software that drives these systems, so it is the success of software that ought to be trumpeted.

If we think about it from an adequate distance—not in all the day-to-day struggles and disappointments we face personally and professionally—software has provided some of the most significant and satisfying advances in modern life.

We can communicate and collaborate, do business and seek distraction, increasingly unconstrained by distance or time . . . all thanks to the power of computing circuitry under the direction of programmed instructions.

Unfortunately, bad news—stories of the unpleasant or the unexpected—tends to crowd out good news. As I tell my wife when she expresses concern about my air travel, the evening news is unlikely to ever begin with the story "10,000 planes land safely today."

I must admit that it is easier to make a striking case study from things that go spectacularly wrong than to try teasing lessons-learned out of projects completed within time, budget, and expectation. My own teaching has drawn on a litany of disasters such as the Therac 25 radiation therapy device that fatally overexposed patients, or the explosion that destroyed the first flight of the Arianne 5 booster rocket.

Even triumphs are sometimes cloaked by the less significant shortcomings. I have used the Patriot missile as a case study not so much for its remarkable transformation, but for one spectacular failure. In a well-publicized incident during the Gulf War, an incoming attacking Scud was not neutralized by the defending Patriot and a number of soldiers were killed in their barracks. The root cause was an unexamined shift in requirements, but the real story was that the Patriot was a victim of its own success: a device designed as an anti-aircraft missile that was transformed by reprogramming into a very different beast, an anti-missile missile.

The most spectacular success of reprogramming has to be that of the Voyager 2 spacecraft. This interplanetary robot was sent out to explore Jupiter and Saturn. After successful high-speed fly-bys of those planets, Voyager 2 was redesigned to encounter the additional planets of Uranus and Neptune, something that had not been planned when it was launched years earlier. The redesign was done literally across the width of the solar system, at distances so great it took hours for speed-of-light signals to travel to and from the rapidly fleeing spaceship. Without the slightest chance of a hardware modification, its mission was transformed by software alone.

These triumphs of software and systems engineering often go unnoticed. Perhaps that is a compliment to the high expectations we have for our technological prowess. Perhaps, as I said before, it is simply because one Tacoma Narrows bridge dramatically tearing itself apart captures the imagination in a way that thousands of safe and reliable bridges used year in and year out cannot.

You have benefited from the triumphs of software, and now you can take an active part in the continuation of that success story. I trust this book has been an aid in that cause. Onward to more successes!

— Taz

Software Quality Engineer Certification (CSQE) Body of Knowledge

The following is an outline of topics that constitute the Body of Knowledge for Software Quality Engineer.

I. General Knowledge, Conduct, and Ethics (24 questions)

    A. Standards

        1. Domestic and international standards and specifications (e.g., ISO 9000, IEEE, Human Factors and Ergonomics Society, graphical user interface guidelines)

        2. Software quality and process initiatives, ventures, and consortia (e.g., SEI, SPICE, bootstrap, ESPRIT)

    B. Quality Philosophies and Principles

        1. Benefits of software quality

        2. Quality philosophies (e.g., Juran, Deming, Crosby)

        3. Prevention vs. detection philosophies

        4. Software total quality management principles and applications

        5. Organization and process benchmarking (i.e., identifying, analyzing, and modeling best practices)

    C. Organizational and Interpersonal Techniques

        1. Verbal communication and presentation

        2. Written communication

        3. Effective listening

        4. Interviewing

        5. Facilitation (e.g., team management, customer-supplier relationships)

        6. Principles of team leadership and facilitation

        7. Meeting management

        8. Conflict resolution

        9. Organization and implementation of various types of quality teams

    D. Problem-Solving Tools and Processes

        1. Root cause analysis

        2. Tools (e.g., affinity diagram, tree diagram, matrix diagram, interrelationship digraph, prioritization matrix, activity network diagram)

        3. Risk management (e.g., project, product, process)

        4. Problem-solving processes

    E. Professional Conduct and Ethics

       1. ASQ Code of Ethics

       2. Conflict of interest issues for a software quality engineer

       3. Ethical issues involving software product licensing

       4. Legal issues involving software product liability and safety (e.g., negligence, customer notification, recall, regulations)

II. Software Quality Management (16 questions)

    A. Planning

       1. Product and project software quality goals and objectives

       2. Customer requirements for quality

       3. Quality and customer support activities

       4. Issues related to software security, safety, and hazard analysis

    B. Tracking

       1. Scope and objectives of quality information systems

       2. Categories of quality data and their uses

       3. Problem reporting and corrective action procedures (e.g., software defects, process nonconformances)

       4. Techniques for implementing information systems to track quality-related data

       5. Records and data collection, storage, maintenance, and retention

    C. Organizational and Professional Software Quality Training

       1. Quality training subject areas (e.g., inspection, testing, configuration management, project management)

       2. Available training resources, materials, and providers

       3. Professional societies, technical associations, and organizations for software quality engineers

III. Software Processes (24 questions)

    A. Development and Maintenance Methods

       1. Software development procedures

       2. Lifecycle or process models (e.g., waterfall, spiral, rapid prototyping)

       3. Defect prevention, detection, and removal methods

       4. Requirement analysis and specification methods (e.g., data flow diagram, entity relationship diagram)

       5. Requirements elicitation methods and techniques (e.g., quality function deployment, joint application development, context-free questioning, needs analysis, focus groups)

       6. Software design methods (e.g., structured analyses and design, Jackson Design method, Warnier-Orr method, object-oriented)

       7. Issues related to reuse, reengineering, and reverse engineering

       8. Maintenance processes (e.g., reengineering, reverse engineering, change management, retirement)

B. Process and Technology Change Management

    1. Software process and technology change management theory and methods

    2. Process maturity models

    3. Software process assessment and evaluation techniques

    4. Software process modeling (e.g., entry and exit criteria, task definition, feedback loops)

    5. Software environments (e.g., development methodologies, tools, data, infrastructure)

    6. Barriers to the implementation or success of quality improvement efforts and quality systems

IV. Software Project Management (16 questions)

  A. Planning

    1. Project planning factors (e.g., quality, costs, resources, deliverables, schedules)

    2. Project planning methods and tools (e.g., work breakdown structures, documentation, forecasting, estimation)

    3. Goal-setting and deployment methodologies

    4. Maintenance types (e.g., corrective, adaptive, perfective)

    5. Software maintenance and adaptability program planning

    6. Supplier management methodologies

  B. Tracking

    1. Phase transitioning control techniques (e.g., reviews and audits, Gantt charts, PERT, budgets)

    2. Methods of collecting cost of quality data

    3. Cost of quality categories (e.g., prevention, appraisal, internal failure, external failure)

    4. Cost, progress, and deliverable tracking (e.g., status reports, lifecycle phase reports)

  C. Implementation

    1. Project management tools (e.g., planning, tracking, cost estimating, reporting)

    2. Methods of reporting cost of quality data

    3. Trade-offs involved in product release decisions (e.g., cost, quality, schedule, customer, test sufficiency, stability)

V. Software Metrics, Measurement, and Analytical Methods (24 questions)

  A. Measurement Theory

    1. Goal, question, metric paradigm for selecting metrics

    2. Basic measurement theory and techniques

    3. Definitions of metrics and measures

    4. Designing measures

    5. Psychology of metrics (e.g., how metrics affect people and how people affect metrics)

B. Analytical Techniques

    1. Issues involving data integrity, completeness, accuracy, and timeliness

    2. Basic statistical concepts and graphical techniques for analysis and presentation of software data (e.g., distributions, confidence intervals, statistical inference)

    3. Quality analysis tools (pareto chart, flowcharts, control charts, check sheets, scatter diagrams, histograms)

    4. Sampling theory and techniques as applied to audits, testing, and product acceptance

C. Software Measurement

    1. Prediction techniques of future maintainability

    2. Applications of measurements to process, product, and resources

    3. Commonly used metrics (e.g., complexity, reliability, defect density, phase containment, size)

    4. Software quality attributes (e.g., reliability, maintainability, usability, testability)

    5. Defect detection effectiveness (e.g., cost, yield, escapes, customer impact)

VI. Software Inspection, Testing, Verification, and Validation (24 questions)

A. Inspection

    1. Inspection types (e.g., peer reviews, inspections, walk-throughs)

    2. Inspection process (e.g., objectives, criteria, techniques and methods, participant roles)

    3. Inspection data collection, reports, and summaries

    4. Methods for reviewing inspection efforts (e.g., technical accomplishments, resource utilization, future planning)

B. Testing

    1. Types of tests (e.g., functional, performance, usability, stress, regression, real-time response)

    2. Test levels (e.g., unit, integration, system, field)

    3. Test strategies (e.g., top down, bottom up, automated testing, I/O first, beta testing, black box, white box)

    4. Test design (e.g., test cases, fault insertion and error handling, equivalence class partitioning, usage scenarios, customer defect reports)

    5. Test coverage of code (e.g., branch-to-branch, path, individual predicate, data)

    6. Test coverage of specifications (e.g., functions, states, data and time domains, localization, internationalization)

    7. Test environments (e.g., tools and methodologies, test libraries, drivers/stubs, equipment compatibility test laboratories)

        8. Test documentation (e.g., test plans, logs, test designs, defect recording, test reports)

        9. Test management (e.g., scheduling, freezing, resources, dependencies, analysis of test results)

        10. Methods for reviewing testing efforts (e.g., technical accomplishments, resource utilization, future planning, risk management)

        11. Methods for testing supplier components and products

        12. Methods for testing the accuracy of customer deliverables including user documentation, marketing and training materials

        13. Traceability mechanisms (e.g., system verification diagrams)

   C. Verification and Validation (V & V)

        1. V & V planning procedures

        2. Methods for reviewing V & V program (e.g., technical accomplishments, resource utilization, future planning, risk management, impact analysis of proposed changes)

        3. Methods for evaluating software lifecycle products and processes (e.g., physical traces, documentation, source code, plans, test and audit results) to determine if user needs and project objectives are satisfied

        4. Methods for performing requirements traceability (e.g., requirements to design, design to code)

        5. Methods for evaluating requirements for correctness, consistency, completeness, and testability

        6. Methods for evaluating interfaces with hardware, user, operator, and other software applications

        7. Methods for evaluating test plans (e.g., system, acceptance, validation) to determine if software satisfies software and system objectives

        8. Methods for evaluating the severity of anomalies in software operation

        9. Methods for assessing all proposed modifications, enhancements, or additions to determine the effect each change will have on the system

        10. Methods for determining which V&V tasks should be iterated based upon proposed modifications and enhancements

VII. Software Audits (16 questions)

   A. Audit Types

        1. Performing internal audits (e.g., quality system, product, process, project, customer)

        2. Performing external audits (e.g., supplier qualifications, certification of supplier systems, auditing testing done by independent agencies)

        3. Functional and physical configuration audits

   B. Audit Methodology

        1. Purpose, objectives, frequency, and criteria of the overall audit program and individual software audits

        2. Procedures, tools, and issues related to conducting audits in specific areas (e.g., software development, project management, configuration management)

       3. Audit steps (planning, preparation, execution, reporting, corrective action, verification follow-up)

       4. Audit process (e.g., objectives, criteria, techniques and methods, participant roles)

  C. Audit Planning

       1. Audit team member responsibilities

       2. Management (auditee and auditor) responsibilities concerning audits

       3. Hosting external audits

       4. Audit program development and administration

       5. Auditing requirements (e.g., industry and government standards)

VIII. Software Configuration Management (16 questions)

  A. Planning and Configuration Identification

       1. Technical and managerial factors that guide software product partitioning into configuration items and components

       2. Release process issues (e.g., supporting multiple versions, feature vs. corrective releases, hardware and software dependencies)

       3. Library control procedures

       4. Configuration identification methods (e.g., schemes, reidentification, naming conventions, versions and serialization, baselines)

       5. Configuration management tools

  B. Configuration Control, Status Accounting, and Reporting

       1. Documentation control (e.g., issuing, approval, storage, retrieval, revision)

       2. Patching issues (e.g., testing, traceability, source updating)

       3. Trade-offs between cost, cycle time, and integrity of software product and rigor and formality of change control process

       4. Source and object code control procedures

       5. Software configuration/change control board processes

       6. Techniques for assessing impacts of proposed software changes

Index